Honouring Our Ancestors

HONOURING OUR ANCESTORS

Takatāpui, Two-Spirit and Indigenous LGBTQI+ Well-being

Edited by
Alison Green and Leonie Pihama

TE HERENGA WAKA
UNIVERSITY PRESS

Te Herenga Waka University Press
Victoria University of Wellington
PO Box 600 Wellington
teherengawakapress.co.nz

Copyright © authors and editors 2023

First published 2023
Reprinted 2024 and 2025 (twice)

This book is copyright. Apart from any fair dealing
for the purpose of private study, research, criticism or review,
as permitted under the Copyright Act, no part may be reproduced
by any process without the permission of the publishers.
The moral rights of the authors have been asserted.

'Does Pain Play a Role?' (p. 240) was originally published in 2014
as 'Racial Discrimination's Influence on Smoking Rates among American
Indian Alaska Native Two-Spirit Individuals: Does Pain Play a Role?', *Journal
of Health Care for the Poor and Underserved*, 25(4), 1667–78.
doi.org/10.1353/hpu.2014.0193. Reproduced with kind permission.

A catalogue record is available at the National Library of New Zealand.

ISBN 9781776920730

Printed by YourBooks, Wellington

Contents

Mihi — 7

1. Introduction — 11
   Leonie Pihama & Alison Green

2. Being Māori, Being Takatāpui — 29
   *Alison Green, Leonie Pihama, Shirley Simmonds,
   Matt Roskruge & Tawhanga Nopera*

3. A Māori Worlded Speculation on Terms 'Sex' and 'Gender' — 43
   Carl Mika

4. He Takatāpui, He Queer, He Mokopuna Rānei — 60
   Kim McBreen

5. Te Whare Takatāpui – Reclaiming the Spaces
   of Our Ancestors — 73
   Elizabeth Kerekere

6. Kaupapa Māori and Designing the Honour Project
   Aotearoa Survey — 97
   *Shirley Simmonds, Alison Green, Leonie Pihama,
   Matt Roskruge, Tawhanga Nopera & Nick Garrett*

7. Te Tatauranga Whakamānawa Takatāpui:
   Honour Project Aotearoa Survey — 111
   *Alison Green, Shirley Simmonds, Leonie Pihama,
   Matt Roskruge, Rebekah Laurence, Tawhanga Nopera
   & Herearoha Skipper*

8. Takatāpui Well-being and Access to Health Services — 133
   *Leonie Pihama, Alison Green, Shirley Simmonds,
   Tawhanga Nopera, Matt Roskruge, Herearoha Skipper
   & Rebekah Laurence*

9. HIV and Indigenous Peoples: Lessons Learned from
   Four Decades of Living in a Pandemic — 153
   Clive Aspin

10.	Tā Moko: Re-imagining Ancestral Skin Carving *Mera Penehira*	163
11.	Tikanga Māori Supports Healthy Māori Communities for Takatāpui Trans People in Aotearoa *Alison Green, Manawaroa Te Wao & Rebekah Laurence*	181
12.	Invoking War Shields of Transformative Resistance and Persistence: Thrivance Among American Indian and Alaska Native Two-Spirit Women *Karina Walters & Michelle Johnson-Jennings*	204
13.	Does Pain Play a Role? The Influence of Racial Discrimination on Smoking Rates among Two-Spirit Indigenous Persons *Michelle Johnson-Jennings, A. Belcourt, M. Town, Melissa Walls & Karina Walters*	240
14.	Body Sovereignty: A Collaborative Reflection on Two-Spirit Methodologies *Sarah Hunt, Sandy Lambert & Alex Wilson*	255
15.	*Gidoo-Imishinkoowenden* ('You Have a Strong Mind'): Reflections on the 2-Spirit HIV/AIDS Wellness and Longevity Study (2SHAWLS) *Randy Jackson, Doris Peltier & David Brennan*	269
16.	Two-Spirit Return: Intergenerational Healing and Cultural Leadership among Mixed-Race American Indians *Andrew Jolivétte*	290
17.	Honouring Our Ancestors: Two-Spirit Resurgence in the 21st Century *Albert McLeod*	304
18.	Unknown Devotions: Trans* and Indigena Freedom Dance *Rafael/a Luna-Pizano*	327

Contributing Authors	342
Index	353

Mihi

Kia tau ngā manaakitanga a te wāhi ngaro	May the strength and life force of our ancestors
Ki runga ki tēnā, ki tēnā o tatou	Be with each and every one of us
Kia mahea te hua mākihikihi	Freeing our paths from obstruction
Kia toi te kupu, toi te mana, toi te aroha, toi te reo	So that our words, spiritual power, compassion and languages are upheld
Kia tūturu, kia whakamaua kia tina! Tina!	Permanently fixed, established and understood!
Hui e, tāiki e!	Moving forward together!

E ngā mana, e ngā reo, e ngā karangatanga maha puta noa te ao, tēnei te reo karamihi ki a koutou, otirā, ki a tātou katoa. Nau mai, tahuti mai ki tēnei whakaeminga kōrero i pupū ake ai i te ngākau whitawhita o ngā iwi taketake, he puna mātauranga, he manawa whenua hei oranga tonutanga mō ō tātou whānau, ō tātou hapori, ō tātou iwi anō hoki.

Acknowledging the independent authorities and languages that distinguish us, and the multitude of connections that bind us together, we welcome you all to this important work. *Honouring Our Ancestors: Takatāpui, Two-Spirit and Indigenous LGBTQI+ Well-being* is a collection of writings that investigate the well-being of American Indian and Alaska Native two-spirit communities in Turtle Island, and the well-being of Māori takatāpui, trans, LGBTQI+ and queer communities here in Aotearoa. We offer this Indigenous knowledge, with themes ranging from reclamation, resistance and healing to persistence, empowerment and transformation, as a wellspring of unlimited potential for Indigenous communities everywhere. Mauri ora ki a tātou!

We would like to acknowledge the many people who have participated in and supported the research project Honour Project Aotearoa. We thank all those who were interviewed or who took part in our many community-based hui and wānanga around Aotearoa. The ongoing support for the continued sharing of the work that has come from the Honour Project Aotearoa has created the opportunity for us to develop this book. We also acknowledge our tuakana, our elder relations, from the Indigenous Wellness Research Institute (IWRI) in Turtle Island; through their work in the HONOR Project, they have provided us with the inspiration to engage in research with takatāpui and Māori LGBTQI+ communities in Aotearoa. In particular, we wish to acknowledge Karina Walters for her unwavering support of our work, and to the wider Honor Project team, for providing us with input and advice from the beginning and hosting us as part of an exchange of ideas. We also acknowledge Linda Tuhiwai Smith, who has provided her ongoing support and advice as needed, Marjorie Beverland, who has been a key support, and our National Advisory group Mera Penehira, Manawaroa Te Wao, Richard Tankersley, Elizabeth Kerekere and Nick Garrett.

We acknowledge the support of the University of Waikato, in particular those people who were a part of these projects during our time at Te Kotahi Research Institute: Herearoha Skipper, Papahuia Dickson and Tammy Tauroa. And we send our appreciation to all of our whānau, who have provided ongoing support and encouragement not only throughout the work of bringing this publication together, but also throughout our work to accomplish the outcomes associated with the studies documented here.

We acknowledge the support of Te Whāriki Takapou, particularly the Trust Board, our colleagues Vernon Waretini, Jillian Tipene, Tawhanga Nopera, Wetini Paul, Rebekah Laurence, Ricky Te Akau, and Ngaire Sandel representing the Ministry of Health. We are indebted to takatāpui and Māori LGBTQI+ networks and organisations, including Kahukura Pounamu from Christchurch, Tīwhanawhana and Gender Minorities from Wellington, Te Rākei Whakaehu online transgender network, and Auckland-based Ahakoa Te Aha, for their advice and support when planning Honour Project Aotearoa and developing the interview and survey questions. Altogether, their promotion of the project after it was launched was crucial to successfully recruiting takatāpui and Māori LGBTQI+ people of all ages, identities and socio-economic backgrounds. We also thank the New Zealand Sex Workers' Collective, the New Zealand AIDS Foundation and Te Pūtahitanga o te Waipounamu for generously hosting meetings with their local takatāpui and Māori LGBTQI+ communities to plan, implement, interview and disseminate study findings.

To all of the authors who have given their time and knowledge to support this publication, we extend our thanks and appreciation for your contribution and for all of the work that you do alongside your respective Māori and Indigenous communities and nations to uplift and affirm the wider aspiration of well-being for our peoples. We hope that *Honouring*

Our Ancestors will provide an opportunity to share more broadly the mātauranga Māori and Indigenous knowledge and practices that support our assertion of tino rangatiratanga (sovereignty) and mana motuhake (self-determination) in regards to the well-being of takatāpui, two-spirit and Indigenous LGBTQI+ peoples in our whānau, hapū and iwi.

Finally, our acknowledgements to the Health Research Council of New Zealand and the University of Waikato for providing funding support to the projects in Aotearoa that enabled us to bring this collection together, and to the publishing team at Te Herenga Waka University Press for their support, enabling the authors to share their knowledge through this publication.

1

Introduction

Leonie Pihama and Alison Green

This publication is inspired by two research projects: the HONOR Project (2007–2010) and the Honour Project Aotearoa (2016–2019). The Honour Project Aotearoa investigated Kaupapa Māori strengths-based understandings of health and well-being in relation to takatāpui/ Māori LGBTQI+ communities. The study and its findings are important because little research has been conducted by takatāpui researchers and community collaborators about takatāpui experiences, wellness and well-being. The first Kaupapa Māori in-depth piece of qualitative research was undertaken by takatāpui researcher Dr Elizabeth Kerekere in her doctoral work *Part of the whānau: The emergence of takatāpui identity – He whāriki takatāpui* (2017). Extending on from that work, the Honour Project Aotearoa is the first Kaupapa Māori national mixed-methods project to investigate understandings of well-being within the takatāpui community and provide insights into processes by which health services can better serve this community.

The Honour Project Aotearoa was influenced by the HONOR Project, a ground-breaking study led by Professor Karina Walters of the Indigenous Wellness Research Institute (IWRI) at the University of Washington, which explored well-being in American Indian and Alaskan Native two-spirit communities (Walters et al., 2011). The term 'two-spirit' – a contemporary rendering of the Northern Algonquin term *niizh manitoag*, 'two spirits' – signifies the embodiment of both the feminine and masculine spirits within one person (Anguksuar, cited in Balsam et al., 2004). The term provides a means for American Indian and Alaskan Native (AIAN) sexual and gender minorities to accentuate and validate a culturally distinct embodiment of their sexual and gender identity (Lehavot et al., 2009). The HONOR Project was the first community-based study of two-spirit American Indians and Alaskan Natives, and involved a nationwide survey that examined the impact of historical trauma, discrimination and other stressors on the health and wellness of Native American men and women who identified as lesbian, gay, bisexual, transgender and two-spirit (LGBTT-S), specifically those living in urban settings.

Both projects were driven by a need to address the almost total lack of responsiveness to the health and well-being of takatāpui, two-spirit and Indigenous LGBTQI+ communities, in terms of equitable provision of quality, sensitive and respectful health services and programmes, and critical research that empowers, enhances the life experience of, and achieves positive transformation for these communities. As has been noted in Aotearoa and internationally, there are significant gaps in service provision to Māori and Indigenous LGBTQI+ populations (Pega & MacEwan, 2010; Walters, 1997). In Aotearoa, the Human Rights Commission (2008) found significant gaps in health services for transgender people, with available services being ad hoc and limited. It was also noted that there was a dire need for more information and education in regard to issues faced by intersex people, in terms of the discrimination faced and knowledge of historical and contemporary medical practices. The HONOR Project and Honour Project Aotearoa provide opportunities to address the invisibility of these communities in these settings. In giving voice to Indigenous expressions, experiences and aspirations for health and well-being, these projects reinforce the belonging of takatāpui/two-spirit and Indigenous LGBTQI+ communities in our present, ancestral and future generations (Walters, 2007).

Gender identity, sexual identity and sexuality are fundamental to our sense of self, our self-esteem and our ability to lead a fulfilling life. However, health and well-being issues in Aotearoa New Zealand are predominantly discussed with a Western heterosexual frame of reference. Health and well-being outcomes vary widely across population groups, including Māori, Pacific peoples and refugees, and lesbian, gay, bisexual, transgender and intersex people. Professional development programmes that are anti-racist, anti-homophobic, anti-transphobic and anti-misogynst are non-existent for healthcare and social service professionals, and very few organisations provide specific services and programmes to Indigenous takatāpui and two-spirit populations (Neville & Henrickson, 2006; Adams et al., 2013).

Well-being is increasingly understood as being culturally and environmentally specific (Panelli & Tipa, 2007), with a strong sense of one's identity – in terms of culture, sexuality and gender – linked to enhanced health status (Aspin, 2007; Pihama et al., 2006; Simoni et al., 2004; Green & Te Wao, 2014). It is essential to the health of takatāpui and two-spirit peoples to have an understanding of our place in the world, to know where we belong and where we stand (Aspin, 2007; Walters, 1997). There is clear evidence that having strong cultural foundations underpins important epistemological, social, economic and health beliefs, attitudes and practices for Indigenous peoples (Durie, 2001). These foundations are also critical in terms of gender and sexual identity (Pihama et al., 2006; Eldred-Grigg, 1984).

Those who do not have regular and ongoing access to contexts that reinforce their sense of self-identity may be at increased risk of negative health outcomes (Pihama et al., 2006; Herewini & Sheridan, 1994). Health and well-being approaches within the dominant Western framework are focused on the individual; they do not accommodate the collective and interdependent values of Indigenous societies (Neville & Henrickson, 2006; Panelli & Tipa, 2007) and our understandings of sexualities and genders (Kerekere, 2017). For instance, sexuality is viewed from the perspective of the individual rather than as an integral component of collective societies (Hutchings & Aspin, 2007), and heterosexuality is constructed as 'normal', with forms of sexuality that sit outside such dominant definitions seen as deviant (McBreen, 2012). In a heteronormative culture, those who identify as gay, lesbian, bisexual, transgender and intersex (LGBTQI+) are positioned as a marginalised minority (McBreen, 2012; Aspin & Hutchings, 2007).

For Māori, such marginalisation occurs not just within dominant mainstream culture but also within some Māori communities, due to colonial values and influences that have been internalised over time (Te Awekotuku 1991; Aspin, 2007; Green & Te Wao, 2014). Moreover, ongoing marginalisation experienced as a result of discrimination and prejudice based on one's sexual identity (Pihama et al., 2006) and gendered identity (Nopera, 2017) is compounded by the prevalence of racism encountered in both mainstream society and LGBTQI+ communities (Aspin, 2007; Green & Te Wao, 2014). This phenomenon can be conceived as being a minority within a minority; or, for example, in the case of those who identify as gender-fluid (Nopera, 2017), transgender or two-spirit (Hutchings, 2007), having a 'multiple minority status' (Balsam et al., 2004, p. 296), or being in 'triple jeopardy' (Lehavot et al., 2009, p. 277). For example, takatāpui suffer discrimination on many levels: within the LGBTQI+ communities because of our cultural identity, within our cultural communities because of sexual and gender identities, and within wider society because of the intersection of sexuality, cultural identity and gender identity (Pihama et al., 2020; Nopera, 2017).

As well as facing discrimination, takatāpui continue to face entrenched stigmatisation (Ashton 2015; Stangl et al., 2019). This is particularly so for those affected by sexually transmitted infections or blood-borne viruses such as HIV (Rua'ine, 2007; Waiti & Green, 2015; Negin et al., 2015). Aside from constituting a breach of human rights (Hutchings, 2007; Waiti & Green, 2014), it is of major concern in terms of well-being that stigma and discrimination impacts not only the person themselves but also their whānau and friends (Pega, 2009; SPINZ, 2013). Consequently, the conceptual unit that is so fundamental to well-being, the whānau, is disrupted, and core Māori values and principles are undermined (Rua'ine, 2007, cited in Waiti & Green, 2015). As a result of stigma and discrimination, Māori living with and affected by HIV experience less favourable treatment at medical centres, less favourable treatment regarding employment, and confidentiality problems regarding their status (Grierson et al., 2004; Sheaf et al., 2011, cited in Waiti & Green, 2014; Te Whāriki Takapou, 2021). For those living with and affected by HIV/AIDS, this manifests as 'a loss of hope' (Pala, 2013, cited in Waiti & Green, 2015), and a reluctance to test for HIV (Miller, 2010, cited in Waiti & Green, 2014).

A pervasive and often covert level of homophobia, heterosexism and violence continues to be promulgated against LGBTQI+ people, which directly affects their health and well-being and that of their whānau and friends (Neville & Henrickson, 2006; Health Research Council, 2010; Green & Te Wao, 2014). This applies particularly to Indigenous/takatāpui women, who may experience higher rates of assault, threats, verbal abuse and workplace discrimination than non-Indigenous LGBTQI+ women (Hutchings, 2007; Rankine, 2001; Balsam et al., 2004). Reynolds and Smith (2012) have established the need for more information regarding access to fertility information and care for takatāpui, while Pihama and Lee (2010) have highlighted the multiple levels of discrimination that takatāpui whānau experience in neonatal intensive care units, including having difficulties in being acknowledged as whānau. Often, sexuality-diverse and gender-diverse people experience discrimination and abuse from within their own families and communities (Birkenhead, 2012; Witten, 2007). For Indigenous sexuality-diverse and gender-diverse people, being excluded from families and communities is a direct result of oppressive colonial histories; individualised approaches to identity, and the concept of a nuclear family have negatively impacted Indigenous collective identities (Dudding, 2017; Reynolds, 2012). Indigenous LGBTQI+ collectives can encourage a sense of whānau connectedness (Dudding, 2017). Anderson (2017) describes a similar form of connectedness for Aboriginal LGBTQI+ people through an urban Indigenous LGBTQI+ sexual health service:

Having people like two-spirits was like ... this is like your mob, you can be Indigenous and queer, it's just like, opened up so many doors for me and made me feel proud of myself. (0.42mins)

Colonisation has had a profound effect on all aspects of Indigenous societies. In their efforts to define and categorise Indigenous peoples, colonisers sought to subjugate and dominate, contributing in a significant way to the marginalisation of Indigenous peoples in contemporary society (Smith, 1999). Aspects of Indigenous cultures that were rendered invisible in the process of colonisation include the diversity of sexual expression. Any variation to heterosexuality was viewed as profane and was actively discouraged. Consequently, we have been left with incomplete understandings of traditional forms of sexuality and diminished cultural resources from which to draw. Not only did colonisers seek to suppress information about Indigenous sexuality, but they also deliberately disseminated false information to prevent people from gaining true and accurate information. Much of this false information drew on people's fears and prejudices about sex and sexuality and contributed to the development of a false and erroneous image of Indigenous people and their relationships. Often, such information was designed to portray Indigenous people as perverted, uncivilised and in need of the superior moral values of the coloniser (Aldrich, 2003).

Zambas and Wright (2016) write that colonialism has impacted Indigenous peoples not only by adversely affecting their health, but also their access to healthcare. Inherited generational trauma and the political-economic effects of disenfranchisement, genocide and military occupation all systematically remove our ability to equitably access services and receive equitable health service outcomes. Some of these, such as interpersonal racism from service providers, operate at an individual level. This could be rectified by training and education for clinical staff and by ensuring that Indigenous healthcare workers are themselves part of service provision for Indigenous patients. Other issues, such as the logistical and financial barriers for Indigenous peoples, are part of the entire political apparatus maintaining the settler colony. For example, Māori may not be able to afford services because our communities have been gutted of economic resources by two centuries of raupatu – the unjust confiscation of iwi and hapū resources. As always, the implicit bias towards the dominant (colonial) culture in the healthcare system means that Indigenous peoples' unique needs (for example, taha wairua or taha whānau) are addenda to an otherwise 'complete' system. A new structure that incorporates tikanga Māori from the outset, premised on absolute social, political, economic equality, is necessary to remove these structurally racist elements of the healthcare system.

Singer (2015) locates the eradication of Indigenous non-binary gender identities in settler colonialism. In this context, the 'beingness' of takatāpui is a political matter, a thing to be overcome, in which settlers supplanted Indigenous cultures with their own. The application of biomedical discourses to takatāpui, such as the 'diagnosis' of 'gender identity disorder' in transgender takatāpui, should be understood as a colonial imposition. Its effect on Indigenous communities – the internalisation of hostile attitudes towards takatāpui and two-spirit peoples – is likewise an internal colonisation. The ways in which colonialism has restructured Māori society has made a healthy existence for takatāpui extremely difficult. Medical discourses to describe the 'beingness' of takatāpui has been part of this restructuring, and so the health and well-being of takatāpui can be achieved only through decolonial politics.

This book seeks to contribute to decolonising and indigenising approaches to issues of gender, sexual identity and sexuality for Indigenous peoples. In these essays, takatāpui, two-spirit and Māori and Indigenous LGBTQI+ writers from Aotearoa (New Zealand) and Turtle Island (Canada and America) contribute their knowledge, theories and experiences of political and social change. These essays challenge existing national and local norms in their discussions of Māori and Indigenous sexuality and gender identity and the impact of colonisation. New pathways for thinking and 'doing' Indigenous sexualities and genders are central to this publication, in particular framing our understandings within and through our own Indigenous knowledges, relationships and practices.

Chapter Overview

The first part of this publication focuses on voices from Aotearoa, known in colonial terms as New Zealand, and provides an overview of key ways in which we as Māori consider the term 'takatāpui' and some of the philosophical discussions of the ways in which naming and locating ourselves is an important cultural process.

Chapter 2: Alison Green, Leonie Pihama, Shirley Simmonds, Matt Roskruge and Tawhanga Nopera, 'Being Māori, Being Takatāpui'

Takatāpui involved in the Honour Project Aotearoa research talked about the importance of reclaiming identity and our cultural ways of understanding ourselves. This essay provides an overview of these discussions. The term 'takatāpui' is understood by many Māori as having been reclaimed from Māori pūrākau (traditional stories) and has become a frame through which Māori LGBTQI+ can speak to aspects of sexuality, gender and cultural identity. This essay shares views about the origins of the term and how it relates to our experiences as takatāpui and LGBTQI+, and also discusses whānau relationships and the importance of a sense of connectedness within our lives and in seeking well-being.

Chapter 3: Carl Mika, 'A Māori Worlded Speculation on Terms "Sex" and "Gender"'

In this essay, Carl Mika argues for a reconsideration of the terms 'sex' and 'gender'. These terms are regularly used in the field of takatāpui health and well-being, but the fundamental ideas or the philosophical platform from which these terms emerge are seldom critiqued. Mika carefully sets out a method for analysis according to an approach that Mika describes as 'worldedness'. This approach proceeds from the position that all things are interconnected by virtue of the primordial ground that, in this instance, gives rise to sex, and ensures that the concept of 'sex' and the materiality of 'sex' (whatever this is determined to be) are not distinct; rather, each constitutes the other and both are constituted by all things in the world. In Western thought, the term 'sex' is delineated through observation, measurement and descriptions from other things in the world. Mika's method of analysis pushes back against this and the drive to separate terms, ideas and things from their materiality. Mika reminds us of the tradition in Māori philosophy wherein things announce their presence (or absence) and, in so doing, claim our attention. In an anti-colonial and Kaupapa Māori tradition, it is important to ask whether the term 'takatāpui' conforms to a Māori worlded metaphysics and why the terms 'sex' and 'gender' claim our attention at this time.

Chapter 4: Kim McBreen, 'He Takatāpui, He Queer, He Mokopuna Rānei'

This essay elucidates the dangers of the dominant culture to those of us who self-identify with minority genders and sexualities. McBreen posits that there are two problems: the immediate threat to our well-being, and the colonising, heteropatriarchal nature of the dominant society. There is tension between addressing short-term needs and long-term vision; building up takatāpui identity and community is one short-term strategy for achieving better well-being, but this doesn't challenge the source of the problem. Instead, it reinforces heteropatriarchy by confirming that Māori who identify with minority genders and sexualities aren't normal. How can we ensure our safety in the short term, in a way that is consistent with dismantling heteropatriarchy in the long term? What does a culture with a healthy understanding of gender and sexuality look like? McBreen writes that we are fortunate to have guidance from our tūpuna. McBreen discusses Māori and colonising understandings of gender and sexuality, and explores how a vision of dismantling heteropatriarchy can support strategies for immediate well-being.

Chapter 5: Elizabeth Kerekere, 'Te Whare Takatāpui: Reclaiming the Spaces of Our Ancestors'

Elizabeth Kerekere, a founding member of Tīwhanawhana Trust, advocates takatāpui telling our stories, building our communities and leaving a legacy. Kerekere uses traditional Māori culture and values to reframe our ways of talking about gender and sexuality in Aotearoa, particularly about gender and sexuality for young Māori. The Whare Takatāpui framework explores conceptual and practical ways in which Māori values can inform takatāpui health and well-being. The framework highlights mana wāhine as essential to restoring the traditional balance between women and men that our ancestors enjoyed so that we may address the historical trauma and gendered violence of colonisation. Doing so provides space and protection for our trans, intersex and non-binary whānau to stand in their own mana. Mana wāhine is the platform for fighting against the homophobia, transphobia and biphobia that impact takatāpui and rainbow health, well-being and relationships.

Chapter 6: Shirley Simmonds, Alison Green, Leonie Pihama, Matt Roskrudge, Tawhanga Nopera and Nick Garrett, 'Kaupapa Māori and Designing the Honour Project Aotearoa Survey'

This essay details the Kaupapa Māori methodological approach to survey development and its Kaupapa Māori underpinnings. An integral part of the research process was to critique commonly used survey methods to ensure they served the aspirations of the project, were consistent with Māori cultural values, and were statistically rigourous. This led to a quantitative dataset that brings a further dimension to the shared personal experiences of the Māori LGBTQI+ community interviewed for this project. As tangata whenua, our right to good health is supported by our right to generate our own data and to critique the statistical tools used to collect, collate, analyse and present our health information. What resulted is a replicable survey development process underpinned by Kaupapa Māori research methodologies, methods and principles.

Chapter 7: Alison Green, Shirley Simmonds, Leonie Pihama, Matt Roskrudge, Rebekah Laurence and Herearoha Skipper, 'Te Tatauranga Whakamānawa Takatāpui: Honour Project Aotearoa Survey'

This chapter provides an overview and discussion of the survey findings about takatāpui and LGBTQI+ understandings and experiences of health, access to primary healthcare services, and well-being. It highlights the importance for Māori of maintaining autonomy over why, what and how health data are collected, analysed and utilised as strategies for determining pathways to rangatiratanga and well-being. Many Māori approach quantitative research with suspicion, often for good reason. To implement a credible survey and report credible data, it was critical to engage with takatāpui and Māori LGBTQI+ people and recognise their priorities, voices and analysis of the data. Some sections of the survey were developed in consultation with specialist organisations and networks, such as the Aotearoa New Zealand Sex Workers' Collective, Gender Minorities Aotearoa, Ahakoa Te Aha and Tīwhanawhana. The researchers assert that the process used to develop the survey will contribute to the growth of Kaupapa Māori mixed methodology, theory and practice. Presently, Kaupapa Māori methodologies are commonly used by Māori undertaking qualitative research but less commonly for quantitative research. Importantly, the survey found that takatāpui and Māori LGBTQI+ participants experienced poor access to primary health services and poor engagement with health professionals. Discrimination in primary healthcare services and in wider society – homophobia, transphobia, misogyny and racism – diminished the health and well-being of survey participants.

Chapter 8: Leonie Pihama, Alison Green, Shirley Simmonds, Tawhanga Nopera, Matt Roskruge, Herearoha Skipper and Rebekah Laurence, 'Takatāpui Well-being and Experiences of Health Services'

This essay focuses on takatāpui experiences of the health system, and provides an overview of three key themes that impact well-being and access to quality healthcare services for takatāpui: (i) homophobia and racism;

(ii) self-harm and suicide; and (iii) difficulty engaging with the healthcare system. Strong links between sexual orientation, gender identity and suicidal behaviours are well established in New Zealand and international literature. It is characteristic of much of this literature, as well as the literature that addresses HIV/AIDS in the LGBTQI+ community in Aotearoa New Zealand, to focus on the negative health outcomes of these communities. Takatāpui continue to face entrenched stigma and discrimination, which impacts not only individuals but also their whānau and friends.

Chapter 9: Clive Aspin, 'HIV and Indigenous Peoples: Lessons Learned from Four Decades of Living in a Pandemic'

This essay provides a brief history of responses to HIV, especially those relating to Māori in Aotearoa. First reported in New York in 1981, HIV was late coming to Aotearoa, with the first recorded case of an AIDS-related death at the Taranaki Base Hospital in 1985. By this time, the virus that led to the condition now known as AIDS had spread throughout the world. The measures that were implemented to curtail its spread focused on people who appeared most at risk: gay men, people who injected drugs, and sex workers. Despite the fact that Indigenous peoples in some countries were identified as vulnerable to HIV, little was done to protect them. As a consequence, Indigenous peoples have recorded higher rates of HIV than their non-Indigenous peers. An analysis of Indigenous HIV initiatives, including research projects, provides compelling evidence that HIV prevention programmes failed to acknowledge the strengths of Indigenous populations. This essay argues that this oversight has been a major contributing factor to the current HIV disparities between Indigenous and non-Indigenous peoples, more than four decades after the inception of the AIDS pandemic.

Chapter 10: Mera Penehira, 'Tā Moko: Re-imagining Ancestral Skin Carving'

This essay examines significant literature regarding the revival of Native and Indigenous skin carving and how it contributes to identity and well-being. Penehira shares the case study of Manu Neho, who is takatāpui and has for over 20 years been journeying with the ancestral skin carving of moko kauwae. In chronicling her experience of attaining and walking in this 'new (but ancient) skin', this case study explores the relationship between this ancestral practice, identity and well-being. However, the revival of tā moko and other Native and Indigenous skin carving is not unaffected by colonial silencing and oppression. This chapter speaks to that and resists its further entrenchment.

Chapter 11: Alison Green, Manawaroa Te Wao and Rebekah Laurence, 'Tikanga Māori Supports Healthy Māori Communities for Takatāpui Trans People in Aotearoa'

This essay proposes that tikanga Māori should inform common law if Aotearoa is serious about eliminating gender-related stigma and discrimination experienced by takatāpui and Māori transgender people. Beginning with an overview of the impact that colonisation continues to have on Māori understandings of gender and associated terminology, the authors discuss tikanga Māori – what it is, its role in Māori communities, and the effects of colonisation. Next, they present the pūrākau as told by Manawaroa, which relates to her gender identity and the renowned kaumatua who, guided by tikanga Māori, confirmed her right to live her life as the person she chose to be. Finally, the authors return to tikanga Māori and its intersection with takatāpui and Māori transgender well-being and human rights. They assert that current rights-informed legislation, policies and standards have failed to eliminate stigma and discrimination and have not upheld the inherent and Tiriti o Waitangi rights of takatāpui trans people to safe, healthy lives in Aotearoa.

∞

Part Two focuses on two-spirit and Indigenous LGBTQI+ peoples and communities in Turtle Island, in particular the countries known in colonial terms as Canada and America. Part Two opens with essays from the team at the Indigenous Wellness Research Institute (IWRI), who give us insight into the HONOR Project. We open with these essays in acknowledgement of the tuakana (elder sibling) status of that research and of our Indigenous relations at IWRI who led the project.

Chapter 12: Karina Walters and Michelle Johnson-Jennings, 'Invoking War Shields of Transformative Resistance and Persistence: Thrivance Among American Indian and Alaska Native Two-Spirit Women'

This essay brings forward the work of the HONOR Project (2007–2010) and highlights the harm that settler colonialism has caused by striving to erase the lived experiences and histories of sexually diverse and gender-diverse (i.e. two-spirit) American Indian and Alaska Native Peoples. Indigenous two-spirit women remain strong and resilient pillars of communities. Often, their stories are missed in public health initiatives as a result of settler colonialism's perpetual drive to erase and silence. Given the ongoing high disparities in violence and trauma exposure, Indigenous and two-spirit scholars and activists have countered this erasure with indigenist research and culturally contextualised narratives of survivance in dealing with historical trauma, microaggressions, ongoing colonialism and related stressors. The term 'survivance' refers to holding on to the deep cultural strands of Indigenous knowledges and practices that endure to this day; however, as the authors propose, 'thrivance' involves weaving those Indigenous knowledge strands (the warp) with the threads of transformative resistance and power of persistence (the weft) into a vibrant fabric of healthful living. Drawing on the national multi-site Honor Project Two-Spirit Health Study (NIMH R01 65871; N=452 surveys; N=65 in-depth interviews) and utilising the listening guide relational voice-centered method, the authors conducted an iterative indigenist qualitative data analysis of 11 two-spirit women's thrivance experiences and narratives. What emerged from the data was a war shield thrivance heuristic, which elucidates the role of Original Instructions (ancient stories/teachings), relational restoration and narrative transformation, as well as ceremony and spirituality in promoting two-spirit women's health and well-being.

Chapter 13: Michelle Johnson-Jennings, A. Belcourt, M. Town, Melissa Walls, and Karina Walters, 'Does Pain Play a Role? The Influence of Racial Discrimination on Smoking Rates among Two-Spirit Indigenous Persons'

The authors of this essay examine the high rates of racial discrimination and non-ceremonial tobacco-smoking among AIAN two-spirit/LGBTQI+ populations and whether pain mediates between racial discrimination and smoking among two-spirits. Two-spirit adults ($N = 447$) from seven urban US locations were surveyed during the HONOR Project. The Indigenist stress coping model was used as a framework in which to conduct descriptive, bivariate and regression analyses. Most participants reported smoking (45.2%) and pain (57%). Pain was found to mediate the association between racial discrimination and smoking. Racial discrimination appears to be a significant factor influencing tobacco smoking and health behaviours within two-spirit populations. Effective tobacco cessation and/

or prevention planning for two-spirits and others who experience frequent racial discrimination, stress, and trauma should consider the influence of pain. Pain may serve as the embodiment of discrimination, calling for future research.

Chapter 14: Sarah Hunt, Sandy Lambert and Alex Wilson, 'Body Sovereignty: A Collaborative Reflection on Two-Spirit Methodologies'

The authors of this essay, three two-spirit activist educators, present diverse approaches to two-spirit research methodologies. They provide pathways into methodology, emphasising principles of relationality, accountability, body sovereignty and gender self-determination. An overview of the impacts of colonisation on Indigenous gender and sexuality is followed by a discussion of changes in the treatment of two-spirit people. The authors provide practical steps for developing methodologies for research projects that focus on two-spirit people or aim to be inclusive of two-spirit people and their experiences. Finally, the authors discuss their visions for future work in this area, encouraging readers to look at their own policies, programmes and leadership models, with the aim of creating culturally safe spaces from which two-spirit ways of being can flourish.

Chapter 15: Randy Jackson, Doris Peltier and David Brennan, '*Gidoo-Imishinkoowenden* ("You have a Strong Mind"): Reflections on the 2-Spirit HIV/AIDS Wellness and Longevity Study (2SHAWLS)'

In the spirit of oral tradition, this essay shares a conversation between three actors: an allied and settler scholar (Brennan), a two-spirit man living long-term with HIV (Jackson), and an *Anishinaabe* knowledge-keeper (Peltier) to discuss ways in which *gidoo-imishinkoowenden* ('you have a strong mind') reframes what we know about resilience. Several years ago an Indigenous two-spirit community organisation expressed a need to better understand why two-spirit men living long-term with HIV were doing so well, when scientific knowledge had focused on disproportionate rates of HIV infection, later uptake of treatment, more illness, and earlier death. Brennan and Jackson designed a study that explored the idea of resilience in this context. Although their study was welcomed because it highlighted the strengths of Indigenous people living in challenging circumstances, it also received criticism. In the words of one community member: 'I never wanted to be resilient in the first place.' Simply exploring resilience – a westernised concept – potentially ignores Indigenous 'worldview and understanding' (*nendaamowin*) of the 'strong mind' (*imishinkoowenden*) that supports people to live their best lives in wellness. Living a strong mind is the honing of Indigenous intellect and applying it in one's life.

Chapter 16: Andrew Jolivétte, 'Two-Spirit Return: Intergenerational Healing and Cultural Leadership among Mixed-Race American Indians'

This essay, from Jolivétte's book *Indian Blood: HIV and Colonial Trauma in San Francisco's Two-Spirit Community* (2016), introduces the concept of Indigenous Cultural Mentoring Networks (ICMNs) among urban American Indian, two-spirit identified community members who are racially mixed. Based on two years of ethnographic research in the San Francisco Bay Area in collaboration with the Native American AIDS Project (NAAP), Jolivétte maps out a strategy using cross-generational mentoring to address intergenerational and historical trauma. Tackling the issues of tradition, culture and interventions, Jolivette argues that tradition is created and is moveable from rural to urban areas. The essay situates urban Indian kinship networks as vehicles for healing and leadership development among two-spirit communities, who build uniquely urban centres of tradition, cultural protocols, and Indigenous/Inter-tribal approaches to wellness.

Chapter 17: Albert McLeod, 'Honouring Our Ancestors: Two-Spirit Resurgence in the 21st Century'

This essay describes the 40-year path towards recognition of two-spirit people in Canada as unique allies in the broader LGBTQI+ community. McLeod writes about his personal journey as an Indigenous gay man living and working in western Canada. Growing up at a time of intense western assimilation of Indigenous peoples and the erasure of Indigenous languages, spirituality and philosophies, McLeod was guided by the resilience of his grandmother, who was born in 1897. Madeline McIvor (née Moose) was a gifted traditional artist. McLeod's inherent and inalienable rights as a two-spirit person were instilled in him by the natural world and ecosystems in which he was raised. He recounts coming out of a hostile, patriarchal hunter society that disdained LGBTQI+ people and going on to establish safer spaces for two-spirit peoples at the highest levels of Canada's colonial structure and Indigenous governance.

Chapter 18: Rafael/a Luna-Pizano, 'Unknown Devotions: Trans* and Indigena Freedom Dance'

This essay explores the 'practice' of being trans from an Indigena perspective, the aim of which is to offer creative ways of remaining connected to land and water despite colonial interruptions. Luna-Pizano posits that Indigenous trans* people have intimate experiences of (dis)embodiment and that our strategies for survival are creative and generative in the face of displacement and assimilation. Consequently, Indigenous trans* people are part of Indigenous freedom-cosmologies and can lead movements, ceremonies and rituals for sovereignty, particularly when our families are willing to learn from our border crossings and respect our elemental power.

References

Adams, J., Dickinson, P., & Asiasiga, L. (2013). Mental health promotion for gay, lesbian, bisexual, transgender and intersex New Zealanders. *Journal of Primary Health Care, 5*(2), 105–113. doi.org/10.1071/HC13105

Aldrich, R. (2003). *Colonialism and homosexuality*. Routledge.

Anderson. (2017, February 10). *Trans, queer and Indigenous*. National Indigenous Television News. [Video]. YouTube. youtube.com/watch?v=b_l8qIT0pZg

Ashton, A. (2015, August 6). *Discrimination ongoing for queer Māori*. Radio New Zealand. rnz.co.nz/news/te-manu-korihi/280696/discrimination-ongoing-for-queer-Māori

Aspin, C. (2007). Takatāpui – Confronting demonisation. In J. Hutchings & C. Aspin (Eds.), *Sexuality and the stories of indigenous people* (pp. 159–167). Huia.

Balsam, K. F., Huang, B., Fieland, K. C., Simoni, J. M., & Walters, K. L. (2004). Culture, trauma, and wellness: A comparison of heterosexual and lesbian, gay, bisexual, and two-spirit Native Americans. *Cultural Diversity and Ethnic Minority Psychology, 10*(3), 287–301. doi.org/10.1037/1099-9809.10.3.287

Birkenhead, A., & Rands, D. (2012). *Let's talk about sex (sexuality and gender): Improving mental health and addiction services for Rainbow Communities*. Auckland District Health Board.

Dudding, A. (2017, June 19). *Welcome to the rainbow world of gender and sexuality*. Stuff. stuff.co.nz/life-style/life/81125652/welcome-to-the-rainbow-world-of-gender-and-sexuality

Durie, M. (2001). *Mauri ora: The dynamics of Māori health*. Oxford University Press.

Eldred-Grigg, S. (1984). *Pleasures of the flesh: Sex & drugs in colonial New Zealand 1840–1915*. A. H. & A. W. Reed Ltd.

Green, J.A., & Te Wao, M. (2014, July 17–19). *Māori values support safer healthier communities for trans Māori in New Zealand* [Paper presentation]. International Indigenous Pre-Conference on HIV/AIDS, Sydney, Australia.

Grierson, J., Pitts, M., Herewini, T. H., Rua'ine, G., Hughes, A., Saxton, P.,

Whyte, M., Misson, S., & Thomas, M. (2004). Mate Aaraikore a muri ake nei: Experiences of Māori New Zealanders living with HIV. *Sexual Health*, *1*(3), 175–180. doi.org/10.1071/SH03008

Herewini, T., & Sheridan, R. H. (1994). *A report on the health needs of Māori gay men*. Public Health Commission.

Human Rights Commission. (2010). *Human rights in New Zealand*. Human Rights Commission. hrc.co.nz/files/7014/2388/0544/Human_Rights_Review_2010_Full.pdf

Hutchings, J. (2007). Hauora, Māori women and HIV/AIDS: Wahine Māori me te Mate Āraikore. In J. Hutchings & C. Aspin (Eds.), *Sexuality and the stories of indigenous people* (pp. 180–188). Huia.

Hutchings, J., & Aspin, C. (2007). *Sexuality and the stories of indigenous people*. Huia.

Kerekere, E. (2017). *Part of the whānau: The emergence of takatāpui identity – he whāriki takatāpui*. Tīwhanawhana Trust. Teipuwhakahauaa.teraumatatini.com/uploads/kerekere/2017/1168_Kerekere2017.pdf

Lehavot, K., Walters, K. L., & Simoni, J. M. (2009). Abuse, mastery, and health among lesbian, bisexual, and two-spirit American Indian and Alaska Native women. *Cultural Diversity and Ethnic Minority Psychology*, *15*(3), 275–284. doi.org/10.1037/a0013458

McBreen, K. (2012). Ahunga tikanga and sexual diversity. In K. McBreen (Ed.), *Ahunga Tikanga* (pp. 21–35). Te Tākupu, Te Wānanga o Raukawa.

Negin, J., Aspin, C., Gadsden, T., & Reading, C. (2015). HIV among Indigenous peoples: A review of the literature on HIV-related behaviour since the beginning of the epidemic. *AIDS and Behavior*, *19*(9), 1720–1734. doi.org.10.1007/s10461-015-1023-0

Neville, S., & Henrickson, M. (2006). Perceptions of lesbian, gay and bisexual people of primary healthcare services. *Journal of Advanced Nursing*, *55*(4), 407–415. doi.org/10.1111/j.1365-2648.2006.03944.x

Nopera, T. M.-L. (2017). *huka can haka: Taonga performing tino rangatiratanga*. [Doctoral thesis, University of Waikato]. Research Commons. hdl.handle.net/10289/11721

Panelli, R., & Tipa, G. (2007). Placing well-being: A Māori case-study of cultural and environmental specificity. *EcoHealth 4*, 445–460. doi.org/10.1007/s10393-007-0133-1

Pega, F., Reisner, S., Sell, R., & Veale, J. F. (2017). Transgender health: New Zealand's innovative statistical standard for gender identity. *American Journal of Public Health*, *107*(2), 217–221. doi.org/10.2105/AJPH.2016.303465

Pihama, L., Green, A., Mika, C., Roskruge, M., Simmonds, S., Nopera, T., Skipper, H., & Laurence, R. (2020). *Honour project Aotearoa*. Te Kotahi Research Institute. tewhariki.org.nz/assets/Honour-Project-Aotearoa-Final-Report.pdf

Pihama, L., & Lee, J. (2010). *He kākano i ruia mai i rangiātea: Māori whānau stories of neonatal intensive care units*. Māori and Indigenous Analysis Ltd and

Rautaki Ltd. babyfriendly.org.nz/resource/he-kakano-i-ruia-mai-i-rangiatea-maori-whanau-stories-of-neonatal-intensive-care-units

Pihama, L., Smith, L. T., Aspin, C., Newth, A., & Mikaere, A. (2006). *He kete kōrero: Historical and contemporary understandings and expressions of Māori sexuality.* The Health Research Council of New Zealand and the Foundation for Research, Science and Technology.

Rankine, J. (2001). The great, late lesbian and bisexual women's discrimination survey. *Journal of Lesbian Studies, 5*(1/2), 133–142. doi.org/10.1300/J155v05n01_09

Reynolds, P. (2012). Trauma and Māori LGBTQ (takatāpui) in New Zealand. *Traumatic Stress Points, 26*(4), 9–10.

Reynolds, P., & Smith, C. (Eds.) (2012). *The gift of children: Māori and infertility.* Huia.

Rua'ine, G. (2007). Takatāpui and HIV – A personal journey. In J. Hutchings & C. Aspin (Eds.), *Sexuality and the stories of indigenous people* (pp. 149–158). Huia.

Simoni, J.M., Sehgal, S., & Walters, K.L. (2004). Triangle of risk: Urban American Indian women's sexual trauma, injection drug use, and HIV sexual risk behaviors. *AIDS and Behavior, 8*(1), 33–45. doi.org/10.1023/B:AIBE.0000017524.40093.6b

Singer, P. (2015). *Colonialism, two spirit identity, and the logics of white supremacy.* Libcom. libcom.org/article/colonialism-two-spirit-identity-and-logics-white-supremacy

Smith, L. T. (1999). *Decolonizing methodologies. Research and Indigenous peoples.* Zed Books and Otago University Press.

SPINZ. (2013). *Rainbow communities and New Zealand suicide prevention action plan.* Unpublished briefing paper for Associate Minister of Health Todd McClay.

Stangl, A. L., Earnshaw, V. A., Logie, C. H., van Brakel, W., Simbayi, L. C., Barré, I., & Dovidio, J. F. (2019). The health stigma and discrimination framework: A global, crosscutting framework to inform research, intervention development, and policy on health-related stigmas. *BMC Medicine, 17*(31). doi.org/10.1186/s12916-019-1271-3

Te Awekotuku, N. (1991). *Mana wāhine Māori.* New Women's Press.

Te Rōpū Rangahau Hauora a Eru Pōmare. (2002). *Mana whakamārama – Equal explanatory power: Māori and non-Māori sample size in national health surveys.* Ministry of Health.

Te Whāriki Takapou (2021, February 6). *Aotearoa New Zealand people living with HIV stigma index: Māori participant report 2021.* Te Whāriki Takapou.

Waiti, J., & Green, J. A. (2014). *Māori strengths-based approaches.* SHopp (14th ed.). Sexual Health Opportunities Aotearoa.

Waiti, J., & Green, J. A. (2015). *He kai ata rau: Māori strengths-based approaches to ending HIV stigma and discrimination.* Conference, July 5–6, 2016. SHopp (15th ed.).

Walters, K. L., Beltrán, R., Huh, D., & Evans-Campbell, T. (2011). Dis-placement and dis-ease: Land, place, and health among American Indians and Alaska Natives. In L. M. Burton, S. A. Matthews, M. Leung, S. P. Kemp, & D. T. Takeuchi (Eds.), *Communities, neighborhoods, and health: Expanding the boundaries of place* (pp. 163–199). Springer. doi.org/10.1007/978-1-4419-7482-2_10

Walters, K. L. (1997). Urban lesbian and gay American Indian identity. *Journal of Gay & Lesbian Social Services*, 6(2), 43–65. doi.org/10.1300/J041v06n02_05

Walters, K. L. (2007). Foreword. In J. Hutchings & C. Aspin (Eds.), *Sexuality and the stories of indigenous people* (pp. 9–12). Huia.

Witten, T. M. (2007). Transgender bodies, identities, and healthcare: Effects of perceived and actual violence and abuse. In J. J. Kronenfeld (Ed.), *Inequalities and disparities in health care and health: Concerns of patients, providers and insurers (Research in the Sociology of Health Care, Volume 25)* (pp. 225–249). Emerald Group Publishing. doi.org/10.1016/S0275-4959(07)00010-5

Zambas, S. I., & Wright, J. (2016). Impact of colonialism on Māori and Aboriginal healthcare access: A discussion paper. *Contemporary Nurse*, 52(4), 398–409. doi.org/10.1080/10376178.2016.1195238

2

Being Māori, Being Takatāpui

Alison Green, Leonie Pihama, Shirley Simmonds, Matt Roskruge and Tawhanga Nopera

Introduction

The term 'takatāpui' has been recovered and reclaimed from historical Māori narratives (Te Awekotuku, 1991); it encapsulates aspects of one's sexuality, gender, and cultural identity. Many, but by no means all, Māori have preferred to use the term takatāpui over 'gay' or 'lesbian' (Kerekere, 2017; Nopera, 2017), not only as an all-encompassing term to describe a diverse minority (Beyer, 2007), but also to assert that gender- and sexuality-diverse Māori have cultural validity and a place in Aotearoa, as well as globally, as Indigenous people. A critical part of being Māori is our whānau relationships. This was highlighted throughout the research where many takatāpui spoke of being Māori and connected to whānau as central to their own sense of well-being. This chapter provides an overview of how takatāpui involved in the Honour Project Aotearoa talked about the importance of reclaiming our identity and our cultural ways of understanding ourselves. We begin with a discussion of reclaiming identity as takatāpui, the origins of the term and how that relates to our experiences as takatāpui. We move then to how those involved in the project talked about whānau relationships and their significance in providing a sense of connectedness and well-being as takatāpui.

Takatāpui: Reclaiming identity

If colonial processes have indeed profoundly shaped Māori sexual identity and expression (Walters, 2007), then reclaiming identity as takatāpui constitutes a deliberate act of agency, of tino rangatiratanga, which is an essential component of hauora Māori (Hutchings, 2007). While western conceptions and terminology such as 'gay' or 'lesbian' have been partly responsible for the shift away from viewing sexuality as an integral part of traditional cultures to seeing it from the perspective of individuals, 'takatāpui', being derived from traditional Māori society, assists with retaining the essence of traditional collective values. As such, it provides a source of strength to deal with and overcome the negative impacts that takatāpui may face in the contemporary world (Aspin, 2007). Moreover, inherent in the concept takatāpui is the central construct of whānau (Reynolds, 2007; Cooper, 2007; Rua'ine, 2007; Kerekere, 2007; 2017), within which connectedness and belonging are encompassed and affirmed. Takatāpui is defined as 'an intimate friend of the same sex' (Te Awekotuku, 1991; Kerekere, 2015a). As such it is a term that encompasses all takatāpui and Māori LGBTQI+. A well-known example is the story of Tutanekai and his relationship with Tiki, who is referred to as his takatāpui. As Te Awekotuku (1991) notes, 'we do have one word, takatāpui. And ironically, this word is associated with one of the most romantic, glamourized [sic], man/woman love stories of the Māori world, the legend of Hinemoa and Tūtanekai. Tūtanekai, with his flute and his favourite intimate friend, his hoa takatāpui, Tiki' (p. 37). Te Rangikaaheke speaks about the intimacy within the relationship between Tūtānekai and Tiki as follows:

> Ka moohio haere a Tuutaanekai ki te takataapui, araa, ki te whakahoa. Ka piri oo raaua wairua ko toona hoa takataapui ko Tiki, anoo he teina, he tuakana raaua. Ko taa raaua nei mahi taakaro he whakatangitangi puu toorino, puu koauau. Kei te ahiahi poo ka piki raaua ki runga i too raaua nei atamira whakatangitangi ai. (Biggs, Hohepa & Mead, 1967, p. 63)

Te Awekotuku (1991) and Kerekere (2015, 2017) stress that such intimacy was considered to be an accepted way of relating within Māori society. Kerekere (2017) notes:

> Tūtanekai may have loved Hinemoa but his heart belonged to Tiki, whom he called 'taku hoa Takatāpui' – my intimate same sex friend – and spoke about at great length (Grey 1971:113). Tūtanekai missed Tiki so much that he moaned to his adoptive father, Whakaue:
>
> 'Ka mate ahau i te aroha ki tōku hoa, ki a Tiki.' (p. 64)

This phrase is translated by Kerekere as 'I am dying for love for my friend, for my beloved, for Tiki', but Grey (1855) gave a translation that was more palatable to colonial views of sexuality at the time: 'I am quite ill from grief for my friend Tiki' (p. 244). The colonial-washing of Māori sexuality and sexual expression has been well documented (Pihama, 2001; Aspin & Hutchings, 2006; Hutchings & Aspin, 2007; Mikaere, 2017). Aspin (2007) regards the denial of the existence of homosexuality as part of the ongoing suppression of non-heterosexual forms of sexuality. Unsurprisingly, the view that 'homosexuality in both male and female was unknown in early New Zealand' (Gluckman, 1976, p. 164) has been rejected by Māori scholars as completely unfounded (Henare, 1988; Te Awekotuku, 1991; Pihama, 1998; Aspin & Hutchings, 2006). Furthermore, Broughton (1996) provides important evidence as to the diversity of sexuality in pre-contact times with his reference to a waiata tangi from Ngati Tuwharetoa that laments the death of a warrior chief and alludes to him having sex with both women and men (p. 187). He also cites the writing of Te Rangikaheke of Te Arawa, which 'recounts the intimate friendship and pledging of love between Tūtanekai and his hoa takatāpui, Tiki' (Broughton, 1996, p. 187). Such examples provide a powerful counterpoint to the tightly constrained definitions of sexuality that early Pākehā commentators have all too often imposed on pre-contact Māori society.

Defining what it means to be takatāpui was one of the first areas of discussion that was undertaken in the qualitative interviews for the Honour Project Aotearoa, and it was also included in the quantitative survey. As noted previously, and notwithstanding the fact that using a term to identify one's sexual and gender identity may indicate the presence of colonialism, there is a strong support for using Māori terms, such as takatāpui, to locate ourselves fully and to highlight the interconnectedness of how we see our sexual identity, gender identity and cultural identity. Participants were invited to share their reflections on the term 'takatāpui' and how they saw the place of the term within their lives. The vast majority spoke positively of the term 'takatāpui', considering it as a way to see themselves through a Māori cultural lens. This section provides a wide range of ways in which those interviewed spoke to the significance of the term takatāpui in their lives.

> 'For me it actually reinforces that we've always been here because it's our language embedded in our culture, it is and does reinforce whakapapa. Takatāpui, like a lot of our words in the Pacific, so, fa'afafine, fakaleitī, māhū, for me what they do is place us within a cultural context that's undeniable . . . way pre-colonisation, so that's what it reinforces for me is that we've existed forever. We are not a construct, which is cool, so it's a powerful word, but I like our word because we are all the same, LGBTQI+ there are so many different, so it's all of us, it is our diversity encapsulated

in one word where we all fit and there is no difference, which is different between the LGBTQI+ community to be honest because they do all see themselves as segments whereas we don't, we are a whole, we are a collective.' [Interview]

'I first heard that term around the 1990s; it was being bandied around then at a hui that we [had] through Women's Refuge. We had a takatāpui thing and it was awesome! So that's when I first heard that name and I didn't care at the time what it meant; I knew that it was about same sex couples and for me it meant yes it was a Māori term that we could use and have for us because those other names that they had I thought were just revolting and yuck and the connotations to it were yuck, but takatāpui had a nice vibe, I loved it, I loved it when it first come out. I thought yeah! Finally, we can attach to something that felt like ours as Māori anyway so I've been saying that ever since . . . Being called a lesbian, dyke it doesn't have the same feeling, the same mana for me personally. I just love that we could have something, if it was a label, everything's got a label but that just seemed to be a word that I got attached to, that I felt really comfortable with.' [Interview]

'Within that word takatāpui . . . So it was like an intimate friend of the same sex and that's how I feel about all of my relationships. If I'm a friend with someone it's at varying levels of intimacy; like it could go into romantic territory, it could go into sexual territory, it can go back it can be with anybody of any gender, of any sex, of any identity . . . So that word takatāpui I use it as part of my identity now, but because it came so late in my understanding of who I am as queer. It's not one that automatically jumps up to the front and still because I have those habits of compartmentalising my identities when I think about being queer I jump to all of those. I guess they're American labels; you know, pansexual, whatever blah blah blah, but when I think about who I am as a whole person, he wahine takatāpui, that's me . . .' [Interview]

It was clearly articulated that the term 'takatāpui' provides a cultural space and way of considering ourselves within whānau, hapū, iwi, Māori communities and the wider world, however participants also spoke of other names and terms that they would use to describe their sexual and/or gender identity. Some noted that they did not use labels to define themselves as they are a part of whānau and that is the key focus in terms of how they see themselves and their identity. The fact that we have available to us as Māori a range of ways of positioning, naming and describing ourselves is an important factor in how we self-identify. It is also an indicator of how we place ourselves within our cultural relationships with others.

'I would say I am bisexual in regards to sexual preference, which just means I could be into anyone. And then gender, I would say I'm takatāpui non-binary and just use pronouns maybe in there, as I don't feel like I fit into any kind of established gender category but I guess I feel more feminine than masculine . . . I think takatāpui means for me a way to find a place in my Māori identity because I was brought up by my Pākehā grandmother and like my relationship with my dad who is the Māori side of my family hasn't been the strongest and I think my queerness was a way into that world for me, a way to start to legitimise myself as a Māori person.' [Interview]

'My gender identity I am wahine and in terms of my sexual orientation I'm takatāpui so I am a lesbian and I am married to my darling wife and I think I've always known that I was "different".' [Interview]

'It's not a term that I ever use comfortably. I don't really like labels like that. I don't even like the word lesbian and it's just when those words are said to me something inside me just doesn't sit right with me. I'm a Māori woman who happens to be in love with another woman and it's interesting because it's the way I feel too . . . We had aunts who were in same-sex relationships; we didn't use any terms it just seems, it was just aunty . . . and cousin . . . and with _____ and I, everyone calls us the Māmās; here comes the Māmās.' [Interview]

'I tend to use a lot of labels that I found off the internet because I never really had a framework growing up and so the way that I self-identify is – what was the first one – gender identity cis woman, cis female; sexuality, pan sexual, pan romantic if that's a distinction that they want to make.' [Interview]

As expected, a considerable range of gender and sexual identities were discussed and the notions of gender fluidity and non-binary identities were highlighted across the project. Another prevalent theme was the high level of assumptions that are made in regards to gender and sexual identity. This includes assumptions of heterosexuality, and that gender and sexual identity is static and defined in ways that fail to affirm or acknowledge the fluidity of experiences that people have within their lifetime. It was clearly voiced that gender and sexual identity are not fixed and as such cannot be reduced to biological understandings or descriptors.

'I describe myself as being a transsexual woman. I was born biologically a male but from the age of between 10 and 12 I realised that obviously I am different and from 12 I ended up deciding that I was going to be a woman. With all things against me I ended up leaving home at a very young age, growing up on the streets in the 70s . . . Growing up in the Māori trans community, we refer to each other as sisters, queens, and girl, that's how we refer to one another . . . Describing myself as a trans woman, to be honest with you, it's been hard you know, because I've conditioned myself for the last 30-odd years to just be me, just be myself without any heading and just be me.' [Interview]

'I usually say I'm a lesbian, gay but then it's sort of changing nowadays as I'm learning about the spectrum and then I do find different days I feel a little different about things, but most of the time I am a lesbian. . . And biologically I'm not really sure how I feel I just say I'm a female I guess.' [Interview]

'Gender identity, I go by male. My sexual identity I go by bi-sexual. When I was still in high school, because of the whole Māori culture aspect of things and how men were supposed to be masculine and women were feminine I didn't really fit into the category of how men are masculine and everything. So, you know with [the] internet being there, a lot of exposure, I came across this category as gender non-conforming and I was like, "Wow", that resonated with me. I was like, I think I am gender non-conforming.' [Interview]

'I am a trans woman, so male to female, I transitioned when I was 17. Transitioning wasn't easy, coming out in such a straight world was quite scary. Thinking about or even knowing that you were different was scary and the thought of being judged or being hurt always occurred to me but in saying that you go through stuff, there are hard times, there are good times and stuff and I think for me it just got better because I knew in my heart that I was a woman, for me in my heart I was born a woman, born in a male's body.' [Interview]

Whānau and takatāpui well-being

For te ao Māori, whānau is central to our identity and sense of connectedness to wider cultural relationships. For takatāpui, being accepted – in particular by whānau – being happy, being grounded are all noted as being at the centre of well-being. A number of people spoke about the need for whānau to provide unconditional love when whānau members share with them.

'Absolutely if they love you unconditionally it doesn't matter what sexuality you are; you are still part of the whānau and they will go to battle for you, so I don't have to ever worry about it.' [Interview]

'My family is very open. My family is very much like you lead your own life, it's your life, however you lead it is completely up to you. You don't have to explain yourself for being who you are and just doing what you want to do, like literally at the end of the day it's your own life.' [Interview]

In talking about whānau it is clear that there is both the desire to ensure connectedness to whakapapa and a need to ensure that there are wider networks that provide support at times when your whānau are not able to fill that role. The importance of whānau and being connected is a common theme throughout all of the interviews; there is no illusion that it is straightforward or easy for all whānau members, but what is clear is the commitment from takatāpui to do all they can to remain connected.

> 'My nan was probably the hardest one so far as well . . . she's 81 [laughs], very old traditional, conservative. I mean before I started transitioning she asked if I was getting married soon? [laughs] Because she was 20 when she got married . . . But also she's just a strong independent woman . . . My Koko died about 36 years ago . . . and my mum was quite young so . . . she's spent so long, you know, looking after her family and just being the glue, and I think she's concerned more. . . but also just doesn't understand and doesn't want to . . . I don't need her to understand I just want her to respect . . . and so she said, "No, you're a girl," and kind of laughed in my face . . . The laughing hurt, but I mean I didn't expect her to be like, "Oh, that's great, good on you!" Yeah, [it's] just her generation . . . So I'm trying, because I love my family and I care about them, and because they've given me so much in my life that it's kind of, how can you forget that just because they don't accept one aspect of your character. You know? And it's a big part because I guess it's guiding some of my journey along the way. But it's, yeah, they're still my family.' [Interview]

> 'My whānau was good, but for one brother, sibling. When I came back to ____ they sort of all just stared at me in shock, I know a lot of them were in shock. Some of the women propositioned me, they were good. I think the worst, negative feedback you could get is from your own whānau, your immediate whānau. From the community, well you really don't care because you are all related and you could have a fight but you could talk about it. Everybody treated me the same and it's because I think, I told them this is what I am and so be it. If ever I did get negative feedback, I would refer back to being propositioned by their wives.' [Interview]

Many participants spoke of the pain of being separated and a deep sense of sorrow and worry at the prospect of isolation from whānau. Similarly a number of people talked about the isolation and grief of not being accepted by their wider iwi or Māori community.

> 'My aunty is a trans woman. She died so young and had such a hard life. I never even got a chance to know her because of the distance that she had to have from her family. My dad has definitely grown but he knew her as Paul, not Cindy, and it's like, "Nah, Dad, she was never really Paul, she wasn't Paul." Everyone else thought she was Paul. I mean I don't actually know how she felt about it, but that's how I think about it to myself. It's

like you find yourself and the rest of the world has to catch up. She had such a fucken hard life; she still found a family and that was the biggest thing for me at her tangi was to see that and I actually stood up and said, "I feel so much sorrow that we weren't there for her, but I see the love in this room and to look around and see that she actually found her family and found her tribe, I'm grateful to all of you and thank you for being here" . . . They put us at the side of the whānau pani and I just thought it was wrong, because yeah, I was grieving and yeah I was related to her but I wasn't there for her when she needed it and that's just how I feel like a lot of our whānau were going through that shit; you know, regardless of where they identify, how they identify, who they identify as and being Māori on top of that and Jesus the lack of care. The lack of understanding that's there.' [Interview]

'So I initially told my mum [I was transgender] . . . she had said that she always just thought I was a lesbian . . . I think I held off . . . Because I didn't want to disappoint her, or burden her and just embarrass her as well. I live in Wellington now, I'm away from everyone that we're always around back home . . . Because I feel like you isolate yourself for such a long time trying to accept yourself and if you don't think you can accept yourself you're not sure if anyone else would. So I think that was the most worrying experience.' [Interview]

'I'll tell you something though this is more to do with ____. When I arrived there I let everyone know I'm gay, "Oh that's good," you know, "We embrace," blah blah blah. Actually they don't; it's quite a homophobic thing there and part of the South Canterbury AIDS network we brought the quilts down to ____ and I announced this at a rūnaka meeting . . . and explained what the quilts were, they're coming into our rohe they need to stay overnight at our marae. Well there was a huge [reaction], it became quite abusive and I thought *That's interesting*. A lot of people supporting the idea and a lot of people against it. No way was that gonna be allowed to happen. So I asked my kaumātua, would you be able to come and mihi for the quilts when we receive them and we're going to open them, you know welcome the quilts into, it was the stadium where we spread them out and he said, oh yes he would but then he said, 'Oh no I can't' So then I asked ____ ; he said, 'oh yes he'd be happy to', closer to the time no he's not happy to, or not able to. You know who came through were the students of the Polytech Māori whānau. They embraced it, they were wonderful. They called us on with them, they were blessed and we spread them out, but that was another little time of people saying, "Yes, it doesn't matter, we embrace you." So this is part of one thing that I'm quite keen about getting involved [in] with this process, this project, because there's part of me that still would like us to be written [about] in our tribal magazine.' [Interview]

A number of participants spoke of the impact of Christianity within their whānau and what that means with regard to being takatāpui. A particular focus they shared was the strength needed to talk to their whānau about their sexual or gender identity. For those raised in Christian homes, which tend to have a much more conservative and uncompromising views of sexuality and gender, the anxiety around such conversations can be magnified. This can mean that people will select specific whānau members to share with before telling the whole whānau.

> 'I was brought up as a Jehovah's Witness. My mum and my dad are still Jehovah's Witnesses so when I kind of got with my first partner and thought oh yeah, okay this is going to happen . . . Yes, I was scared, as I think everybody else [is] . . . coming out, but it was more hard for me to tell my mum because I know she was, well she wasn't pretty staunch in there but I just found it really hard to come out to my mum. Like I could tell my step-dad and I could tell my dad, I told my brother and my sister and all that stuff but I couldn't get myself to tell my mum. So one day I just said to my partner, "I don't know how to bring it to my mum because being a Jehovah's Witness obviously women are women . . . and that's what we've [been] brought up as that it's just Adam and Eve." So it took me like two weeks to get the courage to, because . . . I felt like I was letting her down and it was just so hard. So I finally got to tell my mum and I said, "Hey Mum, I'm going out with a woman" and I could hear it in her voice because she just couldn't stop, she was like, "Oh okay, all right." I knew she wasn't going to go, "Oh, nah, I don't want anything to do with you"; I knew that but it was just actually getting it out to her to say, "Hey Mum, I'm gay and I've got a gay partner." So that was probably one of the ones that stand out . . . was to just to tell my mum that I was lesbian.' [Interview]

> 'Probably for me I had very staunch parents; my mum was a Christian and at the time I was too. So that identity, finding out who I truly was when my children were about 15, probably [it] was way before that, but that was when I stepped out of my Christian beliefs. They were only young men then and when I came out to them was when they were 20, to my children first. But my dad had passed in 1997 and I was his main caregiver and he told me then, he always knew. Well you know they just do and he just told me if you want to be happy you need to be happy in who you are and who you want to be. So that was in 1997 because my mum's sister had been in a lesbian relationship for many years prior to that and she never ever came out openly. My father was the only one that knew about that and it wasn't until he passed that she had spoken to me about that too. So it was really difficult for me because my children were only teenagers, but I knew at 15 when I stepped out of my Christian values that that was the life I was going to pursue and it didn't happen until they were 19, 20, with the partner that

I'm still with today. So it was hard, my family were . . . great with it; my brothers and my one sister and then my mum had spoken to me about that as well. Although she died as a very staunch Christian she said to me that you need to be happy with what you want to be, pretty much the same lines as what my dad had said too, and so life had begun and still there today with my partner.' [Interview]

'Through a church that I belonged to I decided, God knows how, that I could be fixed for being gay because it was generally frowned upon. This was in the mid-60s. So through the church they persuaded me to seek some medical help. They prayed for me, then I could seek some medical help, so through being absolutely stupid – I was old enough to know better – but I was persuaded to seek, and it was still classified then as a mental illness. I had electrodes stuck on the side of my head and they put an electric current through my head . . . You could get so mixed up in your head, but it was a dreadful, dreadful, dreadful time. Because I was so mixed up in my head I didn't understand the impact of what that might do. After that, that was a big turning point in my life, because I made a decision then that I had to be me.' [Interview]

Seeing ourselves

Acceptance and visibility as takatāpui are both linked to the idea of normalisation. One participant reflected on how the term 'normal' has been reframed in ways that marginalise those groups in society that do not fit a predetermined, dominant 'norm'. Others spoke of the normalisation of being takatāpui within whānau and communities as being connected to both self and collective affirmation. Affirmation and acceptance of takatāpui within whānau increases the likelihood of diversity and inclusion for future generations of rangatahi, both by whānau and the wider community.

> 'There are some words that we use in general day-to-day life . . . I thought that I understood them but I am not sure I fully understand the construction of that word when it's used in terminologies to describe us as members of the larger gay community. One of those is 'normal'. That word is bandied around. When I was growing up, normal meant that my mate did the same things that I did. It meant that if I caught an eel and we used a particular lure to put in the water, and he did the same, that was kind of normal between him and I, that was what normal meant for me then. But now I have got to my age and normal is used to describe people and to describe that I've been called not normal . . . the "normal" word that I used as a child was positive but now it's used to describe me as a negative; you are not normal, my relationship is not normal. When I am talking about having a man as my life partner that's not normal – so "normal" has become used in a way that has a sense of negativity and rather than,

growing up as a child, that was a really positive experience, I fitted, I was like a nail that fitted into a hole. Those are the things that I've, I guess I have become more contemplative, I've got time in my head to do that and it's not wisdom, it's just contemplation. So you are thinking about things and how things work. There was a word the other day somebody used as well and I thought about it, that's real sick, but they mean, that used to be a negative word, but actually it's used now in a positive terminology and so my brain doesn't always cope with that.' [Interview]

'I spoke at a rangatahi forum last week, and one of the things I talked about was we have to be proud of who we are, all of us and all of it. And I talked about being takatāpui and [it] doesn't matter where I am and who I'm with I will always acknowledge my wife and be proud of who I am. I mean it's just like that we don't talk to our kids about stuff like that and whoever you are it's a gift from our tūpuna. We all need to embrace it but we don't talk about that actually, and we need to be proactive. I think our tribes need to be proactive and talk about the different identities so it enables our kids to say, "Oh, that's who I am, it's all good, I don't have to be ashamed of myself," because in mainstream it is still a shameful process . . . We need to run it with our iwi because the iwi need to support our takatāpui to be takatāpui and talk about it . . . as part of Auckland Pride Festival, Love Life Fono organised a Pacific panel and . . . one of the things that came out of that was the need to create a Pacific resource that lists all our names – fa'afafine, fakaleitī – all of them takatāpui. As I said before, we exist in our language and our culture; we always have. We are not others; we are a part of it and I see that's the beginning of . . . doing what you want to do with this. But imagine if you could have takatāpui of Taranaki; we need to celebrate, we need to know who these people are.' [Interview]

There was also discussion around whether people were aware of other whānau members who are takatāpui. The silence that often surrounds sexuality and gender identity can make it difficult to know who is takatāpui within whānau, and a number of people spoke about what that meant in their whānau. Much of the discussion centred on finding out about others in the whānau and the ways in which participants supported their whānau members who did come out.

'A nephew of mine, it was his father that wasn't too impressed with it but I supported him. I said, "You can't tell him what feelings he can have and what feelings he can't have," and he was the only one . . . my nephew and he's happy. He's still with his partner and none of us have ever had anything bad to say about him. Just be who you are; don't hide anything. I think when you hide something it just becomes a little bit more, I don't know, you are just not yourself if you are going to try and hide something.

It's like just be open and enjoy life. He's the only one in my family that I know about. But I'm pretty sure that whoever comes out it's just like – "Oh yeah, okay" – that's sort of how our family look at it; we don't begrudge anybody, I haven't had any comeback or negativity.' [Interview]

'I've had very good ones so far with other family and my friends. So my aunties they are, one's my mum's sister and then the other one's her partner. But they have never, you know, claimed that they're together like that.' [Interview]

'When I came out I was staying with a same-sex couple, friends of mine from teacher's college in Wellington and we would just go to the ___ , they had something every month and we'd just go to that and go to Casper's bar in Wellington. I mainly mixed with either the gay men or the queens, because the queens were part of our family in Hastings. That's what we called them at the time, transgender now. There's so many different terms have come to fruition, but they were part of our family.' [Interview]

'The Māori side of my brother, our Māori side was very tough in terms of men being gay and if someone like my uncle, mum's brother – he was pretty harsh. So it's really funny, but he was not supported in our whānau, not with our older generation [and the extended] so he didn't bother going there and actually he ended up cutting himself off and ended up going over to our Pacific Island side, Samoan/Tongan.' [Interview]

Summary

The interviews and stories that were shared for Honour Project Aotearoa enabled in-depth discussions around what it means to identify as and be takatāpui or Māori LGBTQI+ in Aotearoa. Sharing our own definitions of ourselves and our understandings of well-being provides a foundation upon which we can build a future where all sexualities and gender expressions are acknowledged as part of what it means to be Māori. We have been reminded many times throughout this work that to be takatāpui or Māori LGBTQI+ is to be whānau which, in terms of our tikanga views of identity, is to be members of whānau, hapū, iwi and Māori collectives. Sexuality and gender expressions are terms that have been imported through a colonising process; however, the essence of being and of expressing ourselves is embedded within our being Māori. We should not confuse these things. That is clear from those who shared their thoughts for this work. This aligns to the work undertaken by Te Awekotuku (1991), Aspin (2007), Aspin and Hutchings (2006) and Kerekere (2015a; 2017), all of whom have highlighted that to be takatāpui or Māori LGBTQI+ is to be whānau, is to be Māori.

We see much sharing around the need to be visible as takatāpui and Māori LGBTQI+ in order to provide models for those who are feeling isolated, marginalised and alone because of their sexual and/or gender identity. Visibility is in this sense a political project that is required to support those who are 'coming out' into what is often a negative or oppressive situation. As we have been reminded, the idea of being visible as a sexual or gendered identity was not necessarily a practice within the Māori world prior to colonisation as sexual and gender identities were not defining factors in regards to our place within whānau (Kerekere 2015). However, we are in a different, colonised context where oppressive ideologies of misogyny, homophobia and transphobia impact on the lives of many takatāpui and Māori LGBTQI+ communities. What that means is that our whānau, hapū, iwi and Māori communities are critical to ensuring the safety and well-being of takatāpui.

As Māori, we have a strong cultural foundation that is built upon collective well-being and responsibility. This includes an ancestral obligation and expectation that we will ensure the well-being of all within our whānau. It also encompasses a cultural understanding that there are many ways in which sexual and gender identities are expressed amongst our people. As one participant stated, being able to draw on an inner strength of being Māori when facing racism or homophobia was key to their sense of well-being. To be takatāpui is to be Māori and to be a part of whānau. That is a powerful way of seeing ourselves within a world that seeks often to fragment our collective positioning as tangata whenua, as people of the land. The term takatāpui reminds us all that we have always been here and we will always be Māori, takatāpui, and whānau.

References

Aspin, C., & Hutchings, J. (2006). Māori sexuality. In M. Mulholland (Ed.), *The state of the Māori nation: Twenty-first-century issues in Aotearoa* (pp. 227–235). Reed.

Aspin, C. (2007). Takatāpui – Confronting demonisation. In J. Hutchings & C. Aspin (Eds.), *Sexuality and the stories of Indigenous people* (pp. 159–167). Huia.

Biggs, B., Hohepa, P. W., & Mead, S. M. (1967). *Selected readings in Maori*. Reed.

Beyer, G. (2007). Of two spirits: An interview with Georgina Beyer, Member of Parliament. In J. Hutchings & C. Aspin (Eds.), *Sexuality and the stories of Indigenous people* (pp. 70–81). Huia.

Beyer, G., & Casey, C. (1999). *Change for the better: The story of Georgina Beyer as told to Cathy Casey*. Random House.

Broughton, J. (1996). He taru tawhiti: Māori people and HIV/AIDS. In P. Davis

(Ed.), *Intimate details and vital statistics: AIDS, sexuality and the social order in New Zealand* (pp. 187–202). Auckland University Press.

Cooper, T. T. (2007). Why do Māori come out of closets? In J. Hutchings & C. Aspin (Eds.), *Sexuality and the stories of indigenous people* (pp. 141–148). Huia.

Gluckman, L. K. (1976). *Medical history of New Zealand prior to 1860*. L. K. Gluckman.

Grey, G., & Williams, H. W. (Eds.) (1971). *Nga mahi a nga tupuna* (4th ed.). Reed.

Grey, G. (1855). *Polynesian mythology and ancient traditional history of the New Zealand race, as furnished by their priests and chiefs*. J. Murray.

Henare, M. (1988). Standards and foundations of Maori society. In *Nga tikanga me nga ritenga o te ao marama* (Vol. 3). Royal Commission on Social Policy.

Hutchings, J., & Aspin, C. (2007). *Sexuality and the stories of indigenous people*. Huia.

Kerekere, E. (2007). Takatāpui – Where worlds collide. In J. Hutchings & C. Aspin (Eds.), *Sexuality and the stories of indigenous people*. Huia.

Kerekere, E. (2015a). *Takatāpui: Part of the whānau*. Tīwhanawhana Trust and Mental Health Foundation.

Kerekere, E. (2015b, August 13). Waka Hourua National Māori and Pasifika Suicide Prevention Research Symposium. [Video]. YouTube. youtube.com/watch?v=NQ70JKMGKEU

Kerekere, E. (2017). *Part of the whānau: The emergence of takatāpui identity – He whāriki takatāpui*. Tīwhanawhana Trust.

Mikaere, A. (2017). *The balance destroyed*. Huia and Te Tākupu, Te Wānanga o Raukawa.

Nopera, T. M. (2017). *huka can haka: Taonga performing tino rangatiratanga*. [Doctoral thesis, University of Waikato]. Research Commons. hdl.handle.net/10289/11721

Pihama, L. (2001). *Tīhei mauri ora: Honouring our voices – Mana wahine as a kaupapa Māori theoretical framework* [Unpublished doctoral thesis, University of Auckland]. hdl.handle.net/2292/1119

Pihama, L. (1998). Reconstructing meanings of family: Lesbian/gay whanau and families in Aotearoa. In V. Adair & R. Dixon (Eds.), *The family in Aotearoa New Zealand* (pp. 179–207). Addison Wesley Longman.

Reynolds, P. (2007). I'm takatāpui! I'm takatāpui tāne! In J. Hutchings & C. Aspin (Eds.), *Sexuality and the stories of indigenous people* (pp. 110–121). Huia.

Rua'ine, G. (2007). Takatāpui and HIV – A personal journey. In J. Hutchings & C. Aspin (Eds.), *Sexuality and the stories of indigenous people* (pp. 149–158). Huia.

Te Awekotuku, N. (1991). *Mana wāhine Māori*. New Women's Press.

Walters, K. L. (2007). Foreword. In J. Hutchings & C. Aspin (Eds.), *Sexuality and the stories of indigenous people*. Huia.

3

A Māori worlded speculation on terms 'sex' and 'gender'

Carl Mika

Basic premises

Overarching Western assumption: that text and orthodox academia operate neutrally, largely free from their own ancient assumptions.

Therefore: that an analysis of terms is only possible if it is grounded upon the neutral phenomenon of rationalism.

Māori counter-colonial position: that, contrary to rationalism, a Māori analysis tries to expose the ancient metaphysics that text and orthodox academia operate upon; and that a Māori approach will attempt to resurrect a unit of analysis that differs from the West's and synchronises with its own metaphysics.

Introduction

All concepts and their representations – through writing, speech or any other means – are based on an initial metaphysics or set of fundamental ideas.[1] Colonisation has either altered or threatened to completely dissolve those first Māori philosophies, which cannot be determined empirically but only gestured towards through speculative philosophy. These basic principles differ between the West and Indigenous peoples, at least as they are described within the literature. The aim of this paper is to consider some of the terms that are aligned in the West with the area of sexual health, and

---

1   According to Deloria, these sit at the base of any judgement of the world and have consequences for well-being. See in particular Deloria Jnr and Wildcat (2001).

to submit them to a representation that is based on a worlded metaphysics. This concept, 'worlded', is one I use to explain the fact of one thing's constitution by all others (see Mika, 2017b), and it reflects the belief that all things are interconnected or, indeed, one. If a term does nurture a deep view of all things being 'worlded' or co-constitutional, then it may be said to sit well with that most fundamental Māori metaphysics and may then indeed simply *sit well*, not doing harm to the region it is located in or to the representing self. If, however, the term reveals a landscape of strict division and strong individual presence, then it is opposed to that Māori metaphysics, will therefore threaten a Māori ability to represent things in accordance with those initial principles, and will be 'unhealthy' in a Māori sense.

In this paper, I start with a description of worldedness as both a metaphysics and a term analysis (method). This paper proceeds on the premise that, for an Indigenous worldview of worldedness, there are flaws in modes of critique that are sometimes thought of as radical in the West, such as critical discourse analysis[2]. I also explain some of the Māori terminology that equates roughly with worldedness as a concept. I then turn to two terms that arise frequently within the area of takatāpui health – 'sex' and 'gender' with their various assumptions.

Worldedness and language

In Māori thought, the world (ao) is not simply the seen aspect of existence but the totality of all things (Marsden, 2003; Pere, 1982). Ao, interestingly, is also a verb, as in 'ka ao', which most economically could be translated as 'to world', even if 'world' is something different to 'ao' (and here we meet our first difficulty with language between coloniser and colonised and the things that reside within it). To say that something 'worlds' in a Māori context amounts to describing the conceptual and real constitution of a thing by the entirety of the world. Another aspect of 'worlding' is that any object or idea manifests its true nature *as* the world in its totality, and even the individual object's disclosure to the human self is determined by the world. This metaphysics is vastly different to that proposed by the West, which defines an object in its full presence as *the* object, determined firstly by what it will be in advance as an object and then by its properties (Fuchs, 1976). Included in a Māori description of 'things' or 'phenomena' are ideas, thoughts and perceptions, which are just as material as what the West might

2   I highlight CDA here because it is designed to disclose power relations. Yet, if it relies on a notion of language and concept of things that is unholistic, it will perform the same function as more obviously orthodox methods.

call real, material objects. Thinking or experiencing other things thus itself requires thinking about, resulting in a sort of meta-thinking that does not belong in the margins of the page or in footnotes but instead is just as important as the thing being thought about.

We could argue that the possibility worldedness offers is not an option but an ethical responsibility. Certainly, this is my approach to worldedness, which does not simply deal with the description of an object (although it does conduct an assessment) but aims to keep our perceptions and representations intact with the world being discussed at any point. Again, dominant Western thought, with its overwhelmingly antithetic means of fragmenting objects and making them fully what they are through that division, sees ethics as a way of protecting the human self, or maybe the animal, but does not see ideas as 'whakaaro' and hence as evolving, ancestral entities that need to be ethically represented in their own right as ancestral. Arola (2011) therefore argues that the drive for a holistic ontology is beyond simply epistemic; it is more importantly *ethical*. We may gather from him that conceiving of an idea in a Western sense is insufficient for Indigenous approaches.

Most often, the 'hooks' into a worlded analysis are through language. A philosophical analysis is generally accessed through language, but there are distinctions to be made between dominant Western and Māori conceptions of language. Both agree that language can be a mode of communication, although Māori may place more emphasis on silence as a subset of this form of language (Mika, 2017b); silence may influence our senses, either through its unique absence or its ability to allow the world to disclose itself without having to compete with chatter. Where Māori and Western thought diverge is in an emphatic Māori proposition that language belongs to the seen and unseen dimensions of the world as the latter organises itself, whether the human self perceives that self-arrangement or not, whereas in the dominant Western canon the first instance of language is argued as originating from and controlled by the human self. A worlded analysis, then, acknowledges that phenomena provide the cues for thought and, indeed, co-constitute beyond our perception with our ancestor 'whakaaro', among others, to allow the self to articulate or speak at all.

At times, I begin this analysis through the accessibility provided by language, which the West has attempted to define for us simply as a means of logical communication. In this work, we are constantly aware of the colonising philosophies that sit under terms. Hence, sometimes the Indigenous writer must reiterate his or her position constantly and will need to return to the depths of Western thought as much as Māori thought; however, at the same time, I aim to make that excavation into Western thought a Māori event. To this end, we need to keep in mind the following pitfalls of dominant Western thought, all of which actually overlap:

> That, as one talks about things, one is detached from their immediate and formative influence; the discussant or writer is not part of the ground that gives rise to the things being discussed. Where I detect this occurring in language or broader conceptual terrain in this paper, I bracket it with '⌡'; where possible I bold the offending term, and discuss the shortcomings of Western concepts that give rise to the problem as a sort of **subtext**. I have decided to use these hooks instead of footnotes or endnotes as I want to keep the sort of critique they offer on parity with my more proactive assertions. I consider this process of underscoring problematic language an ethical encounter with Western things in the world, as it aims to temporarily destabilise the certainty that Western metaphysics always inserts into representations.

> ⌡ In Māori philosophy, it appears that an utterance could present all things (Mika, 2016); thus, 'subtext' may be a misnomer, as any apparently subservient idea we want to convey would sit immediately within what was being uttered. Here, we begin a critique of Western notions of presence – even within our current discussion. ⌡

> That the West prefers the overwhelming presence of a thing – and, relatedly, the correct identification of its qualities – to its absence.

> That there is no unseen *matter* to a thing that surpasses its material qualities when it is being grasped by the mind. It is simply that thing being discussed. If there is something absent, it is merely *conceptually* absent. On the other hand, matter in Māori thought, in reality and concept, transcends our perception of the thing being discussed.

> That one may often detect a lack of material 'ground' to the concepts and labels used in the West; the ground is simply a 'conceptual' one, set by logic or well-founded facts.

> That things are fragmented rather than preserved as belonging together.

> That rationalistic ways of speaking immediately privilege all these approaches and, more actively, discourage any ways of speaking that prefer Māori concepts and realities of ground.

The uncertain ground of 'sex': Basic premises

Overarching Western assumption: that 'ground' is either conceptual or material, not both at once. That is, a 'ground' in the West is either land or base, or a rationale, never both.

Therefore: that terms such as 'sex' are founded on epistemic certainty.

Māori counter-colonial position: that one's basic mental representations are constituted by a primordial ground (sometimes called 'Papatūānuku'), not simply an *idea* of that ground; and that our representations of 'sex' are obscured by that pervasively material ground (and are therefore not epistemically certain).

A focus on 'ground'

An explicit reference to ground is especially important when we are discussing sexual health, not simply because we do need to establish a set territory of thought to focus on it, but also because there are certain metaphysical entities associated with discussions about sexual health in Māori literature. These phenomena bring into focus 'ground' due to their obvious incorporation within the materiality of earth. We can start with Hinetītama, who is Papatūānuku's granddaughter and Hineahuone's daughter (Jenkins & Harte, 2011) and is therefore constituted by a Māori notion of ground. Hinetītama also delineated certain sexual ethics. Sexual health and its terms must be discussed in light of material ground as much as conceptual ground (although we shouldn't rely on a mention of the ground to discuss it, because it is implicit in all our orientations) and analysed in terms of the co-constitution of one thing by all others. In other words, sexual health, sexuality and discussions about them are immediately saturated with both thinking and real 'ground'.

A particular foundation is established in the West, too. Murphy (2015) reflects on Kitcher's belief that an 'objectivist analysis' of health is '"grounded" on facts about the human body' (n.p.). Murphy's discussion is notable for two reasons: it describes an important approach to the concept and practice of 'health' (and therefore stylistically introduces us, although just through terminology, to a discussion about sexual health in its broadest sense), but even more importantly for this discussion it draws our attention to what the basis of any assertion, including health, is – a particular **'ground'**. The ground Murphy refers to is most definitely a conceptual one, and even though he takes issue with Kitcher's reference to ground, there is nevertheless a ground imputed within his own establishing of fact and argument. Highlighting a thinking ground evinces itself in most writing and logical expression, although the word 'ground' may not be mentioned. There will always be implicit, in most common forms of Western representation, a particular foundation that is not necessarily shared by Māori thought. Thus, a brief explanation is called for when 'ground' is mentioned, because it is not so straightforward for Māori as it appears to be in dominant Western thought.

> The etymology of 'ground' does not particularly signal a division in its spiritual meaning. But its continued use as either conceptual ground or material ground may have so corroded its meaning that the two cannot be unified, at least to the satisfaction of Māori philosophy. If that is true, then a crucial term for this paper (ground) is incapable of disclosing that unification, despite what we intend for that term. Papa, often translated as 'ground', will also be a divider if it is understood in the same way as the divisible 'ground' – as in uses such as a Māori notion of 'ground' forms the 'Papa' of this research, where 'Papa' in fact merely refers to conceptual ground.
>
> Sometimes, on the other hand, terms do reveal an innate, etymological tendency to stand in opposition to a Māori metaphysics. I wrote a book chapter that looked at dominant Western notions of ground and the language of conceptual ground (see Mika, 2017c). The ancient term 'epistēmē' is one that immediately calls for a ground of solidity upon which one stands in order to make utterances of truth about the world. It is one example of a term encrusted with a division between ideal and real from its origin.

Let us start with the ground of 'concept' or 'conceptualising'. We can more precisely group this strong mode of conceptualising under the broad rubric of 'orientation', which may well find its expression in the Māori prefix 'whaka' ('to cause something to be') – an under-theorised particle, in my view. With orientation, all things in the world have their own particular comportment towards the world. We cannot speak about the types of orientation of other things in the world, other than to say that we do know a kōhatu, maunga, awa and so on will have their own turn toward and within the world (see Mika, 2017b) that we cannot possibly know. This is evident in how Kereopa speaks of pipi (a type of seafood) with their own language (Moon, 2003), for instance. For the human self, comportment could comprise rationalising, as well as laughing, worrying, and so on. But the strongly rationalising self, which establishes the extremely vivid conceptual ground and diminishes that ground's simultaneous material self, is the Western way of inserting oneself within the world, because it is precisely the act of rationalising that separates the self from the world. The Platonic Form, which is a transcendent and unchanging phenomenon and which sits in the background as possibly the most highly valued aspect of Western philosophy, is not considered to be a constitutionally real force within all things in the world, giving things their very solid existence – not in a Māori worldview, at least, where the true ground of all things is immediately one and the same with those things.

'Sex' and the problems of its origins

An appropriate place to start an analysis is with the relationship between the most fundamental term in sexual health, 'sex', and a method of division that brings about knowledge. Gordon (2014) traces the link between the terms 'sex' and 'science', through their Latin and Greek origins, with 'science' becoming 'sex' through its etymology of 'to know' ('scire'), 'to divide' ('scindere'), 'to split, cleave' ('skhizein'), and then 'to cut' ('secare') from which arises the term 'sex'. He argues that '[a] link between science and sex brings biology to the fore', with 'concerns over the generation of life initiat[ing] scientific inquiry' (p. 84). The sociological argument that sex has been too deeply equated with biology fits precisely at this point and will not be repeated here, as it is more important for this discussion to indicate that the relationship between sex and biology is a philosophical one as well, with the two phenomena of sex (and its various states) and science evolving from an even more primordial assumption. From the Māori metaphysical perspective, the ground that any dealings with the term 'sex' insists on is divisive. A ground that can be fragmented allows 'scire', 'scindere' and 'skhizein' (Gordon, 2014) to flourish. Indeed, a divisible ground is absolutely necessary for 'sex' as a phenomenon to emerge, given impetus from 'science'.

The division between oneself and one's ground that 'sex/skhizein' and their different forms insist on implies that the human self is a rationalistic entity and that another thing is only possible by virtue of the self's rationalising. For Western philosophers such as Heidegger (1977) and Derrida (1982),[3] thought is calcified through particular representations of the world (a view which many Māori philosophers would probably agree with), but for Māori, to separate the orienting human self away from his or her material ground of existence is a dangerous and colonising undertaking. This amnesia has grave consequences for both the West and Māori. To begin with, the divorce between ideal and real means that all things in the world (including thought, objects and so on) only exist to the extent that they are conceivable. This rupture of a thing from its reality comes about because the thing has been conceived of as a true 'thing', without the materiality of the primordial, material ground to obstruct that true apprehension. For Māori philosophy on its own, there are dire implications for decentring

3 Although extremely useful, neither of these philosophers deal with an Indigenous worldview of co-constitution/worldedness. They may point strongly to the philosophy's tendency to reify the human self, but they do not entertain that the self is materially constituted by all things in the world. Some of Heidegger's later work seemed to hint at worldedness, but not to the extent of Māori philosophy.

what is often called 'Papatūānuku' from thought, but crucially, if thought is to be understood as material, then separating the two will frame and impact on the everyday health of Māori.[4]

A divisible ground in Māori thought has interesting paradoxes: it suggests that the human self's ability to rationalise is implicit in the act, and that any self-division of our ground is immaterial. That is, our ability to control the ground and its reproduction of its things is paramount – this control would amount to an epistemic one that falls into line with 'scire'. If things in the world have their apparent distinctiveness, however, then from that Māori worlded viewpoint there is a self-organisation of ground that is at work and operates as its own sovereign. At no stage in the evolution of any of those Indo-European terms (scire and so on) is there any hint of a ground that constitutes things in the world to the extent that those things are one, and similarly there is no readily accessible language that describes how those things conjoin our and other **things**' comportment to the world.

> In its Western sense, 'thing' is a noun, and is often used in opposition to an animate being (human, animal, etc.). In Māori language, 'mea' denotes both 'to say' and 'thing'. If a thing automatically says, then this may well be a Māori phenomenology in which the world announces itself through a thing (Mika, 2017b), and thus a thing is never as inert as its Western noun-assumption allows. 'Thing' could well be a verb (Mika, 2016).

The sophistication that lies behind the paradox of the Māori ground – where it is both immediately conceptual and material, to the extent that those distinctions should never really be used in relation to it – is put to rest with the science–sex association. As Gordon notes, rationalism cannot tolerate inconsistencies. Scientised thinking takes precedence, and the ground, although in the process of being divided, is only divided insofar as things that are forced to arise from it correspond logically with each other. Here we meet the dilemma that the transferors of empiricist philosophy encounter with so-called irrational philosophies: Cohen (1999), for instance, notes of the downplaying of Spanish philosophy where 'the English, in particular, set their grey, cold, pinched faces against [the vital importance of subjectivity], and proclaimed instead the centrality of "analysis" and importance of detachment' (p. 209). This approach to ground, it should be noted, has implications not only for a discourse of the ground for the

---

4 Wildcat (2001) indicates that Western metaphysics induces instability in the native student. Mika (2017b) similarly argues that the Western lack of materiality to the conceptual ground has repercussions for the long-cherished notion of 'whakapapa'.

self but also for the health of the self. Where Māori may have gladly and healthily co-existed with a ground from which mystery evolved through the complex interrelationship of things, ground through science-sex is ultimately smoothed by human will.

> ❡ 'Self' needs to be signalled in relation to its tendency to individualise the human being. It is well acknowledged that, in Māori philosophy, the 'self' is not the same 'self' as that very term indicates. A Māori individual is both individual- and world-constituted, not solely alone. 'Being' from a Māori existential/metaphysical perspective cannot simply be thought of as the being of the human, but as a co-constitutioned/co-constitutioning entity. ❡

A discussion of 'gender' through 'ira'

Overarching Western assumptions: (1) that a thing demands our attention simply as that thing; and (2) that this call for our attention is from a thing that derives its vitality solely from the human world.

Therefore: that a thing (including an idea of a thing, such as 'gender') is evident and without absence.

Māori counter-colonial speculation: that things are co-constituted by all other things, including the original ground.

Therefore: that one particular 'gender' is saturated with other states of being, including absence and its unstated other.

Having **established** one aspect of the ground of thought and materiality that sex-knowledge operates from, let us now consider the more usual meaning of sex as 'gender' against a Māori worldedness backdrop. It should be remembered, though, that a turn in discussion to 'gender' does not mean that 'knowledge' as an issue has been relinquished. Gender's original sense of 'a class or kind of persons, or things sharing certain traits' (The Sciolist, n.d., n.p.(c)) is a reminder of the West's general attempts to assign constant modes of being to *separate* things in the world. The knowledge ('scire') that those things evolve is based on those permanent properties. There is a significant tradition of Māori **philosophy**, however, that potentially signals the opposite of that explanatory knowledge. This phenomenology is what I would term 'exclamatory knowledge' – one in which a thing in the world organises itself in such a way that we cannot ignore it. It can only do this because it is subject to whakapapa or constitution by all other things in the world. One Māori term, 'ira', signals much more exclamation than explanation.

> ❡ 'Establish' or 'to make firm' is a misnomer, as the ground we operate from is, on its own, larger than cognitive. The Western self may have

slipped into thinking that he/she has reached a final ground (and thus ruled how a discussion is to be continued), but in fact that ground is resistant to 'establishment'. In these instances, it is useful to reflect on one's own ground of origin – that foundation that the West wants us to solidify and make final. This ground is not composed of things that are so easily 'gendered'. For Māori writers, the inability to truly get to the final judgement of a thing may be evidence of a ground that defies control. Moreover, the decision to address that ground's disturbance of one's certainty does not originate from the self.

'Philosophy' is interesting for its original meaning of love of wisdom. However, it has taken on a strongly scientific approach. From a Māori ground of thought, 'philosophy' poses problems due to the fact it has assumed a detachment similar to that of later *theoria* (McNeill, 1999). In order to be valid philosophy, the thinker must now transcend the thing being thought about. This view of higher order thinking was also advocated by Cassirer, who argued that refusing to distinguish between language and the things being discussed amounted to primitivism or 'absolute domination of language by mythological thought' (Brandist, 1997, p. 21). However, that separation of language from its objects is misguided and, ultimately, unhealthy. This highly colonising notion of philosophy means that a philosophy of health, for instance, can only take place against a highly analytic backdrop. How things are represented is not immediately seen as itself a determiner of health. Moreover, for Māori, a conventional mode of philosophising is not capable of deconstructing the assumptions of such terms as 'gender'. Put somewhat rhetorically: philosophy now seeks to explain rather than exclaim.

'Ira' as a scientific phenomenon is highly relevant to our discussion of sexual health, because it is pervaded both with what, in our ordinary discussions, is to do with 'essence' (and thus the set categories that sit behind the term 'gender') and with more concrete elements of 'gender'. In its more conventional or current use, 'ira' takes the form of 'gene' and 'essence'.[5] This default to using highly scientific and essentialist language

---

5   For 'gene', see Hudson et al. (2016) and Mead (2003); for 'essence', see Rameka (2015). In all cases, it is possible that the writers mean different things to the scientific notion of 'gene' and the philosophical notion of 'essence'. However, the dominance of these words perhaps points to the seduction of established terminology which is deeply embedded in Western metaphysics, despite the intentions of the writers. They are not alone in this confrontation with metaphysics through language: the problem is evident in this paper and others. A challenge for Māori writers is to strongly destabilise the metaphysics behind these terms or to invent new terms.

to translate 'ira' is unsurprising, given the ground of certainty that acceptable descriptions are meant to arise from. Western thought prides itself on sorting the world of everyday appearances from pure concept (Bowers, 2007), and so it has established a ground that privileges concept ('ideal'). The further away from the material/spiritual relationship, the better for Western thought. As we have identified, though, Māori have a completely different notion of ground, which throws rationalism into question, and would insist that to exist and then to rationalise is an immediate commissioning of the (apparently, but not really) other ground's sovereignty. Ira has the capacity to undermine the firm foundation that Western terms and their concepts – such as sex, science and gender – ask for because of its tendency to reflect both colonisation and the full reality of the world. It therefore has as part of its essence the Western version of ground *and* the appearance of a thing as it becomes itself (yet it can only become itself because it is subject to whakapapa or co-constitution by the entire world).

Absence and gender

This calls for an explanation. First, I shall speculate on the nature of 'commissioning', which I have argued elsewhere (Mika, 2017a) is the delegation of the entire world within any one thing that our glance falls on. This event is not limited to the sense of ira, and there are various other terms in Māori that have this event as their backdrop: whakapapa, whakaaro, mea, among others.

We should remember that this process is not so much a process as an always-already-saturation-of-one-thing-with-all-others, and is a commissioning (com and mittere – 'to send with') only insofar as there is *not* indeed an orthodox sending, as the world is already the one thing: it has already *sent*.[6] One thing is constituted by all others – it always has been – but the human self's understanding of this is limited and so reduces

---

6 It is sometimes necessary to invent translated terms or hyphenated phrases to question the Western practice of assigning nice, neat and economical definitions to complex Māori terms, and also to attempt to present the sense that the Māori term is trying to convey in English. Derrida's erasure device could be useful in the case of commission: C̶o̶m̶m̶i̶s̶s̶i̶o̶n̶.

this event to a 'process' or 'becoming'.[7] A human understanding of what is essentially unfathomable for the colonised mind comprises the second facet that I mentioned in the above paragraph: that we apprehend the world-evolution of a thing in its commissioned state. One sense of ira that appears to be irrelevant to its hard-and-fast meanings of gene and essence is its interjectory 'look!' Pre-epistemic relationships with things are surprising and mysterious, with their ability to arrange themselves in accordance with their co-constituting world and to ask for our attention (indeed, through their constituting[8] of us). Our glance towards a thing in the world is not incidental; it is only possible because of the fact that a thing-and-world compose the perceiving self.

Ira has implications for its commonly held definition as essence because a thing's essence, in Māori thought, may be the already-commissioning of the world into a thing, including the perception of gender. It has been clearly established that traditional Māori thought and language were less disrupted by strictly gendered categories (Pihama, 2001). 'Ia', for instance, can mean both 'he' and 'she', including their simultaneity. With the cutting that sex conducts, though, a clear distinction is made between the genders. Here, we can see the clarity that dominant Western rational thought tries to pursue. In the sovereignty of presence that the West relies on, a thing draws on a static notion of being (Fuchs, 1976; Mika, 2017b) and is therefore identifiable through its solid and permanent properties. It becomes highly present; it should not be obscured by anything else or its relationship with other things in the world. A strong Māori version of holism suggests that there is the entire world within any one thing, and its precise opposite lies in dominant Western thought, which privileges a thing on its own – sitting in its own category, able to be dealt with through that clarity. With

7   There may be a type of becoming at work, but only if that becoming reflects the always-already. It may therefore be not so much 'becoming' as 'being'. I acknowledge here the writings of Barlow (1991) and Marsden (1985), who argue that Māori have a concept of 'potential' and therefore the thing that always existed was not the phenomenon itself, but its *ability* to become its outcome over time. My position on this is that there may appear to be potential at work, but the thing was forever constituted. 'Potential' and 'becoming' may then be used as a way of managing a fundamentally ungraspable phenomenon, but should be viewed as not presenting its true nature. In the background of my position is my cynicism towards a Western metaphysics of linear time and, from that, *causa efficiens*, which is a scientific explanation for how things come to be.
8   A potential translation of 'constituting' is 'whakapapa'. It is common to hear that one *has* a particular whakapapa, but its beyond-humanness suggests that whakapapa instead has the human self (see for instance Mika, 2017b).

this sharp definition of all things in the world, the human self is deluded into treating gender as absolute and immutable. This trapped falsehood (Andreotti, 2016) results in a dichotomy between the self and the world, between one (apparent) gender and another, and between one thing in the world and another.

To complicate matters, ira marks the designation of darkness or absence[9] to human apprehension. Its fluorescing (Mika, 2015) or disclosure projects its absence as much as its clarity: a thing's lesson for the human self is that it must be regarded in terms of its hidden aspects. There is some precedence, in Hinetītama's change into Hine-nui-te-pō, for us to think of the 'material' as possessing Te Pō which, according to Jenkins and Harte (2011), 'could be out in space in the void where Ranginui remains suspended' (p. xii). We can assess the high presence of gender that we have just discussed – evident, for instance, in Indo-European pronouns such as 'he', 'she', 'it' and so on – against the Māori acknowledgement of the void that we have seen Jenkins and Harte refer to above. The issue here is that both **absence** (te pō/kore) and presence (mārama) in reality ancestrally constitute the world, and so the Māori worldview again collapses the *apparent* with the *real*. In the *apparent*, the notion of gender seems to be highly present; in the *real*, the notion of gender is in fact flooded with both absence and presence. We return at this point to an earlier one: that Māori metaphysics strives for unity between the apparent and the real, a pursuit that is obviously countercolonial (Mika, 2017b).

> And yet even discussing '**absence**' brings it into presence, so that it has validity in a Western sense. Note here that the etymology of 'absence' is 'ab' (away) and 'esse' (essence) (The Sciolist, n.d.(a)); esse is deeply related to the Western classical take on 'ousia', which forms the basis of scientific inquiry; and 'presence' is founded on 'prae' (before) and 'esse' (to be) (The Sciolist, n.d.(d)). These three points indicate that the conceiving self is fundamental to whatever may be said to exist, which itself is founded on presence, with its etymology of 'to stand forth' (The Sciolist, n.d.(b)) – arguably, for the conceiving self. Discussing the absence of a thing is akin to making it present, and henceforth existent, especially in Western academic convention. It necessarily prioritises the human self.

Dominant Western thought understands existence in terms of being (Johnston, 1978), whereas I argue that Māori philosophy attributes material significance to absence as an aspect of being. In cognitive terms, absence surpasses understanding but can be speculated on beyond a

---

9 A synonym could be 'intangibility' or 'mystery'.

state of knowing. But it should be remembered that incomprehensibility is itself a thing, or relation of ours, that constitutes the self. The real and apparent are hence indistinguishable. Similarly, 'he', 'she' and 'it', which denote gender in scientific Western discussions of humans and animals,[10] should really be co-constitutive, not distinctive for their apparent difference. Dominant Western thought and science rely on idiosyncratic, biological categories to assign gender – these categories are unyielding, despite there now being some overlap. Yet, transgender categories themselves rely on demarcation to the same extent as those that allot conservative genders. The etymology of 'he', 'she' and 'it' is the sense of 'this one' in the Proto-Indo-European language,[11] signalling a deep linguistic (and metaphysical) fracture within things in the world. The physical characteristics of a person, especially their sex organs, are uninfluenced by those of the other gender, as they are indeed 'this one', not 'that other', which remains beyond those apparent characteristics but still constitutes them.

Science would therefore prefer that ira point to static essence than to the pervasive uncertainty of things' hiddenness and self-orientation. It is a fascinating activity of 'this one' that gender is being described as close to the cognitive self – 'this', rather than 'that'. It is made manageable and clearer through its proximity to the thinker. A peculiar property of Western thought can be discerned here: a thing is brought within the self's realm of ideas and is thus relevant for the self. Arola (2008) notes:

> If I were an isolated monad, if the way in which I encounter the world were from the perspective of an absolutely individuated 'I', then I must have a particular way of engaging that world which stands outside of me. To think about this world which stands over and against me means to understand that world as something fundamentally other than me, and insofar as I am subject, this means that this world is an object: the *Gegenstand* which literally 'stands against' me. This language points to the interpretative violence that is at stake when humans are conceived of as isolated subjects. I must encounter that which stands against me, the objectivity of things,

10 Gender extends further than just humans and animals, though. In High German, for instance, every noun is assigned a gender (German is a highly genderised language, with three genders – masculine, feminine and neuter). French has two genders. For those learning either of these widespread languages, remembering the correct gender for each thing in the world is necessary. English has largely dropped this sustained reference to gender in inanimate things.

11 For 'she', see *The Sciolist* (n.d. (e)). The other two genders are easily traced from there.

and bring it under concepts – grasp it so as to be able to represent it to myself – so that it becomes thinkable for me (p. 45).

In other words, if I am able to conceptualise a thing then it must be brought closer, appropriated within my sphere of regard, and it therefore takes on immediate importance. This, again, can be contrasted with Māori recognition of absence and beyond-perception, where things do not become relevant through being made into an idea (Mika, 2017b). Jenkins and Harte (2011, p. xii) identify that 'Hinetītama assumed the role Hine-nui-te-pō described in Western terms as the Underworld but the Po does not translate as an underworld place'. In the West, the world is whatever is conceptually close, and it makes sense that Te Pō is then relegated to *under*world – distant, unable to be captured through intellect, and peripheral in terms of its importance.

References

Andreotti, V. (2016). (re)imagining education as an un-coercive re-arrangement of desires. *Other Education: The Journal of Educational Alternatives*, 5(1), 79–88.

Arola, A. (2008). *The movement of philosophy: Freedom as ecstatic thinking in Schelling and Heidegger.* [Doctoral dissertation, University of Oregon]. Scholars' Bank. hdl.handle.net/1794/7231

Arola, A. (2011). Native American philosophy. In W. Edelglass & J. Garfield (Eds.), *The Oxford handbook of world philosophy* (pp. 562–573). Oxford University Press.

Barlow, C. (1991). *Tikanga whakaaro: Key concepts in Māori culture.* Oxford University Press.

Bowers, C. (2007). Philosophy, language, and the titanic mind-set. *Language & Ecology*, 2(1), 1–16.

Brandist, C. (1997). Bakhtin, Cassirer and symbolic forms. *Radical Philosophy*, 85, 20–27.

Cohen, M. (1999). *101 Philosophy Problems* (2nd ed.). Routledge.

Deloria, V. Jnr, & Wildcat, D. (Eds.) (2001). *Power and place: Indian education in America.* Fulcrum Resources.

Derrida, J. (1982). Ousia and grammē: Note on a note from *Being and Time* (A. Bass, Trans.). In *Margins of philosophy* (pp. 29–67). University of Chicago Press.

Fuchs, W. (1976). *Phenomenology and the metaphysics of presence: An essay in the philosophy of Edmund Husserl.* Martinus Nijhoff.

Gordon, L. (2014). Disciplinary decadence and the decolonisation of knowledge. *Africa Development*, 39(1), 81–92.

Heidegger, M. (1977). *The question concerning technology and other essays* (W.

Lovitt, Trans.). Garland Publishing.
Hudson, M., Beaton, A., Milne, M., Port, W., Russell, K., Smith, B., Toki, V., Uerata, L., & Wilcox, P. (2016). *Te mata ira: Guidelines for genomic research with Māori, 2016*. Te Mata Hautū Taketake – Māori and Indigenous Governance Centre, University of Waikato.
Jenkins, K. & Harte, H. (2011). *Traditional Māori parenting: An historical review of literature of traditional Māori child rearing practices in Pre-European times*. Te Kahui Mana Ririki.
Johnston, W. (1978). *The inner eye of love: Mysticism and religion*. Fordham University Press.
Marsden, M. (1985). God, man and universe: A Māori view. In M. King (Ed.), *Te ao hurihuri: The world moves on: Aspects of Māoritanga* (pp. 143–164). Longman Paul Ltd.
Marsden, M. (2003). *The woven universe: Selected writings of Rev. Māori Marsden*. Estate of Rev. Māori Marsden.
McNeill, W. (1999). *The glance of the eye: Heidegger, Aristotle, and the ends of theory*. State University of New York Press.
Mead, H. (2003). *Tikanga Māori: Living by Māori values*. Huia.
Mika, C. (2015). The co-existence of self and thing through 'ira': A Māori phenomenology. *Journal of Aesthetics and Phenomenology, 2*(1), 93–112.
Mika, C. (2016). Worlded object and its presentation: A Māori philosophy of language. *AlterNative, 12*(2), 165–176.
Mika, C. (2017a). Dealing with the indivisible: A Māori philosophy of mystery. *St Paul St Symposium 2017 Ipu ki uta, ihu ki tai* (pp. 5–17). Retrieved December 20, 2022, from stpaulst.aut.ac.nz/symposium/2017-symposium
Mika, C. (2017b). *Indigenous education and the metaphysics of presence: A worlded philosophy*. Routledge.
Mika, C. (2017c). A term's irruption and a possibility for response: A Māori glance at 'epistemology'. In E. McKinley & L. Smith (Eds.), *Handbook of Indigenous education* (pp. 1–19). Springer. doi.org/10.1007/978-981-10-1839-8_20-1
Moon, P. (2003). *Tohunga: Hohepa kereopa*. David Ling.
Murphy, D. (2015). Concepts of disease and health. In *Stanford Encyclopedia of Philosophy Archive*. Retrieved December 20, 2022, from plato.stanford.edu/archives/spr2015/entries/health-disease/
Pere, R. (1982). *Ako: Concepts and learning in the Māori tradition*. University of Waikato.
Pihama, L. (2001). *Tīhei mauri ora: Honouring our voices: Mana wahine as a kaupapa Māori theoretical framework*. [Doctoral thesis, University of Auckland]. Research Commons. hdl.handle.net/2292/1119
Rameka, L. (2015). Te ira atua: The spiritual spark of the child. *He Kupu, 4*(2), 82–92.
The Sciolist. (n.d.)(a). Absence. In *Online Etymology Dictionary*. Retrieved December 20, 2022, from etymonline.com/word/absence
The Sciolist. (n.d.)(b). Exist. In *Online Etymology Dictionary*. Retrieved December

20, 2022, from etymonline.com/word/exist
The Sciolist. (n.d.)(c). Gender. In *Online Etymology Dictionary*. Retrieved December 20, 2022, from etymonline.com/search?q=gender
The Sciolist. (n.d.)(d). Presence. In *Online Etymology Dictionary*. Retrieved December 20, 2022, from etymonline.com/search?q=presence
The Sciolist. (n.d.)(e). She. In *Online Etymology Dictionary*. Retrieved December 20, 2022, from etymonline.com/search?q=she
Wildcat, D. (2001). The schizophrenic nature of Western metaphysics. In V. Deloria Jnr. & D. Wildcat (Eds.), *Power and place: Indian education in America*, (pp. 47–55). Fulcrum Resources.

4

He takatāpui, he queer, he mokopuna rānei

Kim McBreen

Whakapapa is the basis of Māori understandings of who we are and how we fit in our communities. Even someone whose whakapapa isn't or can't be known, someone adopted like me, is understood by their relationships with others and how they behave in those relationships. Or at least we should be. This chapter looks at how colonisation has used gender and sexuality to mess with Māori understandings of ourselves and our relationships, as well as what that means for us now, and how we can respond.

Moana Jackson is a teacher in Ahunga Tikanga courses at Te Wānanga o Raukawa. When I was a student in one of these courses, we talked about gender and sexuality. Moana told us how he'd asked his mother about this word he'd just heard, takatāpui. She didn't know it. He asked what word she would use for people who were gay. She said mokopuna. When I talk with my colleagues, I hear similar stories – where did that word come from? We are all uri. Doesn't matter who anyone is sleeping with. We are understood by whakapapa.

It's hard to talk about sex, gender and sexuality, the language is unavoidably jargony and off-putting. The colonisers' system of gender and sexuality is so normal to them that words like heteropatriarchy have only recently been invented to describe it. And it is so foreign to te ao Māori that our words don't fit, and we have repurposed some and invented others.

Takatāpui is one of the words that has been repurposed for this time when colonisation has made our gender and the genders of our partners so important. And takatāpui identity and community have been invented as a response to that reality. A way for those of us who cannot fit in a heterosexual system based on binary gender to build our own identity and community for well-being. The word is old, but the way it is used now comes from colonisation and heteropatriarchy, not whakapapa. Takatāpui is taking over as the way Māori talk about and organise around genders and sexualities that have been marginalised by colonisation. In this chapter I will argue that we must confront heteropatriarchy, and that building takatāpui identity and community is a strategy that sidesteps the problem. I worry that it is a misstep, because it yields to the colonisers' system of understanding who we are. Instead of challenging heteropatriarchy, it creates a place for us within it. I worry that promoting takatāpui identity and community concedes that heterosexuality and binary gender are normal, and that we who don't fit are not. I worry that it entrenches heteropatriarchy.

This is not an attack on people who use and like the term takatāpui, and I'm not trying to blame any of us for failing to solve heteropatriarchy. I'm talking about strategy – where I want to aim for, and where I think investing in takatāpui identity and community takes us. Because this affects us all.

When my daughter went to kōhanga, the children segregated into boys and girls, and very little was done to bridge that. At five years old, my daughters' friends were being separated into boys and girls for no good reason – to learn rugby versus netball skills, to walk somewhere in two lines, wearing the correct uniform, and who knows what else. From her first year at kura, the boys have used 'sexy' as an insult for the girls. Boys who are friends with girls are shamed into betraying those friendships by other boys. Boys regularly disrupt girls' games, either because they want all the space for their games, or because they want the game to be boys chasing girls. The girls can give in or they can stand their ground, but they can't carry on their own games. Most teachers and parents I've spoken with tell me it is boys being boys, and we wouldn't want it any other way. The few who see it as a problem, either because they worry their boys are learning to bully or because they don't want their daughters taught to accept boys behaving badly, have moved their children to other kura. But I don't think these problems are just at our kura. This is heteropatriarchy. This is where it starts. It is not normal or healthy, and it hurts all of us, whatever our gender or sexual identity.

All of our kids are exposed to heteropatriarchy. Does takatāpui identity and community do anything to help them? Takatāpui as a response doesn't even help all of us who are most attacked for our gender or sexuality, because it doesn't make it into all the homes and schools and other places where we have to survive. It is a very narrow, short-term survival strategy, which doesn't save us all. He waka eke noa – we need a bigger boat. Decolonisation, re-Māorification, tino rangatiratanga. Freedom to be. Isn't that what our whakapapa demands of us?

Of whakapapa and manaaki

Māori gender and sexual organisation before colonisation looked very different from what we have now. Our tūpuna Māori did class people as men or women, and there were some tasks that were seen as mostly for one gender or the other. But most work wasn't divided that way; it was shared, and all work was understood as important community labour. Sex wasn't a big deal, it could be recreational or reproductive, and both men and women could have multiple relationships, or one, or none. Whakapapa and children were a big deal; raising children was a community responsibility, and some special relationships were for the purpose of having children. Those relationships might be expected to be monogamous. There were people who mostly had same-sex relationships or opposite-sex relationships, but the sex of a partner didn't define someone.

We know this, because there are no old words for the categories of gender and sexuality, nor for the people who fit into or break those boundaries. Our tūpuna didn't have words that meant something like queer or gay or lesbian or straight, nor trans* and cis. That says something about the way our tūpuna understood people. It signals that those categories weren't important – they weren't central to social organising or identity. People were understood by whakapapa and the quality of those relationships. We don't get mana from naming all the flash people and places we are related to, our mana comes from how well we take on the responsibilities of those relationships. Our gender, and the gender of who we have sex with, is not who we are nor how we should be judged. I love that. It is almost unimaginable to me.

I want to talk about how we get back there. How do we get to a place where we can be whoever we are, instead of being crushed by the weight of gender expectations? Does takatāpui take us there? I think it takes us on a different, shorter journey to somewhere not unlike where we are now. Heteropatriarchy, with company.

Of families, communities and margins

Whānau and whakapapa are supposed to give us belonging, permanence. But my family didn't feel like a place where I belonged – because of sexuality, ethnicity, temperament and politics. It's become worse as I've become more sure of who I am and what is important to me. My adoptive father disowned me – the final betrayal was that I wouldn't accept his racist theories about history and Māori. Which means my children and I weren't able to see my adoptive parents for several years. He has died since I started writing this, having never met his grandson. At the same time, I don't belong in my birth families because I barely know them. How do you make up for a lifetime spent apart? I don't have the skill or time to reconnect. Many of us as adults have to work out what family means, and try to make it for ourselves. Whānau and other extended families have more potential, if they can resist the pressures to disconnect into separate nuclear families or individuals, especially when the key pakeke die. I am envious of those who have experienced whānau.

I started writing this over the COVID-19 lockdown in 2020. It is Matariki, when life and death, past and future, seem especially close. I am in lockdown with my partner and our children in a house on a quarter-acre section in a small beach town. I never wanted a nuclear family, tiny islands cut off from each other. I believe in community as our source of safety, strength and self-determination. And yet here we are. Pretty much a classic nuclear family fantasy. There's nothing like being trapped in a house with your immediate family for a couple of months to make you think about community and home and belonging. 'We're all in this together' repeats at every news bulletin.

Where is home? Or community? Where do I feel safe to be me and know that I will never be rejected? What are the differences between whānau, family and community? Where do ideas like queer community and takatāpui fit in? I've never found them. Why do I feel uncomfortable when I'm told how important they are to us all?

Colonisation has fucked with home and belonging. The ways it has attacked our homes and whānau will be different for each of us, but there's no avoiding it. I've worked to build community, but I haven't found a home. Wherever I am, the misogyny and racism and normalised oppressive crap gets too much for me to keep pushing. It is too painful. I withdraw, and the spaces that I withdraw to get smaller and smaller. It's not a recipe for health and happiness – it's a last-resort survival strategy. I know, poor me. But many of us have never known what home feels like. How can we even understand community?

I used to believe that a chosen community of friends could fill in for family. But it is too easy to drop out or move away. Without nurturing experiences with enduring, resilient, committed whānau or family relationships, what meaning can I make of community? I have been part of, committed to, contributed to any number of communities. I have walked away from them all with at best a relationship or two. And the gap I leave is filled as quickly as that of a swimmer leaving the ocean, because most of us are bad at community.

Too many of us have only known nuclear families, and nuclear families aren't good examples of community, belonging or permanence. Too often they are small and fragile, and they can't absorb the clashes, messiness and trauma of our lives. Where can you go when you fall out with one of your parents? Many of us only know dysfunction, disconnection and really bad communication and coping strategies, and we bring those to the communities we try to build. Is it any wonder that I roll my eyes when I hear that takatāpui community and identity is important for well-being? How would this community have helped me growing up in my Pākehā Christian family in Whangārei? How does it support the kids in mainstream schools all over these motu because their parents can't speak te reo and feel shut out of 'real' Māori identity? How does it help my kids at their kura with rigid ideas of gender, especially masculinity, and little thought for the effect on children? How does it help any of the young people trapped in bubbles of heteropatriarchal intolerance?

It's not that I think community is unimportant – I know it's all we've got. Without community, there is no way we can disentangle ourselves from this capitalist, heteropatriarchal, colonial shit show. It is only through community that we can imagine and practise all the alternatives we need to try out.

We are already entangled in communities – where we live, where we work, where our kids go to school, where we worship, where we play. What do we gain from inventing takatāpui community? I'm told it is a refuge where we find support, but to me it feels like what I've always done – falling back to my own tiny safest space. Except that space will be shared now. We're withdrawing together, to build a community and decorate our bunker with rainbow-coloured tukutuku and disco lights. There are two meanings to the word retreat: one is a refuge, and the other is conceding the field. Is that what we want?

Those of us who feel marginalised and isolated everywhere we go are unlikely to gain a deep sense of belonging from organising under a word like takatāpui that has been repurposed to give us a sense of history, as if that is the whakapapa we need. And some of us feel even more marginalised and shut out when we are told that this is what we need.

Locked down, sheltering in place until the virus is all but gone, in my family's bubble watching my partner go mad trying by herself to be everything to two children while I sit at my desk 'working from home'. Watching my seven-year-old relax and flourish away from the stress of trying to fit in every day at school. I look out on the world, and I know I don't want a bunker. I want the whole damn world. Okay, not the whole world. But these motu. Or at least my actual community, where I live and work, and my kids learn who they are allowed to be and what it will cost them. I don't want them to think a bunker is all they deserve. That's not the kaupapa I inherited, and it's not what I want to pass on.

I worry that researchers and community workers who find strength and well-being in takatāpui identity and community are building a self-fulfilling prophecy. Advertising to and talking only with those who already identify as takatāpui or rainbow communities, asking them how those labels contribute to their health and well-being, while missing those of us who don't use those labels, who choose not to use them because they feel stifling. And so takatāpui gains traction, the bunker is strengthened. And we are caught between a tiny box, where we are safer but not free, or the unbridled violence of heteropatriarchy.

Am I being unfair? Maybe, and maybe I'm just bitter because I missed my spot in the bunker. But those of us refusing to get with the takatāpui kaupapa aren't the problem. The problem is the attacks on our identity, community and values, and the pressure to conform to Pākehā standards.

Of colonisation and heteropatriarchy

Heteropatriarchy is difficult to talk about because it's so much a part of Western culture that we don't notice it, there aren't common words to describe it — it's just normal. It's been made so normal that it can seem natural — human nature, the way things always are. But it's not. For most of human history, people have lived in small communities, depending on each other (not dominating), and celebrating sexual desire.

Heteropatriarchy's whakapapa started in ancient Greece (Valdes, 1996). As the economy shifted from collector to pastoral to city-state, heavy work became tied to economic and political power, and ideas about male superiority grew. The Romans invaded Greece and took on this thinking. Christianity later added the idea that sex and desire is sinful except for reproduction. And that all added up to heteropatriarchy: men and masculinity were stronger, better, smarter, and sex was only acceptable between a man and his wife to make babies.

For a few thousand years, that's how Western culture understood and shaped people. Each baby was inspected at birth. Based on the size and shape of their genitals they were classed as a boy or a girl, and then they were raised, dressed and educated based on that classification. People who strayed from the expectations of their sex were deviants, dangerous to society. It sounds weird right? But we're still doing it.

When colonisers arrived to these lands a couple of hundred years ago, they brought that way of understanding and organising people, and they have since imposed it on all of us. Our relationships with each other have been attacked through patriarchy (Mikaere, 2003; Smith, 2005) and heteronormativity (Picq, 2019). Wherever we turn, we soak in those messages. I don't know how often I hear that boys and girls are naturally different from birth or earlier. That everything boys do is because they're boys, even if lots of girls do it too. I don't know how many times my seven-year-old daughter has been told that she is so pretty. Or the number of times I have been told what a handful my son will be – it started before he was born.

Heteropatriarchy sounds like a big academic concept, but I find it helpful – it connects some very real and painful ways that people and whānau have been attacked. In a whānau everyone relies on each other, those relationships protect us and allow us to get things done. That doesn't fit well with beliefs in male superiority or the need for cheap workers to exploit. Heteropatriarchy is the reason 'men's work' is more valuable; men have to be protected as providers, which is what makes women dependent and vulnerable; it's hard to get by without a man-sized income. Heteropatriarchy is why men are punished for taking a different path, not being 'manly' enough, choosing 'women's work' or caring for others. It's why the nuclear family is privileged, while the much healthier whānau has been broken down. Heteropatriarchy is why women are punished for choosing to be sexual. That's why I was adopted out – what else could a pregnant 15-year-old girl do? She couldn't raise a baby by herself, and no-one was going to help. She had to learn her lesson. No-one reminded the boy of his responsibilities. How has such an unhealthy, punitive system become normal? And why is it important for a discussion of takatāpui?

First, we need to understand what heteropatriarchy is and where it comes from. It's not 'just normal'. It is an oppressive system that limits and harms people. It was brought here with colonisation, it has been forced on us, and we need to reject it as colonising.

Second, I want to be clear that homosexual and heterosexual categories come from heteropatriarchy. In the same way that 'race is the child of racism, not the father' (Coates, 2015, p. 7), Western understandings of sexuality and gender are the child of heteropatriarchy. There have always been differences among us – we've always had a range of sexualities and flexible genders – but those differences only became important when some people wanted to justify raising themselves above other people. Then they invented categories to fit people into and problematise.

And third, I want to think about what that means for how we understand gender and sexuality now, and how we organise for a healthier way of being. Without heteropatriarchy, categories like homosexuality and heterosexuality don't make sense. Nor queer, nor trans*, nor gender or sexually deviant/marginalised/minority. There is desire and sex. There is reproductive sex and non-reproductive, or recreational, sex. But there is no gay or straight sex, no trans* or cis-gender. There are no queers and straights. Which is just where we started – tikanga Māori.

Without all these categories, where do takatāpui fit in? Everywhere. And also nowhere.

We understand and organise ourselves through whakapapa.

Without heteropatriarchy, there is no need to call ourselves takatāpui.

Of takatāpui and rainbows

In the 1980s, takatāpui was re-invented as a word that celebrates two aspects of our identity – gay and Māori (Te Awekotuku, 1991). It has since expanded to describe all marginalised Māori genders and sexualities.

Takatāpui as an identity has become popular, with many people finding it empowering. It was somewhere to escape racism from our queer circles, and homophobia from our whānau Māori. Elizabeth Kerekere (2015) promotes takatāpui identity as a way that we can find each other, and from there create spaces where we can build and organise. Clive Aspin (2007, p. 164) writes:

> I have found a great source of strength and support from being able to use this term to describe myself. This term locates me firmly in Aotearoa and means that I can stand with pride in a range of different Māori contexts. As well, it gives me the strength to confront the challenges, such as homophobia, marginalisation and oppression, from other quarters.

This shows both how the term takatāpui is a response to heteropatriarchy within Māori and Pākehā spaces, and how it can make confronting heteropatriarchy more possible.

The invention of takatāpui as an identity and community has been an important response to heteropatriarchy. It has reminded us of the possibilities of gender and sexuality within tikanga Māori. But we still need to be cautious of embracing the concept of takatāpui too closely. I worry that it divides us into straight and takatāpui, normal and abnormal. Which is heteropatriarchy. If takatāpui organising keeps people alive here and now, more safe and well than otherwise, then it is useful. It may be a first step towards a goal of taking apart heteropatriarchy. But I worry that by continuing to organise as and for takatāpui, we are conceding to heteropatriarchy, we are reinforcing it. Long-term, I don't know if it is a useful or safe strategy.

Picq (2019, p. 14) says 'Indigenous sexualities are important sites of resistance and resurgence'. They 'expand the political imagination' so we can see beyond heteropatriarchy, beyond colonialism. But takatāpui isn't an 'Indigenous sexuality'. It's a modern invention under heteropatriarchy. Our 'Indigenous sexualities' are the ways our tūpuna were that our colonisers couldn't even see, let alone understand. That's where our power is, and I fear that takatāpui takes us further from it. In fact, Picq (2019, p. 10) warns against framing our sexualities as queer or straight, because that means we have accepted and translated ourselves into the colonising paradigm, and out of our own.

Isn't that exactly what takatāpui does? Even if it's not the intention, it's how I hear people use the word 100% of the time, as an umbrella term for those of us who aren't straight. A Māori version of rainbow or queer. Does that mean we've accepted the colonising understanding of gender and sexuality? 'You can't be straight? You can't be normal? That's okay, you can be takatāpui over there.' Why not focus on releasing everyone from normal?

Because heteropatriarchy affects everyone, wherever we are, however we identify. My children will grow up in it whether we build a takatāpui community and identity or not. My children will be limited by heteropatriarchy whoever they grow up to be and to be with. Does the existence of takatāpui identity and community protect them from the pressure to 'be' their gender correctly? To be a 'proper' boy or girl? Does it shield them from the shame of doing it wrong?

I worry that takatāpui as an identity or way of organising ourselves is a trap. I worry that the more we embrace takatāpui as a community goal, the more essentialised, co-opted and respectable it will become, while doing little or nothing to challenge heteropatriarchy. I worry that while giving us breathing space from the oppressions of heteropatriarchy, takatāpui reinforces that system in Māori communities.

So many worries. My main fears for investing in takatāpui as the solution to heteropatriarchy are:

- That as an identity and a community, takatāpui becomes the alternative to heteropatriarchal Māori identity and community. That it reinforces the binary of normal and other, rather than dismantling it. That instead of challenging the development of a toxic Māori masculinity, entrenched masculine/male leadership, stifling heterosexism, puritanical values and essentialising of binary sex, it is a sidestep. We abandon the majority to their unhealthy choices and live our best takatāpui lives. I see my daughter at kura, and this terrifies me. I think of my son going to kura and I feel sick.

- That as a celebration of what it is to be Māori and queer, takatāpui becomes essentialising and limiting instead of liberatory. I am seeing this in the resurgence of mana wahine and its entanglement with the sacred-feminine earth-mother. I have seen narratives toying with takatāpui as boundary-crossing, deeply spiritual, with specific important roles, aligned with a trans-Indigenous sexuality. I don't need another box to live within.

- That the people most in need of support are outside our networks, isolated and young. Takatāpui is an identity for people who know about it, people who are connected through Māori or academic networks. When I think about the kids I grew up with, none of us were connected in that way. I don't know if takatāpui is something those kids will find or claim.

- That those of us who choose a different path to self-determination are shut out of discussions about Māori sexualities and genders. Over and over we have seen funders, organisers and decision-makers wanting the one correct solution. Many of us have contributions to make, sometimes different or contradictory. In this, as in all resistance, we need many strategies. I very much appreciate the editors of this book making space for my thoughts. How do we ensure that we all have voice, space and resources for our different paths, and avoid building an alternative hegemony?

Of strategies, futures and dreams

Finley (2011) shows that just being queer or takatāpui, no matter how loudly, does nothing to challenge heteropatriarchy, because there is no challenge to power. Lots of conservative people have a flamboyant friend who makes them feel tolerant and worldly without requiring any change. We have to think about what is holding up heteropatriarchy. How do we take apart those systems?

We've seen that the queer movement is liberatory and effective when it is oppositional and confrontational to mainstream heteropatriarchy. That's how we got homosexual law reform, it's why Hero was so beautiful, and why Stonewall is legendary. But when the mainstream is challenged, it tries to absorb and co-opt that resistance. If organisers aim for mainstream acceptance, they quickly slide from resisting the straitjacket of heteropatriarchy, to designing a rainbow straitjacket. Even if we are choosing to wear it, it's still a straitjacket and we are still trapped in it. Anger and rambunctious tendencies are toned down, names and focuses shift. There is less 'movement' and 'liberation', and more business associations and professional membership; embracing pink capitalism and the colonising state as a friendly patriarch, and establishing rainbow wings of political parties, instead of seeing capitalism and the State as the heart of the problem. Hierarchies in the movement come to reflect those they used to resist. The most marginalised of us build a community, carry it on our backs, and are pushed down as it morphs into organisations that speak over and oppress us in the name of unity and celebration.

If we aren't resisting heteropatriarchy, we can slip into reflecting and reinforcing it. We can get sucked into nonsense stories of community unity and the nation state – tolerant kiwis who give everyone a fair go. Our communities mirror mainstream ones, controlled by the most respectable members: white men who now align with mainstream elite, except that they sleep with men. 'Don't rock the boat,' they say. 'We have earned the right to be comfortable.' Meanwhile a young Māori woman is harassed and spat at in a 'rainbow community' meeting for talking about ongoing police brutality and racism.

And likewise, we've seen that Māori resurgence is most liberatory and effective when it is confrontational to colonisation. For example, iwi have resisted the Crown for two centuries arguing for the return of resources and self-determination. The Crown now allocates some resources to iwi to provide services. These arrangements are celebrated as partnerships, despite being dependent on Crown goodwill. They take energy away from the struggle for self-determination, and pit people in that struggle against people providing or needing those services. The pathway to leadership of those iwi often looks much like a mainstream pathway to leadership – men who went to the right schools find their way more quickly than anyone else, no matter how hardworking and committed they may be.

This is not what we want. I fear that by intentionally focusing on building ourselves up, rather than confronting power, it is where takatāpui will take us. I don't want an alternative route to power or another box to pop myself into, where I am expected to be a certain way because of who

I sleep with. For me and my children, I want liberation. How do we make sure we are challenging any essentialising of gender and sexuality?

Let our responses to heteropatriarchy be creative and confrontational, fuelled by love and rage. Let us take on the responsibilities of whakapapa, responsibilities to our tūpuna and our mokopuna.

What is the alternative to takatāpui that I am proposing? It's not an alternative so much as an addition – that we continue to spend our time and energy searching before and beyond the confines of colonisation and its structure for healthy pathways. Colonisation has obscured those paths. I see takatāpui as a clearing rather than a pathway. I don't think it will take us where we want to go, but maybe from there people will find a way that does. I hope that those who choose takatāpui hold it loosely, and let it go when it no longer serves. And I hope that those of us who are searching in different, less clear directions will be recognised and supported as well. We who can never fit into heteropatriarchy are the people who truly understand its dangers. We are the best to dismantle this cornerstone of colonisation. And we will never be free or safe until that work is done – whether or not we choose to call ourselves takatāpui.

I am watching my children grow up in a violent, mean system, just like I did. But it's not just a system, it's us. It's people I like and care about who are trapping my kids, bullying them into being less than they are, allowing others to bully them. All these beautiful unique children, infinite expressions of whakapapa, all sorts of weird and wonderful. And we are slicing away at them, hacking off the bits that don't fit our understandings of gender. Breaking them. What does takatāpui do for them? I don't know what to do. It breaks my heart.

I want to think about how these systems work in our communities so we can work out how to take them apart. I want to build a world where children can grow up free from the confines of gender, where treating each other badly is the only thing that is shameful. Where manaaki, recognising and treating each other with honour, is the expectation. I want them to be safe in their strength and softness. To explore all that they can be. I want that for all of us. We cannot bunker down, imagining there are safe places to retreat to. We have to find ways to bring all our communities with us so that there is no need for takatāpui identity, so that the idea of takatāpui becomes meaningless and unintelligible again. I want a world where whakapapa includes us all, and we can focus on relearning what that means.

Help me work out how to get there.

References

Aspin, C. (2007). Takatāpui: Confronting demonisation. In J. Hutchings & C. Aspin (Eds.), *Sexuality and the stories of indigenous people* (pp. 159–167). Huia.

Coates, T.-N. (2015). *Between the world and me*. Spiegel and Grau.

Finley, C. (2011). Decolonizing the queer Native body (and recovering the Native bull-dyke): Bringing 'sexy back' and out of Native Studies' closet. In Q.-L. Driskill, C. Finley, B. J. Gilley, & S. L. Morgensen (Eds.), *Queer Indigenous studies: Critical interventions in theory, politics, and literature* (pp. 31–42). University of Arizona Press.

Kerekere, E. (2015). *Takatāpui: Part of the whānau*. Tīwhanawhana Trust and Mental Health Foundation.

Mikaere, A. (2003). *The balance destroyed: The consequences for Māori women of the colonisation of tikanga Māori*. International Research Institute for Māori and Indigenous Education, with A. Mikaere.

Picq, M. L. (2019). Decolonizing Indigenous sexualities: Between erasure and resurgence. In M. Bosia, S. M. McEvoy, & M. Rahman (Eds.), *The Oxford handbook of global LGBT and sexual diversity politics*. Oxford University Press. doi.org/10.1093/oxfordhb/9780190673741.001.0001

Smith, A. (2005). *Conquest: Sexual violence and American Indian genocide*. South End Press.

Te Awekotuku, N. (1991). *Mana wahine Māori: Selected writings on Māori women's art, culture and politics*. New Women's Press.

Valdes, F. (1995). Queers, sissies, dykes and tomboys: Deconstructing the conflation of 'sex', 'gender', and 'sexual orientation' in Euro-American law and society. *California Law Review, 83*(1), 1–377. jstor.org/stable/3480882

Valdes, F. (1996). Unpacking hetero-patriarchy: Tracing the conflation of sex, gender and sexual orientation to its origins. *Yale Journal of Law & the Humanities, 8*(1), 161–211. hdl.handle.net/20.500.13051/7687

5

Te Whare Takatāpui – Reclaiming the Spaces of Our Ancestors

Elizabeth Kerekere

Abstract

Tīwhanawhana Trust advocates for takatāpui (Māori with diverse genders, sexualities and sex characteristics) to 'tell our stories, build our communities and leave a legacy'. We use traditional Māori culture and spirituality to reframe gender and sexuality in Aotearoa New Zealand, particularly around how it impacts on our elders and young people. The Te Whare Takatāpui framework explores conceptual and practical ways to address the homophobia, transphobia, interphobia and biphobia that impacts on takatāpui and Rainbow health, well-being and relationships. It is based on the Te Whare Tapa Whā health model and considers whakapapa (genealogy), wairua (spirituality), mauri (life spark), mana (authority/ self-determination), tapu (sacredness) and tikanga (rules and protocols). Te Whare Takatāpui identifies mana wāhine as essential to restoring the traditional balance between women and men that our tīpuna (ancestors) experienced, so that we may address the historical trauma and gendered violence of colonisation affecting us today. I have coined the term 'mana tipua' to denote the inherent mana of trans, intersex and non-binary people, based on the acceptance of gender and sexual fluidity in the spiritual and physical realms of traditional Māori society, and despite the binary constraints imposed by today's cis-heteronormative society. Together, mana wāhine and mana tipua provide the core structure of the ancestral meeting house. In turn, Te Whare Takatāpui can become the tūrangawaewae (place to stand) for all of us with diverse genders, sexualities and sex characteristics, our whānau (extended family) and our allies. We invite you to join us.

Introduction

Te Whare Takatāpui is the health and well-being framework I developed, based on Māori culture and spirituality, to address the homophobia, transphobia, interphobia[1] and biphobia faced by takatāpui and all people with diverse genders, sexualities and sex characteristics.[2]

It came into being as I wondered what takatāpui health and well-being might look like within the Te Whare Tapa Whā model of Māori health and well-being, which likens itself to the four walls of an ancestral meeting house: taha wairua (spirituality); taha hinengaro (psychology and mental health); taha tinana (physical being) and taha whānau (families of birth and choosing) (Durie, 1985).

An outline of Te Whare Takatāpui first appeared in print in my PhD thesis in 2017 and it continues to evolve. I referred to my thesis as 'He Whāriki' (a woven mat):

> This *Whāriki Takatāpui* was intended to be the woven mat that lies inside *Te Whare Tapa Whā* of takatāpui health and well-being. It has been woven based on ancient traditions with contemporary colours and patterns.... the *Whāriki Takatāpui* brings life back to a once vibrant meeting house which has become dusty and run down. As the meeting house is rebuilt, so it will contribute to the transformation of Māori culture – a place where takatāpui are valued and discrimination is unacceptable. Takatāpui will continue to act with agency and speak to power. We will meet challenges with creativity and intergenerational connection. With our whānau [family] and allies we will adorn this *Whare Takatāpui* in a manner befitting its significance; the gardens will be planted and the people resilient and healthy (Kerekere, 2017b, p. 183).

---

1 A term coined by Professor Cary Gabriel Costello, as discussed in 'Interphobia – not cured by hiding us away' (*The Intersex Roadshow*, 12 September 2010, intersexroadshow.blogspot.com/2010/09/interphobia-not-cured-by-hiding-us-away.html).

2 The phrase 'diverse sex characteristics' refers to people born with an intersex variation, who may or may not identify as intersex themselves (see ITANZ, Orchard & RainbowYOUTH, 2017).

I have been working within Rainbow[3] spaces for about 35 years, with a focus on takatāpui and young people. I am founder and chair of Tīwhanawhana Trust (established in 2001) and we advocate for takatāpui to 'tell our stories, build our communities and leave a legacy'. We believe that to uplift takatāpui, we must uplift both our whānau and our Rainbow communities. Tīwhanawhana uses Māori cultural and spiritual values to reframe how society looks at sexuality and gender. We have been operating for over 20 years without government funding, through collaboration, relationship-building and collective vision. Co-chair Kevin Haunui and I respectively lead the cultural and political work, nationally and internationally. Together, we are guided by our Tīwhanawhana whānau; Rainbow people from many different cultures who have found a home with us.

While labouring on my PhD, I distilled my thoughts into two resources – *Takatāpui: Part of the whānau* (2015, in collaboration with the Mental Health Foundation) and *Growing up takatāpui: Whānau journeys* (2017a, in collaboration with RainbowYOUTH). The 2015 publication was the first indigenous LGBTQI+ suicide prevention resource in the world.[4]

From 2017 to 2019, I was privileged to work with the National Collective of Independent Women's Refuges (NCIWR) to help shift the refuge movement from their pillar[5] of 'lesbian visibility' to 'takatāpui nurturing diversity'. I acknowledge Ange Chaney from Te Whare Rokiroki Māori Women's Refuge, who was with me every step of the way. I created a video series and a training manual, and Ange and I delivered training across the country based on Te Whare Takatāpui.

I also acknowledge Jack Trolove, Tom Hamilton and Wai Ho for listening to me read every draft on that video script. Out loud. Week after week. Because I am cisgender, their feedback was critical to ensure my analysis and (English) language related to trans and non-binary people was correct. For (English) language related to intersex people in all my

---

3   I generally use the more poetic term 'Rainbow' in place of versions of the initialism LGBTQIA (lesbian, gay, bisexual, trans, queer, intersex and asexual/allies), except as quoted. Its use is predicated on radical inclusion of all people with diverse gender identities and expressions, sexualities and sex characteristics, from all cultures.
4   This assertion is based on extensive internet searches and network requests. We stand to be corrected.
5   The other three pillars of the Women's Refuge movement are feminism, parallel development (with Māori), and collectivism.

work, I thank legend Mani Bruce Mitchell and Intersex Aotearoa[6] for their guidance and trust.

Throughout that time with the Women's Refuge movement, I discussed my framework with members of Rainbow communities across Aotearoa. In 2019, I used Te Whare Takatāpui as a basis to deliver keynote addresses at the National Rainbow Strategy Hui in Wellington; the first Global Feminist LBQ Women*'s Conference in Cape Town; the United Nations in Geneva; DePaul University in Chicago; the Caribbean Women and Sexual Diversity Conference in Kingston, Jamaica; the United Nations Freedom of Religion and Belief Conference in Bangkok; and Ngā Uri o Uenuku Hui in Nelson. On the basis of this work, I was awarded an Erskine Fellowship at the University of Canterbury in Christchurch just as COVID-19 lockdowns came into being.

In 2020, I was elected to the New Zealand Parliament as one of 12 (cisgender) Rainbow MPs, setting a new world record of Rainbow representation at 10%. With four of ten MPs identifying as Rainbow, the Green Party identifies itself as the 'Proudest Party in the Proudest Parliament'.

I have the privilege of working with our Rainbow Greens and wider Rainbow communities to push for legislative and other change on their behalf. This has included banning conversion practices and enabling trans, non-binary and intersex people to change their birth certificate more easily. Having a strong takatāpui voice in Parliament has raised profile in the media (see Johnsen, 2021), across government, in select committees (see New Zealand Parliament, 2021) and in the House. When we completely reformed the New Zealand health system in 2022, I put the term 'takatāpui' into law for the first time.[7]

Te Whare Takatāpui was used alongside other Māori models to create *Mana Taiohi* (see Ara Taiohi, 2022) – the principles of youth development (Deane et al., 2019). It also forms the basis of the Green Party's new Rainbow Policy (Green Party, 2022) which includes initial work on new sections for Te Whare Takatāpui on whanaungatanga (interconnectedness and relationships) and mātauranga (knowledge and research). I have continued to disseminate and develop Te Whare Takatāpui nationally and internationally including at UN Human Rights Council side-events in 2021 and 2022.

For as long as I have worked on Te Whare Takatāpui, I have promoted a National Rainbow Strategy. I realise now that they are the same thing.

---

6   Intersex Aotearoa: intersexaotearoa.org/
7   Pae Ora (Healthy Futures) Act 2022, s 91.

So, let me introduce to you the culmination of my life's work to date: my framework Te Whare Takatāpui, with storytelling shown in italics.

So, imagine with me, a place of well-being and health for all of us in traditional Māori society – a conceptual Whare Takatāpui. I see a whare (house/meeting house) resplendent with beautiful, intricate whakairo (carvings), of woven tukutuku (latticework), of painted kōwhaiwhai (decorative patterns). Our gardens were abundant. Our tamariki (children) were running around like wild things and our relationships were healthy and strong. The Whare Takatāpui was a place where our tīpuna (ancestors) welcomed people with diverse genders, sexualities and sex characteristics from all over the world.

But then colonisation came along. The missionaries, the puritans, the settlers, the colonisers – they did not appreciate our Whare Takatāpui. They did not appreciate who we were and what we stood for. They pulled down the whakairo, tukutuku and kōwhaiwhai. They caved in the roof and they contaminated our gardens. They tried to erase the fact that we ever existed. They failed. Our tīpuna understood their intent and left clues for us – their descendants – to find. They trusted that we would find our way back to them and to rebuild that Whare Takatāpui from the ground up.

We need help from all our allies to make this happen. I invite you to envisage this Whare Takatāpui and think about your place in it. To think about how you might help rebuild and adorn that whare with the important work you do.

Whakapapa

The word 'whakapapa' literally means 'to make flat' or 'to layer one on top of the other' – in this case, generations reaching back into time (genealogy). Because whakapapa is fundamental to being Māori, it is fundamental to being takatāpui. It is not just a direct line; it spreads out in all directions. And it is not just conceptual. It is absolutely rooted in the whenua (land), our Earth Mother, Papatūānuku.

From our whakapapa, an ancient term was revealed.[8] My definition of 'takatāpui' is:

a traditional Māori word that we have adopted to embrace all Māori with diverse genders, sexualities and sex characteristics including whakawāhine (trans women), tangata ira tāne (trans men), lesbian, gay, bisexual, trans,

8   The term 'takatāpui' was found separately in the writings of Te Rangikāheke (c. 1835) by takatāpui scholars Ngahuia Te Awekotuku and Lee Smith. It was translated in the second edition of the Māori dictionary in 1852 as 'travelling companion'. The translation as 'intimate partner of the same sex' has been consistent in every dictionary since 1871 (Williams, 1871, p. 147).

intersex and queer people. Takatāpui identity is related to whakapapa, mana and inclusion. It emphasises Māori cultural and spiritual identity as equal to – or more important than – those diverse genders, sexualities and sex characteristics (Kerekere, 2017b, p. 25).

To be clear, 'takatāpui' is both an umbrella term and a reclaimed Māori identity. So, if you have Māori ancestry, you can claim it! Regardless of 'how Māori' you consider yourself to be, the colour of your skin, how well you speak te reo Māori, or how well you know your whakapapa, your marae or even your birth whānau.

> Not feeling Māori enough because of whatever reason, it's actually a tool of the coloniser for me to feel that way and to think that way. And it benefits the coloniser – Kassie Hartendorp (Kerekere, 2017a, p. 13).

Takatāpui is a way of bringing all the parts of yourself together.

> Takatāpui just unifies everything. I am Māori. I am queer. I am here to stay. If you have a problem with that well, that's your problem not mine – Morgan Cooke (Kerekere, 2015, p. 8).

> [Takatāpui] means that first and foremost, I'm Māori. Then I'm everything else but together I am everything I am. I am queer, I am Māori and I am tangata ira tāne [trans man]. And I have this entire community backing me up whenever I use that identity – Nathaniel Gordon-Stables (Kerekere, 2017a, p. 27).

Whakapapa is critical because it ensures we never forget where we came from. It means we remember that people with diverse genders, sexualities and sex characteristics have always existed, even if they did not have words for who they knew themselves to be or who they loved. Women were loving each other long before the word 'lesbian' was coined in the 1970s (Faderman, 1985). Takatāpui was used as an affectionate term for same-sex loving centuries before we reclaimed it in the 1980s (Kerekere, 1992; Te Awekotuku, 2005). While many cultures have preserved their traditional terms for people with diverse genders, sexualities and sex characteristics, many other terms have been lost the world over.

We acknowledge those who did not accept the sex they were assigned at birth,[9] who may have transitioned or identified as non-binary. We acknowledge those who did not accept the sex they were designated at birth because of their diverse sex characteristics, who may have identified across

---

9 At the time of writing, the phrase 'assigned at birth' is preferred by trans and non-binary activists, while the phrase 'designated at birth' is preferred by intersex activists. So, I use them both or separately as required.

all gender identities and expressions, and sexualities, including as intersex. We acknowledge those who would have embraced the terms lesbian and gay, and those who might rather have identified as bisexual, pansexual, queer or asexual. We may not know all of their names but we remember them and we honour them.

> My Māoriness is about whakapapa, and even if I can't see it really clearly and I don't have faces necessarily to put to those people, I can feel them 100% and they guide me. They lead me and they support me all of the time – Kassie Hartendorp (Kerekere, 2017a, p. 28).

This way of framing history provides a Te Tiriti o Waitangi[10] context for every other identity. It means that, regardless of where you come from in the world, we recognise that your identities have their own histories, their own languages, their own cultural context, and we honour that.

> *In Te Whare Takatāpui, the walls are up, the roof is secure and finally we can start putting the photographs on the back wall, of those who have passed away. Many of them had no names for who they were but they knew what they wanted, and they knew who they loved. Some found names; takatāpui, whakawāhine, tangata ira tāne, lesbian, gay, bisexual, trans, intersex, queer, non-binary, asexual, aromantic. Some claimed names from their ancient cultures.*
>
> *Some were famous, some were dramatic, some were artists, some were athletes, some had disabilities. Many were parents and guardians. Most of them will never appear in the history books but collectively, we understand that the way to the whare has been paved with their joys, their struggles, and their lives.*
>
> *Mā wai rā e hari taku kauae ki tawhiti?*
> *Who will carry my jawbone into the future? Who will remember me?*
> *Māku.*
> *We will.*[11]

---

10 Te Tiriti o Waitangi is the Māori version of a treaty first signed on 6 February 1840 between representatives of the British Crown and Māori chiefs from the North Island of Aotearoa New Zealand. It is often used interchangeably with 'The Treaty of Waitangi', but the English and Māori versions differ in significant ways.

11 Whakataukī (proverb) cited by Te Awekotuku (1989), in memory of our tūpuna takatāpui. It is originally attributed to Pikiao (Mead and Grove, 2001, p. 292: 1804).

Wairua

'Wairua' refers to the spiritual dimension: the soul or essence we are born with that exists beyond death. It is about our relationship with our atua (gods, deities and higher beings), our tīpuna and the whenua. Wairua is about the interconnectedness of all things in the universe. Literally 'wai' meaning waters and 'rua' meaning two, wairua represents interconnected dimensions. As Dr Rangimarie Turuki Rose Pere (n.d.) describes 'wairua':

> I am a spirit having a physical journey. My spirit is made up of 'two waters'. One 'water' Waiora, is directly linked into the Central Sun, the Divine Spark. Waituhi, the other 'water' records everything that I do, whether it be good or bad.

Because wairua is fundamental to Māori culture, it stands to reason that wairua is also significant for us as takatāpui.[12] In fact, I believe it is *why* we are takatāpui. Our inner sense of self comes from our wairua and most Māori are aware of their gender and sexuality from a very young age (Henrickson, 2006; Kerekere, 2017b; Pihama et al., 2020).

> I have value irrespective of what anyone else says. Based on those things that I've been brought up with, I know what's essentially good for my spirit and my self-worth – Kevin Haunui (Kerekere, 2015, p. 12).

When I gave my definition of takatāpui in the Whakapapa section, I mentioned 'whakawahine', which means the essence of being a woman, and 'tangata ira tāne' which means the spirit or life principle of a man. These are terms for those who were born with the wairua or spirituality of a gender different to the sex they were assigned or designated at birth.

> They [ask] was I born male and I say no, I was born female … the equipment might be wrong. My grandmother knew it. My godmother knew it. So, I know what I am – Jennifer Edwards (Kerekere, 2015, p. 10).

When I first moved home to Gisborne in October 2009, we lived in Te Karaka to meet whānau on my Ruru (grandfather's) side. At Takipū Marae, I met my tīpuna Hine Te Ariki. She was a tipua, a spiritual being who could change form (Mead, 1996a; 1996b). After her death, Hine Te Ariki turned into a marakihau, a water creature (#NotAMermaid) and this is the form she is carved in. Hine Te Ariki became known as the River Mist Maiden and can still be seen moving down the Waikohu (river of mist). I have seen

---

12 I acknowledge Peri Te Wao and Chanel Hati, who shared their transition journeys with me many, many years ago and helped me realise the significance of this. Both are leaders in takatāpui and Rainbow communities.

Hine Te Ariki myself and created artworks about her.

What Hine Te Ariki inspired me to realise is that whakawāhine, tangata ira tāne, trans, intersex and non-binary people are the embodiment of modern-day tipua – spiritual and magical beings who can change gender and form (Kerekere, 2015; 2017a; 2017b; ITANZ, Orchard and RainbowYOUTH, 2017). It is their wairua that gives them the capacity and drive for fluidity and change, and their ability to hold multiple forms at one time:

> Claiming a takatāpui identity is political in a way. Embracing traditional Māori culture is a political act. Colonisation has taken so much, tried so hard to sever those roots. So, claiming takatāpui is an act of power. Māori culture embraces takatāpui, or queer or trans, as normal. Heaps of our old stories in their pre-Christian forms include our atua being takatāpui. That tells us our ancestors were seeing takatāpui around them as good, beautiful, powerful – Ahi Wi-Hongi (Robertson, 2018, p. 10)

Discrimination comes in many and intersectional forms, and that impacts on our wairua. The discrimination I have faced as an older takatāpui who is lesbian femme is very different from the discrimination faced by a non-binary person trying to play competitive sport or by a young intersex person with a disability:

> So, a Māori voice is important when we are trying to enact change and actively advocate for the Intersex community . . . it's often only when going through puberty [that Intersex people start to realise they are different]. For me, things started growing where they shouldn't have and not growing where they should have been. And that was a really tough thing to deal with, without any support or guidance [from] whānau, hapū or iwi. I was automatically misgendered and put into a class that actually wasn't good for my hauora (health). The Takatāpui community suffer impacts, both from societal discrimination and discrimination from whānau, hapū and iwi, as well as organisations within the medical profession, that don't know how to deal with these sorts of things. – Tu Chapman (Hika, 2022)

Being out comes at a price. Being different comes at a price. That price continues to be our livelihoods, our well-being, our safety and our lives (Kerekere, 2015; Robertson, 2018; Clunie, 2018; Veale et al., 2019; Human Rights Commission, 2007; 2016; 2018; 2020; Pihama et al., 2020; Roy et al., 2021; Fenaughty et al., 2022).

The word has gone out. A Whare Takatāpui is being built where people will be welcomed and their wairua can be at peace. They will be celebrated for their true selves in whatever form that might be and however that may change throughout their lives. The pathway towards the Whare is now accessible and people are arriving. We welcome them, we feed them and then together we work.

We train our young people to build the whare as they build themselves. They sit alongside our elders to carve the whakairo. And as they capture our tīpuna, our kaitiaki and our tipua – our ancestors, our guardians and our shapeshifters – so they learn their own stories and they help to record them. Every person sees themselves reflected in the Whare Takatāpui and they know they belong.

Mauri

Mauri is your life spark, that essential quality that is yours alone. Unlike wairua, which exists beyond death, when you die your mauri dies with you. Your mauri encompasses your special skills, talents and superpowers. It is how you present and express yourself to the world: your clothes, your hair, your tā moko (traditional facial tattoo), your tattoos. It is your behaviour, the way you connect with others. It is your presence.

Mauri is in the words you use to describe yourself and how you identify. It is your mauri that wants to put a name to who you are and how you feel. It is your mauri that looks for recognition – that you are seen and you are valued. It is your mauri that is appeased when you see yourself reflected in the world. Many Māori of diverse genders, sexualities and sex characteristics have felt their mauri spark when they first discover the word 'takatāpui' and decide to claim the term:

> The diversity of Māori who hold this identity is I think really beautiful. For me, [takatāpui is] a great word, because I don't have to be specific about how I identify – Morgan Butler (Kerekere, 2017a, p. 27).

Many people with diverse genders, sexualities and sex characteristics are not seen, valued, recognised or reflected even within parts of our Rainbow communities, let alone the rest of the world. The UN Independent Expert on protection against violence and discrimination based on sexual orientation and gender identity (IE SOGI) stated that barriers to improved health outcomes for our communities will only be corrected with a 'radical transformation' in processes for collection data and generating evidence worldwide (Madrigal-Borloz, 2022).

In Aotearoa, Rainbow people have rarely been formally counted in the government statistics that determine positive changes in policy, strategy, funding allocation and legislation. After decades of advocacy, Statistics New Zealand has added questions on sexual identity and gender in the Household Economic Survey since 2020, and from 2023, the Census will include questions on sexual identity, gender, and variations of sex characteristics. A start but not yet the 'radical transformation' we need.

Rainbow people who are Māori, Pasifika or people of colour often feel marginalised and Rainbow people with disabilities are often made invisible (Clunie, 2018; Duder et al, 2018; Robertson, 2018; Veale et al, 2019; Pihama et al., 2020; Roy et al., 2021; Fenaughty et al., 2022). When mauri is not nurtured, that life spark starts to dim and sometimes it will flare out.

> It was a horrifying journey. I didn't know what I was doing but I thought I needed to talk to someone . . . I needed help. I didn't want to exist anymore. It was that bad – Ariki Brightwell (Kerekere, 2017a, p. 15).

The path laid by generations of Rainbow activists has led to a generation of young people who are coming out and transitioning when they are young. They embrace fluidity and have created language we all need to learn (Orchard, 2007). They have established peer-led groups and youth-run organisations all over the country. However, they are paying dearly for their courage.

Young people who have yet to build up strong mental defences suffer significant mental distress because of rejection from whānau and bullying and violence in their schools and communities. They struggle to find the help they need, and many respond with self-harm, depression and suicide (Ara Taiohi, 2015; Kerekere, 2015; 2017a; 2017b; Suicide Mortality Review Committee, 2016; Clunie, 2018; Veale et al., 2019; Fleming et al., 2020; Roy et al., 2021; Fenaughty et al., 2022).

> I don't have an attitude of acceptance or tolerance. I have an attitude of celebration and gratitude for the things our takatāpui youth bring us. It's incredible. It's extraordinary. It's otherworldly. It's beyond tapu. Artistic, intellectual, physical, philosophical, spiritual, sexual . . . I don't believe we have any conception of what's being lost when our young people are lost – Hinemoana Baker (Kerekere, 2015, p. 21).

Sexual minority[13] young people are four times more likely to experience significant depressive symptoms and five times more likely to have

---

13 The Youth 2000 survey series has updated its language over the years from 'non-heterosexual' to 'same- and both-sex attracted' and now to 'sexual minority' to remove the binary connotations. When the data is combined with that of trans and non-binary students, they use 'sexual and gender minority young people'.

attempted suicide in the previous 12 months than heterosexual young people (Lucassen et al., 2014; Fenaughty et al., 2022). Trans young people are four times more likely to experience significant depressive symptoms and five times more likely to have attempted suicide in the previous 12 months than non-trans young people (Clark et al., 2014; Veale et al., 2019; Fleming et al., 2020; Fenaughty et al., 2022). Such figures are worse for Māori, Pasifika and disabled young people (Roy et al., 2021).

I have become familiar with evolving Rainbow-related terminology because for many years I have worked closely with amazing leaders who have diverse genders, sexualities and sex characteristics. Working with and mentoring youth leaders keeps me up to date with their language and politics. As you learn this terminology and talk to people who identify as such, you are less likely to make assumptions. When you see who someone really is; when you ask questions about pronouns and then you use them correctly; when you make sure someone knows they are included and welcomed; you will see their mauri respond. Their life spark will glow and so will yours.

In the Whare Takatāpui, we are building the turapa – the tukutuku panels. The preparation of weaving materials is underway. Alongside the harakeke, the kiekie and the pingao[14] *are ribbons and weaving materials of every colour. We have chosen from traditional patterns and created many of our own.*

Tukutuku – to send, to send back. The stories that have not been told will be captured in a conversation between weavers. Beginners learn beside the experienced and the mauri of the whare glows. Collectively, we weave ourselves back together.

Mana

'Mana' is often translated as 'prestige' or 'authority', and we attribute mana to those we respect and look up to. Mana is something we inherit when we are born, from our iwi (nation/tribe), hapū (sub-tribe) and whānau, and the land that we whakapapa to. We inherit it from our atua, our gods and spiritual beings. Cisgender, trans and intersex women gain mana from our Earth Mother, Papatūānuku, as do those who are able to give birth, including trans men, and intersex and non-binary people.

---

14 Harakeke (*Phormium tenax*), New Zealand flax; kiekie (*Freycinetia banksii*), New Zealand woody climber; and pingao (*Ficinia spiralis*), New Zealand golden sand sedge.

I'm proud of my cultural heritage and my language and everything about being Māori . . . I just love that we have that connection to Papatūānuku [Earth Mother] and Ranginui [Sky Father]. It's just amazing – Cameron Kapua-Morrell (Kerekere, 2017, p. 8).

We also accumulate mana during our lifetime through our words, our deeds, our skills and our achievements. As takatāpui, it is mana that gives us the authority to reject discrimination in all its forms, and to advocate for takatāpui health and well-being.

When the British colonisers and missionaries arrived in Aotearoa, they refused to recognise the mana of Māori women. They could not accept that Māori women were leaders of their people, held land or had equal status with men – despite having a queen themselves. The colonial forces took immediate steps to impose their cis-heteropatriarchal views and nuclear family structure on Māori society in order to dismantle our support structures. They also pathologised and criminalised the sexual and gender fluidity that had been an accepted part of traditional Māori society (Te Awekotuku, 1996, p. 32, Kerekere, 2015, 2017a, 2017b; Pihama et al., 2020).

Colonisation is a systemic and sustained attack from a malevolent force. Misogyny and cis-heterosexism contributed to the historical and intergenerational trauma we now face. It is a cruel and twisted application of feminist privilege[15] that colludes with this history to define who is a 'real' woman and who is a 'real' man based on the sex they were assigned or designated at birth. It tramples on the mana of anyone exercising their right to self-determine their gender identity and expression according to their own whakapapa, wairua and mauri.

An intersectional feminist analysis looks at all the ways that institutional cis-heterosexism discriminates against people who do not fit into the binary it enforces. This includes not only trans, intersex and non-binary people, but also every culture that has more than two genders, including countries in the Pacific, Asia, North America and across the world. Refusing to accept that the definition of 'women' includes trans and intersex women, or that 'men' includes trans and intersex men, or that non-binary people continue to explore preferences for femininity and masculinity, reinforces the colonial construct (Madrigal-Borloz, 2021a; 2021b). So, I believe transphobia and

15 This refers to anti-trans campaigners, including women who identify as – or are perceived to be – TERFs (trans-exclusionary radical feminists). Self-titled 'gender-critical feminists' use so-called 'sex-based rights' to deny the humanity of trans women and cause harm to them, other trans people, their whānau and allies.

interphobia to be inherently racist (Madrigal-Borloz, 2021a). And when discrimination is systemic, change must be systemic.

'Mana wāhine' and 'mana wāhine Māori'[16] were terms originally coined as a form of Māori feminism. Whereas Western feminism focused on fighting the patriarchy for women's rights, mana wāhine reclaims the rights of Māori women to be recognised alongside, and not subservient to, Māori men (Te Awekotuku, 1991; Pihama, 2001; Te Kotahi Research Institute, 2020a; 2020b). Until basic gender equality and sexuality issues are addressed for Māori women,[17] it will be difficult to address the issues specific to takatāpui. On that basis, I have long espoused that mana wāhine is the platform for fighting discrimination against takatāpui, through the restoration of balance between genders in Māori culture (Kerekere, 2015). Without these pou (posts) of wāhine and tāne,[18] we cannot hope to hold space for takatāpui who are trans, intersex and non-binary (Kerekere, 2017a; 2017b).

By the time I first started this chapter in 2020, I came to realise that mana wāhine would not be enough. Even though trans and intersex women are women, by itself, it was a cis-centric concept. When I asked myself how those of us with cis-privilege would uphold the mana of our trans, intersex and non-binary whānau in Te Whare Takatāpui, I realised they needed to be a separate part of the whare structure to reflect their own self-determination.

And so, it came to me from my tīpuna – mana tipua. The inherent mana of trans, intersex and non-binary people, based on the acceptance of gender and sexual fluidity in the spiritual and physical realms of traditional Māori society, and despite the binary constraints imposed by today's cis-heteronormative society. Inside Te Whare Takatāpui, the obvious choice was the tāhuhu: the ridgepole of the meeting house, the backbone of the ancestor. It extends from the front to the back of the house, held up by one or more pou through the centre with the walls at either end. Together, mana wāhine and mana tipua form the core structures of Te Whare Takatāpui.

16 Introduced by takatāpui scholar Ngahuia Te Awekotuku (1991) and developed by many other scholars.
17 Many of the issues facing Māori women have been encapsulated in the Mana Wāhine Kaupapa Inquiry of WAI 2700 – claims against Te Tiriti o Waitangi.
18 The idea of wāhine and tāne being pou, between which all other genders are protected, was told to me by Kevin Haunui, Co-Leader, Tīwhanawhana, in conversations in 2017. In 2019, Soul Mehlhopt raised the idea with me of diverse genders on either side of the pou as well as in the middle – spanning the spectrum.

In turn, Te Whare Takatāpui becomes the tūrangawaewae for all of us with diverse genders, sexualities and sex characteristics, our whānau and our allies.

> *Work is underway restoring the pou and tāhuhu that hold up the mana of Te Whare Takatāpui. The pou representing tāne, the men, is not in bad condition. It only needs minor repairs. The pou representing wāhine, the women, is in an awful state. It needs a lot of work. However, the tāhuhu representing trans, intersex and non-binary people is in the worst condition. Thankfully, we can just make out faint traces of the original designs.*
>
> *Unfortunately, many of the men have forgotten how to repair and restore. They step aside for those women who have always remembered and acknowledge their leadership. Trans, intersex and non-binary people breathe life into the spaces no one else could fill. People of all genders take up roles and responsibilities that suit them and challenge them, and people of all ages contribute to decision-making. They know that between these pou and under this tāhuhu, their mana is upheld. They have found their tūrangawaewae.*

Tapu

Tapu is about those things that are sacred. Things that are prohibited, restricted, set apart or forbidden, things that were under the auspices of our atua. Tapu places restrictions to control how people behave towards each other and the environment, so that society flourishes.

The converse of tapu is noa. It is often translated as 'profane' or 'not sacred', but actually it is the absence of restrictions, limitations or conditions. To remove the tapu or restrictions from something is to 'whakanoa'. Sometimes this is a role for tohunga or religious leaders, but often it is something we can do ourselves. One example is when we sprinkle water over ourselves when we leave the urupā (family cemetery). There may be friends and family in there, but that does not mean we want their spirits wandering around!

One of my favourite artworks is *My tapu head* (1990) by Māori artist Robyn Kahukiwa. In the 1980s, Robyn was the first woman to paint images of the carvings traditionally done by men (Kahukiwa et al., 2005). Let us just say the men reacted badly. *My tapu head* depicts a woman's head with manaia (guardian bird creatures) on either side. What struck me about this painting is that women were inherently tapu. Our physical bodies, and particularly our heads, were meant to be tapu. Our mental spaces were meant to be tapu.

Notwithstanding the ritual warfare of our ancestors, Māori would not violate tapu for fear of incurring the wrath of the atua, because that might result in sickness or catastrophe. Each person was responsible for their own tapu and respecting the tapu of others. The systematic breakdown of Māori culture and spirituality has meant that there is no longer fear of breaching tapu. No concerns for spiritual repercussions. No attempts to appease the atua for wrongdoing. Even though we are still suffering the sickness and the catastrophe. The sacredness, and therefore the safety, is gone.

Individual violence can be physical, psychological, sexual, financial and more. Within a traditional feminist analysis of systemic violence, it is overwhelmingly cisgender men who are breaching the tapu of cisgender women, particularly Māori and those who have disabilities (see Rainbow Violence Prevention Network, rvpn.nz). A more intersectional feminist analysis reminds us it is overwhelmingly cisgender men who are also breaching the tapu of trans, intersex and non-binary people (Mofokeng, 2022). Within takatāpui, this falls disproportionately on whakawāhine and tangata ira tāne (Pihama et al., 2020).

Where tapu has been breached, there is rarely a process for restoration, or for healing. Without support, there is increased likelihood of harmful use of alcohol and drugs, sexual assault and rape, and intimate partner and sexual violence, including within Rainbow communities (Kerekere, 2017b; Clunie, 2018; Veale et al., 2019; Pihama et al., 2020, Fenaughty et al., 2022). Relationships can be fraught and whānau can be complicated. But as much as there may be pain, violence and grief, there will also be love, pride and hope. Frustrating as that can be, we must accept where people are at, without judgement, to support them to make changes for themselves (Kerekere, 2007; RainbowYOUTH, 2014).

Systemic violence within the education, health and mental health sectors affects Rainbow people in myriad ways:

> I remember going to my school counsellor because I'd been outed to my parents by a staff member at the school. I was told that I should focus on my studies and not worry about my sexuality as it would make me more confused and upset. This meant that I didn't get help for years and my mental health got worse. Looking back as an adult, I know this response wasn't good enough. I wish our mental health system empowered queer and gender diverse young people to understand their mental health and not blame it on their gender or sexuality – Toni Duder (Duder and Orchard, 2018, p. 11).

The control of women's bodies is core to the colonial health system, and it extends beyond that into Rainbow communities (Pihama et al., 2020;

Mofokeng, 2022). Rainbow people often struggle for reproductive justice, including access to abortion, contraception, comprehensive sex education, sexually transmitted infection prevention and care, alternative birth options, culturally competent prenatal and pregnancy care, assisted reproduction and other methods for family formation, the resources needed to raise their children in safety and health, and more (Ross, 2017; Kerekere, 2018; Riggs and Bartholomaeus, 2020; Pihama et al., 2020). Recent changes to New Zealand law[19] have decriminalised abortion so that everyone has a genuine choice about whether to be or stay pregnant without fear of poverty, discrimination or violence. That affects cisgender women, trans men and intersex and non-binary people.

Generally, trans, intersex and non-binary people face significant barriers in accessing gender-affirming healthcare, which may include counselling, hormone therapy or surgeries (Liddicoat, 2008; Human Rights Commission, 2016; 2018; 2020; Kerekere, 2017b; Veale et al., 2019; PATHA 2020; Madrigal-Borloz, 2022). Too often, transphobic and interphobic discrimination reduces people to their genitalia. This is exacerbated for takatāpui due to cultural incompetency and a reliance on Western biomedical models incompatible with tikanga Māori (Pihama et al., 2020).

The assault on the bodily integrity of many intersex people starts at birth, while some intersex variations may not become apparent until a person reaches puberty or tries to conceive children. The United Nations Convention on the Rights of the Child[20] has raised concerns about the ethical and human rights issues related to medical and surgical practices on intersex infants and children in this country, when they are too young to provide informed consent (Human Rights Commission, 2016; 2018; 2020; Darlington Statement, 2017; Madrigal-Borloz, 2021a; 2022).

Thinking about whakapapa, it is fundamental that we remember where we came from. Thinking of tapu and how we preserve our bodily and mental autonomy – our sacredness – means we adapt to where we are now. We respond to cis-heterosexist and gendered violence, as it impacts on people with diverse genders, sexualities and sex characteristics, especially when it breaches the tapu of our young people and those who are pregnant. Working together, we may all learn how to heal and assert our own tapu again.

19 I acknowledge takatāpui ally and my Green Party colleague, Jan Logie MP, for her ground-breaking work on this: greens.org.nz/ground_breaking_abortion_law_passes_giving_nzers_compassionate_healthcare
20 See paragraphs 25(b)–25(e) of the concluding observations: crae.org.uk/publications-and-resources/un-crc-committees-concluding-observations-2016

In the Whare Takatāpui, the physical and mental scars of historical and current violations are laid bare. Collectively, we mourn the blood that has flowed, the innocence that was taken, the lives that were lost. Privately, we embrace journeys to heal our wairua and mauri; to restore our sense of self. Private shelters are built for mirimiri (traditional healing/massage), counselling and reflection. Trees and plants are carefully tended for rongoa (traditional medicine). Harakeke is prepared for weaving the wahakura (baby beds).

As mana is asserted over words and deeds, so tapu is asserted over body and mind. In this sacred space, we defy anyone to take it from us again.

Tikanga

Tikanga is a means of social control for interpersonal relationships, how groups meet and interact, and how individuals might identify themselves (Mead, 2003). 'Tika' means 'to be right' so 'tika-nga' focuses on the right way to do something, and what happens if we do something wrong. But who decides what is right and what is wrong? What values or moral judgements are used to make those decisions? And what mātauranga (knowledge) are those decisions based on?

It is tiresome but fair to say that tikanga Māori has been impacted after all these years of colonisation (Hutchings, 2013; Kerekere 2015, 2017a, 2017b; Pihama et al., 2020). The colonists breached our tikanga with their violence against women and children, which was not accepted in Māori society at that time. They also criminalised and punished behaviour that Māori had previously considered tika – such as the fluid expression of gender and sexuality (Te Awekotuku, 2005; Pihama et al., 2020). It can be very uncomfortable to think about how much our own thinking has been influenced, hence the ongoing need for self-reflection and decolonisation. The conviction of our wairua becomes even more important:

> Some people would say, you can't come on [the marae] like this. I'd say are you telling me what I can do in my iwi? Get real! – Jennifer Edwards (Kerekere, 2015, p. 19).

We cannot know how people with fluid genders and sexualities fully participated in traditional Māori society. We cannot know how tikanga was created or adjusted for them within our binary-gendered marae protocols. But we know our tīpuna takatāpui were accepted in traditional Māori society, so they made it work (Te Awekotuku, 1991; 2005; Kerekere, 2017b). The least we can do is come up with some innovative and creative solutions of our own.

Tīwhanawhana Trust has led the way in this area, within Rainbow communities, in collaboration with other sectors and on marae across the country. We work closely with our Rainbow youth leaders[21] and are guided by our elders and our tīpuna. Mana Wāhine and Mana Tipua opens space for takatāpui who are whakawāhine, tangata ira tāne, trans, intersex and non-binary to take their place within whānau, hapū and iwi, in leadership and on the marae (Kerekere, 2015, p. 19).

I hope that my Te Whare Takatāpui framework has offered you something. I hope you will support Rainbow groups across the country who are under-resourced and under capacity but doing the work anyway. If you want to learn more about Rainbow communities, start with *All of us* (Robertson, 2018), *Rainbow communities, mental health and addictions* (Clunie, 2018), *Counting ourselves* (Veale et al., 2019), *Prism* (Human Rights Commission, 2020), *Honour Project Aotearoa* (Pihama et al., 2020), *Identify Survey* (Fenaughty et al., 2022) and check out my resources and the *Takatāpui* website (takatapui.nz).

Most importantly, I hope Te Whare Takatāpui inspires you to create change. Because right now, who does the tikanga include and keep safe in your spaces, and who does it exclude? What challenging conversations are you prepared to have? Having increased your mātauranga, what judgements might you re-examine? What tikanga might you change: in your whānau, in your workplace and in your communities?

> You've got to make an effort . . . if you're part of this whānau. If you don't, what are you doing? What are you here for? – Morgan Butler (Kerekere, 2017, p. 30).

As I like to say, 'why do we get up in the morning, if not to change the world?'

> *In the Whare Takatāpui, the tikanga is being refined. Traditional gender roles and responsibilities are being analysed so we may understand the intentions of our tīpuna and the heart of our culture, while we honour the range of gender identities and expressions amongst us. As our stories are recorded, our mātauranga grows. Those whose behaviour impacts negatively on us are given the opportunity to make amends in order to stay. Because one tikanga is very clear – we will do whatever it takes to keep this whare safe and our whānau strong.*
>
> *And just as the word of our Whare Takatāpui has spread, so we have heard back about other whare who would welcome us, work with us and keep us safe. In a world that does not always acknowledge the joy and wonder we bring and the violence and pain we suffer, I ask you:*

---

21 For an overview of inclusive marae protocols, see Brightwell (2017).

Is that your whare?
Is it you?

Acknowledgements

As an older takatāpui cisgender woman (she/her/ia) who identifies as lesbian femme, I rely on the advice of my friends and colleagues, many of whom are trans, intersex and non-binary – intergenerational activists and leaders all. For the first draft of this chapter and every other project we have been involved in, I give my enduring gratitude to Ahi Wi Hongi, Alex Ker, Ange Chaney, Aych McArdle, Bella Simpson, Duncan Matthews, Frances Arns, George Parker, Georgia Andrews, Georgina Beyer, Jack Byrne, Jack Trolove, Jan Logie MP, Jaye Barclay, Jelly O'Shea, Joey Macdonald, John Fenaughty, Julie McHardy, Kassie Hartendorp, Kate Aschoff, Kevin Haunui, Mani Bruce Mitchell, Meng Zhu Fu, Moira Clunie, Morgan Butler, Rainbow Greens, Ricardo Menendez March MP, Stace Robertson, Tabby Besley, Taine Polkinghorne, the Tīwhanawhana Whānau, Tom Hamilton, Toni Duder and Wai Ho. And to my wife, Alofa Aiono, with whom all things are possible (since 1992 and counting).

This book was delayed repeatedly because of the COVID-19 pandemic. To Penny Leach, who helped edit the second version of this chapter, Taine Polkinghorne for the third, and Julie McHardy, Moira Clunie and Taine Polkinghorne for the fourth and final – thank you so much!

Te Whare Takatāpui is my dedication to all of you and our communities. Ngā mihi aroha ki a koutou!

References

Ara Taiohi. (2015). *Snapshot 2015: A report on the support sector for rainbow young people*. Ara Taiohi.

Brightwell, A. (2017). *Pōwhiri guidebook*. InsideOUT. insideout.org.nz/resources/

Clark, T. C., Lucassen, M. F. G., Bullen, P., Denny, S. J., Fleming, T. M., Robinson, E. M., & Rossen, F. V. (2014). The health and well-being of transgender high school students: results from the New Zealand adolescent health survey (Youth '12). *Journal of Adolescent Health*, 55(1), 93–99. doi.org/10.1016/j.jadohealth.2013.11.008.

Clunie, M. (2018). *Rainbow communities, mental health and addictions: A submission to the government inquiry into mental health and addiction – Oranga tāngata, oranga whānau*. Mental Health Foundation of New Zealand.

Darlington Statement. (2017). Joint consensus statement from the intersex community retreat in Darlington, March 2017. Affirmed by representatives of AISSGA, ITANZ, OIIAU, Intersex Day Project, Bodies Like Ours, Tranz Australia & BEECHAC. darlington.org.au/statement/

Duder, T., & Orchard, S. (2018). *Out loud Aotearoa: Sharing the stories and wishes of queer, gender diverse, intersex, takatāpui, MVPFAFF and rainbow communities around Aotearoa's mental health and addiction services*. RainbowYOUTH and We Are Beneficiaries.

Deane, K., Dutton, H., & Kerekere, E. (2019). *Ngā tikanga whānaketanga – He arotake tuhinga. A review of Aotearoa New Zealand youth development research*. Ara Taiohi. hdl.handle.net/10092/100869

Durie, M. H. (1985). A Māori perspective of health. *Social Science & Medicine, 20*(5), 483–486. doi.org/10.1016/0277-9536(85)90363-6

Fenaughty, J., Ker, A., Alansari, M., Besley, T., Kerekere, E., Pasley, A., Saxton, P., Subramanian, P., Thomsen, P., & Veale, J. (2022). *Identify survey: Community and advocacy report*. Identify Survey Team.

Faderman, L. (1985). *Surpassing the love of men – Romantic friendship and love between women from the Renaissance to the present*. The Women's Press.

Fleming, T., Tiatia-Seath, J., Peiris-John, R., Sutcliffe, K., Archer, D., Bavin, L., Crengle, S., & Clark, T. (2020). *Youth19 rangatahi smart survey, initial findings: Hauora hinengaro / Emotional and mental health*. The Youth19 Research Group, The University of Auckland and Victoria University of Wellington.

Green Party. (2022, November 22). *Rainbow Policy*. greens.org.nz/rainbow

Henrickson, M. (2006). Kō wai rātou?: Managing multiple identities in lesbian, gay and bisexual New Zealand Māori. *New Zealand Sociology, 21*(2), 247–269.

Hika, T. (2022, May 20). Intersex Aotearoa's Tu Chapman: 'I have never met any other Māori intersex'. *Gay Express*. gayexpress.co.nz/2022/05/intersex-aotearoas-tu-chapman-i-have-never-met-any-other-maori-intersex/

Human Rights Commission. (2016). *Intersex Roundtable Report 2016: The practice of genital normalisation on intersex children in Aotearoa New Zealand*. Human Rights Commission. hrc.co.nz/files/5914/8124/9497/HRC_Intersex_Roundtable.pdf

Human Rights Commission. (2018). *Intersex Roundtable Report 2017: Ending the practice of genital normalisation on intersex children in Aotearoa New Zealand*. Human Rights Commission. hrc.co.nz/files/9615/2270/4142/HRC_Intersex_Roundtable_2017.pdf

Human Rights Commission. (2020). *PRISM: Human Rights issues relating to sexual orientation, gender identity and expression, and sex characteristics (SOGIESC) in Aotearoa New Zealand – A report with recommendations*. Human Rights Commission. hrc.co.nz/files/9215/9253/7296/HRC_PRISM_SOGIESC_Report_June_2020_FINAL.pdf

Hutchings, J. (2013). The hetero-patriarchy and the corruption of tikanga. In A. Mikaere & J. Hutchings (Eds.), *Kei tua o te pae hui proceedings Te Wānanga o Raukawa, Ōtaki, 4–5 September 2012* (pp. 31–35). NZCER Press and Te Wānanga o Raukawa.

ITANZ, Orchard, S. & RainbowYOUTH. (2017). *All about intersex*. [Flyer].

Johnsen, M. (2021, March 8). *Conversion therapy ban petition: Takatāpui 'inherent to our culture'*. Radio New Zealand. rnz.co.nz/news/te-manu-korihi/437894/

conversion-therapy-ban-petition-takatapui-inherent-to-our-culture

Kahukiwa, R., Kahukiwa, H., Hilliard, H., Lucie-Smith, E., & Mane-Wheoki, J. (2005). *The art of Robyn Kahukiwa*. Reed.

Kerekere, E. (1992). Preparing the art world for Māori dykes. In H. McPherson, J. King, M. Evans, & P. Gerrish Nunn (Eds.) *Spiral 7: A collection of lesbian art and writing from Aotearoa/New Zealand*. Spiral 7 in association with Daphne Brasell Associates Press. Based on a presentation given on 27 January 1991, Dowse Art Museum, Hutt City, New Zealand.

Kerekere, E. (2007). Takatāpui: When worlds collide. In J. Hutchings & C. Aspin (Eds.), *Sexuality and the stories of indigenous people*. Huia.

Kerekere, E. (2015). *Takatāpui: Part of the whānau*. Tīwhanawhana Trust and Mental Health Foundation.

Kerekere, E. (2017a). *Growing up takatāpui: Whānau journeys*. Tīwhanawhana Trust and RainbowYOUTH.

Kerekere, E. (2017b). *Part of the whānau: The emergence of takatāpui identity – He whāriki takatāpui*. [Doctoral thesis, Victoria University of Wellington]. hdl.handle.net/10063/6369

Kerekere, E. (2018). Takatāpui. *O&G Magazine, LGBTQIA Issue, Royal Australian and New Zealand College of Obstetricians and Gynaecologists, 20*(4), 41–42. ogmagazine.org.au/20/4-20/takatapui/

Kerekere, E. (2019). *Takatāpui nurturing diversity training manual*. National Collective of Independent Women's Refuges.

Liddicoat, J. (2008). *To be who I am: Report of the inquiry into discrimination experienced by transgender people / Ka noho au ki toku anō ao: He pūrongo mō te uiuitanga mō aukatitanga o pāngia ana e ngā tangata whakawhitiira*. Human Rights Commission. ourarchive.otago.ac.nz/handle/10523/8927

Lucassen, M. F. G., Clark, T. C., Moselen, E., Robinson, E. M., & Adolescent Health Research Group (2014). *Youth '12: The health and wellbeing of secondary school students in New Zealand – Results for young people attracted to the same sex or both sexes*. University of Auckland.

Madrigal-Borloz, V. (2021a). *A/HRC/47/27: The law of inclusion – Report of the Independent Expert on protection against violence and discrimination based on sexual orientation and gender identity*. UN Human Rights Council.

Madrigal-Borloz, V. (2021b). *A/76/152: Practices of exclusion – Report of the Independent Expert on protection against violence and discrimination based on sexual orientation and gender identity*. UN General Assembly.

Madrigal-Borloz, V. (2022). *A/HRC/50/27: Report on the right to the enjoyment of the highest attainable standard of physical and mental health of persons, communities and populations affected by discrimination and violence based on sexual orientation and gender identity in relation to the Sustainable Development Goals*. UN Human Rights Council.

Ara Taiohi. (2022). *Mana taiohi*. Ara Taiohi. arataiohi.org.nz/mana-taiohi/

Mead, H. M. (1996a). *Tāwhaki nui-a-hema – Āna mahi whakahirahira*. Reed.

Mead, H. M. (1996b). *Tāwhaki – The deeds of a demigod*. Reed.

Mead, H. M. (2003). *Tikanga Māori: Living Māori values.* Huia.

Mead, H. M., & Grove, N. (2001). *Ngā pēpeha a ngā tīpuna.* Victoria University Press.

Mofokeng, T. (2022). *A/HRC/50/28: Violence and its impact on the right to health – Report of the Special Rapporteur on the right of everyone to the enjoyment of the highest attainable standard of physical and mental health.* UN Human Rights Council.

New Zealand Parliament. (2021, November 1). *Inquiry into Supplementary Order Paper No 59 on the Births, Deaths, Marriages, and Relationships Registration Bill.* Governance and Administration Committee, Fifty-third Parliament. parliament.nz/en/pb/sc/reports/document/SCR_116609/inquiry-into-supplementary-order-paper-59-on-the-births

Orchard, S. (2007). *Queer and trans* 101: A super simple comic guide.* RainbowYOUTH.

PATHA. (2020). *Transgender health briefing to the incoming Minister of Health 2020.* Professional Association for Transgender Health Aotearoa.

Pere, R. T. R. (n.d.). *Te wheke kamaatu – The octopus of great wisdom.* natureplaynz.co.nz/pdf/tewheke_rosepere.pdf

Pihama, L. (2001). *Tīhei mauri ora: Honouring our voices, mana wāhine as a kaupapa Māori theoretical framework.* [Doctoral thesis, University of Auckland]. hdl.handle.net/2292/1119

Pihama, L., Green, A., Mika, C., Roskrudge, M., Simmonds, S., Nopera, T., Skipper, H., & Laurence, R. (2020). *Honour project Aotearoa.* Te Kotahi Research Institute.

RainbowYOUTH (2014). *You, me/us: Ko koe, ko au, ko tāua, ko tātou, ā tātou hunga takāpui, ā tātou hononga.* RainbowYOUTH.

Riggs, D. W., & Bartholomaeus, C. (2020). Toward trans reproductive justice: A qualitative analysis of views on fertility preservation for Australian transgender and non-binary people. *Journal of Social Issues, 76*(2), 314–337. doi.org/10.1111/josi.12364

Robertson, S. (2018). *All of us: Minority identities and inclusion in Aotearoa, New Zealand.* Stace Robertson with support from Vodafone.

Ross, L. J. (2017). Reproductive justice as intersectional feminist activism. *Souls, 19*(3), 286–314.

Roy, R., Greaves, L.M., Peiris-John, R., Clark, T., Fenaughty, J., Sutcliffe, K., Barnett, D., Hawthorne, V., Tiatia-Seath, J., & Fleming, T. (2021). *Negotiating multiple identities: Intersecting identities among Māori, Pacific, Rainbow and Disabled young people.* Youth19 Research Group, The University of Auckland and Victoria University of Wellington.

Suicide Mortality Review Committee. (2016). *Ngā rāhui hau kura: Suicide Mortality Review Committee feasibility study 2014–15. Report to the Ministry of Health, 31 May 2016.* Suicide Mortality Review Committee.

Te Awekotuku, N. (1989). *Tahuri.* New Women's Press.

Te Awekotuku, N. (1991). *Mana wāhine Māori: Selected writings in Māori women's art, culture and politics.* New Women's Press.

Te Awekotuku, N. (1996). Māori: People and culture. In D. C. Starzecka (Ed.), *Māori art and culture.* David Bateman in association with British Museum Press.

Te Awekotuku, N. (2005). He reka anō: Same sex lust and loving in the ancient Māori world. In A. J. Laurie & L. Evans (Eds.), *Outlines: Lesbian and gay histories of Aotearoa* (pp. 6–9). Lesbian and Gay Archives of New Zealand.

Te Kotahi Research Institute (2020a). *Mana wahine reader: A collection of writing 1987–1998. Volume I.* Te Kotahi Research Institute.

Te Kotahi Research Institute (2020b). *Mana wahine reader: A collection of writing 1998–2019. Volume II.* Te Kotahi Research Institute.

Te Rangikāheke, W. M. (c. 1835). *Hine-Moa.* GNZ MMS 51 in Special Collections, Auckland Public Library.

Veale, J., Byrne, J., Tan, K., Guy, S., Yee, A., Nopera, T., & Bentham, R. (2019). *Counting ourselves: The health and wellbeing of trans and non-binary people in Aotearoa New Zealand.* Transgender Health Research Lab, University of Waikato.

Williams, W. H. (1871). *A dictionary of the Māori language* (3rd ed.). Government Print.

6

Kaupapa Māori and Designing the Honour Project Aotearoa Survey

Shirley Simmonds, Alison Green, Leonie Pihama, Matt Roskruge, Tawhanga Nopera and Nick Garrett

For Māori, the Indigenous population of Aotearoa, maintaining autonomy over health data is important in determining pathways to well-being. Monitoring progress towards optimal health requires the ongoing production of high-quality, appropriate data that reflects diverse health realities.

Most standard statistical methods used to generate data have been introduced, developed and implemented by the non-Māori colonial group in our society. These methods have served as tools of colonisation, subjecting the Māori population to surveillance and scrutiny as part of the colonising agenda (Smith, 2005, p. 87), and contributing greatly to mistrust and vulnerability in the research environment. However, for some time now, Māori researchers have been challenging Westernised quantitative methods of knowledge creation, finding ways to ensure that Māori population data is visible in academic and policy-creation environments, critiquing statistical tools, and ensuring that high-quality Māori health data is available (Harris et al., 2007; Keefe et al., 1999; Reid et al., 2017; Robson et al., 2007; Te Rōpū Rangahau Hauora a Eru Pōmare, 2002). Implementing Kaupapa Māori as a research theory and methodology ensures that Māori knowledges are prioritised, Māori aspirations are centralised, Māori voices privileged, and Māori values and philosophies are upheld throughout data generation and the entire research process. This requires Kaupapa Māori researchers to be vigilant and to scrutinise existing tools and methods to ensure they meet the needs of Māori. To accept and apply epidemiological tools to Indigenous data without critique risks reproducing the colonial approach to data creation.

This paper describes the process of assessing a commonly used statistical method – a cross-sectional survey – before its application to a specific Māori population. Each step in the survey development is examined for its appropriateness to the study population and for its contribution to the aims of the study. The process is guided by Māori cultural values and practices. It is a process of transformation and self-determination, of seeking to disrupt norms in the statistical research environment, and of reclaiming power in an Indigenous knowledge creation space (Cram & Mertens, 2015).

The overall aim of the Honour Project Aotearoa is to investigate the life experiences of takatāpui[1] and Māori LGBTQI+, and to understand how their experiences impact their health and well-being. Specifically, the project aims to gain insight into understandings of health and well-being, and to explore issues of access to, and appropriateness of, healthcare and other services for this specific Māori community.

The Honour Project Aotearoa was inspired by the HONOR Project, a groundbreaking study that explored well-being within the American Indian and Alaskan Native two-spirit community. The study was conducted by Karina Walters of the Indigenous Wellness Research Institute at the University of Washington.

A quantitative Kaupapa Māori research project

Surveys enable the gathering of qualitative data (such as opinions and experiences) from a specific population, which can then be aggregated for quantitative analysis (such as proportions or percentages). For the Honour Project Aotearoa, data were gathered using two main methods: key informant interviews and a national survey, both informed by a review of relevant literature. It is intended that the quantitative survey data provides a complementary perspective to accompany the more in-depth qualitative data from the key informant interviews, thus presenting a comprehensive picture of the health and well-being of takatāpui and Māori LGBTQI+ in Aotearoa.

A cross-sectional survey is a method commonly used to gather epidemiological data from a population at a certain point in time. Typically, it involves collecting information from members of the population using well-

1 A term used by some Māori to describe their identity, whether gay, lesbian, bisexual, transgender, intersex or part of the rainbow community.

defined concepts, methods and procedures to gather, analyse and summarise data (Statistics New Zealand, 2015). These concepts, methods and procedures are rarely challenged; rather, they are accepted as given, and the underlying values that inform the process are not necessarily made explicit.

The Honour Project Aotearoa is the first national survey to be designed specifically for the takatāpui Māori LGBTQI+ community, aiming to address a dearth of much-needed information. As a Kaupapa Māori research project, the Honour Project Aotearoa is initiated and led by Māori researchers, most of whom are also members of the takatāpui LGBTQI+ community. The project engages closely with the Māori takatāpui LGBTQI+ community, and is guided by a Māori advisory group. It is therefore research conducted by Māori, for Māori and with Māori (Smith, 2015).

As with all Kaupapa Māori research, the Honour Project Aotearoa has tino rangatiratanga, or self-determination, at its core (Smith, 2015). The pursuit of autonomy is common to Indigenous populations who have experienced colonisation, and in a research setting this means that Māori cultural practices and processes are prioritised throughout the process, from inception to dissemination of results. Any epidemiological method considered for application in research must be examined and critiqued for its appropriateness to Māori data, context and communities.

This paper describes the process of developing the national survey for the Honour Project Aotearoa. It is largely a methodological paper, and doesn't intend to discuss the overall study results, as these will be described elsewhere. In general, the key steps of a survey are as follows:

1. Develop the aims and objectives
2. Define the target population
3. Decide sample size
4. Select survey mode
5. Develop survey questions
6. Pre-test, pilot, amend
7. Recruit participants
8. Conduct survey
9. Analyse information
10. Report and disseminate findings

Developing the survey required Kaupapa Māori researchers to critique of each step and the processes involved, therefore navigating the space between Kaupapa Māori and survey design.

Developing the aims and objectives

Most survey development guides recommend that the research question is clearly defined at the outset (Coggon et al., 2003; Statistics New Zealand, 2015). While this might seem a logical place to start, it is useful to refine the research aims into measurable objectives with the close involvement of the research team and advisory group. From the beginning, the Honour Project Aotearoa had clear overall aims, modelled on those of the HONOR Project: to explore understandings of hauora (health and well-being), and to gain insight to experiences of this specific community and how well their health needs were being met (or not) by existing services. Two further processes were required at this stage: to ensure the aims were contextualised to Aotearoa, and to explore Māori perceptions of health and well-being.

Wānanga

To delve deeper into understandings of hauora, a wānanga was conducted. This is a traditional style of group learning and knowledge exchange, where participants are engaged in the process of sharing and reflecting upon understandings of a topic, allowing a creative consciousness to emerge and a 'commonly held and satisfying understanding' to be achieved (Royal, 2009). Wānanga allows time to tītiro (look), whakarongo (listen) and kōrero (speak) during the research process. These are characteristics that typify Kaupapa Māori research (Cram, 2001). In this way, the concept of hauora was explored by the Māori research team, who stood as representatives of their families, communities and disciplines. What emerged was a broad and thorough shared understanding of hauora that was inclusive of many concepts unique to Te Ao Māori – the Māori world.

The practice of wānanga was continued throughout the project, particularly for decision-making and for navigating the space between Kaupapa Māori practices and statistical methods. Holding wānanga ensured that a range of expertise and experience – such as mātauranga Māori (Māori knowledges), statistical know-how, and the realities of the takatāpui LGBTQI+ community – were available to draw upon throughout the research journey. This helped the research team to find balance, sometimes discussing compromises and trade-offs in a research project that brought several different (and at times conflicting) worlds together.

Tuakana/teina

Centring the project on hauora also ensured that from the outset the project was contextualised to Māori realities and understandings. Professor Walters of the HONOR Project guided the initiation and development of the Honour Project Aotearoa, and remains an advisory to the research. In this way, a tuakana/teina role is established between the two projects and research groups. These are Māori terms that describe the relationship between a tuakana – a (usually older) relative, who has more experience and expertise in an area – and the (usually younger) teina. In a modern context, the tuakana/teina relationship is often implemented in education, healthcare and workforce development as a form of mentorship in which the mana, or prestige, of both parties is upheld and advanced (Winitana, 2012; Ratima & Grant, 2007; Curtis at al., 2014). This provided a model for the relationship between the two research groups.

A Kaupapa Māori framework

During the wānanga on the concept of hauora, participants' thoughts and contributions were collated and then loosely thematically grouped. Four components of hauora emerged from this process and became the framework for the survey and the wider research project. These concepts aligned directly with *He Korowai Oranga,* the Māori Health Strategy (Ministry of Health, 2014) and centre on the overarching concept of ora, or life, health and well-being. They are: mauri ora, whānau ora, waiora and pae ora.

Mauri ora refers to the physical, mental, emotional and spiritual health and well-being of the individual. 'Mauri' translates as 'life principle' (Williams, 1991). Whānau ora pertains to the collective health and well-being of a group such as family, extended family, social group or community, and therefore explores the nature of relationships and connectedness. Waiora considers the external impacts on health and well-being such as the environment, social impacts, and access to, and appropriateness of, health and other services.

Pae ora encompasses the other three concepts, which are interconnected and mutually reinforcing (Ministry of Health, 2014). 'Pae ora' translates as the 'horizon of health' and, as the highest standard of well-being for Māori individuals, families and communities, it is the collective aim. As an aspirational goal, pae ora resists a deficit focus and encompasses hope and positivity.

Following the confirmation of the survey framework for the Honour Project Aotearoa, eight key objectives were identified, as detailed in Table 1.

Rangatiratanga refers to self-determination and Māori empowerment to determine Māori futures. Mana motuhake describes Māori autonomy. The practice of guardianship of the land and environment is referred to as kaitiakitanga, a role of considerable importance to Māori. Mātauranga Māori describes traditional Māori knowledges and ways of knowing.

Table 1: Honour Aotearoa Project survey objectives

Mauri ora	The current status of the physical, mental, spiritual and emotional health of takatāpui and LGBTQI+ Māori. The experiences of takatāpui and LGBTQI+ Māori when using services that provide for physical, mental, spiritual and emotional health.
Whānau ora	The current status of connectedness for takatāpui and LGBTQI+ Māori including relationships with whānau, hapū, iwi, kaupapa whānau, whenua and self. The experience of services that impact upon connectedness, and how these support, or do not support, connectedness.
Waiora	The components of the health ecosystem that are not provided for in current services for takatāpui and LGBTQI+ Māori. These may include physical environments, settings and virtual spaces. The experiences of the health ecosystem components on the health of takatāpui and LGBTQI+ Māori.
Pae ora	The systems and pathways that takatāpui and LGBTQI+ Māori use to achieve rangatiratanga, mana motuhake, kaitiakitanga and mātauranga. Ways that service provision could improve for takatāpui and LGBTQI+ Māori to achieve rangatiratanga, mana motuhake, kaitiakitanga and mātauranga.

Defining the target population

The target population for the Honour Project Aotearoa is the takatāpui Māori LGBTQI+ community living in Aotearoa, aged 18 and over. The survey included those who self-identified Māori as their sole ethnic group, or one of their ethnic groups, as determined by the standardised ethnicity question (Statistics New Zealand, 2009a) *and who also* identified that they were descended from a Māori, using the Census Māori descent question (Bycroft et al., 2016). Many epidemiological studies use ethnicity alone as an identity marker; however, ethnicity is a social construct whereby individuals self-identify their affiliation to one or more social groups (Krieger, 2001; Reid et al., 2017). Māori descent, on the other hand, identifies whakapapa or genealogical links to a Māori ancestor or ancestors (Kukutai, 2004; Reid et al., 2017). The research team decided that both whakapapa (ancestral descent) and identity choice were important defining factors for the Māori population.

In the absence of a validated question for either gender or sexual identity, respondents were asked, 'Which of the following best describes the group you belong to?' A range of possible answers were provided (such as gay, lesbian, bisexual, transgender) and a free-text box. Allowing for all possible responses to identity is consistent with the principle of rangatiratanga; the freedom to define oneself is central to self-determination.

Deciding sample size

To obtain survey results with adequate statistical power, an ideal sample size of 500 was specified, with a minimum of 350. As there is no current collection of data on this specific population, many of the usual methods used to access potential respondents, such as electoral roll or other databases, were not available. It was acknowledged at the outset that it might be difficult to access survey respondents.

Selecting the survey mode

The survey was administered online, in hard copy, and by interviewer-assisted hard copy. The potential impact of 'mode effect' caused by using different modes for one study was considered of lesser importance than the need to increase the response rate through the provision of choice for respondents, and the need to increase opportunities to access this community.

Developing the survey questions

Following the confirmation of the survey objectives (Table 1), survey questions were developed by adapting the HONOR Project questions, sourcing validated questions from other surveys to support comparison, and crafting new questions. The key principle of mana – an individual's inherent prestige and esteem – was carefully considered in this process. A fundamental aim is to avoid reducing the mana of an individual, in this case, the survey respondent (Cram, 2001). To this end, questions were formulated in a strengths-based manner to ensure the mana of respondents was upheld or uplifted. The sequence of questions was also carefully considered to provide a lead-in to more personal questions, and a clear rationale for each question was developed to justify its inclusion. Questions that didn't directly contribute to the survey aims were excluded, minimising respondent burden.

Provision of contact details for emotional support was included for respondents if required, acknowledging that the survey might trigger responses from past trauma. To some extent, this provided for the emotional safety of respondents, which is similar in essence to the 'wāhi haumaru' or safe space described by Stephenson (2018) in research on Māori experiences of harm or loss around birth.

Where possible, respondents were empowered to make their own decisions, particularly in the selection of answers, with open text options provided for many of the questions. While this added to the analysis burden for the research team, maintaining a level of decision-making power for respondents was considered more important, and is consistent with the philosophy of rangatiratanga or self-determination and autonomy.

The finalised questionnaire received ethics approval.

Pre-testing, piloting and amending the survey

Consistent with best practice survey development, the questions were pre-tested, then piloted on a sample of the target population (Statistics New Zealand, 2015), in order to finalise the wording, check understanding, and provide an estimate of time required to complete. The pool of potential respondents for this study is relatively small and the lack of a database or similar provides a challenge in identifying and accessing respondents. An individual who has been involved in the pre-testing cannot undertake the questionnaire itself, therefore some of the pre-testing of survey questions was undertaken by those outside the takatāpui or Māori LGBTQI+ community in order to maximise the pool of respondents for the final survey. The final questions were loaded into Qualtrics, an online survey tool.

Recruiting participants

During recruitment of participants, the research team implemented the process of whanaungatanga (relationship building and networking). This involved using existing relational networks of the project researchers, advisory group and associates, then accessing further networks that individuals are connected to, in order to identify potential survey respondents.

In many cases, respondents were contacted personally, using a kanohi kitea (face to face) approach that is favoured in Kaupapa Māori research (Cram, 2001). Kanohi kitea allows a researcher and potential survey respondent to develop trust, and serves to maintain whanaungatanga. Kanohi kitea has been described as an 'honest instrument', as expressions and emotions are difficult to hide when researchers and respondents are physically present (Rewi, 2014; Paine et al., 2013). It also adds a level of accountability for the researchers, acknowledging their responsibility to the communities they are researching.

Confidentiality and anonymity were assured and maintained, and data kept under strict security, accessed only by researchers on the project, in accordance with the Statistics Act 1975. Geographical bias was minimised by ensuring a reasonable spread of respondent location (determined by the District Health Board), and recruitment efforts were targeted in areas (such as the South Island) to ensure adequate representation.

Conducting the survey

The original survey open time of six months was extended to 18 months in order to maximise the response rate. During this additional time, a stronger focus was placed on kanohi kitea engagement with participants. A Māori research assistant was employed to undertake researcher-assisted interviews and to promote the survey through wider networks and groups.

These strategies greatly contributed to reaching the final target of 368 respondents. The research team decided that the need to increase the response rate outweighed the importance of gathering data in the 'narrow' time period more consistent with cross-sectional surveys.

Discussing, analysing and distributing the findings

Retaining sovereignty of Indigenous data is a decolonising process for Indigenous populations, and requires that the decision-making power of data collection, analysis and distribution remains with Indigenous researchers. Te Mana Raraunga, the Māori Data Sovereignty Network, advocates for the involvement of Māori in the governance of repositories of

Māori data (Kukutai, 2019). In this respect, the Honour Aotearoa Project research team made a clear decision to retain governance of data collected from this survey, making it unavailable for use outside of the project without the agreement of the Principal Investigators.

In recent years, several surveys have been conducted among the Māori population in topics such as the Māori language (Te Puni Kokiri, 2007), experiences of health services (Jansen et al., 2008), infant sleep patterns (Jones et al., 2017), education (Ministry of Education, 2013), identity (Houkamau & Sibley, 2010), and health workforce (McClintock et al., 2019).

Te Kupenga, the largest and most comprehensive national survey of Māori, was first conducted post-census in 2013, then repeated in 2018. Te Kupenga was developed using principles and processes grounded in a Māori worldview, and involved collaboration across key government organisations and close engagement with Māori leaders and communities in order to arrive at its key themes for exploration (Statistics New Zealand, 2009b). As a survey to collect data on the health and well-being of the Māori population, Te Kupenga includes practices and outcomes that are specific to Māori, gathering data that had never before been prioritised for collection. It provides key statistics on four areas of Māori well-being: wairuatanga (spirituality), tikanga (Māori customs and practices), te reo Māori (the Māori language), and whanaungatanga (social connectedness) (Statistics New Zealand, 2014). In developing the framework for Te Kupenga, statisticians and researchers made explicit the four core values of the survey.

Similarly, Stevenson (2018) describes five key values that researches can use to underpin a survey of Māori families, and the survey on housing and well-being described by Henry and Crothers (2019) incorporates key Kaupapa Māori principles to form a quantitative research model. The Honour Project Aotearoa is firmly grounded in Māori cultural principles and values that serve to continue ancestral philosophies, applying them in a quantitative research context.

It is perhaps no coincidence that following the initial wānanga on the concept of hauora, the research team agreed to adopt the four values of Māori health that are at the pinnacle of Te Korowai Oranga: Māori Health Strategy. These include mauri ora (healthy individuals), whānau ora (healthy families), waiora (healthy environments) and pae ora (aspirational well-being). The values contained in He Korowai Oranga were developed through rigorous consultation with Māori communities in 2002, and updated following further consultation in 2014 (Ministry of Health, 2014).

The Honour Project Aotearoa research is strengthened by this framework, ensuring that a wider perspective of health is embedded in the survey and is consistent with the core values of the Māori Health Strategy.

Researchers who have designed other surveys for Māori have also involved the target community in the design process, drawing on expertise and experience at a gathering similar to the wānanga described here, or using an advisory group, or combining both methods (Stevenson, 2017; Henry & Crothers 2019; Ward et al., 2017; Jansen et al., 2008). Rameka (2015) describes a 'weaving' of participants' contributions, Kaupapa Māori theory, technologies and knowledge in the context of early childhood research. In a similar vein, the Honour Project Aotearoa project drew together three areas of expertise; Kaupapa Māori research, takatāpui and Māori LGBTQI+ experience, and statistical survey expertise, in order to develop a framework, a survey instrument, and a research protocol for the duration of the project that was inclusive and met the needs of all parties.

The practice of whanaungatanga, or drawing on existing connections and relationships, has been used as a recruitment tool in other Kaupapa Māori surveys (Rewi, 2014; Jones et al., 2017; Henry & Crothers, 2019; Stevenson, 2018; Te Rau Matatini, 2019). It was particularly suited to the Honour Project Aotearoa, because of the absence of a national collation of data for this population. In drawing on relationships based on trust, it also ensured a level of safety for respondents.

A guiding principle of this research is that of tino rangatiratanga: self-determination and autonomy. This was facilitated by involving the target research group, giving close consideration to the right to self-identify, and inviting freedom of expression within the confines of the survey research tool. Key to the success of this process was the establishment of a research team and advisory group with membership of target communities, expertise in quantitative investigation and Kaupapa Māori research, and perhaps most of all, expertise in their own health and well-being and that of their families and communities. This produced a robust, ongoing critique of a commonly used epidemiological tool, ensuring that statistical rigour was maintained while Indigenous autonomy was upheld.

References

Bycroft, C., Reid, G., McNally, J., & Gleisner, F. (2016). *Identifying Māori populations using administrative data: A comparison with the census.* Statistics New Zealand.

Coggon, D., Rose, G. A., & Barker, D. J. P. (2003). *Epidemiology for the uninitiated.*

BMJ Books.
Cram F. (2001). Tona tika, tona pono: The validity and integrity of Māori research. In M. Tolich (Ed.), *Research ethics in Aotearoa New Zealand: Concepts, practice, critique* (pp. 35–52). Longman.
Cram, F., & Mertens, D. (2015). Transformative and Indigenous frameworks for multimethod and mixed methods research. In S. N. Hesse-Biber & R. B. Johnson (Eds.), *The Oxford handbook of multimethod and mixed methods Research Inquity* (pp. 91–109). Oxford University Press.
Curtis, E., Reid, P., Jones, R. (2014). Decolonising the academy: The process of re-presenting Indigenous health in tertiary teaching and learning. *Māori and Pacific Higher Education Horizons, Diversity in Higher Education 15*, 147–165. doi.org/10.1108/S1479-3644201415
Harris, R., Purdie, G., Robson, B., Wright, C., Zhang, J., & Baker, M. (2007). Appendix 3: Estimating Māori hospitalisations and cancer registrations. In B. Robson & R. Harris (Eds.), *Hauora IV: Māori standards of health: A study of the years 2000–2005* (pp. 249–259). Te Rōpū Rangahau Hauora a Eru Pōmare.
Henry, E., & Crothers, C. (2019, May). Exploring Papakāinga: A Kaupapa Māori quantitative methodology. National Science Challenges: Building Better Homes, Towns and Cities. Kāinga Tahi, Kāinga Rua, project 8 – Papakāinga Whenu 3. BBHTC.
Houkamau, C. A., & Sibley, C. G. (2010). The multi-dimensional model of Māori identity and cultural engagement. *New Zealand Journal of Psychology, 19*(1), 97–110. doi.org/10.1037/a0031113
Jansen, P., Bacal, K., & Crengle, S. (2008). *He Ritenga Whakaaro: Māori experiences of health services*. Mauri Ora Associates.
Jones, H., Barber, C. C., Nikora, L. W., & Middlemiss, W. (2017). Māori child rearing and infant sleep practices. *New Zealand Journal of Psychology, 46*(3), 30–37. hdl.handle.net/10289/13397
Keefe, V., Ormsby, C., Robson, B., Reid, P., Cram, F., Purdie, G., & Ngāti Kahungunu Iwi Authority Incorporated (1999). Kaupapa Māori meets retrospective cohort. *He Pūkenga Kōrero, 5*(1), 12–17. hauhake.auckland.ac.nz/record/197237
Krieger, N. (2001). A glossary for social epidemiology. *Journal of Epidemiology and Community Health, 55*(10), 693–700. doi.org/10.1136/jech.55.10.693
Kukutai, T. (2004). The problem of defining an ethnic group for public policy: Who is Māori and why does it matter? *Social Policy Journal of New Zealand* (23), 86–108.
Kukutai, T. (2019). Reflections on Indigenous sovereignty. *Journal of Indigenous Wellbeing Te Mauri – Pimatisiwin. 4*(1), 3–4. journalindigenouswellbeing. co.nz/journal_articles/reflections-on-indigenous-sovereignty/
McClintock, K., Stephens, S., Baker, M., & Huriwai, T. (2019). *Te iti me te rahi, everyone counts – Māori health workforce report*. Te Rau Matatini. terauora.com/te-iti-me-te-rahi-everyone-counts-survey-and-report/
Ministry of Education. (2013). *Māori Medium Kaiako Survey*. Ministry of

Education. educationcounts.govt.nz/publications/schooling/140016

Ministry of Health. (2014). *The guide to He Korowai Oranga – Māori Health Strategy*. Ministry of Health. health.govt.nz/publication/guide-he-korowai-oranga-maori-health-strategy

Paine, S. J., Priston, M., Signal, T. L., Sweeney, B., & Muller. D. (2013). Developing new approaches for the recruitment and retention of indigenous participants in longitudinal research: Lessons from E Moe, Māmā: Maternal sleep and health in Aotearoa / New Zealand. *MAI Journal, 2*(2), 121–132. journal.mai.ac.nz/content/developing-new-approaches-recruitment-and-retention-indigenous-participants-longitudinal

Ratima, M., & Grant, B. (2007). Peer commentary 1 – Thinking about difference across and within mentoring. *MAI Review 3*.

Rameka, L. (2015). Whatu: A Māori approach to research. *Waikato Journal of Education, 20*(2), 39–48. doi.org/10.15663/wje.v20i2.204

Reid, P., Paine, S.-J., Curtis, E., Jones, R., Anderson, A., Willing, E., & Harwood, M. (2017). Achieving health equity in Aotearoa: strengthening responsiveness to Māori in health research. *The New Zealand Medical Journal, 130*(1465), 96–103.

Rewi, T. (2014). Utilising Kaupapa Māori approaches to initiate research. *MAI Journal, 3*(3), 243–254.

Robson, B., Purdie, G., Cram, F., & Simmonds, S. (2007). Age standardisation – an Indigenous standard? *Emerging Themes in Epidemiology, 4*(3). doi.org/10.1186/1742-7622-4-3

Royal, C. T. A. (2009). *Wānanga: The creative potential of mātauranga Māori*. MKTA.

Smith, L. T. (2005). On tricky ground: Researching the native in the age of uncertainty. In N. K. Denzin & Y. S. Lincoln (Eds.), *The Sage handbook of qualitative research* (pp. 85–107). Sage Publications.

Smith, L. T. (2015). Kaupapa Māori Research – Some Kaupapa Māori principles. In L. Pihama & K. South (Eds.), *Kaupapa Rangahau: A reader: A collection of readings from the kaupapa Māori research workshop series* (pp. 46–52). Te Kotahi Research Institute.

Statistics New Zealand. (2009a). *Final report of a review of the national Official Ethnicity Statistical Standard 2009*. Statistics New Zealand. statsnz.contentdm.oclc.org/digital/collection/p20045coll1/id/3642

Statistics New Zealand. (2009b). *He kohinga whakaaro: Māori social survey discussion document*. Statistics New Zealand. stats.govt.nz/consultations/he-kohinga-whakaaro-maori-social-survey-discussion-document/

Statistics New Zealand. (2014). *Te Kupenga 2013 English – corrected*. Statistics New Zealand.

Statistics New Zealand. (2015). *A guide to good survey design, 4th ed*. Statistics New Zealand.

Stevenson, K. (2018). A consultation journey: developing a Kaupapa Māori research methodology to explore Māori whānau experiences of harm and loss around birth. *AlterNative: An International Journal of Indigenous Peoples, 14*(1), 54–62. doi.org/10.1177/1177180117744612

Te Puni Kōkiri. (2007). *The health of the Māori language.* Te Puni Kōkiri.

Te Rōpū Rangahau Hauora ā Eru Pōmare. (2002). *Mana whakamārama – equal explanatory power: Māori and non-Māori sample size in national health surveys.* Report for Public Health Intelligence, Ministry of Health.

Ward, A. L., Wyeth, E. H., McGee, R., Freeman, C., & Cameron, C. (2017) Found in (survey) translation: Lessons learned while engaging with a wharekura in Southland, New Zealand. *Kōtuitui: New Zealand Journal of Social Sciences Online 13*(1), 70–81. doi.org/10.1080/1177083X.2017.1421978

Williams, H. W. (1991). *Dictionary of the Māori Language.* GP Publications Ltd.

Winitana, M. (2012). Remembering the deeds of Māui: What messages are in the tuakana-teina pedagogy for tertiary educators? *MAI Journal 1*(1), 29–37.

7

Te Tatauranga Whakamānawa Takatāpui: Honour Project Aotearoa Survey

Alison Green, Shirley Simmonds, Leonie Pihama, Matt Roskruge, Rebekah Laurence, Tawhanga Nopera and Herearoha Skipper

The Honour Project Aotearoa nationwide survey was the first of its kind to be conducted with and for takatāpui and Māori LGBTQI+ communities. The survey was informed by the original HONOR Project survey undertaken by Professor Karina Walters and her team from the Indigenous Wellness Research Institute (University of Washington, Seattle), with a key focus on Māori and our experiences and positioning in Aotearoa. The survey addressed the current dearth of information about takatāpui health and well-being. The process used to develop the survey, the researchers assert, contributes significantly to the growth of Kaupapa Māori mixed-method methodology, theory and practice. To this end, the researchers critiqued each of the steps commonly used to construct a statistical survey. The aim was to ensure that every stage of the survey development process met the needs and aspirations of the takatāpui and Māori LGBTQI+ communities.

The survey was completed by 368 takatāpui and Māori LGBTQI+ people. (The methodology and methods are discussed in the previous chapter.) Of 368 participants, just over 60% described their sexual and gender identities as takatāpui; 24% identified as gay, 21.5% as bisexual, 16.6% as lesbian, 12.8% as queer, 8.7% as rainbow, 7.3% as transgender, 5.4% as non-binary, 4.9% as whakawāhine, and 3.8% as gender-diverse; 5.7% described themselves as 'other', and 38 participants or 10.3% described themselves using a variety of terms ('queen', 'dyke', 'butch', 'whakatane', 'intersex', 'intersex variation', 'cross-dresser', 'pan-gender', 'MSM', and 'transvestite'). The average age of survey participants was 35.6 years, the oldest participant was 77 years, and the youngest 18 years. Nearly half of all participants lived in a major city, while 34% lived in a secondary urban area (i.e. small city or town), and 20% lived in a rural town or a rural area.

This chapter provides an overview and discussion of the survey's findings. The findings offer insight into participants' understandings and experiences of health and well-being, including their access to healthcare and their experiences with health professionals, and insight into the impact of discrimination on takatāpui.

Mauri ora: Takatāpui and Māori LGBTQI+ health and well-being

Current New Zealand well-being measures fall short of acknowledging Māori relationships to things that are tangible and intangible. Things that are tangible – observable and measurable – include relationships with mountains, rivers, whenua (land/earth) and wharenui (ancestral houses). Things that are intangible – not observable or measurable – include but are not limited to people's relationships with 'terms' for self-identification of one's sexuality and gender, and components of tikanga (practices and protocols) and mātauranga (Māori knowledge and ways of knowing) such as mauri (life force) and wairua (spirit). These are things that are unrecognised in other New Zealand surveys. The Honour Project Aotearoa team developed a conceptual framework for considering the contribution of tangible and intangible things to takatāpui and Māori LGBTQI+ individual and collective well-being. The framework drew on components of well-being as described in *He Korowai Oranga: Māori Health Strategy* (Ministry of Health, 2022; 2018). The Whānau Rangatiratanga Measurement Framework developed by the Families Commission (2015) also informed the framework.

The significance of the relationships that takatāpui and Māori LGBTQI+ survey participants have to things that are intangible, and the value of these relationships to health and well-being, cannot be overstated. Such relationships, for the most part, cannot be fostered and maintained without close and enduring connections to stable Māori collective entities and thriving natural environments, both of which are arguably key foundations of the health and well-being of all Māori. Takatāpui and Māori LGBTQI+ participants reported that achieving healthy futures for themselves required relationships with the following, in order of importance: wairuatanga (Māori spirituality); mātauranga Māori and tikanga Māori (Māori knowledge and cultural practices); rangatiratanga (leadership and self-determination); te reo Māori (the Māori language); kaitiakitanga (guardianship concerning metaphysical, physical and human realms).

Regarding healthy futures for whānau (extended family), takatāpui and Māori LGBTQI+ participants reported they require, in order of importance: kāinga (communal home and homelands); and whanaungatanga (relationships); kai (food); whakapapa (ancestral lineage); connectedness; whānau and kaupapa whānau (extended family structures and common interest groupings); tuakiri (identity). Takatāpui and Māori LGBTQI+ participants also reported the following as important for their own health: kāinga (communal home and homelands); whanaungatanga (relationships); connectedness; tuakiri (identity); kaupapa whānau (groups of common interest); and whakapapa (ancestral lineage).

Positively, more than 70% of takatāpui and Māori LGBTQI+ participants reported wairuatanga (spirituality) was very important to their health and well-being (Figure 1), compared with 66% of Te Kupenga 2013 (Statistics New Zealand, 2013) respondents.

Also positive was that 70% of survey participants reported they were happy all of the time to be Māori, 64% reported they were happy to be takatāpui or Māori LGBTQI+, and 85% thought it was important for takatāpui and Māori LGBTQI+ people to have positive role models.

Takatāpui and Māori LGBTQI+ survey participants rated whanaungatanga, having a home to live in, feeling connected, and having a strong sense of identity as most important for their health. Considering the high proportion of takatāpui and Māori LGBTQI+ survey participants

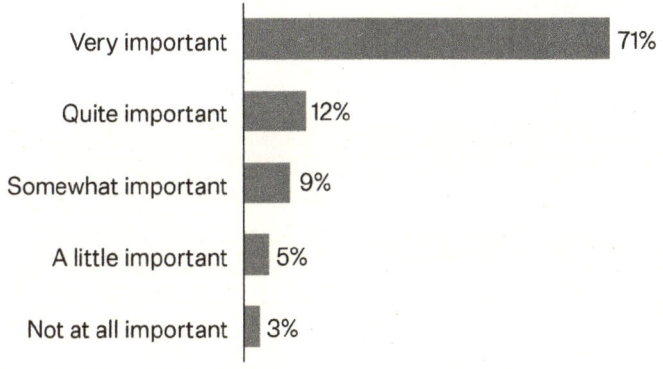

Figure 1: How important is wairuatanga or spirituality to your health?

reporting homelessness (20%) and insufficient income to meet their and their families' everyday needs (55%), it is unsurprising that participants reported that these were high priorities. It is also important to note that takatāpui and Māori LGBTQI+ participants rated whakapapa and whanaungatanga highly. These could be understood as enabling whānau relationships to be practised, quite possibly helping some takatāpui and Māori LGBTQI+ people to navigate the impacts of homelessness and insufficient income.

A number of survey questions focused on self-perception of physical, mental and sexual health. Adopted from the New Zealand Health Survey (2017), responses were analysed and compared with responses from Māori to the same questions. Most survey participants reported they felt satisfied with their overall health, rating it as 'good', 'very good', or 'excellent'. However, of significant concern is that almost one quarter (24.5%) of takatāpui and Māori LGBTQI+ participants rated their health as 'fair' to 'poor' (Figure 2). Approximately 10–20% of participants experienced some difficulty seeing, hearing, walking and climbing steps, concentrating, managing self-care, and being understood.

Also of concern were those participants (27%) who, when asked how much control they felt they had over their lives, reported they felt they had only 'some' or 'no' control. These responses suggest that more than a quarter of takatāpui and Māori LGBTQI+ survey participants will struggle to achieve a sense of control and self-determination over their lives, a factor that is vital to achieving healthy futures for themselves and their whānau.

One's self-identified sexual identity is a core component of tuakiri or overall Māori identity. Regarding the contribution that public health services make to fostering Māori identity and maintaining health, the

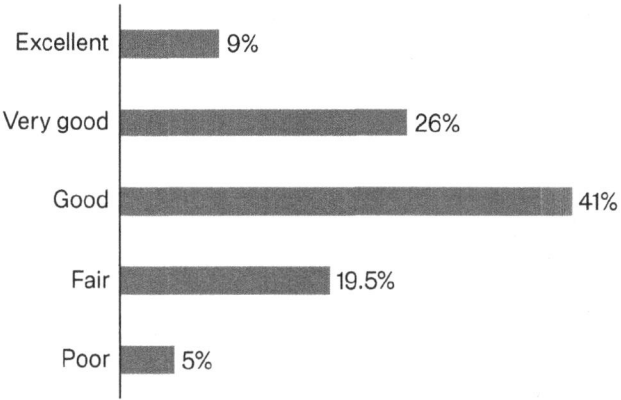

Figure 2: How would you rate your overall health?

Honour Project Aotearoa team developed questions designed to find out whether participants' general practitioner (GP) – the public health service professional most frequently utilised in Aotearoa – knew of their sexual identity and, if so, how their GP had obtained that information. Sexual identity is a self-identified umbrella term for a person's sexual orientation, sexual attraction and sexual behaviour (New Zealand Health Survey, 2017). Nearly half (47%) of all takatāpui and Māori LGBTQI+ survey participants reported that they were unsure if their GP knew their sexual identity or that their GP did not know their sexual identity or had not enquired as to their sexual identity (Figure 3).

These responses suggest that participants' GPs may not be providing proactive, inclusive and safe primary care services such that takatāpui and Māori LGBTQI+ people feel safe to disclose their sexual identity and request health interventions that may indicate their sexual orientation (such as an HIV test). Furthermore, 53% of takatāpui and Māori LGBTQI+ participants reported that their GPs used terms to describe their sexual identity that caused them to feel uncomfortable. Reflecting on the study by Ludlam et al. (2015), it seems that this area of health service practice requires attention to ensure that takatāpui and Māori LGBTQI+ have early access to preventative healthcare and, in turn, to ensure a reduction in health inequities.

Further, takatāpui and Māori LGBTQI+ people may not be receiving the range of gender-related health services they need and, therefore, struggle to foster and maintain their health and well-being. Inability to disclose one's sexual or gender identity due to fear of stigma and discrimination has implications for the sexual health inequities that exist between takatāpui and Māori LGBTQI+ people and the Pākehā LGBTQI+ population, and between the Māori and Pākehā populations of Aotearoa.

Survey questions about discrimination (racism, transphobia, homophobia and misogyny) were influenced by the HONOR Project, which reported responses from 447 two-spirit Native Americans over 2005–

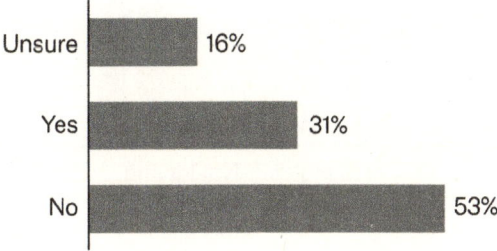

Figure 3: Does your current GP know your sexual identity?

2007. The project's main goal was to report on the impact of historical trauma, discrimination and other stressors on the health and wellness of the participants. A comparative analysis of data from the Honour Project Aotearoa and the HONOR Project is underway.

In the meantime, 43% of takatāpui and Māori LGBTQI+ survey participants reported using alcohol in the last 12 months (monthly, weekly and more often) to manage stress related to homophobia, transphobia and discrimination. Similarly, 43% of takatāpui and Māori LGBTQI+ participants reported using recreational and prescription drugs in the last 12 months (monthly, weekly and more often) to manage stress arising from homophobia, transphobia, misogyny and discrimination. In total, 77% of takatāpui and Māori LGBTQI+ survey participants reported experiencing distress some, most, or all of the time as a consequence of homophobia, transphobia and misogyny. By comparison, the HONOR Project survey participants reported that 31% of participants injected drugs, 38% experienced alcohol dependence, and 44% were bothered by some form of discrimination arising from their two-spirit identity.

Asked how often they were distressed because they felt that they had to be 'on guard', because they were fearful of being bullied or attacked, because they lacked positive role models, or because whānau and friends avoided discussion about their sexual or gender identities, takatāpui and Māori LGBTQI+ survey participants indicated that they lived with unhealthy levels of stress. Taken together, 78% reported they felt they had

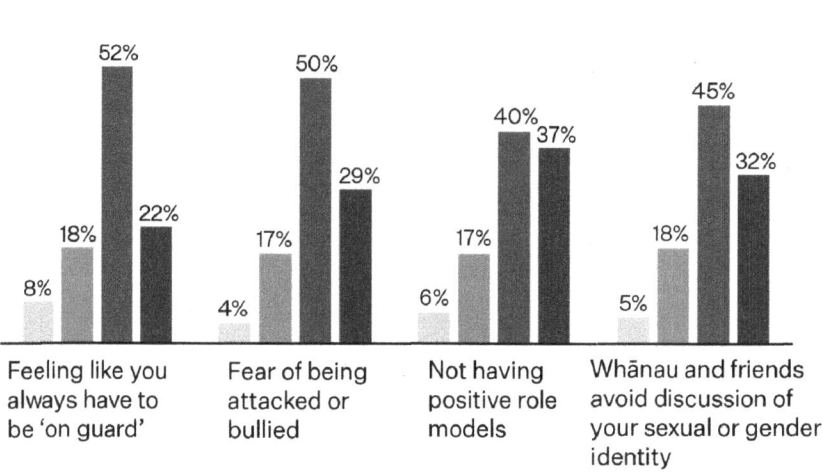

Figure 4: As a takatāpui or Māori LGBTQI+ person, how often are you distressed by . . . ?

to be 'on guard' for 'all', 'most' or 'some of the time' (Figure 4). Further, 71% reported fear of being bullied or attacked 'all', 'most' or 'some of the time', and 63% reported they lacked positive role models 'all', 'most' or 'some of the time'. Lastly, 68% reported that they were distressed by whānau and friends avoiding discussion of their sexual or gender identities 'all', 'most' or 'some of the time'. Unsurprisingly, 45% of participants reported that they were 'not open', or only 'sometimes open', in their day-to-day lives about being takatāpui and Māori LGBTQI+. The four most common reasons participants gave for not being open were, in order, 1) fear of discrimination, 2) fear of rejection, 3) people are homophobic, and 4) fear for safety. Further, when asked whether they had experienced violence or the threat of violence because they are takatāpui and Māori LGBTQI+, 49% reported they had; physical, sexual, psychological and emotional abuse were the most commonly experienced forms or threats of violence.

When asked whether they were distressed about a lack of legal rights and protections related to being takatāpui and Māori LGBTQI+ people, 44% reported they were 'somewhat distressed', 'very distressed' or 'extremely distressed' (Figure 5).

It is unacceptable that takatāpui and Māori LGBTQI+ people are unable to express their tuakiri or their identity and exercise their rangatiratanga for fear of violence, abuse and discrimination related to their Māori, sexual and gender identities. A recent Kaupapa Māori study of HIV-related stigma and discrimination experienced by Māori people living with HIV (Māori PLHIV) – many of whom identify as takatāpui and Māori LGBTQI+ – further confirms that Aotearoa has a serious problem with regard to stigma and discrimination towards Māori (Te Whāriki Takapou,

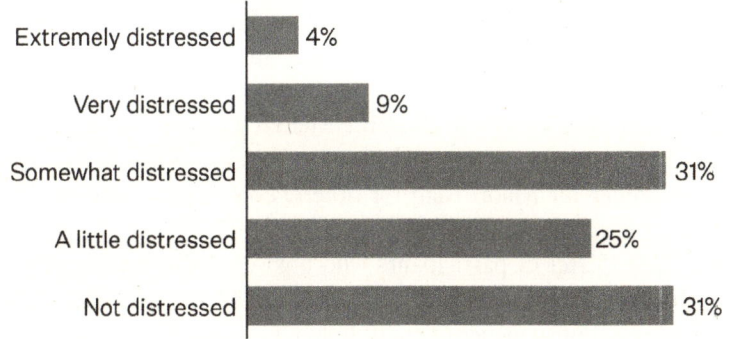

Figure 5: In the last 12 months, how distressed were you by the lack of legal rights and protection because you are takatāpui or Māori LGBTQI+?

2021). Specifically, three-quarters of participants reported that in the last 12 months they had experienced some form of HIV-related stigma and discrimination. Over that period, more than a third had been verbally harassed, and just under a quarter had been refused employment.

The way in which current human rights legislation is promoted and implemented in Aotearoa does not meet the needs of takatāpui and Māori LGBTQI+ communities, and this issue requires attention. The process for taking a complaint against a person for alleged discrimination is described by Māori as complicated, leading to fear of retaliation and low confidence of a positive outcome (Te Whāriki Takapou, 2021). However, Aotearoa is a signatory to an international human rights framework that includes the United Nations Declaration on the Rights of Indigenous Peoples. The right to freedom from any kind of discrimination is addressed in article 2, and articles 13 and 15 address the right to redress associated with the subjugation of mātauranga Māori approaches to gender and sexual identities (United Nations, 2007). It is, therefore, completely unacceptable that national legislation and international rights frameworks are unable to deliver the suite of rights and protection that will support the individual and collective self-determined identities of takatāpui and Māori LGBTQI+ communities.

The final section of the 'Mauri Ora' component of the survey invited takatāpui and Māori LGBTQI+ participants to answer questions about self-harm and suicide with regard to their own and other's health and well-being. In total, 19% of survey participants made the decision to skip this section. This was the only section where participants could choose to opt out and then re-join the survey. The decision to survey self-harm and suicide among participants was made following hui in Auckland, Wellington and Christchurch, where takatāpui and Māori LGBTQI+ community leaders told the researchers that one of the most destructive consequences of homophobia, transphobia, misogyny and discrimination was self-harm and suicide. The decision to include questions about self-harm, suicide and access to support services was confirmed by an earlier study, Te Rau Hinengaro: New Zealand Mental Health Survey, which found that the prevalence of suicidal ideation, suicide plans and suicide attempts was higher for Māori than for others, even after adjustment for sociodemographic correlates (Oakley Browne et al., 2006).

Just over half (53%) of participants who answered this section of the survey had had a whānau member or friend who had thought about self-harm or suicide as a consequence of transphobia, homophobia, misogyny or discrimination because of their sexual or gender identities. Most participants reported that their whānau member or friend had received support from friends, whānau, a GP, or someone else. Alarmingly, 16% of participants thought their whānau member or friend had received no support, or they didn't know if support had been obtained. Further, 51% of takatāpui and Māori LGBTQI+ people reported that a whānau member or friend had self-harmed or suicided as a consequence of transphobia, homophobia, misogyny or discrimination associated with their sexual or gender identities, and support, if and when this was obtained, mainly came from friends and whānau. Again, 16% of participants thought no support was obtained, or they didn't know if there had been support. When participants were asked whether they themselves had ever thought about self-harm or suicide, 45% reported they had and that support had come from friends and whānau, although 13% reported they had no support during this distressing time of their lives. Lastly, just over a third (33.96%) of respondents reported that they had self-harmed or attempted suicide, citing friends and whānau as their most likely sources of support.

Concluding this section, questions from the General Social Survey (Statistics New Zealand, 2018), Te Kupenga: 2018, the HONOR Project, and the Honour Project Aotearoa focused on survey participants' mental and spiritual health. Most (55%) takatāpui and Māori LGBTQI+ participants reported that over the last four weeks they had felt calm 'most of the time' or 'all of the time'. However, the remaining (45%) participants did not feel calm and peaceful at all (6%), or only 'some of the time' (25%) or 'a little of the time' (14%).

Whānau ora: The health of whānau

This section builds on the conceptual framework that was developed to gather information about the health and well-being of takatāpui, Māori LGBTQI+ and their whānau, using distinctly Māori indicators. As expected, takatāpui and Māori LGBTQI+ participants reported that their whānau included multiple generations of people descended from common ancestors. Mothers, aunts and older female members were most likely to be reported as whānau members (93%), followed by parents (89%), tūpuna/ tīpuna (ancestor, elder, grandparent) (88%), kaumātua (88%), cousins (88%) partners (87%), sisters (85%), children (84%), kaupapa whānau (81%), and brothers (79%). Unexpectedly, but possibly as a consequence of the number of survey participants who reported they did not have children (70.5% of participants were without children, compared with more than 70% of Māori households include children), takatāpui and Māori LGBTQI+ survey participants were less likely to report children and grandchildren as whānau members, and friends were as likely to be reported as whānau members as tīpuna/tūpuna and kaumātua.

When comparing the Honour Project Aotearoa whānau composition to the composition of whānau reported by Te Kupenga 2013, it appears that takatāpui and Māori LGBTQI+ participants may have different whānau compositions. For example, Te Kupenga participants (94%) reported whānau as most likely to include parents, partners, children, brothers and sisters, whereas Honour Project Aotearoa participants were more likely to report older women, parents, tīpuna/tūpuna, kaumātua (elders), cousins and partners as whānau members. Despite an apparent difference with regard to whānau composition, 82% of takatāpui and Māori LGBTQI+ survey participants reported that they felt connected or strongly connected to their whānau (Figure 6).

Approximately 70% of takatāpui and Māori LGBTQI+ survey participants reported their whānau as doing well or extremely well, compared to 83% of Te Kupenga participants. Low level of income, homelessness and discrimination may affect how well the Honour Project Aotearoa survey participants reported the well-being of their whānau.

Of the survey participants, 70.5% of takatāpui and Māori LGBTQI+ individuals had not been a parent. Of the 29% who had parented a child, 58% had become a parent with a friend, partner or spouse, 34% had raised a whāngai child, and 21% had been a step-parent. Assisted reproduction at home had enabled 7% of takatāpui and Māori LGBTQI+ survey participants to become parents, and 2% had utilised external fertility services in order to conceive a child. Counting Ourselves, a study of the health and well-being of trans and non-binary people in Aotearoa, reported 16% of survey

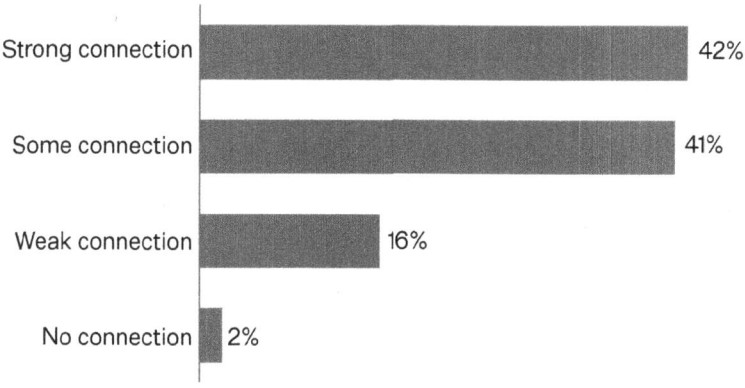

Figure 6: How connected do you feel to the whānau group you were thinking about?

participants were parents, including being a foster or adopted parent. For the Māori participants, 32% reported wanting to be a parent, nearly twice the level of the study's Pākehā participants (Veale et al., 2019).

Takatāpui and Māori LGBTQI+ parents reported that they are faced with challenges arising from racism, homophobia, transphobia and misogyny when raising their children. Of concern is that 29% of participants reported that someone had threatened custody of their children because of their (the parent's) sexual or gender identity, 18% had experienced rejection by whānau members and others, and 44% had had their right to be a parent questioned by others.

When accessing a health service for their children, 40% of survey participants had had their right to parent a child questioned by the health service, which is a clear breach of the obligations and duties of health services as set out in New Zealand's Code of Health and Disability Services Consumers' Rights. Half of survey participants (50%) who were or who had been a parent reported they had experienced discrimination for being a takatāpui or Māori LGBTQI+ parent, and 36% reported that their child had experienced discrimination as a consequence of having a takatāpui or Māori LGBTQI+ parent.

Kerekere (2017) notes that children can feel discrimination keenly, even when they might not understand the reason for the discrimination, such as homophobia, transphobia and misogyny. Kerekere proposes that one of the effects of children witnessing or directly experiencing discrimination may be to limit the development of their own sense of being Māori, and of being themselves. Asked how they might become a parent in the future, 52% of takatāpui and Māori LGBTQI+ survey participants wanting to be parents reported that they preferred to whāngai a relative's child, 21% would prefer to adopt a child, and 15% thought they would like to parent a partner's child. At 52%, the preference for raising a relative's child can be interpreted as indicating the importance of whakapapa – of continuing one's whānau descent lines – for takatāpui and Māori LGBTQI+ people.

Ngā hononga: Cultural connections

Survey participants reported on a number of questions to do with te reo Māori and participation in Māori and iwi, hapū and whānau cultural activities and events. Some questions were adopted from Te Kupenga 2013, and others were developed by the Honour Project Aotearoa team. Briefly, 10% of takatāpui and Māori LGBTQI+ survey participants reported that te reo Māori was the language most often spoken in their home (Figure 7).

By comparison, 2.6% of adult Māori respondents in Te Kupenga 2013 reported that te reo Māori was the main language at their home, and a further 20.5% reported that te reo Māori was spoken regularly at home.

Regarding te reo Māori proficiency, takatāpui and Māori LGBTQI+ survey participants reported their ability to speak Māori in day-to-day conversations as high, in fact higher than Te Kupenga 2013 participants, although participants in both surveys reported almost the same level of ability to understand spoken Māori. Takatāpui and Māori LGBTQI+ survey participants reported higher levels of reading and writing proficiency than their Te Kupenga 2013 counterparts. Higher te reo Māori proficiency reported by takatāpui and Māori LGBTQI+ survey participants may be associated with numbers attending kōhanga reo, kura Kaupapa Māori, and Māori-medium education settings. Survey findings on te reo Māori proficiency are positive and suggest takatāpui and Māori LGBTQI+ participants place a high value on te reo Māori. Data require further analysis, but on the face of it, we can infer that resources to support the revitalisation of te reo Māori would likely be supported by takatāpui and Māori LGBTQI+ households.

Questions focusing on engagement with Māori, iwi, hapū and whānau activities and events were derived from Te Kupenga 2013. In total, 93% of takatāpui and Māori LGBTQI+ participants reported that they knew their iwi, 44% reported regular participation in iwi events, and 62% had been to their ancestral marae in the last 12 months. By comparison, 89% of Te Kupenga 2013 respondents knew their iwi, and 62% had been to their ancestral marae in the last 12 months.

Regarding socio-economic barriers and facilitators to Māori development,

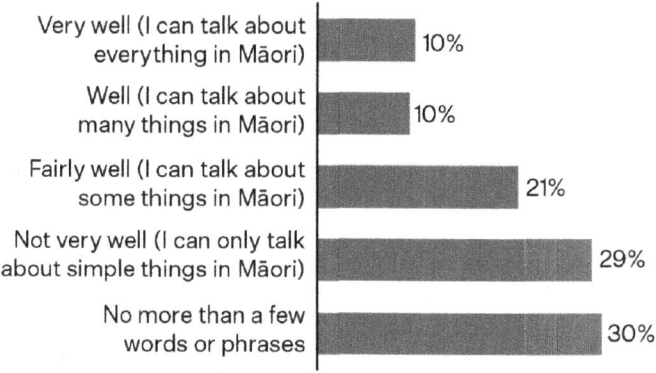

Figure 7: How well are you able to speak Māori in everyday conversation?

the Honour Project Aotearoa team wanted to know what barriers prevented takatāpui and Māori LGBTQI+ people from connecting with their iwi and hapū. Specifically, survey participants were asked how often they had gone to their ancestral marae in the last 12 months, and whether discrimination was a barrier to participation (Figure 8). For takatāpui and Māori LGBTQI+ survey participants, the most common barriers were cost, distance or transport problems (46%), followed by no occasion or no invitation (42%). Taken together, 22% of takatāpui and Māori LGBTQI+ participants reported that fear of experiencing homophobia, transphobia, misogyny, discrimination, violence or bullying (and prior experience of these) were reasons for not going to their ancestral marae in the last 12 months. A further 27% of survey participants reported not going to their ancestral marae because they felt out of place. This response could be interpreted in many ways, including the possibility that, in spite of takatāpui and Māori LGBTQI+ people being connected to marae through whakapapa, some ancestral marae are heteronormative settings, which can create formidable barriers to them.

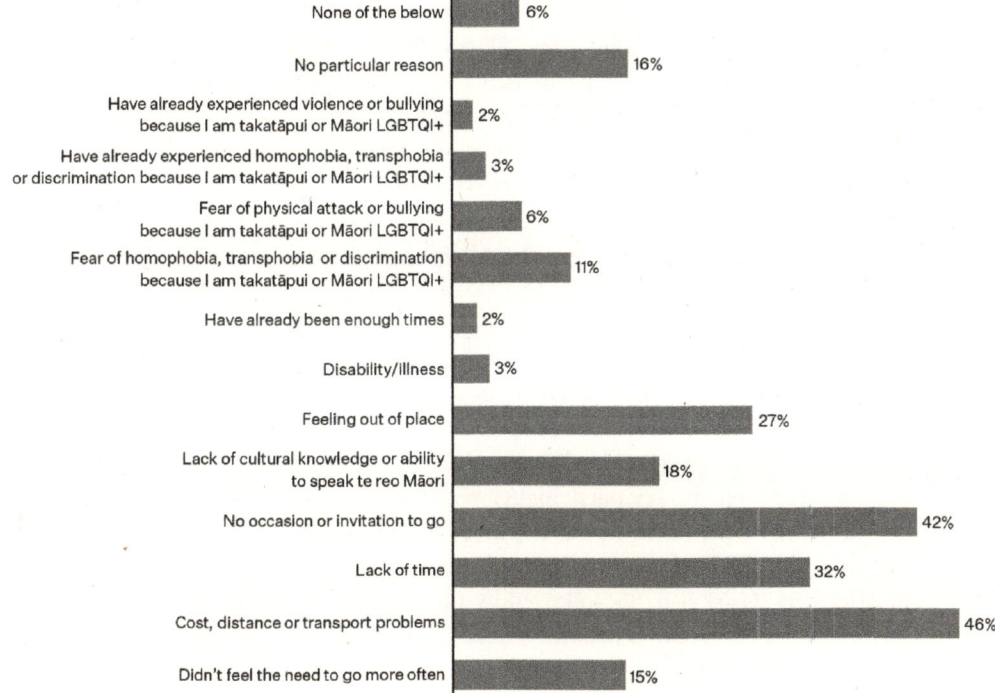

Figure 8: In the last 12 months, what were the reasons you didn't go to your ancestral marae?

Discriminatory barriers and socio-economic challenges notwithstanding, 92% of takatāpui and Māori LGBTQI+ survey participants reported that it was 'somewhat', 'quite', or 'very' important for them to be involved in things to do with Māori language and culture, compared with 70% of Te Kupenga 2013 respondents. A positive finding was that 50% of our takatāpui and Māori LGBTQI+ survey participants reported carrying out a range of well-respected cultural roles (such as ringawera, kapa haka kaiako and kaitiaki taiao). The high value of culture to Indigenous LGBTQI+ peoples was noted by HONOR Project two-spirit survey participants for whom 90% reported they felt good about their Indian identity, and 95% reported that Indian culture has many strengths. Furthermore, 85% of HONOR Project two-spirit survey participants felt a spiritual connection to the land, and 89% reported feeling at peace with their American Indian identity.

The Honour Project Aotearoa team developed four questions to find out where takatāpui and Māori LGBTQI+ survey participants sought their social support. Sources of support, in order of popularity, were 1) friends, 2) whānau, 3) online social media support groups, 4) kaupapa whānau, 5) takatāpui and Māori LGBTQI+ organisations, 6) Pākehā LGBTQI+ organisations, 7) work colleagues, 8) counsellor health services, and 9) Māori organisations. Survey participants were also asked which LGBTQI+ settings they had visited in the last 12 months. In order of popularity were 1) online LGBTQI+ networks, 2) clubs and bars, 3) the Auckland Pride Parade and Big Gay Out, and 4) other (free text).

Wai ora: How health and social services affect health and well-being

This section of the survey report focuses on health and social services (i.e. lived environments) as key determinants of the health and well-being of takatāpui and Māori LGBTQI+ people. In total, 64% of survey participants reported using some type of health and social service in the last 12 months in order to keep well. Survey participants were asked to report all services they had used for their health. By far the most common services that takatāpui and Māori LGBTQI+ survey participants reported using were general practitioners (GPs) at 87%, followed by pharmacists (47%), mental health services (24%), and sexual health services (21%). Most takatāpui and Māori LGBTQI+ survey participants (91%) reported that their GP was their main healthcare professional. This is not unsurprising, given that for two decades the Ministry of Health and District Health Boards have promoted primary healthcare and GPs as the first point of entry into the health and disability system. However, only a third (36%) of survey participants thought they were registered with a primary healthcare organisation (PHO), although the Ministry of Health estimates 84% of the total Māori population are enrolled with a PHO (Ministry of Health, 2021).

Although 36% of takatāpui and Māori LGBTQI+ survey participants thought that they were registered with a GP and 87% reported their GP as the person they saw most often for their health needs, only 9% reported their main healthcare professional as very knowledgeable in terms of meeting their needs as Māori, and only 8% reported that they were very knowledgeable meeting their needs as a takatāpui or a Māori LGBTQI+ person. This suggests that despite two decades of primary healthcare sector development, the knowledge of GPs is not well developed in terms of meeting their takatāpui or Māori LGBTQI+ patients' needs. There may be a connection between the small number (9%) of survey participants reporting their GP as very knowledgeable and our other findings about survey participants' relationships with their GPs: 47% reported that their GP did not know their sexual identity and 20% that their GP did not know their gender identity, and a significant number reported that their GP and other health professionals used sexuality-related terms and gender identity-related terms that made them feel uncomfortable (53% and 33% respectively).

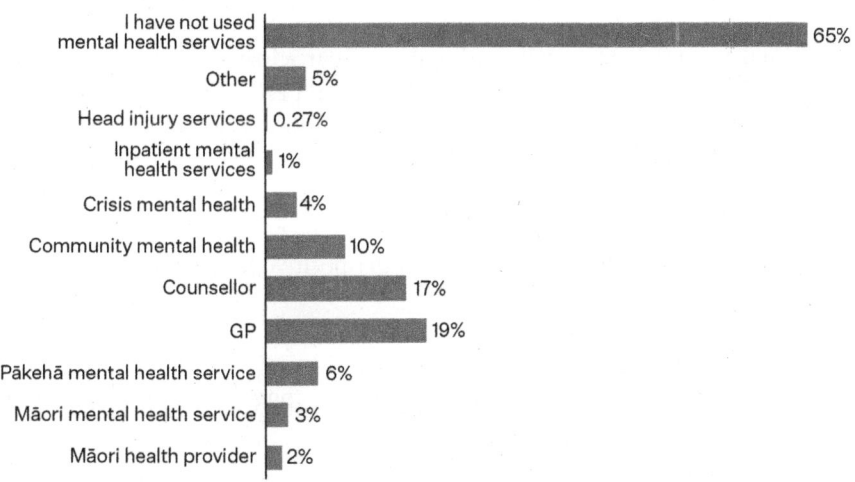

Figure 9: In the last 12 months have you accessed any of the following services for mental health care?

Of those survey participants who accessed services for their mental health (Figure 9), 47% reported that they were required to have a mental health diagnosis in order to access services. Given the high levels of sexuality-based discrimination and gender-based discrimination that takatāpui and Māori LGBTQI+ experience, the distress associated with feeling like they must always be 'on guard', the fear of being attacked or bullied, an absence of positive role models, and whānau and friends' avoidance of talking about one's sexual and gender identities, access to no-cost mental health services is critical for the health and well-being of takatāpui and Māori LGBTQI+ people.

Lastly, survey participants were asked about how well their healthcare professional explained health conditions and treatments so that they could understand. Most takatāpui and Māori LGBTQI+ participants (48.1%) reported that their healthcare professional's explanations were 'good' or 'very good'. Of concern were the 18.2% who responded 'poor' or 'very poor'. Taken together, while the Primary Health Strategy emphasises prevention and aims to improve access to GPs and other primary health services, it is clear that the barriers to these positive outcomes for significant numbers of takatāpui and Māori LGBTQI+ people include a lack of knowledge, a failure to provide health information that aligns with patients' health literacy, and the cost of health services.

In the meantime, 32% of takatāpui and Māori LGBTQI+ survey participants sought out Māori healing services, particularly Rongoā (70%), Mirimiri (68%), Karakia (66%), and Wai (43%). Similarly, the HONOR Project two-spirit survey participants reported that traditional healing, spirituality and ceremonial and cultural participation were protective against the harmful effects of stress and trauma. Lastly, 43% of participants reported that if they could, they would use a support person to help them get the health services they need. This simple strategy could make a difference in terms of reducing discrimination stemming from racism, homophobia and transphobia for takatāpui and Māori LGBTQI+ people seeking culturally affirming and sexuality-positive and gender-positive health services.

Impacts of discrimination

Discrimination against takatāpui and Māori LGBTQI+ people is not only a significant barrier to their use of health services, but also to participation and success in education, employment and well-being in public places. It is concerning that 51% of takatāpui and Māori LGBTQI+ survey participants reported experiencing discrimination for being Māori in multiple settings:

at school (81%), in public places (70%), in shops (61%), on the street (56%), at work (54%), when seeking employment (53%), and in restaurants (43%).

Discrimination because of sexual identity was experienced by 46% of takatāpui and Māori LGBTQI+ survey participants in public places such as parks, libraries and recreation settings (76%), on the street (60%), at school (54%), at work (43%), in shops (28%), in tertiary education settings (22%), and in restaurants (21%). Discrimination because of gender identity was experienced by 20% of takatāpui and Māori LGBTQI+ survey participants in public places (64%), at school (60%), at work (60%), on the street (58%), when seeking employment (38%), in shops (37%), at restaurants (26%), and in tertiary education settings (23%).

Some takatāpui and LGBTQI+ survey participants (18%) reported experiencing discrimination while using health services. While this is not as poor as the results for other public services, racism in health services is unacceptable and constitutes a breach of legislative and health standards, negatively affecting Māori health outcomes. Focusing on health services as sites of discrimination, takatāpui and Māori LGBTQI+ survey participants reported experiencing racism at hospitals (22%), GP medical centres (19%), emergency departments (18%), and after-hours medical centres (8%). Discrimination at health services because of sexual identity was experienced at GP medical centres (17%), hospitals (15%), Māori providers (11%), emergency departments (9%), community mental health services (8%), and sexual health services (6%). Discrimination at health services

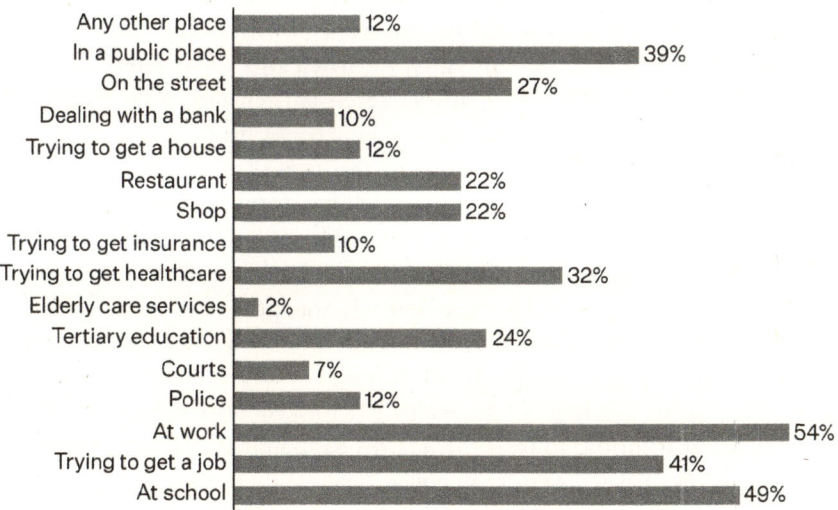

Figure 10: Have you experienced discrimination because of disability-related issues?

because of gender identity was experienced by survey participants at GP medical centres (25%), hospitals (25%), emergency departments (12%), after-hours medical centres (10%), medical specialists (10%), and Māori providers (8%) and women's health services (8%).

Discrimination arising from disability-related issues was reported by 11% of takatāpui and Māori LGBTQI+ survey participants (Figure 10). Sites where disability-related discrimination was experienced by participants were the workplace (54%), at school (49%), when seeking employment (41%), in public places (39%), trying to get healthcare (32%), on the street (27%), at tertiary education settings (24%), at shops (22%), and at restaurants (22%). Takatāpui and Māori LGBTQI+ survey participants with disabilities reported experiencing disability-related discrimination at GP medical centres (34%), emergency departments (20%), community mental health services (20%), hospitals (15%), medical specialists (12%), after-hours medical centres (10%), and in-patient mental health services (10%).

Discrimination is experienced by many Māori who are subject to the criminal justice system. Evidence of discrimination against prisoners can be seen in the disenfranchisement or blanket ban on all prisoners' right to vote. For Māori, who comprise 50% of the adult prison population in Aotearoa, disenfranchisement means that their individual rights, and their socio-political Treaty rights as members of iwi, hapū, whānau and Māori collectives, are disproportionately affected (Just Speak, 2019). Discrimination was experienced by takatāpui and Māori LGBTQI-+ survey participants who reported having spent time in prison. In total, 24 takatāpui and Māori LGBTQI+ survey participants (7%) reported that they had been to prison, and a further seven participants (2%) preferred not to answer the question. And while they were in prison, most reported they had not been able to access the health services they needed.

Te Kupenga 2013 explored Māori adults' patterns of trust in six institutions – media, systems of government, education, courts, health, and police. Te Kupenga 2013 described the aim of these public institutions as to promote a well-functioning society. It was proposed that if people do not trust these institutions, it is unlikely they will make use of their services which, in turn, limits the institution's ability to foster individual and collective well-being. Te Kupenga 2013 asked respondents whether they trusted institutions to treat them fairly. Respondents reported that the institutions they trusted most were police, health, and the courts, and those they least trusted were the media and systems of government. Te Kupenga 2013 found that as Māori respondents' material well-being increased, so too did their level of trust in the police. Further, the more highly qualified Māori are, the lower their level of trust in the media.

By comparison, takatāpui and Māori LGBTQI+ survey participants reported that the institutions they trusted most were education (46% of participants), followed by health (39% of participants) and social services (33% of participants). For religious institutions, a trust level of 7+ (high trust) was held by just 11% of survey participants, and 17% for the media. Takatāpui and Māori LGBTQI+ participants' responses in the Honour Projet Aotearoa were different from Te Kupenga 2013 responses; specifically, education was the most trusted institution, rather than the police. Trust levels of 7+ (high trust) for the police, justice, immigration and courts were held by around 27% to 28% percent of Honour Project Aotearoa survey participants – significantly lower than levels of trust in the same institutions reported by Te Kupenga 2013. A closer analysis will be required over the coming months in order to understand the significance of this data.

Finally, survey participants were asked which factors contributed to positive health service experiences for takatāpui and Māori LGBTQI+ people, their whānau and friends. Most highly rated was 'a welcoming space' (97% of participants), followed by 'awareness of sexual identity' (94%), 'awareness of gender identity' (93%), 'a respectful GP / healthcare provider' (93%), 'clear communication of health information' (93%), and 'a nurturing environment' (90%). Survey participants also rated the following as important: 'I feel comfortable talking about being Māori' (89% of participants), 'I feel comfortable talking about being takatāpui or Māori LGBTQI+' (88%), 'Pronunciation of te reo Māori' (86%), 'Knowledge of tikanga Māori' (85%), 'Visible Māori staff' (81%), 'Knowledge of te reo Māori' (76%), 'Visible takatāpui staff' (76%), 'Physical contact is appropriate' (73%), 'Traditional rongoa is supported' (73%), 'Alternative medicines are supported' (71%), and 'Karakia is practised' (66%). These factors are all required by current health service legislation and policy, professional practice standards, and the Code of Health, yet many takatāpui and Māori LGBTQI+ participants reported that their healthcare professionals failed to deliver services that were compliant.

Summary

The Honour Project Aotearoa survey was developed in collaboration with advisors from the HONOR Project, and takatāpui and Māori LGBTQI+ communities and non-government organisations. A total of 368 Māori self-identified takatāpui and Māori LGBTQI+ people completed the survey.

Asked to rate factors that support their health and well-being, participants reported that having a home, having enough good food, and experiencing whanaungatanga and connectedness were high priorities. Whakapapa whānau and kaupapa whānau were important sources of positivity and support for takatāpui and Māori LGBTQI+ survey participants. While the composition of takatāpui and Māori LGBTQI+ whānau may differ from the composition of whānau Māori identified by Te Kupenga 2013, the majority of takatāpui and Māori LGBTQI+ survey participants reported that they felt connected or strongly connected to their whānau, and their whānau as doing well or extremely well.

Discrimination experienced by takatāpui and Māori LGBTQI+ survey participants – whether when using health and social services, or in public places – is gravely unacceptable and induces unhealthy and at times life-threatening levels of distress. Racism, homophobia and transphobia demand national and international action. High levels of discrimination, violence and abuse in Aotearoa indicate that racism, homophobia and transphobia are entrenched, persistent and systemic. It is intolerable that takatāpui and Māori LGBTQI+ people are unable, for fear of violence or abuse, to express their tuakiri (cultural, sexual and gender identities) and exercise their rangatiratanga or their Treaty of Waitangi self-determining rights. Survey participants reported that the stress caused by society's response to their cultural, sexual and gender identities contributed to self-harm and suicide. If any support was received by those who had contemplated self-harm and suicide and for those who had self-harmed and attempted suicide, it came largely from friends and whānau. In spite of the serious levels of discrimination experienced by takatāpui and Māori LGBTQI+ participants, a high number reported they were happy all of the time to be Māori, and happy to be takatāpui. It is important for takatāpui and Māori LGBTQI+ people to have good role models to help foster and maintain positive identities.

Survey participants raising children reported being faced with a number of challenges. Involvement with Māori language and culture was high amongst takatāpui and Māori LGBTQI+ participants. They reported higher levels of reading and writing proficiency than their Te Kupenga 2013 counterparts, the majority indicated knowledge of their iwi, and they reported significant cultural engagement with iwi and marae. They reported carrying out a range of well-respected cultural roles at their marae or for their iwi, hapū and kaupapa whānau. However, fear of experiencing homophobia, transphobia and discrimination, or prior experience of these, were reasons why some had not gone to their marae in the last 12 months.

Turning to health services and health systems, the picture is grim. Although the majority of takatāpui and Māori LGBTQI+ survey participants were registered with a GP and reported their GP as the person they saw most often for their health needs, only a small proportion reported their main GP as knowledgeable in terms of meeting their needs as Māori, and even fewer reported that their GP was knowledgeable in terms of meeting their needs. Lack of knowledge about takatāpui and Māori LGBTQI+ people coupled with a failure to provide health information and reduce the cost of health services are significant barriers to prevention and well-being for takatāpui and Māori LGBTQI+ people.

Discrimination that stems from racism, homophobia, transphobia and misogyny is not only a significant barrier to health service utilisation, but also to participation and success in education, employment, and well-being in public places. Just over half of takatāpui and Māori LGBTQI+ survey participants reported experiencing discrimination for being Māori in multiple settings.

These responses suggest that inequities exist for takatāpui and Māori LGBTQI+ people relative to other Māori and other New Zealanders in Aotearoa. Homelessness, insufficient income, and unacceptably high levels of discrimination negatively impact one's sense of identity, mental health, parenting, access to most health and social services, and trust in government institutions. As well, legislation and government strategies appear to be failing takatāpui and Māori LGBTQI+ communities. Notwithstanding the significant distress experienced by takatāpui and Māori LGBTQI+ survey participants in the face of discriminatory health and social services, schools, shops, restaurants, and other public places, their determination to foster and maintain their identities as valued members of iwi, hapū and whānau inspires self-determination and courage for the future.

References

Botha, D. (2019, June 12). The prisoner voting ban continues to silence the voices that matter the most. *Just Speak*. justspeak.org.nz/ourwork/the-prisoner-voting-ban-continues-to-silence-the-voices-that-matter-the-most

Kerekere, E. (2017). *Part of the whānau: The emergence of takatāpui identity – he whāriki takatāpui*. Tīwhanawhana Trust.

Ludlam, A., Saxton, P., Dickson, N., & Hughes, A. (2015). General practitioner awareness of sexual orientation among a community and internet sample of gay and bisexual men in New Zealand. *Journal of Primary Health Care, 7*(3), 204–212. pubmed.ncbi.nlm.nih.gov/26437044/

Ministry of Health. (2016). *New Zealand health strategy 2016: Future direction.* Ministry of Health. health.govt.nz/publication/new-zealand-health-strategy-2016

Ministry of Health. (2021). *Enrolment in a primary health organisation.* Ministry of Health. health.govt.nz/our-work/primary-health-care/about-primary-health-organisations/enrolment-primary-health-organisation

Oakley Browne, M. A., Wells, J. E., & Scott, K. M. (Eds). (2006). *Te rau hinengaro: New Zealand mental health survey.* Ministry of Health.

Statistics New Zealand. (2015). *A matter of trust: Patterns of Māori trust in institutions 2013.* Statistics New Zealand. archive.stats.govt.nz/browse_for_stats/people_and_communities/Māori/te-kupenga/matter-of-trust.aspx

Statistics New Zealand. (2018). *General Social Survey 2018: Final content.* Statistics New Zealand.

Statistics New Zealand. (2018). *Te Kupenga: 2018 (final) – English – tables.* Statistics New Zealand. stats.govt.nz/information-releases/te-kupenga-2018-final-english

Social Policy Evaluation and Research Unit. (2015). *Families and Whānau Status Report 2015.* Families Commission. thehub.swa.govt.nz/resources/families-and-whanau-status-report-2015/

Te Puni Kōkiri. (2011). *Ngā whānau me ngā kainga Māori.* Te Puni Kōkiri.

United Nations. (2007). *United Nations declaration on the rights of Indigenous peoples.* un.org/development/desa/indigenouspeoples/declaration-on-the-rights-of-indigenous-peoples.html

Veale, J., Byrne, J., Tan, K., Guy, S., Nopera, T., & Bentham, R. (2019). *Counting ourselves: The health and wellbeing of trans and non-binary people in Aotearoa New Zealand.* Transgender Health Research Lab, University of Waikato.

8

Takatāpui Well-being and Access to Health Services

Leonie Pihama, Alison Green, Shirley Simmonds, Tawhanga Nopera, Matt Roskruge, Herearoha Skipper and Rebekah Lawrence

Introduction

The Honour Project Aotearoa was driven by a need to address the almost total lack of responsiveness to the health and well-being of the takatāpui community in terms of equitable provision of quality, sensitive and respectful health services and programmes, and critical research that empowers takatāpui communities, enhances their experience of tino rangatiratanga and achieves positive transformation for these communities. This project is distinctive because it gives voice to takatāpui expressions, experiences and aspirations for health and well-being, thereby reinforcing takatāpui belonging – in the whānau and iwi, and in ancestral and future generations (Walters, 2007). Further, the project has provided the research team with an opportunity to engage with Indigenous critiques of colonialism and the role of colonial ideologies in the construction of identity (Durie, 1995; Moeke-Pickering, 1996; L. T. Smith, 1999). This was significant when understanding the positioning of takatāpui within te ao Māori and the ways in which colonial discourses have disrupted our understandings of diversity within whānau, hapū and iwi.

There is compelling evidence internationally that people who identify as lesbian, gay, bisexual, transgender, queer, intersex and otherwise (LGBTQI+) experience poorer mental health than heterosexual populations, as well as higher rates of depression, anxiety and substance and alcohol abuse (Adams et al., 2013; Balsam et al., 2004; Pega & MacEwan, 2010). Strong links between sexual orientation, gender identity and suicidal behaviours have been well established in the New Zealand and international literature (Adams et al., 2013; Fenaughty & Harré, 2003; Fergusson et al., 1999; Veale et al., 2019). Characteristically, much of this literature, as well as the literature that addresses issues around HIV/AIDS in the LGBTQI+ community in Aotearoa New Zealand (Grierson et al., 2011, cited in Waiti & Green, 2014; Te Whāriki Takapou, 2021), focuses on the extent to which these communities are unwell; that is, it focuses on negative health outcomes.

Along with discrimination, takatāpui have faced and continue to face entrenched stigmatisation (Ashton, 2015; Stangl et al., 2019). This is particularly so for those affected by sexually transmitted infections, or blood-borne viruses such as HIV (Negin et al., 2015; Rua'ine, 2007; Te Puni Kōkiri, 1995; Te Whāriki Takapou, 2021; Waiti & Green, 2015). Aside from constituting a breach of human rights (Hutchings, 2007; Waiti & Green, 2014), it is of major concern in terms of well-being that stigma and discrimination impacts not only the person themselves but also their whānau and friends (Pega, 2009; RainbowYOUTH et al., 2013). Consequently, the conceptual unit that is so fundamental to well-being, the whānau, is disrupted, and core Māori values and principles are undermined (Nopera, 2017; Rua'ine, 2007, cited in Waiti & Green, 2015). As a result of stigma and discrimination, Māori living with and affected by HIV experience less favourable treatment at medical centres, less favourable treatment regarding their employment, and confidentiality problems regarding their status (Grierson et al., 2004; Sheaf et al., 2011, cited in Waiti & Green, 2014; Te Whāriki Takapou, 2021). For those living with and affected by HIV/AIDS, this manifests as 'a loss of hope' (Pala, 2013, cited in Waiti & Green, 2015) and a reluctance to test for HIV (Miller, 2010, cited in Waiti & Green, 2014).

The kōrero that took place showed common themes with regard to takatāpui well-being and access to health services. The kaikōrero (those interviewed) also highlighted other themes around takatāpui identity: knowing who you are; whānau (extended family structure); role models; visibility; homophobia and negative experiences; self-harm and suicide and engaging health services. The themes that relate to whānau, identity, visibility and role models are noted in Chapter 3, 'Defining ourselves'.

This essay provides an overview of three key themes that affect takatāpui well-being: (i) homophobia and racism; (ii) self-harm and suicide; and (iii) difficulties accessing and engaging with the health system.

Homophobia and racism

Māori LGBTQI+ people, in particular Māori transgender people, experience high levels of discrimination, hate speech, violence and hate crimes (Birkenhead & Rands, 2012; Clark et al., 2013; Delahunt et al., 2016; Dudding, 2017; Laurence & Temese, 2021; Pega et al., 2017; Pitts et al., 2009; Reisner et al., 2016; Richard et al., 2015; Witten, 2007). Richards et al. (2015) explain that being transgender in itself is not a cause of distress, but rather 'can be largely explained by a hostile, phobic culture, which may result in harassment, abuse, victimisation and discrimination' (p. 310). This contributes to what is described as 'minority stress' (Richards et al., 2015), which impacts transgender people at a macro social scale and through the delivery of services particular to transgender needs (Reisner et al., 2016). These can include medical, legal, social welfare, mental health, sexual and reproductive health, dental, physiotherapy, gender presentation services, speech pathology, specialist cosmetic services, employment and housing services (Gender Minorities, 2016; Pitts et al., 2009). Munson and Cook (2016) consider factors that contribute to the recognised trend of lesbian and bisexual women under-accessing sexual health services. The presumption of heterosexuality, and a concomitantly heteronormative service, alienates many queer women. Similarly, overt homophobia is an issue.

Issues surrounding the intersection of racism and homophobia are raised by Pihama and Lee (2010) and Reynolds and C. Smith (2012) as experienced by takatāpui accessing both fertility treatment and neonatal intensive care services. Homophobia, the hatred of people who do not fit a colonial heterosexual defined norm, and experiences of racism, were highlighted in varied and often multi-layered ways. The Honour Project Aotearoa kaikōrero responded that even as children they had experienced high levels of homophobia, transphobia and misogyny.

> 'When I went to Intermediate [. . .] I used to get made fun of, laughed at, called a homo now and again, bloody idiot, a geek, a weirdo, homo, fag, looked at funny you know, so I used to get a lot of mamae and hurt and used to want to run away all the time.'

> 'I was always ostracising myself from people. I avoided anything like that, I used to wag school for long periods of time, I never went to school for a whole year even, I just hid, like a weirdo if you like, a loner, a nobody, that's how I felt. I felt scared, I felt like hideous, like I need to not be around anyone, I can't be around anyone, I can't make friends with anyone, I will just go to school and eat my lunch and just stay away from everyone and force myself to go to class to learn things.'

Interviewees described daily homophobic experiences, from name-calling, being demeaned, and dealing with homophobia within their own communities, through to having to move to another city or country, incarceration in a mental institution, and electric shock treatment.

> 'For me I knew that I had to go somewhere and I used to have dreams actually, dreams of men kissing, I'd never seen men kissing, you know, it was quite strong in my being that I was gay [but] didn't even know the word gay [. . .] I went overseas travelling with a friend and my main object was to get somewhere and to be able to come out even though I didn't know what coming out was. I ended up immigrating to Canada, we travelled in the States and Mexico. He went on to England, we travelled by ship in those days so we had a booking from Montreal to Southampton, so I arrive and of course I'm staying at the YMCA.'

> 'I did get a letter of apology from the government for what they [had] done to me in the sixties. That was part of the apology for the abuse I suffered, so they acknowledged what they had done trying to shock us, so I wasn't alone, there were quite a few of us queens in Oakley and Tokanui that were put in there for that same reason. We can cure that homosexual by giving [them] shock treatment. So, there we were, shipped off to Tokanui and Oakley, which was for the criminally insane. Thrown in there with them. Electrodes on the head.'

For takatāpui, acceptance and inclusion within whānau, hapū, iwi and Māori organisations is critical to overall well-being. Kerekere (2017) highlights the importance of whānau support for takatāpui and the implications of the removal of that support:

> Instead of the strength of whānau support, takatāpui rangatahi can be isolated or made invisible. They can be the butt of jokes or even kicked out of home. This can lead to drug and alcohol addictions, unwanted pregnancies, depression, self-harm and suicide. (p. 144)

The interviews for the Honour Project Aotearoa emphasised that experiences of discrimination within whānau or Māori contexts was extremely painful for takatāpui. Given the impact of racism upon our people, it was considered even more distressing.

> 'There wasn't really anyone else because my main war at that time was with myself. My second war was with my family. I was home-schooled and I didn't want to dump it on the few friends that I did have left so the isolation was really difficult, so Lifeline then was fucking amazing. I do remember that when I was specifically going through all this stuff about being

polyamorous. I was suicidally depressed and that was two years ago and I didn't think that would happen to me again but I did get there and then I pulled myself out of it. The suicidal thing [. . .] was for a very short period of time because I was like, "This is not okay, we're not going back here again," [. . .] I would have really loved to have someone just helping me out.'

'While I have been here _____ , you would think being predominantly Māori that there would be an empathy towards difference, but just like racism [. . .] I've had to put up with a lot actually, here. A lot of discrimination, a lot of snide remarks.'

Self-harm and suicide

Many kaikōrero shared stories about self-harm and suicide. This aligned with an earlier study, Te Rau Hinengaro: New Zealand Mental Health Survey 2006, which found that Māori have a higher prevalence of suicidal ideation, suicide plans and suicide attempts than others, even after adjustment for sociodemographic correlates (Oakley Browne et al., 2006). Kerekere (2017) highlights the impact of homophobia and increased risk of self-harm and suicide:

> Specific statistics on non-heterosexual Māori find they are significantly more likely to experience bullying, unwanted sexual attention and sexual and mental health problems than both their Pākehā and heterosexual counterparts. This has culminated in negative body image, increased risk-taking behaviour, self-harm and suicide (p. 20)

We heard much discussion around the need to be visible as takatāpui and Māori LGBTQI+. This visibility helps provide models for those who are feeling isolated and alone in their sexual and/or gender identity or who are marginalised by others. In this sense, visibility is a political project that is required to support those who are 'coming out' into an often negative or oppressive situation. As we have been reminded, prior to colonisation, sexual and gender identities were not defining factors within the Māori world in regards to our place within whānau, and as such, there was a focus on roles and obligations rather than sexuality or gender identity (Kerekere, 2015).

However, we live now in a different, colonised context in which oppressive ideologies of misogyny, homophobia and transphobia impact on the lives of many takatāpui and Māori LGBTQI+ communities. The discussions around self-harm and suicide, and negative experiences within the health service system are indicators of this, as well as of the need for takatāpui,

Māori LGBTQI+ people and our whānau to continue to challenge misogyny, homophobia and transphobia in all forms. In *Takatāpui: Part of the whānau*, Kerekere (2015) highlights the consequences of failing to do so:

> Gender and sexual stereotypes impact negatively on all Māori but have a heightened risk for takatāpui. Ideas that takatāpui can be 'turned straight' or could 'choose to be normal' are direct insults to the wairua we inherit from our tūpuna. All of our whānau are affected when disconnection and discrimination leads takatāpui to isolation, addictions, unwanted sex and pregnancies, depression, self-harm and suicide. It may be uncomfortable to talk about these things and acceptance of takatāpui might mean going against the teachings of your church. What is more uncomfortable is standing at the tangi of takatāpui in your whānau who have taken their own life because they could not be who they are. (p. 20)

The majority of those interviewed for this project spoke of the impact of bullying, homophobia, rejection and internalised self-hatred. The impacts included depression, self-harm, suicidal ideation and having close friends or whānau take their own lives. Kaikōrero who shared these stories spoke of seeking help from friends or whānau or professional support such as counselling, but help wasn't always available or appropriate:

'My partner has been very important recently and I am able to talk to someone about it [. . .] In the past I used to self-harm a lot but I haven't done that for a long time, so it's good, though I do still think about it when I get to a certain place where there's anger and self-hatred [. . .] but I think it's also helped being in a relationship, like, I stopped before that [. . .] Well, the realisation, like, a few years ago, I would think I wouldn't do this to anyone else, even people I really hate I wouldn't do that, I'd maybe want certain things to happen to them but I wouldn't run a knife along their wrists [. . .] and I was like, why do I deserve worse than the people I hate, what is happening there? That compounded with being in a relationship and I'm like, this person really loves me and all of me and I don't want to hurt them, like I would never do that to them, which if I cut myself or anything like that would be doing it to them because if I get on the other side and see the people I really hurt so far, that's just dumb.'

'I went through a time when I felt because of that pressure of not being able to be who I was, I felt, it wasn't really depressed but I was contemplating suicide, and it just really annoyed me that I should even be contemplating killing myself just because there's a law that says basically I don't exist. That made me really angry that I'd got to that place where I was even contemplating doing that and [...] it politicised me in a way, because I'm thinking, if this is a law that affects me like this, what the hell are a lot of the other laws [doing] that are out there that we all kind of take for granted, you know what I mean?'

'There's a lot of us out there and it's quite hidden, and when we're hiding it, I know what it was like when I was hiding it. How hard it was to hide that from myself and what a relief it was when I was able to [...] begin the journey of accepting. How many of our young people out there, then how many of our young people are still like I was, not just contemplating suicide but actually suicidal. I mean we are living in a homophobic culture, we are, even though it's not as hard as it used to be, it still exists.'

'I used to bottle up a lot of my emotions and I had a couple suicide attempts [...] just because I didn't want to deal with my emotions anymore and also just the shame of being Māori and what that would mean and, you know, could I go back to my marae? And could I see my family? And where would I go to be away from them? So then I didn't embarrass them.'

As in the wider context of the high numbers of Māori suicides every year (Coronial Services of New Zealand, 2020), there is the view, also supported by the Honour Project Aotearoa, that we need to talk about suicide as takatāpui in order to understand its prevalence. We also need to develop strategies to reduce the risk of suicide among takatāpui and Māori more generally (Aspin, 2020).

'I suppose a kaupapa that is important to Māori, particularly the numbers, is suicide and I've never seen any statistics and I don't know how you get this information in terms of Māori who identify as takatāpui who are committing suicide. I think about it, I think, well, how do we know? We don't know and I hear kōrero, it's something that you don't talk about, if we don't talk about it how are we going to know, and then how do we set up systems and safe places for particularly our youth and people like myself who were adults going through that transition of identifying who I am, how I identify and where I can go because of the experiences that I've had in the past.'

'I think that they should absolutely be employing more [takatāpui] [...] looking at maybe making them more available and there for people to access [...] so that our young ones have got access, especially our young men, because those suicide rates are so high and that whole thing around their sexuality when they are young. I just think they need someone to go and kōrero to if they can't do it at home; they need somewhere they can go to.'

Difficulty accessing and engaging with health services

Beavis et al. (2015) outline steps that can be taken in healthcare training to ensure that service providers have an understanding of colonialism and its effect on their practice. This knowledge is an important part of providing equitable service to all Indigenous peoples, including Māori. Focus is given to the inseparability of social, political and historical factors from contemporary healthcare practice. By situating colonialism in the present, Beavis et al. (2015) propose that healthcare professionals can develop the critical conscience necessary to provide culturally safe care. There is a poor level of cultural competency among service providers to LGBTQI+ communities (Birkenhead & Rands, 2012) and, in particular, service providers to Māori transgender people (Reynolds, 2012; Veale et al., 2019). Overall, it has been established that there is a serious lack of culturally safe and informed healthcare service provision for Māori (Waitangi Tribunal, 2019) and inadequate services for takatāpui (Kerekere, 2015; Veale et al., 2019).

Kaikōrero discussed the ways in which they had received care and treatment, both as Māori and as takatāpui. Many had had both positive and negative experiences, depending on who they were dealing with, the type of engagement, whether culturally appropriate or tikanga-based service was provided, the health professional's philosophies, beliefs or assumptions and their knowledge about takatāpui, and the service itself. Many negative experiences were underpinned by discriminatory beliefs, assumptions or practices, stemming from both racism and homophobia.

> 'The issues I've had have been more about me being Māori than about me being in a same-sex relationship and that's just more about the way I've been treated, I could take [child's name] and be treated quite differently to [my Pākehā partner] taking [child] and getting quite a different service.'

> 'I didn't let people know that I was in the hospital because I didn't feel safe; it wasn't a safe place for me. I reached out to the rōpū kaitiaki who are a Māori health provider in the hospital, a nurse said to me, "Oh, you're Māori, right," and he said, "Oh, I'll get this organisation to contact you," and they did and a kuia turned up on the first day and was talking to me. I was away with the fairies with the morphine but she did karakia and made me feel safe.'

At times, discrimination was clearly evident; at other times, it was felt through deficit-based or pathologising approaches. In health services with takatāpui staff or with health professionals who held cultural or decolonising knowledge and whose practices were informed by that knowledge, kaikōrero spoke about having positive experiences. However, a number of kaikōrero spoke about the impact of what they considered judgemental reactions from medical staff.

'I found [my doctor] to be quite judgemental because I was an ex-intravenous user and I wanted hormones and I felt that he looked at me in a different light. He was very judgemental [. . .] yet his job description was working with transgender. He was like a specialist in hormones and stuff like that, but yet he judged me because I was an ex-intravenous user. I was right in the beginning of my journey of recovery, and he was a cunt, but most experiences have been good [. . .] Because I think he thought, I don't know, I think he thought that he was judging the fact that I was using needles and that I had Hep C and I wanted hormone pills, which he probably thought in his mind that was a waste of time, because he thought that I would just go straight back to being on the needle, which wasn't his place to judge really.'

'I've been to _____ after-hours medical centre as well, and I had a nurse that wasn't very nice [. . .] I don't think she knew that it would come across offensive. It's just she asked me why I would want to transition because I'm quite old [. . .] So it was kind of really bizarre, and so she asked me why I'm transitioning at my age and how long I'm on the medication? Which I don't really feel comfortable talking about because I don't need to disclose that and also, I don't really want to explain why, because I mean I did in the end. I just told her that I would need to take testosterone for the rest of my life to just help me to be myself and it might not be in this form later on in life, and she said, "Well, wow, that's a long time, are you sure?" [. . .] I just hope there's no one else that came in after me needing the same thing and saw her, because I mean, I can handle that kind of thing but just [for] someone else it might be quite devastating.'

'I remember going to the doctor a couple of times and just, I don't know, just saying inappropriate things to me, like asking me was my relationship with my dad, that's why I wore a dress. I was like WTF and that didn't have anything to do with why I was there [. . .] that makes me apprehensive to go back.'

Kaikōrero noted that the particular philosophy of a health service, especially a service run by a religious organisation or from a different cultural background, could make them less likely to disclose their gender or sexual identity.

'When we were younger, we still played the facade of being "related" [. . .] here, most of the services are like, "Oh yeah, Māori, they are all related, they all live together." That's how they think, so they never ever questioned us, and it depended on how safe you might have felt [. . .] A lot of it centred around the kids, but there wasn't a lot of services that were very supportive back in the day and we tended to stay close to takatāpui circles.'

A number of kaikōrero discussed the importance of being listened to when they spoke about their health needs, and in particular the importance of feeling safe and affirmed in the ways that providers met their health needs.

'[. . .] there's a real failing for people in general, queer and Māori people especially, especially takatāpui people because we're misunderstood on two fronts. Why should we come in here and be misunderstood at the very least and degraded and humiliated at the very worst?'

Some kaikōrero expressed a preference for Māori health providers, since such services are culturally appropriate. However, others could not access Māori services because these were not publicly funded (Waitangi Tribunal, 2019).

'I've only ever engaged in Māori services when I've wanted to use services and I always make a point of saying okay so, is there a Māori? I always do that just because I think I would rather [go to our] own people first, that's just how I feel.'

'I think now that I'm older in age that an organisation that caters for and understands your cultural heritage and background is the way of the future.'

'Compassion, understanding, [. . .] I guess culture, guess it's tapu to us [. . .] Just having respect and just seeing us as equal.'

'I had to teach them my kaupapa and get them to understand and accept where I was coming from. Everybody's individual, you can't just say we're all same because we're takatāpui, but I found that they were very caring, like the Māori people that they are [. . .] No, I haven't found any problems in the health sector, because the first cousin was the head nurse up there.'

Throughout the interviews, kaikōrero commented on providing self-care and being as independent and self-reliant as possible in their well-being. Many spoke of attending services only if they really needed to. This included dealing with significant trauma or bouts of depression, either in themselves or whānau or friends. What this indicated is that critical changes must be made if some takatāpui are to utilise health services. A number of kaikōrero spoke of challenging homophobia and seeking change over the past 40 years.

'I go to the community blood lab to get an HIV antibody test and I look at the requisition sitting on the desk: in big letters it said HIV antibody test, it had "homosexual" written right across the requisition for the blood thing and the nurse just looked terrified. She was double-gloved and masked, and took the blood and [. . .] gave me the cotton to put on my arm, she wasn't even gonna touch my arm, [. . .] well, honestly, I felt like a leper [. . .] so it was kind of a wake-up call for me that I was allowed to, so then I became involved with the AIDS Network and then with the AIDS Foundation.'

Publicly funded specialist sexual health services were considered important, as they provide free, accessible HIV and STI testing and treatment services, although such services are mostly located in cities and bigger towns.

'I used to go out to the Burnett Clinic in Auckland just to have tests. I should be able to go to my local GP and they should be able to give me a test and I get the results straight away, shouldn't I? It has progressed that far, but I don't think you can do that in [this town]. I think they have to send it in to Whakatāne and it takes a while, you know. So, I am wondering to myself what happened to these instant tests that you can see whether you are positive or negative or whatever. I think a lot of people still don't know how to talk to gay, takatāpui, they still don't know how to, and of course being in the country it's very heterosexual, isn't it. It's quite stifling.'

Another issue was the failure of health professionals to communicate fully with whānau, including with partners.

'The only time I think I've felt that there was something odd was when I was actually at my partner's bedside in hospital, where I felt like information wasn't given to me because that particular health professional didn't feel that they should give it to me. I think that's the only thing that has impacted on me, but I wasn't the one receiving the service [. . .] I don't think I personally felt discriminated against that I can recall, apart from that one incident where you got quite a bad situation of a very unwell partner and a doctor that blatantly ignored my request for information and we didn't actually discuss why. But the nurse quickly came back, knowing who I was, and told me everything, so one was great. The other, I mean, it was a bit sort of tricky when you have got an aunty who can walk in and get you whatever you want but the partner that is sitting at the bedside at the time the doctor walks in is not willing to talk. I think that was the one time I really felt I should matter.'

When asked how health services could be improved for takatāpui, a large proportion of kaikōrero spoke about the need for greater education and training about Māori health needs more generally and the needs of takatāpui specifically.

'It's just like, I think, more education and you need to know people. You can't just be like a theoretical label in your head, you need to go find a face and build a relationship. It's not that hard to find. We are here, we are queer and get used to it. We like bright shiny things. Then there is also [. . .] making sure that you befriend the quiet emo gay as well, or the quiet emo queer. Basically, it's education, understanding, communication. That's fuckin' fundamental. And relationships, build relationships within the community. You can't separate yourself from it, you can't separate the humanity out of the theoretical shit that you've learnt and I think that's so important and maybe just sensitivity training; that would be a good place to start.'

'There wasn't a place where I could actually, when I filled out the form I could identify myself as takatāpui, I wasn't asked that question. I don't know if I would have replied to it yes [. . .] because I don't know how safe it is. Would I be given the right respect and care as a human being if I identified myself as being heterosexual or homosexual? I had a couple of nurses who were Māori, but I didn't go down that path in terms of explaining well, actually, I'm takatāpui, I didn't go there.'

'Understanding and a little bit more knowledge [. . .] as a nurse I did my training, I graduated seven years ago; there was nothing that was really discussed in three years of training of how to work with those in the takatāpui, rainbow community. I don't recall any specifics; it may have been a little something here and there of acceptance and things but nothing that I can recall.'

An open and non-judgemental approach was also considered essential to quality healthcare provision.

'They have to have an understanding of the gay community people [. . .] when the caregiver comes into my house, I always make sure that Disability Resource Centre have explained to them my gender, my sexuality and to ask them if they personally have a problem with it. Because even though it can be legal on the paper but you can't change people's minds and opinions [. . .] But I've found no problem within my care and that's been over six years.'

'First and foremost, I think they need to be non-judgemental and they need to have an open mind as to who they are working with and be very delicate because I know as a takatāpui woman we are quite delicate, so treat us as you would treat anybody else, we are not asking for royalty, we are just asking to be treated as everybody else would be treated.'

A number of kaikōrero spoke about healthcare professionals having an awareness of sexual and gender identity for Māori, and the cultural needs that come with that.

'I would say just attempting to pronounce names properly would be good. I mean Māori is quite a nice and easy language to learn even if they tried, you know, and even if the attempt wasn't the best or they didn't say it right. That would be better than not saying it at all or maybe not referring to you just with pronouns or something because they feel too uncomfortable to say the name. So, I'd start with the name. Also just being willing to listen because it takes a lot of courage for a lot of people to seek the health services they need, whether they're takatāpui or just need a flu shot or just a general health check-up, and probably to try to learn more [. . .] coming from a background in anthropology that's [. . .] yeah, I've enjoyed those, I'm always willing to learn about people and I think that if you're willing to learn you are constantly growing in yourself and just your understanding of people [. . .] we're around so much people why wouldn't you want to know more? Whether they think the same or not. I think just that willingness to learn, to be more confident in the knowledge that they have to be resourceful, because you know, some people might be isolated. That might be their only health service; they could be in a small town. They don't really have other options; they might have to travel to get to their major city or something. So I think just [. . .] even doing some you know basic research [on] what does transgender mean? What does takatāpui mean? What would they need?'

Kaikōrero also raised the critical need for more takatāpui and Māori health professionals within the health sector.

'I think there needs to be just more trans health professionals in general. [. . .] The counsellor I saw in Wellington, I only saw them for like two or three sessions, they are non-binary so that was just like, okay, you get it, I don't need to explain it to you, like different experiences obviously but it's just, I don't need to feel like I have to prove something. There should definitely be more people like us in those professions but then also [more allies too], yeah, also to make sure that there is more information that's not just however many hours you said [in] a year's course, it's ridiculous.'

'I think that they should absolutely be employing more [takatāpui] [. . .] looking at maybe making them more available and there for people to access [. . .] so that our young ones have got access, especially our young men, because those suicide rates are so high and that whole thing around their sexuality when they are young. I just think they need someone to go and kōrero to if they can't do it at home; they need somewhere they can go to.'

'One thing I'd like them to have is more Māori to begin with; that makes a difference, and one of the most important things they need to have is life skills, like that they're sitting in place themselves as being accepting who they are. Whoever that health practitioner is, needs to be sitting in a place that they know themselves well; if you know yourself well then you can be receptive to whatever is coming at you or whatever the situation may be. I don't know that it can be taught. To me it's one of those things, I've worked with people who were just in the health system who were just naturally [. . .] great nurses, and that's a thing that can't be taught, you know.'

Some kaikōrero noted that once they connected positively with a health service provider or general practitioner, they tended to remain with them. This highlights the importance of positive and affirming relationships.

'I only go back to my same [GP]. She's been amazing, I take my hat off to her, my GP, especially with me being her first one to put through it and she did all the background work as well, researched it and what have you, and what were the better options for me financially to take with my meds and stuff. So I take my hat off to her. The psychologist I had he was great, they were fine, I had no hassle, no dramas or anything with them [. . .] as far as I am concerned all the questions they asked weren't awkward, they just wanted to know stuff so I just told them, just answered their questions, whatever they asked.'

'Yes, right up to this day, so it's quite good. I have a wonderful doctor who is quite understanding and I am still currently on hormones to this day.'

If they are to build strong and respectful relationships with their takatāpui patients, health practitioners must be non-discriminatory, non-judgemental, Treaty of Waitangi-informed, and open to taking time to build the relationship. All health practitioners are required to adhere to the code of ethics associated with their profession and the Code of Health and Disability Services Consumers' Rights (1996) (Came et al., 2021). However, kaikōrero suggest compliance is weak and that health funders, policy-makers and practitioners need to address this issue with urgency. One kaikōrero talked about this with regard to mihimihi (cultural greetings) and whanaungatanga (relationships).

'The initial thing, that mihimihi, sitting down and taking the time to connect with someone and let them know who you are and have the time to do it. This is something that we would always bring to whatever group we were working with and of course they would say we don't have the time, and I'd say well you've got to make the time because this is going to be a time saver [. . .] Take the time, introduce yourself, sit down. That mihimihi is most important, I think, and that can cross over to every culture for anyone [. . .] I don't know how they need to get this. I think there's a part that would be very valuable in the health system and that's to have a group of gay, lesbian and transgender people coming and talking to the nursing staff [. . .] We mentioned before whakawhanaukataka, and where is that happening, you know. We had that little group of people that came for that one day [. . .] last year, there was a whakawhanaukataka happening; there was that sense where people felt connected and felt safe to be able to talk about things.'

'It is a bit hard to say because what I would say is it's just something that I would generally expect of them. Just make it obvious that you know, you literally, as a therapist you can't be closed minded, you have to be open minded and you need to make them feel comfortable and let them know straight off the bat that you do accept them and that they can open up to you. Because when people feel like they can't open up to you there are restrictions. You have got to make sure that they don't feel restricted; like they can just go on and on about the boy or the girl that they like or those who non-conform or whatever the gender is, sorry. It's literally just what I expect to open up the floor and make the room an inviting environment to express how you feel and to not be judged. Literally that is all our community ever fights for is acceptance and to just be seen as normal.'

When healthcare professionals are respectful and take time to build trusting relationships, it is more appropriate for them to ask patients about their sexual and gender identities – rather than simply guessing.

Summary

The qualitative components that were shared for the Honour Project Aotearoa enabled in-depth discussions of what it means to be takatāpui and Māori LGBTQI+ in Aotearoa. Sharing our own definitions of ourselves as takatāpui and Māori LGBTQI+, and our understandings of well-being, provides a foundation upon which we can build a future where the acknowledgement of the place of all sexualities and gender expressions are a part of what it means to be Māori. Throughout this work, we have been reminded many times that to be takatāpui and Māori LGBTQI+ is to be whānau which, in terms of our cultural views of identity, is to be members of whānau, hapū, iwi and Māori collectives.

'Sexuality' and 'gender expression' are terms that have been imported by colonisation. However, the essence of being and of expressing ourselves is embedded within our being Māori. We should not confuse these things. That is clear from those takatāpui and Māori LGBTQI+ who shared their thoughts for this work. This aligns to the work undertaken by Te Awekōtuku (1991), Aspin (2000), Aspin and Hutchings (2006), and Kerekere (2015, 2017), all of whom have expressed that to be takatāpui and Māori LGBTQI+ is to be whānau – is to be Māori.

We see much sharing around the need to be visible as takatāpui and Māori LGBTQI+ in order to provide models for those who are feeling isolated and alone in their sexual and/or gender identity or are marginalised by others. Visibility in this sense is a political project that is required to support those who are 'coming out' into what is often a negative or oppressive situation. As we have been reminded, the idea of being visible as takatāpui and Māori LGBTQI+ was not necessarily a practice within the Māori world prior to colonisation, as sexual and gender identities were not defining factors in regard to our place within whānau (Kerekere, 2015). However, we are in a different, colonised context where oppressive ideologies of misogyny, homophobia and transphobia impact on the lives of many takatāpui and Māori LGBTQI+ communities. The discussions around self-harm and suicide, and negative experiences within the health service system are indicators of this and the need for takatāpui, Māori LGBTQI+ people and our whānau to continue to challenge misogyny, homophobia and transphobia in all of their forms. The need to increase healthcare professionals' knowledge of Māori health generally and takatāpui and Māori LGBTQI+ health needs specifically was clearly expressed, including the need for more takatāpui and Māori LGBTQI+ practitioners within the health workforce. The concept of health and well-being for takatāpui and Māori LGBTQI+ people is broad and inclusive of all parts of ourselves as Māori.

References

Adams, J., Dickinson, P., & Asiasiga, L. (2013). Mental health promotion for gay, lesbian, bisexual, transgender and intersex New Zealanders. *Journal of Primary Health Care*, 5(2), 105–113.

Ashton, A. (2015, August 6). Discrimination ongoing for Queer Māori. Radio New Zealand. rnz.co.nz/news/te-manu-korihi/280696/discrimination-ongoing-for-queer-Māori

Aspin, C. (2000). *Trans-Tasman migration and Māori in the time of AIDS* [Unpublished doctoral thesis]. University of Otago.

Aspin, C., & Hutchings, J. (2006). Māori sexuality. In M. Mulholland (Ed.), *State of the Māori nation: Twenty-first-century issues in Aotearoa* (pp. 227–236). Reed Books.

Aspin, C. (2020, October 30). *Unpacking the issues in Māori suicide mortality review for takatāpui rangatahi – Clive Aspin* [Video]. YouTube. youtube.com/watch?v=_0SpJ-uO6mY

Balsam, K. F., Huang, B., Fieland, K. C., Simoni, J. M., & Walters, K. L. (2004). Culture, trauma, and wellness: A comparison of heterosexual and lesbian, gay, bisexual, and two-spirit Native Americans. *Cultural Diversity and Ethnic Minority Psychology, 10*(3), 287–301. doi.org/10.1037/1099-9809.10.3.287

Beavis, A. S. W., Hojjati, A., Kassam, A., Choudhury, D., Fraser, M., Masching, R., & Nixon, S. A. (2015). What all students in healthcare training programs should learn to increase health equity: Perspectives on postcolonialism and the health of Aboriginal Peoples in Canada. *BMC Medical Education, 15*(155). doi.org/10.1186/s12909-015-0442-y

Birkenhead, A., & Rands, D. (2012). *Let's talk about sex (sexuality and gender): Improving mental health and addiction services for Rainbow Communities.* Auckland District Health Board.

Came, H., Kidd, J., Heke, D., & McCreanor, T. (2021). Te Tiriti o Waitangi compliance in regulated health practitioner competency documents in Aotearoa. *New Zealand Medical Journal, 134*(1535), 35–43.

Clark, T. C., Fleming, T., Bullen, P., Denny, S., Crengle, S., Dyson, B., Fortune, S., Lucassen, M., Peiris-John, R., Robinson, E., Rossen, F., Sheridan, J., Teevale, T., Utter, J. (2013). *Youth'12 overview: The health and wellbeing of New Zealand secondary school students in 2012.* The University of Auckland.

Code of Health and Disability Services Consumers' Rights 1996.

Delahunt, J. W., Denison, H. J., Kennedy, J., Hilton, J., Young, H., Chaudhri, O. B., & Elston, M. S. (2016). Specialist services for management of individuals identifying as transgender in New Zealand. *New Zealand Medical Journal, 129*(1434), 49–58.

Dudding, A. (2017, June 19). Welcome to the rainbow world of gender and sexuality. *Stuff.* stuff.co.nz/life-style/life/81125652/Welcome-to-the-rainbow-world-ofgender-and-sexuality

Durie, M. (1995). Tino rangatiratanga: Māori self-determination. *He Pūkenga Kōrero: A Journal of Māori Studies, 1*(1), 44–53.

Fenaughty, J., & Harré, N. (2003). Life on the seesaw: A qualitative study of suicide resiliency factors for young gay men. *Journal of Homosexuality, 45*(1), 1–22. doi.org/10.1300/J082v45n01_01

Fergusson, D. M., Horwood, L. J., & Beautrais, A. L. (1999). Is sexual orientation related to mental health problems and suicidality in young people? *Archives of General Psychiatry, 56*(10), 876–880. doi.org/10.1001/archpsyc.56.10.876

Gender Minorities Aotearoa. (2016). *Gender Minorities Aotearoa.*

Grierson, J. Pitts, M., Herewini, T. H., Rua'ine, G., Hughes, A., Saxton, P., Whyte, M., Mission, S., & Thomas, M. (2004). Mate Aaraikore a muri ake nei: Experiences of Māori New Zealanders living with HIV. *Sexual Health, 1*(3), 175–180.

Hutchings, J. (2007). Hauora, Māori women and HIV/AIDS – Mana wahine me te mate araikore. In J. Hutchings & C. Aspin (Eds.), *Sexuality and the stories of Indigenous peoples* (pp. 180–188). Huia Publishers.

Kerekere, E. (2015). *Takatāpui: Part of the whānau*. Tīwhanawhana Trust and Mental Health Foundation.

Kerekere, E. (2017). *Part of the whānau: The emergence of Takatāpui identity – He whāriki takatāpui* [Doctoral thesis, Victoria University of Wellington]. ResearchArchive@VUW. researcharchive.vuw.ac.nz/xmlui/handle/10063/6369

Laurence, R., & Temese, C. (2021, October 29–30). *Discrimination among takatāpui and Māori LGBTQI-plus people in NZ GP clinics* [Paper presentation]. The 42nd NZ Sexual Health Society Conference 2021, Virtual Conference, New Zealand.

Moeke-Pickering, T. (1996). *Māori identity within whānau: A review of literature*. hdl.handle.net/10289/464

Coronial Services of New Zealand. (2020). *Annual provisional suicide statistics for deaths reported to the coroner between 1 July 2007 and 30 June 2020*. Ministry of Justice. coronialservices.justice.govt.nz/assets/Documents/Publications/2020-Annual-Provisional-Suicide-Statistics.pdf

Munson, S., & Cook, C. (2016). Lesbian and bisexual women's sexual healthcare experiences. *Journal of Clinical Nursing, 25*(23–24), 3497–3510.

Negin, J., Aspin, C., Gadsden, T., & Reading, C. (2015). HIV among Indigenous peoples: A review of the literature on HIV related behaviour since the beginning of the epidemic. *AIDS Behaviour, 19*(9), 1720–1734. doi.org/10.1007/s10461-015-1023-0

Nopera, T. M.-L. (2017). *huka can haka: Taonga performing tino rangatiratanga* [Doctoral thesis]. University of Waikato. Research Commons. hdl.handle.net/10289/11721

Oakley Browne, M. A., Wells, J. E., & Scott, K. M. (2006). *Te Rau Hinengaro: The New Zealand Mental Health Survey*. Ministry of Health.

Pega, F. (2009). Policy discourses that exclude lesbian, gay, and bisexual populations from public health policy in Aotearoa, New Zealand. In *Culture, Health & Sexuality: Vol. 11* (p. 75). Routledge Journals, Taylor & Francis.

Pega, F., & MacEwan, I. (2010). *Takatāpui, lesbian, gay and bisexual scoping exercise: Report to the Alcohol Advisory Council of New Zealand*. Alcohol Advisory Council of New Zealand. hpa.org.nz/sites/default/files/imported/field_research_publication_file/TLGB_Scoping_Exercise.pdf

Pega, F., Reisner, S., Sell, R., & Veale, J. F. (2017). Transgender health: New Zealand's innovative statistical standard for gender identity. *American Journal of Public Health, 107*(2), 217–221. doi.org/10.2105/AJPH.2016.303465

Pihama, L., & Lee, J. (2010). *He kākano i ruia mai i rangiātea: Māori whānau stories of neonatal intensive care units*. Māori and Indigenous Analysis Ltd.; Rautaki Ltd. babyfriendly.org.nz/ā/Documents/Research_Report_-_Whānau_Stories_of_NICU_.pdf

Pitts, M., Couch, M., Mulcare, H., Croy, S., & Mitchell, A. (2009).

Transgender people in Australia and New Zealand: Health, well-being and access to health services. *Feminism & Psychology, 19*(4), 475–495. doi.org/10.1177/0959353509342771

RainbowYOUTH, OUTLine NZ, GenderBridge, Intersex Trust Aotearoa New Zealand, New Zealand AIDS Foundation, Affinity Services, Mental Health Foundation of New Zealand, Lucassen, M., Henrickson, M., Fenaughty, J., & Lindberg, W. (2013). *Rainbow communities and the New Zealand Suicide Prevention Action Plan: Briefing paper for Associate Minister of Health Todd McClay*.

Reisner, S. L., Poteat, T., Keatley, J., Cabral, M., Mothopeng, T., Dunham, E., & Baral, S. D. (2016). Global health burden and needs of transgender populations: A review. *The Lancet, 288*(10042), 412–436. doi.org/10.1016/S0140-6736(16)00684-X

Reynolds, P. (2012). Trauma and Māori LGBTQ (Takatāpui) in New Zealand. *Traumatic Stress Points, 26*(4), 9–10.

Reynolds, P., & Smith, C. (Eds.) (2012). *The gift of children: Māori and infertility*. Huia Publishers.

Richards, C., Arcelus, J., Barrett, J., Bouman, W. P., Lenihan, P., Lorimer, S., Murjan, S., & Seal, L. (2015). Trans is not a disorder – but should still receive funding. *Sexual and Relationship Therapy, 30*(3), 309–313. doi.org10.1080/14681994.2015.1054110

Smith, L. T. (1999). *Decolonizing methodologies: Research and Indigenous peoples*. Zed Books; Otago University Press.

Stangl, A. L., Earnshaw, V. A., Logie, C. H., van Brakel, W., C Simbayi, L., Barré, I., & Dovidio, J. F. (2019). The health stigma and discrimination framework: A global, crosscutting framework to inform research, intervention development, and policy on health-related stigmas. *BMC Medicine, 17*(1), 31. doi.org/10.1186/s12916-019-1271-3

Te Awekōtuku, Ng. (1991). *Mana wāhine Māori: Selected writings on Māori women's art, culture, and politics*. New Women's Press.

Te Puni Kōkiri. (1995). *Hui whai māramatanga, whai oranga: Report of the hui on Māori reproductive health and HIV AIDS* [Hui held at Papakura Marae, Tāmaki Makaurau, on March 21–24]. Te Puni Kōkiri.

Te Whāriki Takapou. (2021). *Aotearoa New Zealand people living with HIV stigma index: Māori participant report 2021*. tewhariki.org.nz/article/health-research/aoteoaroa-new-zealand-people-living-with-hiv-stigma-index-Māori-participants-report-2021/

Veale, J., Byrne, J., Tan, K., Guy, S., Yee, A., Nopera, T., & Bentham, R. (2019). *Counting ourselves: The health and wellbeing of trans and non-binary people in Aotearoa New Zealand*. Transgender Health Research Lab. countingourselves.nz/index.php/community-report/

Waitangi Tribunal. (2019). *Hauora: Report on stage one of the health services and outcomes inquiry* (Report No. Wai 2575). waitangitribunal.govt.nz/inquiries/kaupapa-inquiries/health-services-and-outcomes-inquiry/

Waiti, J., & Green, J. A. (2014). *Māori strengths-based approaches.* SHopp, Edition 14 (Sexual Health Opportunities Aotearoa).

Waiti, J., & Green, J. A. (2015, July 5–6). *He kai ata rau: Māori strengths-based approaches to ending HIV stigma and discrimination.* [Conference presentation]. SHopp, Edition 15.

Walter, K. L. (2007). Foreword. In J. Hutchings & C. Aspin (Eds.), *Sexuality and the stories of indigenous people* (pp. 9–12). Huia Publishers.

Witten, T. M. (2007). Transgender bodies, identities, and healthcare: Effects of perceived and actual violence and abuse. In J. J. Kronenfeld (Ed.), *Research in the sociology of health care: Vol. 25. Inequalities and disparities in health care and health: Concerns of patients, providers and insurers* (pp. 225–249). Emerald Group Publishing.

9

HIV and Indigenous Peoples: Lessons Learned from Four Decades of Living in a Pandemic

Clive Aspin

Introduction

HIV arrived in Aotearoa New Zealand a few years after it first surfaced in New York City in 1981. By the time of the first notification in this country in 1984, levels of fear and anxiety had risen exponentially, especially among people considered to be at high risk. The shorthand term 'the Four Hs' was coined in the US to identify those who were considered the most vulnerable: 'homosexuals, heroin users, hookers, Haitians'. This had two outcomes – one being that perceived members of the four categories bore the brunt of stigma, discrimination and prejudice, a legacy that remains with us today. The other outcome was that people who considered themselves as being outside those categories believed themselves to be immune from infection and that, therefore, there was no need for them to take precautions.

In the early days of the HIV response, the importance of maintaining a strong community focus was overlooked. Instead, the focus was on the virus, the cause of AIDS. The complexity of human behaviours, especially those related to sexual behaviour and drug use, presented significant challenges, and endeavours to understand and overcome these challenges were slow. However, early gay community activism was instrumental in sharing information and promoting awareness of this new illness, and saw the design and implementation of prevention programmes that focused on the population groups at highest risk of infection – gay men and other men who have sex with men.

The first notification of an AIDS-related death in New Zealand occurred in 1985 at the Taranaki Base Hospital. Like many of the diseases and infections that have affected Māori since first contact with colonisers, this first case of HIV infection came from outside New Zealand. In his account of the early impact of HIV on Māori, John Broughton (1996) refers to HIV as 'he taru tawhiti', or 'an imported disease'. As he explains, HIV is a modern-day manifestation of other historical events that have had a negative impact on the lives of Māori. He cites the decline in the Māori population from 150,000 in 1835 to 42,113 in 1896 as evidence of the drastic effect of new illnesses for which Māori had no immunity.

Despite early warnings that Indigenous peoples were vulnerable to HIV, minimal efforts were made to ensure their protection (Orellana et al., 2013). Instead, Indigenous peoples came to be defined according to their deficiencies rather than their strengths. Research efforts focused on describing their vulnerability to HIV and identifying the risk factors that contributed to that vulnerability. This deficit-based approach to research into the impact of HIV on Indigenous peoples has done little to reduce the rates of diagnoses among Indigenous communities. Rather, as the volume of literature of this nature has increased, so too have the rates of HIV diagnoses among Indigenous peoples in some parts of the world. As Negin et al. (2015) have shown, the number of deficit-focused articles increased exponentially between 1990 and 2009, with most articles generated in Canada and the US. At the same time, rates of HIV diagnosis have risen among First Nations people in provinces such as Saskatchewan, where HIV rates outstrip some of those in some of the most resource-poor parts of the world (Public Health Agency of Canada, 2014).

A comparison of HIV diagnoses among the Indigenous peoples of Australia, Canada and New Zealand produced clear evidence of the HIV disparities that exist in the three countries, with these being especially stark for the Indigenous peoples of Canada (Shea et al., 2011). The analysis showed that rates of HIV diagnosis were far greater for First Nations, Inuit and Métis people than for non-Indigenous Canadians. Australia and New Zealand also recorded disparities in HIV between Indigenous peoples and non-Indigenous peoples, though they were not as extreme as those in Canada. Nevertheless, this comparative study clearly showed that Indigenous peoples in three countries that share similar histories of colonial expansion have been ill-served by HIV prevention strategies.

The Aotearoa New Zealand experience

In Aotearoa New Zealand, the first government response to the perceived vulnerability of Māori came from Te Puni Kokiri, with the release of their report *Mate Arai Kore, Mate Ketoketo* in 1994, almost a decade after the first recorded AIDS-related death in 1985 (Te Puni Kokiri, 1994). The report identified key determinants of health that increased the vulnerability of Māori to HIV: low incomes, lack of information and poor access to services and resources. The report also identified trans-Tasman migration as a factor that increased vulnerability.

Te Rōpū Tautoko Trust, a community-based AIDS organisation funded to provide care and support for Māori living with HIV and AIDS, played a key role in raising awareness of the impact of HIV on Māori (Smith, 1989). In response to appeals from within the Māori community, Te Rōpū Tautoko Trust convened the first international Indigenous HIV conference in Auckland in 1991. This was instrumental in creating an international Indigenous response to HIV that, more than 30 years later, continues to mobilise communities around the world.

Te Rōpū Tautoko Trust warned that AIDS would have a devastating impact on Māori and Indigenous communities internationally if measures were not implemented as a matter of urgency. Te Aoterangi McGarvey, a prominent Māori activist and leader in the Māori HIV community, stressed the importance of community leadership and unity:

> If we do not take responsibility and start the dialogue between family members and hapū and iwi at every marae occasion, the impact of this new disease is going to be ten times worse. Don't live in ignorance, because it has a cost. The cost is the impact on our whakapapa. We want to be able to protect our whakapapa. It's about survival and about continuation. (Te Puni Kōkiri, 1995)

A report produced by Lee Smith (1989) and commissioned by Te Rōpū Tautoko Trust pointed out that the dearth of knowledge about HIV within Māori communities made it difficult to develop and implement HIV prevention programmes for Māori. The report called for prevention and education programmes for Māori as a matter of urgency.

At the same time, government agencies were drawing attention to the potentially negative impact that HIV and AIDS would have on Māori communities. Two short-lived agencies, the National Council on AIDS and the Public Health Commission, pointed to the heightened vulnerability of Māori and called for dedicated resources to meet the anticipated HIV-related challenges faced by Māori (National Council on AIDS, 1989; Public

Health Commission, 1994). The National Council on AIDS (1989, p. 59) identified young Māori as vulnerable because of 'sexual and drug-taking experimentation common in adolescence'. Given that more than 50% of the Māori population at this time were aged under 20 years, the Council rightly identified an increased need for appropriate community or field workers to promote awareness of HIV. At the time, Te Rōpū Tautoko Trust employed only three workers to cover the whole of New Zealand, with those workers providing care and support for people living with HIV. Te Rōpū Tautoko Trust was not funded to provide prevention programmes, despite this being a crucial component of HIV care and support programmes. In the same report, the Council generated some confusion when they stated 'Māori are not considered to be at higher risk of HIV than non-Māori' (1989, p. 19), despite the youthfulness of the Māori population. Similar confusion was generated by the Public Health Commission (1994) when they stated, 'Workers acceptable to Kaumatua and able to speak on marae are needed' (p. 19). This simplistic solution overlooked many factors that needed to be considered in confronting the challenges HIV posed to Māori.

Limitations of data

As in many aspects of healthcare, efforts to understand the impact of HIV on Māori have been driven by interpretations of quantitative data. The principal source of quantitative data related to Māori is held by the AIDS Epidemiology Group, University of Otago, where notifications of HIV and AIDS have been collected since the first recorded case in 1985. Processes to collect ethnicity data were implemented in 1996, when a retrospective study was conducted to determine the number of Māori diagnoses (Carlson, Skegg & Paul, 1991). Given the nature of this study, it is reasonable to question the accuracy of the determination that only 11% of all diagnoses were Māori, somewhat less than the population threshold of 15%. It is well known that Māori data are often underreported or misreported when a third party is asked to record Māori ethnicity, as occurred in this study. While these quantitative analyses provide some indication of the numbers of people diagnosed with HIV and AIDS, they provide an incomplete picture. Data such as these have been used to justify predictions of vulnerability and heightened risk of Māori to HIV.

A consequence of limited analysis is that much of the research into the impact of HIV on Indigenous peoples has sought to understand the factors that contribute to vulnerability. A team of researchers sought to identify these factors by conducting a comprehensive review of the literature spanning more than 20 years, beginning in 1993 – the publication year of the first article examining the vulnerability of Indigenous peoples to HIV (Negin et al., 2015). The team examined 107 articles from Australia, Canada, New Zealand and the United States, countries where Indigenous populations endure ongoing health and social disparities. Articles in all four countries identified childhood abuse, family harm, social disadvantage, substance use and mistrust of health professionals as factors that increased HIV risk.

This emphasis on negative aspects of Indigenous lives meant that early research efforts to understand the impact of HIV on Indigenous peoples failed to acknowledge the inherent strengths and resilience factors that underpin Indigenous communities and peoples. Today, hundreds of years after the inception of colonisation, Indigenous health and well-being derives strength from its resistance to colonial paradigms and influences. By exercising tino rangatiratanga over their lives, Māori and other Indigenous peoples have continued to flourish and ensure their survival for generations to come (Penehira et al., 2014), yet this is not reflected in the body of research into Indigenous peoples and HIV.

International Indigenous networks

A collaboration between Australia, Canada and New Zealand has been instrumental in generating cross-country evidence of HIV disparities in the three countries. In response to the rising rates of HIV among Indigenous peoples, community activists have established international networks to confront the HIV-related challenges to the well-being of individuals and communities. This activism has led to a raft of community-based initiatives to confront the impact of HIV on Indigenous communities, nationally and internationally.

The spearhead of this activism is the International Indigenous Working Group on HIV and AIDS (IIWGHA), an alliance that evolved from the group that was convened to organise an Indigenous pre-conference at the International AIDS Conference, held in Toronto in 2006. Since then, IIWGHA has grown to represent Indigenous communities in North and South America, Africa, Asia and Oceania, and has been responsible for ensuring Indigenous HIV issues are discussed and addressed at international AIDS conferences. All international AIDS conferences are now preceded by an Indigenous pre-conference, which has led to the development of strategic measures to address the impact of HIV on Indigenous communities around the world. Through their presence at international meetings, including those of the United Nations, members of IIWGHA have ensured that the needs of Indigenous peoples remain firmly on the agendas of those agencies charged with ensuring the good health of people affected by HIV.

These conferences have led directly to building the capacity of Indigenous communities to address HIV. Networks of Indigenous researchers have done crucial work on the impact of HIV on Indigenous communities and have identified strategies for confronting HIV-related challenges.

The Toronto Charter

A significant Indigenous-led initiative from the 2006 International AIDS Conference saw the launch of the Toronto Charter – An Indigenous Peoples' Action Plan on HIV/AIDS. Developed in a consultative process leading up to the conference, the charter continues to be a focal point for Indigenous HIV-related initiatives around the world. It provides guidelines for policy-makers, community workers, health services and Indigenous communities affected by HIV. It focuses on the need to collect robust data on the impact of HIV on Indigenous communities which, in turn, informs the design and implementation of prevention programmes.

> It is essential that HIV/AIDS data on Indigenous peoples be collected, analysed and reported in a manner that is respectful of the needs of Indigenous peoples as identified by Indigenous peoples themselves. (Toronto Charter, 2006)

The Toronto Charter calls for surveillance systems that are capable of collecting and disseminating up-to-date HIV-related information to enhance the health and well-being of Indigenous peoples. These systems must engage with Indigenous communities to allay the fear and anxiety that still surrounds HIV. Similar patterns of anxiety are apparent in Indigenous communities today, in the context of COVID-19.

'Sowing Seeds'

The record of inappropriate and inadequate research into the impact of HIV on Indigenous peoples underlines the importance of ensuring that Indigenous peoples are closely involved in all stages of the research process. Since the inception of colonisation, Indigenous peoples and communities have been scrutinised according to paradigms designed and implemented by the coloniser (Smith, 1999). During a pandemic, in a time of heightened uncertainty and anxiety among our communities, researchers resort to the methodologies that exclude and marginalise Indigenous ways of understanding the world. This was apparent at the beginning of the HIV pandemic, when health professionals identified particular at-risk groups. Almost four decades later, these efforts are echoed by our present responses to COVID-19, which have been marked by the generation of false information which led some communities to exclude people considered at risk of infection – just as the descriptor 'the Four Hs' led to the exclusion of significant numbers of people from their usual health and social support mechanisms.

In efforts to counter the harmful impact of research based on Western paradigms, Indigenous scholars have developed culturally appropriate frameworks to guide research into the impact of HIV on Indigenous peoples (King et al., 2017). The protocols that the 'Sowing Seeds' research team have developed call on others to conduct research in a manner that acknowledges the harmful impact of colonisation, and the associated intergenerational trauma, on Indigenous peoples. Importantly, the protocols call on researchers to place an Indigenous worldview at the front and centre of their research with Indigenous peoples.

As paraphrased below, the 'Sowing Seeds' research term identify six principles that must underpin HIV-related research with Indigenous peoples.

> Indigenous peoples, and specifically those living with HIV, must be included in all stages of the research process.
>
> Researchers must engage with Indigenous peoples in a spirit of good faith that recognises ancestral wisdom and based on free, prior, informed consent.
>
> Researchers must acknowledge the impact of Indigenous determinants of health on the lives of Indigenous peoples and communities.
>
> Researchers must recognise the strengths and vibrancy of Indigenous peoples and their cultures, and seek solutions that are culturally grounded.
>
> Research processes must be informed by the multiple Indigenous Ways of Knowing, including ancestral understandings.
>
> Local Indigenous knowledge and approaches must be acknowledged.

These protocols provide an essential framework for research with Indigenous peoples as we enter the fifth decade of HIV. These principles and are also highly relevant to the broader context of research into the health and well-being of Indigenous peoples.

Lessons learned

In 2016, Indigenous leaders and activists gathered in Ottawa to share knowledge and insights into the impact of HIV on Indigenous communities (Aspin et al., 2018). Community leaders from Australia, New Zealand, Uganda, Norway, Peru, Chile and South Africa, as well as representatives of First Nations, Inuit and Métis peoples, shared and documented lessons learned from four decades of living with HIV.

Overwhelmingly, there was agreement that the impact of HIV has been exacerbated by the impacts of colonisation and intergenerational trauma. Delegates reported significant HIV disparities, poor access to HIV-related services and resources, and marginalisation and entrenched stigma and discrimination – all of which posed significant barriers to adequate care and support for Indigenous communities.

These barriers were greater for Indigenous peoples living with HIV, who reported experiences of racism, stigma and discrimination. These systemic barriers are compounded by a reluctance on the part of health professionals to recognise the importance of traditional ceremonies and medicines in the lives of Indigenous peoples. Delegates called on health services and professionals to adopt a people-centred approach to HIV prevention and care, based on respectful engagement with individuals and their families. By disrupting conventional methods of care through the adoption of a holistic approach to HIV, health services are better placed to confront many of the social determinants that undermine the health and well-being of Indigenous peoples affected by HIV. Central to an holistic approach is the respectful engagement of Indigenous peoples living with HIV, who hold crucial knowledge that might inform solutions to the challenges HIV poses to communities.

A clear message from this gathering was that Indigenous peoples themselves must be at the front and centre of initiatives to prevent the transmission of HIV among their communities. For this to happen, structural and systemic barriers to care and support must be removed and communities must be adequately resourced to design and implement sustainable programmes. The development and consolidation of international Indigenous HIV networks play a major role in building long-term resilience, both domestically and internationally. The IIWGHA is an example of how an organisation can play a major role in confronting the impact of HIV on Indigenous communities worldwide.

Towards the future

As we prepare to enter our fifth decade of living with HIV, it is imperative that we apply what we have learned from the past to our future initiatives, especially in the context of a world that has been changed by COVID-19.

In contrast to early efforts that focused on risk and vulnerability, more recent Indigenous-focused initiatives have sought to identify the inherent strengths of Indigenous peoples and communities. By exercising tino rangatiratanga and control over their own lives, Indigenous peoples are best placed to address the problems caused by HIV. Their strength and leadership in HIV prevention, care and support are crucial in overcoming the challenges that HIV presents to Indigenous peoples, other minority groups and the wider community. The insights of Indigenous peoples will also be invaluable in supporting their communities through the COVID-19 pandemic and potentially others in the future. The building and consolidation of Indigenous networks have given us firm foundations from which to navigate, and the lessons we have learned from the HIV pandemic will serve us well amid the current pandemic and those to come.

References

Aspin, C., Rogers, B. J., Swift, K., van der Woerd, K., Amirault, M., & Masching, R. (2018). *Documenting lessons learned and measuring progress towards global targets for HIV, tuberculosis, viral hepatitis, and sexually transmitted infections in Indigenous communities*. Ottawa: Canadian Aboriginal AIDS Network and the Public Health Agency of Canada.

Carlson, R. V., Skegg, D., & Paul, C. (1991). Occurrence of AIDS in New Zealand: The first seven years. *New Zealand Medical Journal, 104*(909), 131–134.

King, A., King, M., Montalvo, P., Stratton, T., Yac, J., Moliner, R.B., Olivera, S.P., Aspin, C., & Masching, R. (2017). *Conducting research on HIV among Indigenous peoples: Values, approaches and guidelines*. Vancouver, BC: Canadian Aboriginal AIDS Network for the International Indigenous Working Group on HIV & AIDS.

National Council on AIDS. (1989). *The HIV/AIDS epidemic: Towards a New Zealand strategy. A policy discussion paper*. Wellington: Department of Health.

Negin, J., Aspin. C., Gadsden, T., & Reading, C. (2015). HIV among Indigenous peoples: A review of the literature on HIV-related behaviour since the beginning of the epidemic. *AIDS Behaviour, 19*(9), 1720–1734. doi.org/10.1007/s10461-015-1023-0

Orellana, E. R., Alva, I. E., Cárcamo, C. P., & García, P. J. (2013). Structural factors that increase HIV/STI vulnerability among Indigenous people in the Peruvian Amazon. *Qualitative Health Research, 23*(9), 1240–1250.

doi.org/10.1177/1049732313502129

Penehira. M., Green, A., Smith. L. T., & Aspin, C. (2014). Māori and Indigenous view on R & R: Resistance and resilience. *MAI Journal 3*(2), 96–110. hdl.handle.net/10289/10016

Public Health Agency of Canada. (2014). *HIV/AIDS EpI Updates. HIV/AIDS among Aboriginal people in Canada.* Health Canada.

Public Health Commission. (1994). *HIV/AIDS. The Public Health Commission's Advice to the Minister of Health 1993–1994.* Public Health Commission.

Shea, B., Aspin, C., Ward, J., Archibald. C., Dickson, N., McDonald, A., Penehira, M., Halverson, J., Masching, R., McAllister, S., Smith, L. T., Kaldor, J. M., & Andersson, N. (2011). HIV diagnoses in Indigenous peoples: Comparison of Australia, Canada and New Zealand. *International Health, 3*(3), 193–198. doi.org/10.1016/j.inhe.2011.03.010

Smith, L. T. (1989). *A survey of the Māori population with respect to attitudes and knowledge of HIV transmission and AIDS. Report #1.* Tauranga Te Roopu Tautoko Trust.

Smith, L. T. (1999). *Decolonising Methodologies: Research and Indigenous peoples.* Zed Books.

Te Puni Kōkiri (1995). *Hui Whai Māramatanga Whai Oranga. Report of the Hui on Māori Reproductive Health and HIV/AIDS.* Te Puni Kōkiri.

Te Puni Kōkiri (1994). *A report about HIV/AIDS and Māori: Mate Ketoketo/Arai kore.* Te Puni Kōkiri.

Toronto Charter (2006). *The Toronto Charter: Indigenous Peoples' Action Plan on HIV/AIDS 2006.* caan.ca/wp-content/uploads/2021/05/Toronto-Charter-english.pdf

10

Tā Moko: Re-imagining Ancestral Skin Carving

Mera Penehira

Introduction

This essay examines significant literature regarding the revival of Native and Indigenous skin carving, with a particular focus on how this contributes to identity and well-being. This discussion will lead us to the story of Manu Neho, who is in her 21st year of journeying with the ancestral skin carving of moko kauwae.[1] In an interview, she describes her experience in both attaining and walking in this 'new (but ancient) skin'. Her story allows us to explore the relationship between this ancestral practice, identity and well-being.

The revival of tā moko and other Native and Indigenous skin carving is not devoid of the impact of colonial silencing and oppression. This essay speaks back to that and resists its further entrenchment.

Mouri moko: Mouri ora!
The life essence of ancestral skin carving!

Mouri is most simply described as the energy source of one's life essence and is well known to Māori (Penehira, 2011). Other Indigenous nations have equivalent ways of discussing this concept (Cajete, 1994; Wickstrom, 2008). This essay examines the mouri evident in the process of moko and

1   Moko kauwae, also known as moko kauae, is the ancient tradition of skin carving on a woman's chin. The ancestral knowledge depicted in the kauwae reflects the wearer's tribal connections, whakapapa and genealogy. In addition, the designs may reference other points of significance for the wearer.

in moko itself, and ultimately, the relationship that has with the mouri of the moko recipient.

Does mouri moko exist and in what ways is that evidenced? For Māori, moko carries with it the mauri of our tūpuna, of whakapapa, and of our identity. It is its own narrative, telling its own stories using the language of Māori visual art and spirituality. As Ngahuia Te Awekotuku and Linda Waimarie Nikora (2007) explain, moko symbolises an ideal which includes 'bloodlines and life lines, about being Māori. And being more' (p. 158).

As noted, life essence is one of the most common ways of describing mouri. It is a natural assumption that because the notions and practice of moko include bloodlines and life lines, and are to do with whakapapa and identity among other things, there is indeed evidence of 'mouri moko', and that this mouri provides and enhances expression of the individual wearer's existing mouri.

Given this, many potential wearers of moko choose the placement of their moko very carefully. Most agree that facial moko are particularly significant; one's personal identity, view of themselves and value of themselves are all factors in determining whether they will select facial moko. Consciously or unconsciously, a potential moko receipient must think about how their moko aligns with their mouri. That is, the recipient determines the relationship between their mouri and the moko, perhaps in order to ensure a natural and effortless forging of the two. For some people, however, it is as if the moko already exists within themselves or within their whakapapa. As such, many would view the moko as enhancing and giving outwards expression to their mouri. Others, however, view moko as a new addition to themselves that requires building a relationship with their existing mouri. The wearer thinks about how they want to represent themselves, their identity (and all that is included in that), in the moko to be carved and which they will wear permanently in their skin. Te Awekotuku and Nikora (2007) state that many of the participants in their study were 'sensitive about whether they "deserved" it, and learned a lot more as they questioned this' (p. 176). Te Awekotuku and Nikora go on:

> For us, it is more than skin deep; neither pumped in, nor painted on, it is a resonance through the blood that rises to the surface, it stains the needle and blends with the ink, it marks the chisel; it moves with heart rhythm and breath . . . For the wāhine mau kauae, tāne rangi paruhi, Māori mau moko, it is about life. (p. 209)

Moko is a multi-layered journey, carrying with it a multiplicity of meaning for both the 'creator' and the recipient:

Moko has many meanings to those who carry it. Moko is about identity; about being Māori in a Māori place, being Māori in a foreign place, being Māori in one's own land and times, being Māori on Māori terms. It is about survival and resilience. It reflects Māori relationships with others; how they see Māori, and more importantly, how Māori want to be seen. (pp. 208–209)

When we link the physical and metaphysical relationships that exist among us and in the moko journeys themselves, this helps us to better understand the relationship between physicality and spirituality. Te Awekotuku and Nikora explain:

Wearers become experts in communication, exponents of the art of explaining symbol and significance, because the outsider needs to be reminded that Māori are different. Different from them, and different from one another, and in this difference there is celebration, on a metaphysical as well as physical level. (p. 209)

Given that 'health' is one of four cornerstones of the Māori principle of well-being (Mana Kaitiakitanga),[2] it could be suggested that when one's health is poor, so is one's mouri (Penehira, 2011).

Traditional healing practices and tā moko

In the present political context of colonial transformation, re-claiming our own healing knowledges is a catalyst for affirming our own power because it locates the source of our power 'within' ourselves. (Reinfeld & Pihama, 2008, p. 25)

We continue to reclaim our own healing knowledges across Indigenous nations and among Native peoples, often referencing this as reclaiming *traditional healing practices*. In examining this, the following questions are useful: What counts as healing, what counts as traditional, and what is their significance? What are Māori views about illness and wellness and the broad expanse of healing in between? What are Māori views and experiences of moko and how do these situate and allow moko to claim the space of 'healing intervention', alongside other Māori and Indigenous healing tools and methodologies? Using mana kaitiakitanga, the Māori principle of well-being framework (Figure 1), how valid is it to present moko as a healing intervention?

2 Mana Kaitiakitanga is discussed in full in the author's doctoral thesis, *Mouri Tū, Mouri Moko, Mouri Ora: Moko as a wellbeing strategy* (Penehira, 2011).

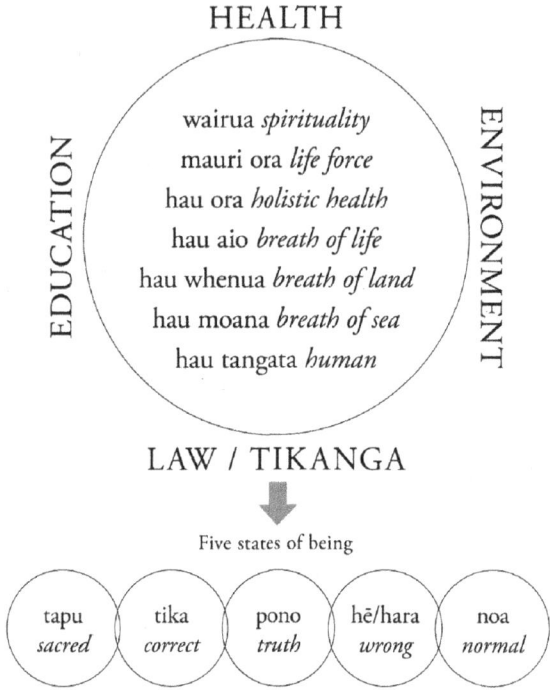

Figure 1: Mana Kaitiakitanga – Māori principles of well-being

In a Māori world view, healing is a multi-layered notion. It is part of a whole that relates to our humanity and wellness as Māori and as Indigenous peoples. It is important to note at the outset of this discussion that to enter into the discourse of Māori healing is to engage in the discourse of well-being. To consider 'healing' in isolation from well-being risks positioning healing as something undertaken only when one is 'unwell', or when there is an imbalance. However, as those who work in this area have noted, the sorts of things that are considered part of the Māori healing 'package', are more often than not part of a lifestyle:

> Rongoā Māori centralises the importance of healthful and balanced relationships with self, universe and gods – whatever we perceive these to be. They may also continue to include direct relationships with tribal lands and environs or they could be shared due to the multi-affiliate character of many Māori descendants today. (Reinfeld & Pihama, 2008, p. 37)

Tohunga can be considered the centre point of traditional Māori healing. Paul Moon (2005), who has explored the life and experiences of

Hohepa Kereopa, describes tohunga as those who possess a great depth of knowledge about traditional Māori life:

> Tohunga traditionally possessed this knowledge not because of some ancient, forgotten cultural norm, but because it was fundamental to the community's survival [. . .] tohunga amassed knowledge not only in practical aspects of day-today living, but they were also the arbiters on matters of tapu, the metaphysical realm, and the complex relationships between people and their environment. (p. 13)

The tohunga and their implicit knowledge and practice of Māori healing are clearly more than something simply 'enjoyed' by our people but rather something critical to our survival. Rongoā and healing were as much a part of daily life as eating and drinking, as opposed to contemporary understandings of medicine and health interventions.

From the time of settler arrival, Māori have naturally explored and taken on Western health interventions, initially as a matter of curiosity, latterly as an essential response to the onset of Western ills that beset our communities with settler arrival, and at times in conjunction with our own traditional knowledge. One man known to have traversed the junctions between Māori and Western health systems is Dr Golan Maaka. Although trained in a Western framework of health, Dr Maaka understood and respected the knowledges of tohunga and Māori healing.

He believed greatly in the efficacy of Māori medicines and often sent Māori back to their old people to be cured by their parents who knew the traditional remedy for their ailment. He knew that the old Māori medicines used by many of his young patients' grandparents would cure their ailments much better than any modern medicine he could prescribe ... Golan would send people away with the Māori cure for their ailment, which they were to apply for a week. After a week he would study the reaction and if there was no change, he would apply the western equivalent. (Haami, p. 136)

In their study of healing knowledges in Taranaki, Reinfeld and Pihama (2008) write that Māori healing includes, but is not exclusive to, Rongoā Māori, which they posit as reflecting an Indigenous and holistic view of health:

> Rongoā Māori encapsulates a desire for holistic health and in doing so can also be interpreted as a means of reinforcing long held tribal beliefs regarding the legitimacy and efficacy of whakapapa shared with atua Māori, Te Ao Tūroa and te tangata whenua. In this sense it can be understood as being another cultural marker and means of reinforcing a select group membership. The positive focus of rongoā Māori in restoring

whole relationships is reason enough to take an active interest in it. Rongoā Māori is neither magic nor exceptional. It is basic and practical to living a balanced existence with 'all our relations'. Such a view is shared by many Indigenous peoples still living close to the land base, forests and oceans. (p. 39)

The reclamation of Rongoā Māori and indeed anything deemed to fit within the realm of Māori healing, whether through practice or research, has an importance that stretches into an even broader view of health and well-being. That is to say, it has a political importance: reclaiming and practising Māori healing is part of a return to our traditional, pre-colonised ways of living. It is a decolonising action, and an action which could play a vital role in the return of Māori to the self-determining collective that we once were.

What counts as traditional?

> Traditional world views provide an historical example of the complexity of Māori beliefs and understandings of the world ... Māori knowledge represents the body of knowledge which, in today's society, can be extended, alongside that of existing Western knowledge. (Smith, 1999, p. 175)

Understanding moko as part of Māori traditional knowledge, and indeed understanding what is meant by 'traditional knowledge', lays the foundation for considering moko as a healing intervention. Naming something 'traditional', however, has inherent risk. As Tereki Stewart (1997) explains, there is a

> propensity to view Māori society as (a) cultural artefact, and to dichotomise it into the 'traditional' and the 'contemporary'. As a consequence, the significance of Māori is relegated to an artefact of the past with no relevance to the present. (p. 82)

Moko has claimed a visible space in contemporary society, but it was borne from Māori traditional custom and practice, and as such it has been at risk of being labelled an 'artefact of the past'. Prior to its present-day resurgence, traditional moko has reached 'near extinction', particularly facial moko (Te Awekotuku, 2006).

In her thesis on matters of colonisation and iwi development, Cheryl Smith comments on traditionality:

> what they [early writers on Māori society] have articulated as 'traditional' was viewed as a fixed entity rather than an evolving, dynamic society within

a colonised context. This view legitimates the notion that Indigenous groups are part of the old world, it is the Europeans that bring civilisation, progress, development and modernity. (1994, p. 58)

It is this 'incorrect' view that we need to consider in our current reflections and representations regarding traditional knowledge. The literature shows that many Māori and other Indigenous writers use a variety of terms interchangeably with, or in place of, 'traditional knowledge'. These include but are not exclusive to: Indigenous knowledge, Native knowledge, Indigenous knowledge systems, Indigenous technical knowledge, local knowledge, Mātauranga Māori, tribal knowledge, and community knowledge (United Nations Environment Programme, 2007). For example, Hart (2007) notes that:

> Such knowledge is holistic, personal (subjective), social (dependent upon inter-relations), and highly dependent upon local ecosystems. It is also intergenerational, incorporates the spiritual and physical, and heavily reliant on Elders to guide its development and transmission. (p. 85)

Professor Lee Brown (2004), a First Nations academic from the University of British Columbia, also engaged with this discourse in his doctoral research on Aboriginal emotional competencies:

> Battiste and Henderson articulate that it is the 'social process of learning' in the emotional realm that makes traditional knowledge traditional. It is this social process of acquiring and sharing knowledge that is unique to each tribe and nation. Thus, knowledge acquisition is based on 'social relations' that are founded on emotional development. (p. 20)

An Indigenous view of knowledge in itself encapsulates a broad view of knowledge and the relationships required in the acquisition, use, development, and dissemination of knowledge.

> Indigenous Knowledge can be broadly defined as the knowledge that an Indigenous (local) community accumulates over generations of living in a particular environment. This definition encompasses all forms of knowledge – technologies, know-how skills, practices and beliefs – that enable the community to achieve stable livelihoods in their environment. (United Nations Environment Programme, 2007, p. 1)

Removing the word 'traditional' enables us to view the knowledge without bias and consider it in the context of today's people and societies. To an extent, this also lessens the risk that our knowledge will be 'mystified' (Smith, 2009). When we shroud something in mystery, we severely limit others' access to it. Ngahuia Te Awekotuku (1991) was one of the first Māori women to identify the dangers and impact of mystifying our knowledge:

> [P]rohibitions have nevertheless become much more mystified, and their origins, apart from the roots of obvious male fear, sadly obscured. Much of the mystification comes from the colonising health system which has effectively disallowed one traditional – and essential – link of the Māori woman with the earth. (p. 68)

Te Awekotuku explores the implications of colonisation for the female traditions (especially) of Māori, showing that these traditions have suffered great obscurity throughout colonisation by a patriarchal society that continues to entrench such values in our lives today.

In more general terms, in Māori and other Indigenous cultures, people often must 'prove' themselves 'worthy' of attaining Indigenous knowledge. Although 'proof of worthiness' is part of the protection and dissemination of knowledge for Indigenous peoples, it is the de-contextualisation and misuse of this practice that limits knowledge progression and dissemination in ways that are detrimental to us as a people. Therefore, while protecting Indigenous or traditional knowledge is important, as well evidenced in the literature (see Mead, 1994), we need to ensure that this protection does not hinder our own people's reclamation of our knowledge. To create this barrier is to increase the likelihood of 'traditional knowledge' being perceived as a 'thing of the past', just as the anthropological approach has done. As Hart (2007) indicates, the reliance on elders – and, I would add, on those who hold the knowledge who are not always elders – is a significant protection measure in itself.

Charles Royal (2005), who has contributed significantly to the literature and development of Mātauranga Māori, a term often used in Aotearoa interchangeably with traditional or Indigenous knowledges, suggests that:

> [T]he revitalisation of traditional knowledge of Indigenous communities – challenges us to think carefully about a range of matters including:
>
> Why is cultural knowledge associated particularly with a population of people so vital to a people's wellbeing and prosperity?
>
> Why is heritage, and particularly memory, so important to a people's health?
>
> Do we endanger the wisdom of generations at our peril? (p. 5)

These questions guide us to consider the place, space and significance of our traditional knowledge. With specific reference to the present study, and Royal's first question, I would suggest that the cultural knowledge of moko is particularly associated with our (Māori) well-being and prosperity for a number of reasons. Firstly, moko is an identity marker for Māori, and the links between identity and well-being for Māori have been well documented (Penehira, 2011; Durie, 2004). Secondly, to engage in a process that requires significant effort and commitment to one's culture, such as moko, from the position of being an Indigenous person living in a colonised society, further indicates the bigger picture of well-being. That is to say, those who engage in traditional moko processes are engaging in self-determining behaviours, and as many Māori and other Indigenous writers have discussed (hooks, 1990; Meyer, 2008; Reynolds, 2004; Smith, 1994; Smith, 1999; Te Awekotuku, 1991; Walker, 1987), being self-determining is critical to the well-being of Indigenous peoples.

Royal's second question suggests connections between heritage, memory and health. Traditional moko is part of our Māori heritage, and many have personal memories of family members and ancestors who have carried moko. The creation of 'traditional' moko is the re-creation and the remembering of who we are and where we have come from. The following well-known whakataukī or proverb is evidence of the strength and place that remembering has in our well-being:

E kore au e ngaro, he kākano i ruia mai i Rangiātea

This whakataukī reminds us that because of our history and ancestry, our knowledge, our selves, are to be remembered and cannot be lost nor stolen. We know from oral history, from whakapapa (genealogy) records, from waiata, and from many other historical records, that our ancestors were strong and healthy people. It makes sense, therefore, that by engaging in, remembering and re-creating our ancestral ways of being, we are more likely to maintain ourselves as strong and healthy people. In her significant work on the effects of historical trauma suffered by Indigenous peoples through colonisation, Karina Walters (2009) highlights the importance of remembering Indigenous ways of being pre-colonisation, pre-trauma. For example, in her work with First Nations communities to identify health interventions specifically targeting those affected by diabetes, she has found that the most powerful approach is to assist people to think about why they eat the way they eat and to remember when and why their people changed from traditionally healthy foods. People were able to identify and make links between colonisation and the introduction of fast and fatty foods. They were able to remember or recall ways and types of eating that aligned closely to the 'original instructions', the values and principles, of their ancestors. They were then able to self-determine a change back to healthy eating more easily, simply because they were able to contextualise it as something that was Indigenous to them. The 'new diet' was actually a return to something already known, of their own heritage, as opposed to something from a Western framework of health, the same Western framework that was the likely cause of many of their health problems. This is an excellent example of the importance of the connections between heritage, memory and health of Indigenous peoples.

Royal's (2005) final question is a caution about traditional knowledge revitalisation 'endangering the wisdom of generations at our peril'. This serves as a useful reminder about the fine line between protection and 'gate-keeping'. It highlights the importance of creating safe landscapes, safe environments, in which we can remember, resurface, develop, and share our traditional knowledges. This makes salient the relationship of protection and the resurgence of moko, the safe landscape for moko being the preparation and groundwork that occurs prior to its application.

He reo māreikura: A conversation with Manu Neho

Manu's narrative gifts are presented in the below interview transcript, in which she chronicles her experience in attaining and walking in this 'new (but ancient) skin'. The relationship between this ancestral practice, identity and well-being is woven into the conversation.

Manu: 'I am an amazing mix of cultures – Māori and English, from my father's genes and Samoan from my mother's genes. Along with the genes come the cellular memory of all things that have occurred in both genealogical lines. This is the template left for me to follow and to improve upon. I am the eldest of ten – eight sisters and two brothers. I am the mother of three – two daughters and a son, all of whom are in their 40s. I have been blessed with 14 grandchildren and 11 great-grandchildren. My blessings are many and responsibility is great because of these numbers. My life purpose is to live my divine design, living by design in this dimension, doing what I am passionate about. Creating balance with my spiritual being and my temporal being. My passion is to see humanity standing in their sovereign light. To continue the path of my spiritual sovereignty and to assist those who want to learn about the process. The journey is a very personal one and can only be travelled alone. When an individual is ready to be in the world and not of it the journey becomes effortless. It is my vision to achieve my 1000-year strategic plan, see the joy in the lives of humanity, and assist humanity to achieve spiritual sovereignty. I am the incarnation of my tupuna [ancestors]. I am the quintessence of my mokopuna [grandchildren]. I am them, they are me. I am now!'

Mera: 'It's a journey of 21 years in this realm and I'm really interested in whatever you want to share about your journey with moko.'

Manu: 'It was just, wake up one Saturday morning and two weeks later I was wearing it! It was actually an inspiration that moved incrementally over the years and being with [my partner] Tuhi at that time was a path that enabled that to happen. To be sitting in Māori activism and re-birthing of all things Māori and the renaissance of!

'And having said that, one of those things that I am really clear about is that it was a journey for me, not just me personally, but for my whakapapa. Now as it transpired in 2002/2003 I began my "1000-year strategic plan" at a conscious level. But actually if I go back, the initiation of that was the taking of moko kauwae in 1999. And so that was a journey that was taken at warp speed if you think about it. Waking up on a Saturday morning in the first week of October in 1999, and in the third week of October, having my moko kauwae done!'

Mera: 'Wow!'

Manu: 'And so it was all sorted! It would have been that very weekend except that the artists, the tohunga, weren't available until Labour weekend. And so that was warp speed, really. I woke up! Had the inspiration! And you know I didn't have it by myself! It came and I agreed! Without question! So there was nothing to reference it, because I had never grown up with seeing moko kauwae, live up close and personal in Ngāpuhi or anywhere in fact except in books.

'There's no reference, and without that reference one can only assume that it was inspired from the other side. And so having taken that and moved it from the realm of thought to the realm of form and actuality, it was a simple journey. It was really simple! Because what I have found over the years is that when you ask somebody for permission, they're not going to give it! And I didn't need to ask permission from anyone, including my mother, or my elders!

'When you're sure about something, everybody supports that because you give no room to question. *Your* acceptance of it is the acceptance by everybody. So when you accept it as I accepted the taking of moko kauwae, there is nothing for anybody else to say except to accept it. And there were innuendos and little side comments like: "What did you do to your beautiful face?" And I said: "I've made it more beautiful!" And so the statement is not so much about my action as it is about their inability to be that forthright with their own sovereignty.

'Anything anybody said was never about me, it was always about them. The more I was comfortable about and with [my moko kauwae], the more it made others feel comfortable to be with it. It has been a journey. For years, and it still happens, where people will actually be staring and I'm not sure I'm always aware of it, but they do stare! And I love that there are so many women now who wear it, who wear moko kauwae.

'In 2003 I started my 1000-year strategic plan, which unbeknownst to me actually began in 1999 if I think about it. My plan has been going for 21 years.'

Mera: 'So you became conscious to it in 2003?'

Manu: 'Yes! And so from that came a whole lot of things. Wearing moko kauwae is not about being seen, it is definitely not about being part of a crowd, it is not a statement as much as it is about who I am! And that who I am is represented in so many ways that the markings are the physical representation of that plan of who I was to become having been sown in Rangiātea!

'Ko au he kakano i ruia mai i Rangiātea, e kore kore au e ngaro! It's about that. And this [pointing to particular part of the skin carving], which remarkably are the seed pods which happen to be in those thousand years that all of these mokopuna are being born.

'This is just coming to me now as I'm talking to you, because I'm reflecting on what it is. I know now that when [tohunga/artist] Gordon was drawing and designing this, we had this conversation but I didn't have *this* particular conversation with him. Just that it was to represent my children, my mokopuna and coming generations. I'm only just aware now, today conscious of the fact that, actually it is the 1000-year plan, it is about all of these seeds that are sitting in this pod waiting to be born, who have been born if we look at the continuum, they're existing now 500 years down the line. And it's about the protection of all of those. So the protection of them if when you're looking at the seed pods, they're sitting in the pod and they are still growing and still happening.

'It is to protect that! It's so important to me. Because this is not just about markings, it's not about how Māori you are. It's about the continuation of a whakapapa line, and that I need to get things right. Part of that comes from a line that have left templates. And this here and now, it is my responsibility to make cellular changes so that the babies in 500 years' time, or in a 500-year span, those mokopuna, those uri whakatipu are now thriving, in this very now! Not just because of moko kauwae, but because their kuia did something to make some changes in their lives. Put in place steps and measures so that they have protection. And just like them [pointing to skin carving], being the little seed that sits in the pod, I've ensured their safety. Around all of them is a coveted space, it's a place where they are protected and that's my responsibility.

'I thought I'd said everything about my moko but I haven't. Because we're still yet to discover what else it has [planned], and every time I look at the markings I know where they are, I can touch them on my chin, and I can tell you that every time I talk about it something different comes up. And so the conversation today is one that I've never had before. It will continue to extend because as it unfolds the reality of what was now in 1999, was the overwhelming feeling of rebirth and of something that was nearly lost. But it's not about the art form. It's about the unfolding of the individual within that moko kauwae. As it unfolds, as I become more at one with it, it's not just about wearing it; it's about actually feeling what it is and how it opens you up. The fact that 1) you are game enough to wear it in public, 2) it is without compunction or distinction that you do it, and, 3) you do not ask for permission to have it, to be wearing it, that you take it as your right. This is a huge part of understanding oneself, because as you understand yourself at a deeper and more spiritual level, then the [unfolding] of what your moko kauwae is, becomes you. Or you become it.

'There are lots of hidden spaces in there [kauwae], there's lots of hidden stories in there that are yet to [unfold]. In 1999 my moko kauwae was out there up close and public, and that's how it was, and as it's become the overlay, the externalising of my spirit, is what it is! The externalising of my spirit has become a connectivity that I feel to every individual on the planet. Because when you think about that karakia:

Kia tau kia tatou katoa te atawahai o tou tatou ariki me te aroha o te atua me te whiwhingatahitanga o te wairua tapu. (Bestow apon us the grace of Christ, our elder brother.)

'Not being Christian or anything, but he was one of the great masters that walked the earth, "and the unconditional love of God", whoever that might be for anybody, "Io" or whomever.

The most poignant part of that karakia is "me te whiwhingatahitanga o te wairua tapu", and that interconnectedness that every individual on this planet has through spirit.

'That kōrero about wairua, that's where moko kauwae takes me – to that place of wairua and to that connectivity. That I'm a flavour and you're a flavour, I'm a note and you're a note, and everybody's a note. When we're singing our notes in perfect pitch, there's a harmony that happens in humanity. And when we are singing our own note, leaving others to sing their own, you're the happiest in that place. And these are the places that I've come to with moko kauwae.'

Mera: 'Which really resonates with context of this book and its focus on takatāpui. I think that's a really poignant comment about singing our own notes. And when we allow everyone to sing their own notes then there perhaps comes together the harmony that you referred to. That's a neat metaphor for being takatāpui in this realm.'

Manu: 'Yes, it actually fits with anything and everything, you can apply that everywhere! It takes away the boundaries, because for me moko kauwae has given me an insight to limitlessness, and living life without limits! I resist the word lesbian for many reasons. But I am who I am! And understanding life without limits means that I can transcend any gender group, ethnic group, political group! Because I am who I am regardless of where somebody wants to place me outside in those limits. I will not be bound basically! I will not be this, at the detriment of being that. I'm all of that. So when I'm here with this group I'm fine with this group, when I'm there with that group I'm fine with that group. And the thing that makes it okay is that I understand who I am, and I don't live with a dichotomy in my life.'

Mera: 'Wonderful! It's easy to focus on how moko kauwae is a reflection of, and contributes to your own identity and well-being. And in talking about the seed pods you've started to talk about how that extends to ngā uri whakatipu. Do you want to talk a little bit more about how moko contributes to the well-being of whānau?'

Manu: 'When a group of people have been in a place of struggle, and in this instance Māori, have been placed in a space of "unsureness", and have over just about 200 years been told that you're pretty much not worth much –

being part of a group of people who have been minimalised, marginalised and, you know, under-represented in all places – moko kauwae gives permission, actually! It's the doorway to finding one's rangatiratanga! Because it's a symbol that they can wear.

'On the day that I had my moko kauwae, two of my children got sleeves and Shane started his puhoro, and it was like the doors opened and there it was. I remember on the second day when my brother came, and his wife and my niece came. They were so thrilled, they were overcome with joy and the wairua that was there. We had 70 people in and out of the house, and there were countless numbers of men and women having work done. My brother came the next day, and though they're devout Mormons he said, "I'm blown away by the wairua, and it could get me to question my beliefs." But it didn't [laughs]. However, he didn't think that that level of spirituality or wairua could be achieved anywhere else other than at church.

'So what does it do for whānau? It gives them an opportunity to take without resistance, without question: First the symbols and ability to place those symbols on their skin. As was done, as a recognition of their sovereignty. Yet if we are totally connected, and when we are totally connected, it's much more than that. It's beyond that. It is a spiritual happening that takes you to places beyond the physical realm. And it takes you to places where you question deeply what you do and why you do it. All of this is subliminal, because you can't see the moko unless you're looking in the mirror. It's always been on my chin. It became visible in 1999, and it is constantly working as a physical metaphor for the spiritual journey. And so what it's done for my family is that it has raised them up to be proud of who they are without question. It has raised them up.

'One of the things that I want to say is that wearing moko kauwae comes with a huge responsibility. To be true! To be authentic! To be absolute! To be tika and pono about the things that you do. And until an individual can say this is why I've got it, this is what I do with it, this is how I feel about it – then it's just another adornment. And that's okay. That's putting your eyeshadow on and that's okay. But when we can live what we are 24/7, I think that's a measure. That's not to say that we don't have slips, because we all have slips, and there's always the endeavouring to be better the day after than we are the day before. And we all recover! We all recover the next day from the day before, so you know it's no biggie, we all have slips, just recognise it, get over it, and be better the next day.

'So what has it done for my family? It's opened doors for them to be who they are without question. And if I'm that matriarch and I'm leading in a way that says I don't need anybody else's permission, then that's what they're going to do. Having said that, it comes with humility. You need to be humble! You have to be humble! However, there's a fine line between humility and stupidity and one should never cross over that, but that doesn't mean one should subjugate oneself to something else either. It is about sovereignty with spirituality in physical form in terms of ensuring that my uri whakatipu, of which there will be 5000 in 1000 years minimum! Based on how generations are happening at the moment. Every 20 years, sometimes every 15 years depending on how fast they are procreating [laughs].

'Yes, so that's what it's done, it's a doorway, it's a doorway! It's a doorway to freedom, it's a doorway to self-realisation, it's a doorway to spirituality, to wairuatanga, it's a doorway to atuatanga.'

Mera: 'I like how you talked about how it's "raised them up", when you're talking about your children. It's "raised them up", rather than simply "raising children". It enables a different way of conceptualising our responsibilities. I also really like how you talk about the responsibilities that come with moko kauwae, because it talks back to the more prevalent lot of responsibilities that people have talked about in these colonised years perhaps. Around our responsibilities to be a good speaker of the reo, to be a non-smoker, to be all those other things that you're meant to tick in order to attain or wear moko kauwae in the way some people perceive you should. Your discussion about responsibilities speaks back to that and brings it to a more tūturu space of being pono and tika and all of those things. Those are what our responsibilities are. Thank you!'

Manu: 'It's that level of clarity. It's not for me to say who should be doing what, but this is what I feel that it's about for me, and who am I to talk about what others should be doing. I need to be doing what I'm doing, but what I will not do is ask permission of you to be who I am. And if I know who I am and I stand in my sovereign light and my sovereign being wearing moko kauwae, understanding that what I do now affects the generations down, 1000 years! Making cellular changes through wairuatanga is a great responsibility! In doing that, the healing will happen. The traumas of our past generations that sit in our family will heal as I get to heal those in this present time. And moko kauwae helps to do that. It is not for me to do a kauwhau about what people should be doing. It is my reality, and in my reality and on my planet that's what I'm doing. So there's no positive or negative, it just is! And that's what moko kauwae is for me. It just is *everything*.

'One of the things that in 1990 I wrote was: "I am the incarnation of my tūpuna and the quintessence of my mokopuna. I am them and they are me. And I am now!" It talks about that continuum, the only place I can do anything is now! I can't change the past, the future is yet to come, and what I do now affects that.'

Conclusion

A person's 21st year is traditionally acknowledged as a rite of passage – a time in life when one reaches adulthood and is considered ready to receive the 'key to the world'. This chapter concludes as a celebration of 'Manu's 21st', and a looking forward to the continued unlocking of doors with the key to the world. May there be many more 21st celebrations of women walking with their 'new (but ancient) skin'. May all of the doors be unlocked by takatāpui as we reclaim our keys to the world.

References

Brown, F. L. (2004). *Making the classroom a healthy place: The development of affective competency in Aboriginal pedagogy.* [Unpublished doctoral thesis, University of British Columbia, Canada].

Cajete, G. (1994). *Look to the mountain: An ecology of indigenous education.* Kivaki Press.

Durie, M. H. (2004, September 15). *Indigeneity, and the promotion of positive mental health* [Conference presentation]. Third World Conference for the Promotion of Mental Health and Prevention of Mental and Behavioural Disorders, Auckland.

Haami, B. (1995). *Dr Golan Maaka: Māori doctor.* Tandem Press Ltd.

Hart, M. (2007). Indigenous knowledge and research: The míkiwáhp as a symbol for reclaiming our knowledge and ways of knowing. *First Peoples Child and Family Review, 3*(1), 83–90. fpcfr.com/index.php/FPCFR/article/view/26

hooks, b. (1990). *Yearning: Race, gender, and cultural politics.* South End Press.

Penehira, M. (2011). *Mouri tū, mouri moko, mouri ora! Moko as a wellbeing strategy.* [Doctoral thesis, University of Auckland]. Research Commons. researchcommons.waikato.ac.nz/handle/10289/5945

Reinfeld, M., & Pihama, L. (2008). Matarākau: Ngā kōrero mo ngā rongoā o Taranaki. Report submitted to HRC.

Reynolds, P. (2004). *Ngā puni whakapiri: Indigenous struggle and genetic engineering.* Unpublished PhD Thesis, Simon Fraser University, Vancouver, Canada.

Royal, C. (2005, June 25). *Exploring Indigenous knowledge.* [Conference presentation]. The Indigenous Knowledges Conference: Reconciling Academic Priorities with Indigenous Realities, Victoria University of Wellington,

Wellington. charles-royal.nz/papers-reports

Smith, C. (1994). *Kimihia te māramatanga: Colonisation and iwi development.* [Unpublished MA thesis]. University of Auckland.

Smith, G. H. (2009). Personal communication. Auckland.

Smith, L. T. (1999). *Decolonizing methodologies: Research and Indigenous peoples.* Zed Books Ltd; University of Otago Press.

Stewart, T. (1997). Historical interfaces between Māori and psychology. In P. M. T. Te Whaiti, M. B. McCarthy, & A. Durie (Eds.), *Mai i rangiātea: Māori wellbeing and development* (pp. 75–95). Auckland University Press with Bridget Williams Books.

Te Awekotuku, N. (1991). *Mana wāhine Māori: Selected writings on Māori women's art, culture and politics.* New Women's Press Ltd.

Te Awekotuku, N. (2006). Mata ora: Chiseling the living face – Dimensions of Māori tattoo. In E. Edwards, C. Gosden, & R. B. Phillips (Eds.), *Sensible objects: Colonialism, museums, and material culture* (pp. 121–140). Berg.

Te Awekotuku, N., & Nikora, W. (2007). *Mau moko: The world of Māori tattoo.* Penguin.

United Nations. (2007). *United Nations Declaration on the Rights of Indigenous Peoples.* United Nations. un.org/development/desa/indigenouspeoples/declaration-on-the-rights-of-indigenous-peoples.html

United Nations Environment Programme. (2007). What is Indigenous knowledge? Retrieved from www.unep.org/ik

Walker, R. (1987). *Ngā tau tohetohe: Years of anger.* Penguin Books.

Walters, K. (2009, November 9). Conference presentation. Sensitive Issues Symposium, Ngā Pae o te Māramatanga, Ellerslie, Auckland.

Wickstrom, S. (2008). Cultural politics and the essence of life: Who controls the water. In D. V. Carruthers (Ed.), *Environmental justice in Latin America: Problems, promise, and practice* (pp. 287–319). MIT Press.

11

Tikanga Māori Supports Healthy Māori Communities for Takatāpui Trans People in Aotearoa

Alison Green, Manawaroa Te Wao and Rebekah Laurence

Manawaroa and I (Alison) begin this chapter with the assertion that tikanga Māori (Māori customary laws, values, practices) can make an important contribution to building healthy Māori communities and reducing stigma and discrimination experienced by Māori or takatāpui who also identify as transgender. We are interested in tikanga Māori that fosters and maintains healthy Māori communities in which everyone, regardless of gender identities, roles and expressions, is valued and has a role to play. We propose that these were the tikanga that shaped our communities before colonisation.

In this essay, we provide an overview of the impact that colonisation has had and continues to have upon Māori understandings of gender and associated terminology. We follow this with a discussion of tikanga Māori – what it is, and its role in Māori communities – and the effect of colonisation on tikanga Māori, also described as the first law of Aotearoa. We note work underway by Māori lawyers, Māori development experts and kaumātua to bring tikanga Māori into the common law in Aotearoa. Next, we present the pūrākau as told by Manawaroa, which relates to her gender identity, and the renowned kaumātua who, guided by tikanga, confirmed her right to live her life as the person she chose to be. We then recount the gender-based stigma and discrimination that Manawaroa and her friends experienced in the 1970s in Aotearoa and the stigma and discrimination that takatāpui and Māori transgender people have told us they experience today. Lastly, we return to tikanga Māori and its intersection with takatāpui and Māori transgender well-being and human rights. We propose that, if we are serious about eliminating gender-based stigma and discrimination experienced by takatāpui and Māori transgender people in this country, tikanga Māori should inform common law in Aotearoa.

Our essay draws upon two sources of data. The first is the pūrākau told by Manawaroa about the renowned elder who, in the 1980s, utilised his knowledge of tikanga Māori and responded positively to Manawaroa's question about her gender identity and traditional role in her community. The elder's response had a profound, positive effect on Manawaroa's life as a takatāpui person who has self-identified as a trans woman for many years. The elder's response also positively impacted the life of the small rural community that Manawaroa belongs to.

The second source of data comes from Māori participants (n = 86) of the Honour Project Aotearoa survey who identified as transgender, non-binary, gender-diverse, pan-gender, whakawahine (to become a woman) and whakatāne (to show manly qualities, act like a man). Participants were a subset of a nationwide, non-representative sample of takatāpui and Māori LGBTQI+ people (n = 368) who took part in the Honour Project Aotearoa survey of health and well-being in Aotearoa in 2019. This project was informed by Māori health inequities that are partly a result of high levels of gender identity-related and sexual identity-related stigma and discrimination that takatāpui and Māori transgender people told us they experience.

Who are we?

Manawaroa descends from the West Coast tribes of the Waikato region, from Whatawhata to Whaingaroa, and since returning to Aotearoa New Zealand in the 1980s she has lived her life as a takatāpui transgender woman, with the support of her home community. Manawaroa is a mother, grandmother and respected elder of her iwi. She is a long-time advocate for the rights and well-being of takatāpui transgender people – primarily younger Māori from her home community (as shared in an interview published by Kaupapa Rangahau, 2019). Manawaroa has worked on a number of projects that aim to advance the rights and well-being of takatāpui transgender people.

I descend from the East Coast tribes of the Bay of Plenty region and am takatāpui and cisgender. I am a mother and grandmother, and my partner and Manawaroa are closely related. I work with Manawaroa and other takatāpui transgender people on takatāpui and Māori transgender rights because transphobia and its related stigma, discrimination and other forms of colonial violence – racism, homophobia and misogyny – are not the responsibility of takatāpui transgender people alone to address. It is the responsibility of all Māori to foster and promote healthy Māori communities. Those were the goals of our ancestors, and these must be our goals today.

As part of our advocacy for the health and well-being of takatāpui transgender people, Manawaroa and I co-authored a presentation for the International Indigenous Pre-Conference on HIV/AIDS 2014 in Sydney, Australia. Delivered by Manawaroa, the presentation took the form of a pūrākau that described her life as a young person growing up in a small rural Māori community, her time in Sydney, the HIV/AIDS epidemic, the discrimination she encountered in Sydney, her return to her home community, the tikanga or value of respect expressed by the renowned kaumātua or elder when he heard Manawaroa's wish to live as a woman, and her experiences raising her daughter and granddaughter.

From 2017 to 2019, Manawaroa and I were part of the Honour Project Aotearoa study, Manawaroa as a member of the advisory group and myself as a principal investigator. The Honour Project Aotearoa was the largest nationwide mixed-methods study of takatāpui and Māori LGBTQI+ health and well-being in Aotearoa. The study was led by takatāpui Kaupapa Māori researchers, and leaders and advocates from takatāpui and Māori LGBTQI+ networks and communities. In 2019, I interviewed Manawaroa about her life, and a video of our interview was produced as part of the digital storytelling project for the Honour Project Aotearoa (available at tewhariki.org.nz/article/health-research/takatapui-health-and-wellbeing/digital-storytelling/). As evidenced by Manawaroa's pūrākau, it was tikanga Māori in the form of older, pre-colonial Māori knowledges that helped her and her community to navigate destructive, colonising stigma and discrimination, and to foster older Māori understandings of gender.

Colonisation of Māori gender identities

Before colonisation of Aotearoa, health inequities as an outcome of gender-based hierarchies were likely not a feature of Māori life. Mikaere (1998) writes:

> The absence of any gender hierarchy in pre-contact Māori society is reflected in the Māori language. The language is gender-neutral in the sense that there is no he/she (ia) or his/hers (tana/tona) in Māori. (p. 85)

Similarly, Te Aho (2007) asserts that:

> before 1840 Māori women were significant leaders, organisers and nurturers at both whānau and hapū level. They were explorers, poets, composers, chiefs and warriors, heads of families, and founding ancestors ... Much has come to be written about the complementary nature of the roles of men and women prior to colonisation, that neither gender was necessarily superior to the other. (p. 3)

The colonisation of Māori understandings and practices associated with gender began in the late 17th and early 18th centuries, when European settlers brought their religious doctrines, morals and cultural values and practices to Aotearoa and forced these upon Māori, the first peoples of Aotearoa (Aspin & Hutchings, 2007). In 1840, a treaty called Te Tiriti o Waitangi was signed by Māori leaders of tribes and sub-tribes and representatives of the British Crown. Most Māori signed Te Tiriti o Waitangi, which was the Māori language version of the treaty. Māori understood the Māori-language text as a guarantee of their right to maintain authority over themselves and their lands, knowledges and important possessions. They understood that by signing Te Tiriti they were merely delegating the authority required by the Crown to deal effectively with lawlessness among its own citizens – the European settlers, traders, missionaries, and everyone else who wasn't Māori (Durie, 1996).

Next, the Crown established a Westminster-system of sovereign government and, according to Mikaere (2005), 'the challenge was to stamp out any trace of Māori belief systems and to replace them with their own' (p. 143). To this end, settler governments passed legislation and promoted policy that subjugated mātauranga Māori (Māori knowledge) in almost every facet of life, including what nowadays would be described as pre-colonial understandings and tikanga (values and practices) associated with gender identity, gender roles and gender expressions. Parliament, the legal system, churches, schools, workplaces and wider Aotearoa society promoted racist Western patriarchal, binary and heteronormative knowledges and practices concerning gender. The power to confirm a person's gender identity and its associated roles and expressions was wrested from Māori communities and given to the Western medical profession who, upon sighting a newborn baby's genitals, assigned a gender – either male or female – to the child.

The expectation was that a child's assigned gender identity would conform to what Western societies worldwide deemed acceptable. Furthermore, it was the view of the medical profession and of society that a person's gender identity, role and expression would remain the same throughout their life. In fact, one of the roles of wider society in Aotearoa was – and arguably still is – to monitor and enforce, both publicly and privately, socially constructed gender roles and expressions so that they correspond with one's gender assigned at birth.

By comparison, early accounts of Māori understandings and practices associated with a person's gender identity, role and expression indicate that they were fluid and less tied to a person's genitalia (Hutchings & Aspin, 2007). In short, one's genitalia might not have limited their role or expression of their gender identity in the way that it does nowadays. This may have been the case for high-ranking persons in particular. For example, the well-known and oft-repeated tribal saying 'Kia whakatāne au i ahau', made by Wairaka in the 1350s, can be understood in more than one way. Wairaka, a young woman of high rank, saved her people's great ocean voyaging canoe, *Mataatua*, from drifting out to sea (Barrett, 2018). The tribal saying – sometimes used today to commend a woman's successful endeavours – celebrates Wairaka's astute thinking, physical strength and self-confidence. While tikanga might ordinarily have required the action of securing a canoe to be performed by a man, in the absence of a man, Wairaka's high rank – derived from her whakapapa or birth lines – accorded her the legitimacy to save the canoe whilst also ensuring that tikanga was maintained.

Mikaere (1998) writes that missionaries disagreed with tikanga Māori and its concern with maintaining a gender balance between Māori men and women. Unlike European women of the time, Māori women held significant political and social roles, and in the 17th and 18th centuries their authority as leaders was recognised and revered by their people. Historical oral and written accounts indicate the role and expression of gender identities among Māori males and females at this time were determined by whakapapa (Kerekere, 2017) as much as by skills and aptitude (Kupenga et al., 1990). Māori men and women cared for and raised children, Māori men and women engaged in warfare, and those Māori men and women with mana or authority were recognised as skilled and strategic leaders in their iwi, hapū and whānau (Kupenga et al., 1990; Mikaere, 1998).

This state of affairs seriously challenged European men's understanding of gender roles and expressions because European women, even those from families of rank, were, by law, the property of European men (Te Aho, 2007). As expressed in their writings in the 1800s, European men had racist, patriarchal, binary and heteronormative worldviews of Māori. Mostly they wrote about Māori men, distorting what Māori men did and said and silencing Māori women. Despite the immense mana held by so many Māori women across Aotearoa in 1840 when Te Tiriti o Waitangi was signed, Mikaere (1998) posits that the Crown encouraged more Māori men than women to sign Te Tiriti. An example of the shift of political and economic power away from Māori women and the unbalancing of the relationship between Māori men and Māori women can be seen in the actions of Meri Te Tai Mangakāhia, a woman of rank. In 1893 she became the first woman to speak at Te Kotahitanga, the Māori Parliament. Mangakāhia spoke to her own motion, which was that Māori women ought to have the right to elect members to Te Kotahitanga. About this, Ballara (1993) wrote:

> She requested not only that Māori women be given the vote, but that they be eligible to sit in the Māori parliament, thus going a step further than the contemporary aims of the European suffrage movement. She argued on the grounds that many Māori women owned and administered their own lands, either because they had no male relatives or because the women were more competent. She claimed that although chiefs had appealed to Queen Victoria over Māori problems, Māori women had received no advantage from these appeals.

By the 20th century, and as a consequence of having had their knowledges of gender subjugated, tikanga, which ensured a balanced and respectful relationship between Māori men and women, also became subjugated. According to Te Aho (2007):

> There are many examples of how Māori adopted or 'internalised' colonial values, or how these values were imposed, and how various tikanga and kawa and ways of doing things changed as a consequence. (p. 4).

Māori communities adopted aspects of Western understandings of male and female gender identities and associated gender roles and expressions. According to Kupenga et al. (1990):

> Under the Pakeha (European) system the only demand was for [Māori] males. Gradually, the attitudes of Māori men began to change. They began to model themselves on their Pakeha bosses and workmates, regarding their earnings as belonging to themselves, and thus deciding what portions were to be meted out and to whom [. . .] Pakeha did not accept [Māori] women's autonomy. This is evident in Māori women's herstory which reflects the attitudes of Pakeha society. The demand for land, together with assimilationist policies, personal and institutional racism, cultural genocide and urbanisation, had an adverse effect on all Māori people, with Māori women being pushed constantly to the bottom of the heap. The net result was that te mana me te tapu o te wahine was eroded. (p. 11)

Adopting hierarchical Western understandings of gender identity, roles and expressions narrowed the spaces and places in Māori communities and wider Aotearoa where Māori could fully express themselves as the autonomous, whakapapa-based individuals and collectives that Te Tiriti o Waitangi supported them to be. Māori – who sought to express their gender identities in ways that did not always match the genders they'd been assigned at birth or the roles and expressions of gender as determined by Western legislation, policy and practices – found themselves pushed to the margins of Aotearoa, and to the margins of Māori communities too (Aspin, 1996).

Terminology

In this section, we provide a brief description of the terms 'takatāpui' and 'takatāpui transgender' as we have used these, and we signal opportunities and challenges that are associated with both. The Māori language term 'takatāpui' has its origins in iwi, hapū and whānau knowledges and understandings. Kerekere (2017) writes that the term 'takatāpui' is traditional and has been reclaimed after it was discovered in the 1980s by Māori scholars Ngāhuia Te Awekōtuku, and by Lee Smith, in the historical writings of Te Rangikāheke. Kerekere (2017) provides a detailed account of the reclamation and meaning of the term 'takatāpui' as described by contemporary Māori scholars. While there is not a Māori consensus on the origins of the term or its English language interpretation, nevertheless from the 1980s onwards it has been used by Māori who are writing and researching Māori sexualities and gender identities. The term is used by many who identify as Māori and gay, lesbian, bisexual, transgender, queer, intersex, non-binary, and of diverse gender identities and sexualities (Kerekere, 2016; Wall, 2007). Kerekere writes:

> Takatāpui is an umbrella term that embraces all Māori with diverse gender identities, sexualities and sex characteristics including whakawāhine, tangata ira tāne, lesbian, gay, bisexual, trans, intersex and queer. Takatāpui identity is related to whakapapa, mana and inclusion. It emphasises Māori cultural and spiritual identity as equal to – or more important than – gender identity, sexuality or having diverse sex characteristics (Kerekere, 2017, as cited in Statistics New Zealand, 2020, p. 10).

Kerekere (2017) notes that from the 1990s the practice of adding a gendered qualifying term to the term 'takatāpui' became popular. Kerekere problematises the practice of adding 'wahine' and 'tāne' to the term 'takatāpui', and we agree that the practice is contrary to the description of takatāpui as an umbrella term that embraces all Māori whose genders and sexual identities are diverse and not fixed throughout one's life.

Nevertheless, Manawaroa and I use the phrase 'takatāpui transgender' so that our readers know the group of people from the takatāpui community for whom we are writing about and for. This group is comprised of people who are Māori and identify with one or a number of genders (Kerekere, 2016). If we had taken a pre-colonial approach, we might refer to this group of people according to their iwi, hapū and whānau identities as determined by whakapapa or descent from specified ancestors. Or we might have taken a contemporary decolonising approach, pushed back on the Western obsession with fragmenting the Māori collective, and simply used the diverse gender-inclusive and sexuality-inclusive term 'takatāpui'. Instead, we were guided by the Māori participants who were part of the Honour Project Aotearoa and who chose to self-identify as Māori and as transgender, non-binary, gender-diverse, whakawahine, whakatāne, and pan-gender (n = 86). The number of survey participants is likely an undercount of those participants with diverse genders. Some participants may have chosen to identify more simply as takatāpui, or as a woman or man.

Having a critical awareness of the terms that the Honour Project Aotearoa participants used to describe themselves is important. Terms that participants used in 2018 and 2019 when the survey was undertaken are different to the terms participants used to describe themselves a decade or two decades earlier. One reason is that terms emerge from specific times and contexts. In Manawaroa's pūrākau, she used the English language terms 'sissy boy', 'transexual' and 'transvestite' to describe herself in her younger years, but more recently she has chosen to use 'trans woman', 'rainbow' and 'takatāpui'.

Manawaroa is not alone in her changing use of terms to describe herself. Terms reflect the broader national and international decolonising political and social processes underway in Māori and Indigenous communities and nations. Manawaroa's pūrākau and the responses of the Honour Project Aotearoa survey participants indicate that many takatāpui transgender people are choosing a reo Māori or Māori language term to describe who they are. For some, the decision to use reo Māori terms such as whakatāne, whakawahine and takatāpui can be interpreted as an intention to break from Western colonising understandings of gender and to assert tino rangatiratanga or the right to self-determination of their own identity. For others, the use of te reo Māori terms is an action that talks back to the colonising binary terms – 'male' and 'female' – which underpin the structures and systems of the Western world. Still others likely use te reo Māori terms to hold space and validate the older, pre-colonial application of Māori knowledges and tikanga which value and respect a person's whakapapa, gender identity, gender roles and gender expressions.

The reo Māori terms 'whakawahine', 'tāhine', 'tangata ira tāne' (Veale et al., 2019), 'hinehi' and 'hinehua' (Human Rights Commission, n.d.), and 'whakatāne' (Pihama et al., 2020) have all been described as reclaimed terms. Other reo Māori terms have been created by takatāpui transgender people. Reclaimed and new reo Māori terms for gender identity can be found in reports, programmes, services, articles, social media and research undertaken by takatāpui transgender people and their allies. Māori will not be surprised by the decision of takatāpui transgender leaders to assert their mana or authority over Māori language terms that they use to describe themselves. Recently, Te Taura Whiri i Te Reo Māori (the Māori Language Commission) endorsed the decision of takatāpui transgender leaders to introduce a new term, 'tāhine', to describe themselves (Oliphant et al., 2018). The decision to reclaim and create new reo Māori terms, and to name and rename oneself, is common practice within contemporary Māori communities. It is an assertion of mana motuhake (Māori separate identity, self-government) and tino rangatiratanga (autonomy, self-determination) guaranteed by Te Tiriti o Waitangi in 1840.

Positive as all this seems, naming oneself according to one's gender identity rather than by whakapapa or descent to one's hapū and iwi is, we propose, a contemporary response to the colonisation of gender. However, Manawaroa and I propose that it will take far more than today's use of te reo Māori terms like whakatāne, whakawahine, tāhine and takatāpui to decolonise and rebalance strictly gendered, binary and heteronormative approaches to Māori gender identities in Aotearoa. One of the actions which supports takatāpui transgender people by re-establishing balanced and respectful gender relationships is to utilise decolonised tikanga Māori values and practices.

Tikanga Māori and contemporary gender identities, roles and expressions

Esteemed Ngāti Awa elder, author and tribal leader Sir Hirini Moko Mead describes tikanga Māori as Māori customary values and practices, habits and correctness. More broadly, tikanga is normative. It is an ethical and dynamic system of Māori customary common law, proper procedures, and rules and regulations. Mead (2016) proposes the following definition:

Tikanga refers to the ethical and common law issues that underpin the behaviour of members of whānau, hapū and iwi as they go about their lives and especially when they engage in the cultural, social, ritual and economic ceremonies of their society. (p. 25)

Mead notes that while tikanga changes over time, adhering to tikanga is important. The role of teaching tikanga and scrutinising the practice of tikanga is, according to Mead, a role that most often falls to older Māori. Their years of lived experience and knowledge from participating in their own tikanga and observing others practising their tikanga ensures that tikanga is fostered and maintained to a high standard and valued by whānau, hapū and iwi. Mead (2016) writes:

Older individuals generally have a greater familiarity with and knowledge about tikanga because they have participated in tikanga, have observed interpretations of the tikanga at home and other tribal areas. The kaumātua and kuia, the elders, are often the guardians of tikanga (p. 27).

Mead notes that when tikanga was not practised to the high standard that was expected, the mana or the authority of whānau, hapū and iwi could be called into question. So important is it that tikanga is performed to the highest standard that many Māori believe that if tikanga is not carried out correctly, misfortune will follow.

However, as the colonial process advanced across the generations and mātauranga Māori – the base from which tikanga Māori proceeds – was subjugated by European understandings about gender, it seems that some Māori saw no good reason why tikanga Māori about gender identity, roles and expressions should not mirror those of European or Pākehā people. We whole-heartedly agree with Mikaere (1998), who writes:

A crucial part of restoring Māori law [tikanga Māori] must be the realisation that ... the privileging of men over women was never part of tradition. Māori men must confront the fact that colonisation has made them collaborators with the colonisers against their own women. (p. 97)

Confronted with European hierarchies of gender identity, many Māori became less able to confidently use tikanga Māori as a guide to revitalising and re-establishing older, gender-balanced customary values and practices. Instead, Māori took up European societal approaches such as shunning and discriminating against Māori women, Māori LGBTQI+ people and takatāpui transgender people. These important members of whānau, hapū and iwi were marginalised and discriminated against because their gender identities, roles and expressions did not maintain the Western fiction that these are only ever binary and heteronormative; that is, male and female and heterosexual. Over time, any other form of gender identity, role and expression was described as an abomination.

Shunning and discriminating against one's own whānau and others' whānau members are practices which are contrary to tikanga Māori and can be seen to undermine the mana or the authority of whānau, hapū and iwi (Mead, 2016). However, for more than 100 years, in Aotearoa and in Māori communities, there has been a practice of shunning and discriminating against Māori who self-identify as trannies, transexuals, transvestites, takatāpui transgender, non-binary, gender diverse, pan-gender, whakawahine and whakatāne. Now more than ever, in this era of restoring mātauranga Māori, we need to revitalise tikanga Māori to ensure that the mana of Māori men and women – however they choose to identify their gender identities, roles and expressions – is rebalanced. While acknowledging the difficulties of restoring pre-colonial tikanga Māori in contemporary colonial Aotearoa, we agree with McBreen (2012) that tikanga will be maintained if relationships between people 'are based on mutual respect, manaakitanga and aroha, [and if that is the case] then they are tika, irrespective of anything else' (p. 59).

Just as our kaumātua would have done, we need to scrutinise tikanga Māori to make sure that it reflects Māori customary principles, values and practices rather than distorted and hierarchical European beliefs and practices. We need to ensure that contemporary tikanga Māori rejects transphobia, homophobia, misogyny and other forms of gender-based stigma and discrimination. Rejecting gender-based stigma and discrimination will not be an easy task; it will require effort from all of us. Change will require leadership from kaumātua in partnership with leadership from takatāpui transgender, non-binary, gender diverse, pan-gender, whakawahine and whakatāne people, whom Kerekere (2017) describes as simply 'part of the whānau'.

And whereas traditionally it is the domain of kaumātua to ensure that tikanga is correctly maintained in Māori communities, discussion is now underway as to whether it is possible to maintain tikanga Māori in the courts, legislation and policy. According to Ngāti Awa lawyer Natalie Coates:

> Tikanga is the first law of Aotearoa. In the last 40 years we have moved on from the period of rejection and active suppression, have accepted that tikanga is part of the common law, and are now engaged in testing the bounds of recognition on a case-by-case basis. The challenge going forward more broadly is how tikanga can inform the state legal system in ways that

are genuine, meaningful and culturally safe. (New Zealand Law Society, 2020)

As members of takatāpui transgender and Māori LGBTQI+ communities, Manawaroa and I have a keen interest in advocating for decolonised tikanga Māori to inform the common law in Aotearoa in ways that are tika (correct) and that prevent recolonising and commodifying tikanga Māori. Our interest is for tikanga Māori in common law to assist in eliminating the marginalisation and discrimination of takatāpui transgender people, and in restoring the balance between Māori men and women, regardless of their gender identities, roles and expressions. To date, in terms of eliminating or even reducing high levels of transphobia experienced by takatāpui transgender people, the common law of Aotearoa appears to have contributed little of help to Manawaroa and her community and to the Honour Project Aotearoa participants.

The right to be takatāpui

Regardless of our earlier assertion that before colonisation there was likely no need for a Māori person to self-identify as anyone other than as a member of their whānau, hapū and iwi, we strongly support the right of Māori to identify as transgender, non-binary, gender-diverse, whakawahine, whakatāne and pan-gender. As noted, the Western, patriarchal, Christian, binary and heteronormative colonising processes deliberately subjugated whānau, hapū and iwi knowledges that had enabled Māori, in accordance with the framework of whakapapa and tikanga, to express themselves as they and their collectives saw fit. Outside Māori communities, the key mechanisms by which takatāpui transgender people might reclaim healthy Māori identities and eliminate gender-based stigma and discrimination are not sourced in tikanga Māori but are located in government legislation, policy, codes and standards.

The Crown, as the signatory to the Treaty of Waitangi 1840, has the responsibility of affirming the right of takatāpui transgender people to 'be who I am' (Liddicoat, 2008). The WAI 262 report by the Waitangi Tribunal (2011), which ruled that Crown policy breached the Treaty of Waitangi right of Māori to their culture, identity and traditional knowledges, also confirms the Crown's responsibility to ensure that all Māori – including all takatāpui transgender people – have access to relevant mātauranga Māori, te reo Māori and tikanga Māori. This right is also affirmed by the United Nations Declaration on the Rights of Indigenous Peoples (UNDRIP) (United Nations [General Assembly], 2007). However, to our knowledge no claim has been made to the Waitangi Tribunal that government policy has subjugated Māori understandings of gender identity, roles and expressions and caused generations of takatāpui transgender people to be shunned and discriminated against by wider society and by their own Māori communities. Given high levels of stigma and discrimination experienced by takatāpui transgender people, it is not surprising that a claim hasn't been taken to the Waitangi Tribunal. However, there is no excuse for the failure of government agencies to deliver on the rights of takatāpui transgender people to decolonised health, education, employment and social services that affirm pre-colonial Māori approaches to gender identities. To wait for a claim to the Waitangi Tribunal in order to force change in the health and social sectors is abusive and a breach of articles two (rangatiratanga) and three (protection) of Te Tiriti o Waitangi, and principle four (equity) of the Treaty of Waitangi.

The Crown is responsible for ensuring that policy protects and advances the health and well-being of takatāpui transgender people, including protection from stigma and discrimination. Legislation within Aotearoa and international agreements to which Aotearoa is a signatory all require the Crown, represented by the government of the day, to adhere to these instruments. However, a key finding by the Honour Project Aotearoa is that the Human Rights Act (1993) and the Code of Health and Disability Services Consumers' Rights (1996) (the Code) have not been effective mechanisms for reducing the marginalisation and discrimination that takatāpui transgender people experience in the public domain and in primary health services. The narrow-mindedness that Manawaroa describes as characteristic of Aotearoa in the 1970s and 1980s appears to be unchanged, despite the Human Rights Act and the Code. Progress toward eliminating transphobia and its intersection with homophobia, misogyny and racism has been imperceptibly slow. By comparison, as illustrated in the pūrākau told by Manawaroa, tikanga Māori that is decolonised and implemented in Māori communities by well-respected kaumātua can be an effective mechanism for reducing gender-based discrimination and building a foundation of respect and value for everyone within whakapapa-based Māori communities. Nonetheless, beyond the scope of Māori communities, we need legislation, policies and practices. This is why we believe that engaging decolonised tikanga Māori with specific pieces of legislation could support the process of eliminating the marginalisation and discrimination that takatāpui transgender people experience.

Manawaroa's pūrākau

Manawaroa and her family live on tribal land in their semi-rural home community in Whatawhata, where their ancestors have lived for many generations. Manawaroa is related to almost everyone who lives on her road. She says that everyone in her home community grew up together, went to the same school and participated in community dances, weddings, birthdays and funerals. She says that when she was a child, it was not unusual for three or four generations of a family to live together in the same house.

> I was born in the early 1950s, the fifth child of ten. The body I was born with was biologically that of a boy, but as far back as I can remember, I felt I was a girl. My mother let me dress up in girls' clothes, but my father wasn't so accepting. My brothers and sisters, cousins and aunties and uncles pretty much accepted me. When I got older, maybe some of them were not as accepting. Outside my home community, living as a woman was unacceptable.

Manawaroa's experience growing up was that outside of her family and home community it was dangerous for her to live as the gender she always felt she was. This was a common experience among takatāpui transgender people in Aotearoa New Zealand in the 1950s (Beyer, 2007). Almost three generations or 75 years later, takatāpui transgender, non-binary, gender-diverse, pan-gender, whakawahine and whakatāne participants who were part of the Honour Project Aotearoa reported that they too experience high levels of shunning and discrimination. Of the survey participants, 47% had experienced gender-based discrimination in parks, at beaches and pools, in libraries and on public transport; 43% had experienced discrimination on the street. Participants also reported discrimination in schools (37%), in the workplace (30%), and in restaurants (19%) (Pihama et al., 2020).

In Manawaroa's home community, Whatawhata, in the 1950s, tikanga Māori or traditional Māori values and practices were strong. As Mead (2016) notes, kaumātua whose role was to foster and maintain tikanga were highly respected. Kaumātua knowledge and perspectives on the world set the standards by which Māori communities lived, including in Whatawhata. Helping others, caring for children, respecting each other, and looking out for the whole community were key values, and Manawaroa says that everyone was expected to live by those values. Respecting kaumātua and their knowledge and experience in making good decisions and caring for their people, knowing who you descended from, knowing who your relations are, and enacting your responsibilities for your whānau, hapū and iwi were central.

When Manawaroa was growing up, she thought it was normal that she wanted to live as a girl:

> I remember some kids at school calling me a 'sissy'. The kids knew that my older brothers would step in and sort them out if the teasing got too bad. There's a photo of me – maybe I was 16 years old? I'd finished school and I'm wearing a padded bra because I wanted breasts. I thought I was pretty neat! But outside my home community I knew that it was safer if I was dressed as a man. Dressing as a woman was OK, unless you got 'sprung' and then things could turn nasty. Back then, it wasn't easy to get a job if you were living as a woman in a man's body, especially if you got 'sprung'. You lost your job, you could lose your flat, and doctors and nurses could be cruel. The police treated you like you were a criminal. New Zealand in the 1970s was very small-minded. People called us 'trannies', short for 'transexuals' and 'transvestites'. They called us 'faggots', sometimes worse.

Manawaroa at about 16 years old.

Leaving narrow-minded Aotearoa for Sydney

Like many other Māori who experienced discrimination due to their gender or sexual identities, Manawaroa moved to Australia. She recalls that when she got there, she 'came out' to herself, making the decision that she would live her life full-time as a woman. She encountered many other Māori who had left New Zealand to get away from the small-mindedness and the pile-up of racism, homophobia, transphobia and misogyny. In Australia, Manawaroa says, Māori gay, lesbian and transgender people could find employment and lifestyles that they could not dream of having back home. They were also able to get hormone treatment and gender reassignment surgery.

> I joined a large community of trans women, and many were Māori just like me. Unfortunately, the only work we could get in Australia was sex work. Some of us worked on the streets and others in parlours. Sometimes the work was dangerous, so we used a lot of drugs to help us get through. And we spent a lot of time avoiding the police. There was a photo of me taken when I was in my 20s. Standing next to me was a Māori trans woman who travelled to Egypt for gender reassignment surgery. We were good friends. Around the time the photo was taken I had had breast implants done in Adelaide. The surgery was pretty rough, so later I had another set of implants and felt happier with the surgery. As well as the implants, I also started oestrogen treatment. The Australian doctors didn't care who you were or what you wanted. They did the surgery, they wrote the scripts, and we took the pills.

Aspin (1996) describes the prejudice that transexuals, transvestites and gay Māori men faced in 1970s Aotearoa, which drove them overseas. Writing about Carmen and other Māori transvestites, transexuals and gay men moved to Sydney, Aspin (1996) states,

> Transexuals and transvestites were allowed to manage and operate businesses [in Aotearoa] so long as they did not overstep the boundaries that society imposed. Carmen['s] ... story is to some extent an example of the path followed by many gay men in the 1970s. The public pressure eventually became too much and she, like many others in the 70s, left the country to take up residence in [Sydney,] a city that was more accepting of her flamboyant style. (p. 3)

Unknown to Māori transexuals, transvestites and gay men at the time, moving to places like Sydney, San Francisco and New York would expose them to HIV and AIDS (Aspin & Hutchings, 2006). Some died and were buried far from home. Others risked discrimination for themselves and their families, and came home to Aotearoa to die.

Many Māori and Australian trans women showed Manawaroa 'the ropes' in the sex industry and looked after her. Sadly, many of the good friends she made in Australia have since passed away. She recalls a gay Australian friend she had in Adelaide. Years later, Manawaroa found out he had died of AIDS.

> Back then we didn't know about HIV and that it was transmitted by having unprotected sex and sharing needles. At some point in the early 1980s I realised that if I didn't go home soon, I'd be going home in a coffin.

In the 1980s, Manawaroa returned to Whatawhata. She was surprised to learn that two of her younger relations were also living as trans women; their presence helped her to feel stronger.

Manawaroa in her 20s with a friend who was also a Māori trans woman.

The esteemed kaumātua who supported Manawaroa's right to be a woman

Around this time, Manawaroa went to a large meeting held at her home community wharenui (traditional ancestral meeting house). A group of esteemed Waikato kaumātua were travelling through the region with the goal of strengthening tribal tikanga or Waikato traditional tribal values and practices. Manawaroa remembers the wharenui being packed. At some stage during the meeting the kaumātua began talking about the traditional roles of men and women. With her heart pounding, Manawaroa stood up and asked a question of the most senior kaumātua, Te Whatinga Tamati, who had been born in 1885: 'What about the role of transsexual people like me? What are our roles?'

Manawaroa said that at first the kaumātua didn't understand her question. When she repeated it, he asked her the meaning of the word 'transsexual'. Manawaroa explained that being transsexual meant that she had been born with a boy's body but had always felt she was a woman; she wore women's clothes and she did women's things.

The kaumātua replied, 'If you want to wear a dress and you feel like you are a woman and live your life as a woman, then you are a woman!' She recalled feeling amazed at what the kaumātua said, as was everyone else at the meeting. The pronouncement by Te Whatinga Tamati was held in high regard by her home community. Manawaroa says the tikanga is still remembered and talked about today. The kaumātua's respectful affirmation of who she was gave her permission to live her life as a woman in her home community, taking up the traditional roles and practices of women. That Te Whatinga Tamati's pronouncement would be adopted by the community was never in doubt: he was recognised as a kaumātua with deep knowledge and experience of traditional ways. Manawaroa and everyone else at the meeting accepted his pronouncement as tika, and adopted his values and practices of respecting the right of transgender people to be who they are.

For Manawaroa, the response of the elder was a pivotal moment in her life and in the lives of other takatāpui transgender people in her home community. Te Whatinga Tamati's response also highlighted the value of whakapapa, whereupon a person belongs to a community because of their descent from a common ancestor and they are respected and valued accordingly. Their gender identity, gender roles and expressions of gender are theirs to determine and their home community's to respectfully endorse. Looking back, Manawaroa says that discrimination of a Māori person because of their gender identity, roles and expressions has no place in healthy Māori communities where tikanga operates and where everyone is respected.

Raising her daughter and granddaughter

Not long after this important community meeting, a relation who was pregnant asked Manawaroa if she would like to raise her baby daughter. Raising a relation's child is a traditional Māori practice that was very common in Māori communities. Manawaroa's family were very supportive and encouraging, and so Manawaroa agreed and raised her relation's daughter as her own. As her daughter grew, there were times when other children at school teased her, saying that her mother was a man and not a woman. As her daughter matured, Manawaroa told her about the body she had been born into and her decision to live her life as the woman she had always felt she was. Manawaroa also told her daughter what the kaumātua, Te Whatinga Tamati, had said at the community meeting many years ago and the support she had received from her community ever since.

Today, Manawaroa is a mother, a grandmother, an aunty, a sister, and a respected member of her tribes. She is now raising her daughter's child – her

Manawaroa in recent years, with her daughter and granddaughter.

mokopuna (grandchild). Manawaroa contributes to the operations of the large communal kitchen at her marae. Now in her 70s, she is a weaver, and as could be expected she carries out traditional roles undertaken by the kuia (knowledgeable older women). She is also a support person for takatāpui who are considering changing their gender, and a strong advocate for Māori who are gay, lesbian, bisexual, transgender, intersex, and other genders and sexualities.

Tikanga Māori and takatāpui transgender health and wellbeing

While the rights of takatāpui transgender people to live safe and satisfying lives are in theory protected by national and international instruments, such as the Human Rights Act and the Code, in practice they have not been supported or protected. Takatāpui transgender people still face harsh, gender-based discrimination and other forms of discrimination in employment, education, health, public facilities and public spaces today, as the Honour Project Aotearoa indicates. Instruments that might protect and support takatāpui transgender people are likely hindered at a number of levels, from development to implementation and resourcing, monitoring to revision.

We assert, therefore, that the Human Rights Act and the Code should be updated and strengthened, and an action plan and budget should be developed to address legislation, policy and actions across all key sectors of government. The goal of revising the Act and the Code – as far as takatāpui transgender people are concerned – would be to engage tikanga Māori with human rights and health legislation as a mechanism for eliminating gender identity-based discrimination experienced by takatāpui transgender people. The newly drafted Pae Ora (Healthy Futures) Bill engages tikanga Māori in key clauses and, once the public consultation and Māori Select Committee processes are complete, may provide a guide for a new-look Human Rights Act and Code of Health and Disability Services' Consumer Rights.

Before embarking upon a revision of these instruments so that they engage with tikanga Māori, we first recommend convening a wānanga of esteemed kaumātua and takatāpui leaders to explore tikanga Māori and pre-colonial positions on gender identities, gender roles and gender expressions. We recognise that tikanga Māori – like mātauranga Māori – has been subject to colonisation (Kupenga et al., 1990; McBreen, 2012; Mikaere, 1998) and to misappropriation by people who are not Māori. As lawyer Natalie Coates notes (New Zealand Law Society, 2020), it is critical to ensure the cultural safety of tikanga Māori when it is brought into the realm of public policy and implementation. With these caveats, we offer the pūrākau told by Manawaroa as a referent for a wānanga process. Lastly, we encourage other takatāpui transgender people to share their own positive experiences of tikanga Māori.

In summary, gender identity-based discrimination has the potential to severely limit the quality of life and expectations of takatāpui transgender people and their whānau. Discrimination erodes their inherent rights, Te Tiriti rights and UNDRIP rights to be themselves. Evidence from the Honour Project Aotearoa survey indicates that the marginalisation and discrimination experienced by takatāpui transgender people in Aotearoa is as bad as it was at least three generations ago. Manawaroa's pūrākau shows that decolonised tikanga Māori can support Māori communities to recognise takatāpui transgender people as valued and respected members of whānau, hapū and iwi. Beyond the borders of small Māori communities, we encourage kaumātua and takatāpui transgender leaders to wānanga the engagement of decolonised tikanga Māori in the Human Rights Act, the Code of Health and Disability Services and other relevant legislation and policy. Eliminating gender-based marginalisation and discrimination through careful engagement with decolonised tikanga Māori has the potential to foster and maintain healthy Māori communities where everyone, regardless of gender identities, roles and expressions, is valued and has a role to play.

References

Aspin, C. (1996). Te whanaketanga o te iwi whānui takatāpui ki Aotearoa me te hauora o ngā takatāpui tāne i tēnei wā: Gay community development in New Zealand in the 1970s and implications for the health of gay Māori men in the 1990s. *Social Policy Journal of New Zealand: Te Puna Whakaaro, 7,* 42–51.

Aspin, C., & Hutchings, J. (2006). Māori sexuality. In M. Mulholland (Ed.), *State of the Māori nation: Twenty-first-century issues in Aotearoa* (pp. 227–236). Reed.

Aspin, C., & Hutchings, J. (2007). Reclaiming the past to inform the future: Contemporary views of Māori sexuality. *Culture, Health & Sexuality, 9*(4), 415–427. doi.org/10.1080/13691050701195119

Ballara, A. (1993). *Mangakāhia, Meri Te Tai*. Te Ara – The Encyclopedia of New Zealand. teara.govt.nz/en/biographies/2m30/mangakahia-meri-te-tai

Barrett, T. A. (2018). *School leadership for Māori succeeding as Māori: A Mataatua perspective* [Doctoral thesis, University of Waikato]. Research Commons. https://hdl.handle.net/10289/12101

Beyer, G. (2007). Of two spirits. In J. Hutchings & C. Aspin (Eds.), *Sexuality and the stories of indigenous people* (pp. 70–81). Huia Publishers.

Durie, M. (1996). Identity, conflict, and the search for nationhood. *Australian Psychiatry, 4*(4), 189–193. doi.org/10.3109/10398569609080487

Human Rights Commission. (n.d.). *Trans people: Facts & information.* hrc.co.nz/our-work/sogiesc/resources/trans-people-facts-information/

Hutchings, J., & Aspin, C. (Eds.). (2007). *Sexuality and the stories of indigenous people.* Huia Publishers.

Kaupapa Rangahau. (2019, September 10). *Manawaroa Te Wao – Honour Project Aotearoa* [Video]. YouTube. youtube.com/watch?v=gtdD4UyThlI

Kerekere, E. (2016). *Takatāpui: Part of the whānau.* Tīwhanawhana Trust and Mental Health Foundation.

Kerekere, E. (2017). *Part of the whānau: The emergence of Takatāpui identity – He Whāriki Takatāpui* [Doctoral thesis, Victoria University of Wellington]. ResearchArchive@VUW. researcharchive.vuw.ac.nz/xmlui/handle/10063/6369

Kupenga, V., Rata, R., & Nepe, T. (1990). Whaia te iti kahurangi: Māori women reclaiming autonomy. In *Puna Wairere: Essays by Māori.* New Zealand Planning Council.

Liddicoat, J. (2008). *To be who I am: Kia noho au ki tōku anō ao.* Human Rights Commission. hdl.handle.net/10523/8927

Mead, S. M. (2016). *Tikanga Māori: Living by Māori values.* Huia Publishers.

McBreen, K. (2012, September). *It's about whānau – Oppression, sexuality, and mana* [Paper presentation]. Kei Tua o Te Pae, Ōtaki. academia.edu/4052281/Its_about_whānau_oppression_sexuality_and_mana

Mikaere, A. (1994). Māori women: Caught in the contradictions of a colonised reality. *Waikato Law Review, 2,* 125–149.

Mikaere, A. (1998). Collective rights and gender issues: A Māori woman's perspective. In N. Tomas (Ed.), *Collective human rights of Pacific peoples* (pp. 79–99). International Research Unit for Māori and Indigenous Education, University of Auckland.

Mikaere, A. (2003). *The balance destroyed: Consequences for Māori women of the colonisation of tikanga Māori.* University of Auckland.

Mikaere, A. (2005). Cultural invasion continued: The ongoing colonisation of Tikanga Māori. In A. Mikaere (Ed.), *8.2 Yearbook of New Zealand jurisprudence: Special issue. Te Purenga* (pp. 134–172). University of Waikato School of Law. waikato.ac.nz/__data/assets/pdf_file/0003/32799/Yearbook-of-NZ-Jurisprudence-vol-8-issue-2-2005.pdf

New Zealand Law Society. (2020, December 1). Tikanga in 2020: An interview with Natalie Coates. *LawTalk,* 994. lawsociety.org.nz/news/lawtalk/lawtalk-issue-944/tikanga-in-2020/

Oliphant, J., Veale, J., Macdonald, J., Carroll, R., Johnson, R., Harte, M., Stephenson, C., & Bullock, J. (2018). *Guidelines for gender affirming healthcare for gender diverse and transgender children, young people, and adults in Aotearoa New Zealand.* Transgender Health Research Lab, University of Waikato.

Pihama, L., Green, A., Mika, C., Roskruge, M., Simmonds, S., Nopera, T.,

Skipper, H., & Laurence, R. (2020). *Honour Project Aotearoa*. Te Kotahi Research Institute.

Statistics New Zealand. (2020). *Sex and gender identity statistical standards: Consultation*. Statistics New Zealand. stats.govt.nz/consultations/sex-and-gender-identity-statistical-standards-consultation

Te Aho, L. (2007). He tikanga e pā ana ki a Tainui – Tikanga: Some Tainui experiences. In L. Te Aho (Ed.), *10 Yearbook of New Zealand Jurisprudence: Special issue. Tikanga Māori me te mana i Waitangi. Māori laws and values, Te Tiriti o Waitangi, and human rights* (pp. 10–14). University of Waikato School of Law. waikato.ac.nz/__data/assets/pdf_file/0014/32801/Yearbook-of-NZ-Jurisprudence-Vol-10-2007-print.pdf

Te Wao, M. (2019, September 10). *Manawaroa Te Wao – Honour Project Aotearoa* [Interview]. YouTube. youtube.com/watch?v=gtdD4UyThlI

United Nations (General Assembly). (2007). *Declaration on the Rights of Indigenous People.* un.org/development/desa/indigenouspeoples/declaration-on-the-rights-of-indigenous-peoples.html

Veale, J., Byrne, J., Tan, K., Guy, S., Yee, A., Nopera, T., & Bentham, R. (2019). *Counting ourselves: The health and wellbeing of trans and non-binary people in Aotearoa New Zealand*. Transgender Health Research Lab. countingourselves.nz/index.php/community-report/

Waitangi Tribunal. (2011). *Ko Aotearoa tēnei: A report into claims concerning New Zealand law and policy affecting Māori culture and identity* (Report No. Wai 262). waitangitribunal.govt.nz/news/ko-aotearoa-tenei-report-on-the-wai-262-claim-released/

Wall, L. (2007). Takatāpui: An identity of choice of a gift from my tūpuna? In J. Hutchings & C. Aspin (Eds.), *Sexuality and the stories of indigenous people* (pp. 44–54). Huia Publishers.

12

Invoking War Shields of Transformative Resistance and Persistence: Thrivance Among American Indian and Alaska Native Two-Spirit Women

Karina Walters and Michelle Johnson-Jennings

The story of Apanukfila (Whirlwind), also known as Apela ('helper'), Apalachi ('giving help') and Apeli ('act of storming'), is a Choctaw Okla Hannali (Six Towns people) story. This rendition is shared through the Choctaw family of Dr Johnson-Jennings.

The Story of Apanukfila (Whirlwind)

Long time ago, two children were orphaned. The elder sister cared for her brother. She hunted and provided their food. They were well. Then one day the sky darkened; the sister failed to return home from her hunt. Then the clouds came, the skies roared, and in nearby lands they watched the whirlwind come and cause great devastation to the villages. They say that the boy grew so worried about his sister that he set off to find her. After several nights, he heard someone crying in a nearby tree. As he climbed up to the hollow, he found his beloved sister. 'Go away and be safe,' she told him. He begged her to come home, but she could not. She explained that during her last hunting expedition she had been sexually assaulted by neighbouring villagers. In her all-consuming rage she transformed into the whirlwind (Apunukfila) and took revenge on the men and others. She begged her brother to flee, as she would turn into the whirlwind again. He asked her to come home, as he loved her. She refused as she was now Apunukfila but transferred to him her hunting skills. They say that the boy frequently visited his sister, bringing her gifts of food during the day. While his sister raged over the lands, he became known as the best hunter in the village and readily shared his meat with all. As his reputation spread, he was welcomed as a potential son-in-law to many. He visited his sister and shared the news of his success with her. He asked if she needed anything, and she said that she was lonely and wished that she too could have a partner. He offered to find a partner for her. He met with the maternal uncle of a prospective wife and asked for her hand in marriage. The prospective wife agreed to the marriage, but when they left the village he told her the truth – that he was hoping she would marry his sister who is the whirlwind. The prospective wife agreed, as long as she could meet her and determine for herself if they were a love match. Apanukfila and her betrothed met, and they agreed to marry. Over time, she and her beloved wife grew a strong partnership and through love, Apunukfila was able to transform her pain and heal. As she healed, Apanukfila's power of whirlwind transformed into restoring balance with the earth, turning up vegetation and land, and not destruction and pain. One day her brother visited and she told him to tell others to place tobacco outside their home so that she would miss their homes when she came through to rebalance the earth. From this day forward, this is why tobacco is put down during a tornado, or so they say. Yohmi ho.

As the Choctaw Okla Hannali story of Apanukfila reminds us, two-spirit women have stories of existence and transformative power among American Indian and Alaska Native Nations (hereafter referred to as Native), despite settler colonialism's attempt at erasure. Two-spirit women[1] have existed in tribal societies as well in the hearts and minds of our ancestors, as revealed in stories handed down since time immemorial. Though sometimes only fragments and whispers of stories remain, they provide critical insights, values and teachings for future generations. From an indigenist health perspective, Apanukfila reminds us of the transformative power of love and

1   The term 'two-spirit women' is used in this essay to describe lesbian, bisexual and women-loving Native American women. We acknowledge that the term 'two-spirit', as formally adopted at the 1990 Native American/First Nations Gay and Lesbian conference in Winnipeg, is a placeholder for tribally specific terms and roles and is used more inclusively for gender diversity irrespective of sexual identity (see Wilson, 1996). As Elm et al. (2019) write: 'Two-spirit is a contemporary, unifying, intertribal term adopted by some AI/ANs, First Nations, and Aboriginal people to signify their spiritual, sexual, gender, cultural, and community identities [. . .] the term [. . .] has been known to facilitate an individual's reconnection with tribal understandings of non-binary sexual and gender identities, as well as traditional spiritual or ceremonial roles that two-spirits have held [earned].' (p. 2).

relationality in healing from trauma. Kinship practices and responsibilities can provide a space for healing to evolve and healthful, restorative practices to emerge.

American Indian and Alaska Native communities have suffered from cumulative and chronic exposure to violent, historically traumatic attacks (such as massacres and boarding schools; Walters et al., 2011; Evans-Campbell, 2012) and contemporary targeted attacks on land or community (such as the Dakota Access Pipeline (DAPL) and missing and murdered Indigenous women), as well as other forms of ongoing discrimination and microaggression distress (such as sports team mascots). On top of historical and contemporary traumatic events, Native communities have been plagued by inequities in access to quality medical care (historically underfunded, inaccessible and inadequate), appropriate housing (substandard, overcrowded), healthful food access (food desert environments), clean and accessible water, and electricity. They have endured exposure to damaging environmental hazards, pollutants and toxins, all of which produce cumulative and chronic adverse health outcomes that are in place even before discriminatory events based on sexuality or gender diversity strike. These environmental factors drive the disproportionately high chronic physical health and mental health disease burden (such as diabetes, heart disease, PTSD and substance misuse) and corresponding elevated morbidity and mortality rates observed in Native communities.

Research has indicated that two-spirit people in particular have suffered disproportionate historical and contemporary forms of trauma and discrimination (Balsam et al., 2004; Evans-Campbell et al., 2012; Johnson-Jennings et al., 2014; Parker, Duran & Walters, 2017; Walters & Chae, 2009) and corresponding behavioural health challenges (such as PTSD, anxiety, substance misuse; see Parker et al., 2017; Johnson-Jennings et al., 2014; Yuan et al., 2014; Pearson et al., 2013; Nelson et al., 2011; Pantelone et al., 2011; Cassels et al., 2010; and Walters et al., 2002). For example, two-spirit people who attended boarding school have reported high levels of physical violence (34%) and sexual violence (39%) while attending the schools (Evans-Campbell, 2014). Additionally, after controlling for contemporary trauma including childhood physical and sexual abuse, as well as adult military combat exposure, empirical studies indicate that historically traumatic land-based events (such as forced relocation, loss of land and land desecration) have a significant effect on contemporary mental and physical health among Indigenous two-spirit populations (Walters et al., 2011). Two-spirit women in particular bear the burden of exceptionally high prevalence of sexual assault (85%) and physical assault (78%) (Lehavot et al., 2009; Walters et al, 2006). As Elm and colleagues note (2019), the 'cascade of eco-social chronic stressors, with proximal and distal historical traumas, has the potential to lead to prolonged suffering, including depression and anxiety symptoms and substance misuse' (p. 3). However, Indigenous two-spirit researchers have sought to move from a deficit-oriented approach to an indigenist-culture-centred approach, re-contextualising behavioural health concerns to more accurately amplify the strengths, resilience and survivance of two-spirit people.

Erasure of two-spirit experiences and histories is a tool of settler colonialism. Throughout history, settler colonialism has endeavoured to erase the lived experiences and histories of sexually and gender-diverse (two-spirit) Native Peoples. With the advent of rapid forced Christianisation, two-spirit people were targeted for erasure by Indian agents, missionaries and boarding school teachers, among other settler colonial representatives. For example, Lang (2016) writes that in 1879 the last surviving 'Hidatsa miati (male in a woman's role) was forcibly stripped of her/his female attire by the local government agent, who also dressed her/him in men's clothes and cut off his braids' (p. 300). As Tuck and Wang (2012, p. 9) note, 'everything within a settler colonial society strains to destroy or assimilate the Native in order to disappear them from the land'. Yet Indigenous two-spirit women remain strong and resilient pillars of their communities. Often, as a result of settler colonialism's perpetual drive to erase and silence, these stories are missed in public health initiatives. Johnson-Jennings and colleagues (2021) explain that Indigenous women still hold these stories today: 'We know that there will be a sacrifice of pain, at times, and sacred giving. Yet we also know that contributing to the past, present and future generations is our honoured position and responsibility as [Indigenous] women.'

Given the ongoing high disparities in violence and trauma exposure, Indigenous two-spirit scholars and activists have countered this erasure with indigenist research as well as culturally contextualised narratives of resilience and survivance in dealing with historical trauma, microaggressions, colonialism and related stressors. For example, Elm and colleagues (2016) identify a braided resiliency framework to elucidate the multi-layered abilities, processes and resources involved in two-spirit women's road to recovery from substance use and addiction. Similarly, Walters and colleagues (2006) have identified Indigenous world views that facilitate healthful identities and authentic representation of self in relation to family, ancestors and community (such as coming out), as well as navigating stress associated with racist violence, homonormativity and heterosexism among two-spirit women.

As established by Native scholar Vizenor (1994, 1995, 2008), this essay recognises that the term 'survivance' involves uplifting the visibility of Indigenous Peoples, supporting the continuation and regeneration of Indigenous Knowledges and stories, and renouncing notions of powerlessness, victimisation and invisibility. Survivance includes growing the deep cultural strands of Indigenous Knowledges and practices that endure to this day. Building on the work of Brayboy (2005), Walters and colleagues (2019) coined the phrase 'transformative resistance' to dynamically represent health-based decolonisation processes, such as resisting settler colonialism and activating change in others. Specifically, transformative resistance is a conscious process of engaging with and critiquing settler colonial conditions and identifying overt and covert strategies of resisting internalisation of those messages. Transformative resistance is built on conscious acts of decolonisation practices within and across Indigenous and settler colonial contexts. Acts of transformative resistance counter colonisation and, actively sustain Indigenous health beliefs, world views, presence and survivance across generations. Indigenous Knowledges provide the stability through which transformative resistance and persistence are woven (Johnson-Jennings et al., 2019; Walters, Johnson-Jennings et al., 2020).

'Thrivance', then, as the authors propose, involves weaving those survivance and Indigenous Knowledge strands (the warp) with the threads of transformative resistance and power of persistence (the weft) into a vibrant fabric of healthful living (Figure 1). Thrivance grows from ancestral knowledges and wisdoms, which then actuate healthful practices and well-being (Johnson-Jennings et al., 2019; Johnson-Jennings, Billiot, & Walters, 2019; Walters et al., 2020). Just as Indigenous weavers use backstrap

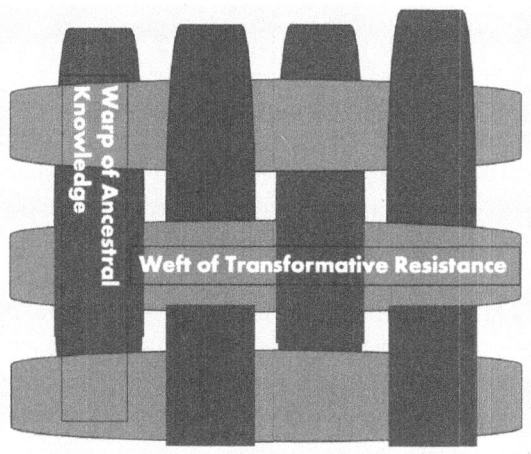

Figure 1: Basket of thrivance

weaving – using the weight of the weaver's body to control the tension of the loom – so too do Native two-spirit people navigate the embodiment and expression of thrivance. As we contextualised, read, and listened to the narratives of two-spirit women in the present study, we identified the overlapping threads of thrivance.

Methods

Drawing from the national multi-site HONOR Project Two-Spirit Health Study (NIMH R01 65871; N = 452 surveys; 65 in-depth interviews) and utilising the listening guide relational voice-centred method (Walters, 2010; Petrovic et al., 2015), the authors conducted an iterative indigenist qualitative data analysis of 11 two-spirit women's thrivance experiences and narratives. Respondents were recruited as part of a multi-site cross-sectional national health survey of Native two-spirits from seven metropolitan areas in the United States: Seattle-Tacoma, San Francisco-Oakland, Los Angeles, Denver, Tulsa – Oklahoma, Minneapolis-St. Paul, and New York City. Complementing the survey portion of the project and the mixed methods design, qualitative data was gathered to supplement and deepen the survey findings relative to key turning points in two-spirit health and well-being. The HONOR Project personnel worked closely with local and regional two-spirit advisory boards as well as agency partners in identifying community-recognised American Indian or Alaska Native two-spirit leaders for the qualitative portion of the study. As a result, over 65 diverse (by age, gender) two-spirit community leaders were identified by their respective communities and interviewed, using qualitative, in-depth, semi-structured methods. The qualitative approach employed indigenist methods providing opportunities for Native leaders to share their 'testimonios' – a type of narrative method or life story approach that supports authentic narratives and allows a person to transform narratives of past experiences of trauma, suffering and injustice into new narratives that can inform future generations and address injustices (Bishop, 2005; Huber, 2009; McMahan & Rogers, 2013; Smith, 2005).

Sample

Eligibility criteria included: (1) nominated as a two-spirit leader by their local Native community; (2) self-identified as American Indian, Alaska Native or First Nations; (3) self-identified as gay, lesbian, bisexual, transgender or two-spirit; (4) 18 years or older; (5) resided, worked or socialised in one of the urban study sites.

The study for this chapter is an extension of the original parent study, the HONOR Project, and met university and human subject research requirements. To protect confidentiality, all data were anonymised, and participants' quotes are used with pseudonyms. The sample for the present study focused on sampling female-identified leaders (including one self-identified transgender woman). This yielded a sample frame of 23 two-spirit women. All transcriptions were then 'listened' to relationally (Gilligan, Spencer et al., 2003) to identify two-spirit women who exhibited narratives of thrivance (invoking Indigenous Knowledges to overcome stressors as well as to conduct transformative resistance and/or survivance strategies). After examining all 23 transcripts, we found that 11 participants provided complete data on thrivance. These participants are the data analytic sample for the present study. Ages of interviewees ranged from 20s through late 50s.

Data analysis

The two American Indian women authors, one of whom is two-spirit, used the Listening Guide (LG) method (Gilligan et al., 2003; Petrovic et al., 2015) and conducted an iterative indigenist qualitative data analysis of 11 two-spirit women's thrivance experiences and narratives. The LG method is a relational, voice-centred method of analysing qualitative research data. It involves listening carefully to and for themes; in this case, the authors listened for themes of thrivance in the two-spirit women's narratives.

Per the LG method, the first author, who is two-spirit, reviewed and extracted all narratives at each LG step (1. Listening for the plot; 2. Constructing I-poems; 3. Listening for contrapuntal voices; and 4. Composing the analysis). The first author listened for plots, metaphors and prevailing themes within and across narratives, colour-coding the transcripts while keeping reflexive notes. During the second step of the LG method, the first author reviewed and underlined each first-person singular 'I' pronoun, 'we' (first-person plural), 'you' (second-person plural), and 'they' (third-person plural) poems, thus creating a poetic structure for deeper listening. The I-poems (inclusive of we, you, they) deepen analytic possibilities and provide participants' shifting perceptions of self, community and ancestors relative to the emergent theme.

The second author then reviewed the I-poems, extending construction of initial themes as well as verifying and providing convergent mapping of themes. Finally, both authors reviewed the emergent themes and the I-poems, 'listened' for contrapuntal voices (such as 'they' as ancestor voice/teachings), and composed final analyses through consensus and synthesising. Both also considered all interpretations and reflexive notes. (See Petrovic et al., 2015 for a more detailed description of this data analytic methodology.) The LG iterative steps provided an opportunity for deep, layered 'listening' and identification of thrivance strategies embedded in the narratives. As Brayboy (2005) notes:

> Stories as 'data' are important, and one key to collecting these data is 'hearing' the stories [which] means that the value is attributed to them and both the authority and the nuance of stories are understood [. . .] stories often are the guardians of cumulative knowledges that hold a place in the psyches of the group members, memories of tradition, and reflections on power. (p. 440)

Choctaw names are given as pseudonyms to further protect confidentiality.

Results and discussion

By examining the warps of survivance/Indigenous Knowledges and the wefts of transformative resistance, we were able to analyse the narratives of two-spirit women and identify the themes of thrivance. After the first data listening, we found five major organising themes through which to understand thrivance as well as the processes that emerged from their narratives. In the quotes that follow, we illuminate thrivance findings through the themes of: (1) Setting the context: Settler colonialism and historical trauma; (2) Original Instructions (ancient stories/teachings); (3) relational restoration/generation; (4) narrative transformation; (5) ceremony and spirituality. Within each theme, we examine examples of thrivance (Indigenous Knowledges, survivance, transformative resistance, and persistence). We conclude with a war shield thrivance heuristic, which consolidates the relational processes of Original Instructions, relational restoration, narrative transformation, ceremony and spirituality in promoting two-spirit women's health and well-being.

Settler colonialism and historical trauma

Two-spirit women have had their health and well-being systematically attacked by colonial systems since settler invasion (Wilson, 1996), which was voiced in the present study. United States settler colonialism consists of the policies and practices (systems/structures) that facilitate Native land dispossession and erasure of Native peoples and identities. As Tuck and Rowe (2017) note, this has meant the genocide of Indigenous peoples and the 'reconfiguring of Indigenous land into settler property'. Settler colonial policies and structures (such as Manifest Destiny and Doctrine of Discovery) are designed to distort historical realities and free future settler generations from guilt and accountability; rationalise and normalise continuous settler attempts to erase or disappear Indigenous histories and realities from the land, history, and contemporary society; and disavow ongoing settler colonial violence by obfuscating violence as inevitable. Thus, settler colonialism is an ongoing structure with circumscribed values that normalise continuous occupation through land dispossession, while straining to erase Indigenous people from the land and the colonial imagination. Erasure is a fundamental tool of settler colonialism. While settler colonialism is the structure, historical trauma is the set of unfolding events and impacts that uphold settler colonial systems.

Historical trauma is conceptualised as an event or set of events perpetrated on a group of people with a shared identity. The trauma significantly impacts the community, and it compounds as multiple traumatic events occur over generations, forming a legacy of intergenerational assaults (Evans-Campbell, 2008). Historically traumatic events are designed to eradicate a people, tribe or community (genocide); and/or eradicate their lifeways (ethnocide), such as their culture, language, identity, ceremonies; and/or eradicate their thoughtways (epistemicide), such as their world views, Indigenous Knowledges, epistemologies, and ways of knowing; and/or to devastate Native ecologies (ecocide), such as by polluting or destroying lands, waters and air quality (Johnson-Jennings, Billiot, & Walters, 2019; Walters et al., 2020). While all Native people have experienced settler colonialism and its corresponding historical trauma, two-spirit people have been targeted for elimination since first contact with Europeans (see de Bry's 1594 etching *Balboa's dogs attacking a group of Panamanian sodomites*). This press to eradicate sexual and gender expression was particularly salient throughout missionary-run boarding schools where any expression of physical affection or gender nonconformity was often met with physical punishment (Roscoe, 1988). Roscoe (1988) notes that boarding school punishments inverted traditional values where, for example, there is documentation of re-captured runaway boys being forced to wear girls' dresses as a form of humiliation – thus reconfiguring a once normalised traditional practice for some third/fourth gendered tribal people as a mark of dishonour and shame. Simultaneously, inculcation of traditional Indigenous stories and knowledges of sex or gender roles was strictly forbidden in these settings. Boarding schools were charged with erasing Indigenous Knowledges, traditions, and cultural practices and replacing them with Christian dogma and settler colonial heteronormative and patriarchal European norms and practices. The confluence of removing young children from their territories, placing them in a militarised, enforced Christian heteronormative and patriarchal dogmatic environment coupled with physical violence and torture if they expressed any cultural connectedness left a generation bereft of traditional stories about two-spirit lives. Despite such attempts at erasure, two-spirit people endured and their stories persisted, even if they went underground for cultural protection. For two-spirit peoples, settler colonial erasure coupled with ongoing historical trauma has left its mark on the present generation, as the I-poems of Chunkash and Ahnichi reflect. Both poems suggest that there is a time of emergence and a time to wake up culturally and to bring tools back for the healing of the people. These poems suggest that two-spirit people have a place and role in collective healing for all.

I-Poem (Chukʋsh/Chunkash)
There has been, as in the whole Indian community,
a whole phenomenon of disaster.
Huge, huge trauma
told they were less than . . .
Configuration of savage . . .
Women had no place.
The men were drained by filling them with alcohol
moving them and taking their weapons.
During that time,
they had ghost dancers.
Any spiritual thing going on was murdered.
It was killed.
It was devastated.

The only thing that stayed with us was our spirit.

Two-spirits were trained to take care of the spiritualness.
They were supposed to take care of the community.
Here, now they are told . . .
You are nothing.
You're stupid.
You don't have any right to live.
What are you?

Let's do some genocide here.

Two-spirits back then were looking at a community
who already hated the sight of Indians.

I'm sure that historical trauma was there.
You feel it.
You feel it today.
I think we all feel that historical distrust.
We carry around that dominance is still in our lives.
The two-spirit people back then were probably needing to go underground
or they were eliminated.
Until there was a time . . .
Other people could recognise them,
two-spirits themselves. (1038)

I-Poem (Ahnichi)
It's hard to break through and really bring about healing.
I know that our ancestors gave their lives for us.
I know that my ancestors sacrificed their lives. So . . .
I could be here today.
There are tools.
Some of the tools are out there, they're kind of hiding . . .
People have to go out there and find them.
You got to be persevering in doing it,
then you might find a tool that's broken or shattered.
It still has energy.
You have to go out,
find those people,
bring them back,
wake them up again
to ask their help for a clear path for healing.
To get through these traumas.
Really call it for what it is.
Start naming it.

Original Instructions

Settler colonialism is designed to disrupt Indigenous ways of knowing and the corresponding ability of Native people to fulfil their Original Instructions – that is, ancient teachings handed down since time immemorial (Walters et al., 2020). As Johnson-Jennings et al. (2021) note:

> disruptions of intergenerational knowledge transfer inhibit a people's ability to fulfil their Original Instructions (ancient teachings) and responsibilities – thus impacting well-being. Original Instructions are tied to land and cosmos and require a relationship between person and place with specific obligations and responsibilities. (p. 2)

Original Instructions are grounded in Indigenous Knowledges. These instructions provide protocols, practices and responsibilities to the natural and spiritual worlds as well as to past, present, and future generations (Nelson, 2008; Walters et al., 2020). Original Instructions are expressed through stories, songs, chants, dances, ceremonies and calendar cycles as well as traditional kinship and governance systems (Nelson, 2008). As noted by Walters et al. (2020):

> Embedded in IK and enacted through OI are place-based teachings, relational worldviews, and ways of being, knowing and talking in the world [. . .] how we think, communicate, and act all carry power as well as intergenerational responsibilities taught through OI. (p. 6)

Original Instructions also involve teachings (such as trickster stories) that relate to playful, healthful, diverse sexual and gender expressions (such as third genders or transforming back and forth across genders) (Ballinger, 2000) and healthful ways of being in the world, including healing from trauma (as in the story of Apanukfila) or addressing sexual or gender-based violence (such as the story of Deer Woman). As noted earlier, while there have been disruptions in Original Instructions related to two-spirit people, many communities and families have held on to enduring threads of knowledge and practices related to two-spirits.

A hallmark of healing from historically traumatic events is building health and well-being based on Original Instructions. This battles the erasure and invisibility of two-spirit peoples; and for two-spirit women, activates being 'seen' and belonging to family, community and tribe. By attempting to sever Indigenous collective identities and disrupt their views of self as connected to land, community and tribal ways, settler colonial policies sought to extinguish not only Indigenous cultures (Johnson-Jennings et al., 2021; Walters et al., 2011), but two-spirit peoples from Native cultures, histories and communities. This systematic disruption to Indigenous two-spirit history and knowledges has not only rendered two-spirit peoples invisible, but also inflamed anti-two-spirit attitudes still present in some Native circles today.

In the poem below, Ahnichi identifies two critical elements: firstly, that there was a name for two-spirit people as her aunt had noted, though the name is not remembered. Secondly, we exist, and according to Indigenous Knowledges we would belong and we would have purpose.

I-Poem (Ahnichi)
My aunty said, 'Oh, we have a name for people in our community like you.'
I remember that she called back home to [tribal community] and

the elder said
'Well, we don't really have those names, and we don't have people like that.'
My aunty was totally shocked that the response would be that.
She couldn't remember the name.
I was totally shocked.
It's like, well then, how could that be?
If you don't have people like that in our communities, then how come . . .
I am.
You know . . . those questions.
How can I be in this world if I don't exist?
I'm in this world.
I'm here for a reason.
There's many of us who are in the world who are not supposed to exist, but we exist.

Belonging is an essential component of Native identity and well-being (Roberts et al., 1998). Belonging gives people a sense of rootedness within a community and across generations. It is bi-directional, encompassing a sense of purpose and place within the larger community and in the circle of life (Hill, 2006). The term 'two-spirit', in and of itself, describes 'the inseparability of the experience of their sexuality from the experience of their culture and community' (Wilson, 1996, p. 303). For two-spirit women, belonging is tied to understanding the historical roles and place of two-spirit people as naturally manifesting through social or ceremonial roles as helpers and mediators, or other roles held historically in tribal communities (Wilson, 1996).

The role of service is a core Indigenous value and world view. For two-spirit people, the most common role across more than 250 tribes is caretaker or mediator, meaning a person who bridges or mediates between worlds (human/political, physical and/or spiritual). This person is one who can stand in the in-between place, from which they have a unique vantage point that serves the people, and/or one who is a caretaker for the community (such as carrying out funerary rites, or helping with children and medicines). Indeed, some tribal names for two-spirit people translate literally as 'one who stands in the middle' (such as the Muscogee/Creek term *Envrkepv-huerv* or *Envrkepv-huervlke*; Briggs Cloud, 2010). In the Mvskoke language, the term represents the stitching design at the centre, where two straps of the bandolier medicine bag are stitched together. The term symbolises 'the medicine gifted to the *envrkepv-huervlke* that holds the community together'; historically the term was used to recognise those who carry the roles and responsibilities associated with their innate ability to see from both male and female perspectives (Briggs Cloud, 2013).

I-Poem (Ahnichi)
I believe that there have always been roles.
I believe that each Nation has had names for people like us.
It was just a way of life . . .
We didn't have to explain who we were,
we didn't have to justify our existence.
Within myself today,
I see it happening.
I don't have to think about it,
I just fall into some role.
I don't say, yeah, I'll do that.
It just happens . . .
I always believe there have been roles for us.
Those roles, either spoken or unspoken . . .
just naturally filling in those gaps.

Throughout their narratives, many two-spirit women identified helping roles. In her I-poem, Apela describes being mentored by another two-spirit person through that person's modelling of serving others and assisting wherever needed. Apela's mentor instilled in her *noblesse oblige* – the Indigenous value of responsibility and obligation to serve the community and help others in need. Importantly, Apela's narrative reflects the transmission of Indigenous Knowledge and values of generosity and service. It is an example of how helping roles continue through two-spirit mentors in Native communities. Apela also reflects on how she was loved and embraced by the whole tribe, not just her family. This is critical to her sense of place and belonging.

I-Poem (Apela)
My Native people accepted me and loved me.
It wasn't just my family,
it was the whole tribe.
It doesn't matter what your sexual orientation is . . .
There were always two-spirited people in our tribe.
People just didn't talk about it.
They were treated as well as anybody else.
A lot of times better simply because . . .
they were good, productive, helpful, generous people.
My dear two-spirit friend was always there
if someone was sick or needed something, anything, groceries.
He'd take a trunk load of groceries to somebody.
He'd instilled in me *noblesse oblige*
We have an obligation to our people

to help take care of them if we could.
I would, in time
carry on where he left off.
He kinda groomed me to do that
I don't know why, but he just did . . .

Original Instructions are passed down through formal and informal teaching processes across generations (Nelson, 2008; Walters et al., 2020). Many of the two-spirit women in this study talked about naturally falling into helping roles. They equated this 'falling into' with ancestral predestiny or a manifestation of the remnant, embodied ties to historical roles of two-spirit peoples in their tribal nations.

This next I-poem, from Maiya, captures how contemporary two-spirit people naturally fall into health support roles. Maiya shares knowledge of historical two-spirit roles (such as carrying out funerary rites and praying over the sick) in her tribal nation and how this anchored her understanding of her role in supporting friends who were terminally ill with AIDS. She identifies the courage and fierceness of two-spirit women as they step in to care for people, where others have been fearful or failed to do so. Finally, she identifies her sense of belonging, her role and her place.

I-Poem (Maiya)
Before colonisers came, the gay and lesbian individuals in [my tribe]
were the people responsible for praying over the sick.
Helping the dying to die right and appropriately.
In a good way.
To take care of the dead after they are gone . . .
I feel like that's what I do . . . teaching, healing . . .
I've always felt pulled in this direction . . .
I had friends who in the early 80s were dying of AIDS.
I helped take care of them, because back then nobody would touch them.
When my [relative] was dying
I took care of her.
I was with her when she died peacefully . . . none of her kids could do
that for her.
See, my family turns to me for those kinds of things a lot.
It just comes naturally.
In a lot of ways
I've grown into who I'm supposed to be
Who my ancestors expected me to be when they put me here . . .
I think
I was put here for a reason.
My ancestors placed me in this place for a reason.
And my grandma knew it.

Original Instructions manifest in Native communities and two-spirit families today through rite of passage ceremonies. In her I-poem, Pʋlali describes women coming together to talk about sex and self-respect. As Pʋlali notes, these powerful rites establish positive communication patterns between mothers and daughters, for present and future generations.

I-Poem (Pʋlali)
In almost every traditional [family/community] that I have encountered
there has been some sort of rite of passage for a child from childhood
into young adulthood . . .
Those ceremonies still exist in some form or another . . .
what are the values around someone's health . . .
When [daughter] started her moon [menstrual cycle],
all of the women, over 20 of them, came to the ceremonial ground.
Every woman talked [with my daughter] about
the first time that she had sex . . .
talked about how you say 'no',
how you respect yourself – what that means . . .
She has a real clear idea of what her responsibility to herself is.
It's made it a lot easier when . . .
we talk about sex.
We talk about HIV and STDs.
It all ties in with mental health.
I think that's important . . .
If we're going to talk about health –
our health –
part of our future generations' health –
it's important that those young people know it.

As the I-poem of Tombi demonstrates, Indigenous Knowledges, values and spirituality provide a critical foundation for survival in troubled times. Tombi acknowledges the role of Original Instructions and notes that a foundation of Indigenous Knowledge and spirituality, instilled in her from an early age, has helped her to face challenges.

I-Poem (Tombi)
Creator's plan was mapped out long before me.
Getting through each moment, riding each wave.
Knowing that when the waters are calm,
that doesn't mean there ain't a shark right underneath you.
When the waters are rough,
that doesn't mean that's not the best ride that you're about to take ever.
Coming out of that tunnel of water . . . where

you could easily have your back broken and drown
could just as easily be that moment of triumph ... where
you make it through that tunnel.
So, trying to get through
each rough moment
I go in.
Knowing that this is part of those Indigenous values and spirituality
that were given to me ...
from a very young age ...
allowed me to have full access to Indigenous spirituality and understanding.

Relational restoration

For Indigenous peoples, relationality is about deep reciprocal connectedness across space and time. Human beings are part of a vast web of life and are inextricably linked to all others in the natural and spiritual worlds, just as all others are linked to back to human beings, as captured in the maxim 'all our relations' (Cajete, 1999). Moreton-Robinson (2000) labels relationality as 'kindredness' across space, time, place, and all beings.

Settler colonialism and historically traumatic events are designed to disrupt relational connectedness. Thus, restoring relational ways of being in the world – to peoples, body, ancestors, mind and knowledges, environment/natural and spiritual worlds – and generating healthful relational processes is a key to healing and promoting Indigenous health and well-being.

Restorative remembering is a critical component of relational restorative practices. As Maiya notes, she was 'lucky' to have a great-grandmother who remembered traditional ways and knowledges.

> **I-Poem (Maiya)**
> The Christian impact has been really harsh.
> That's a huge challenge for people who want to know what
> their traditions are
> To be able to go back and be
> accepted.
> I was lucky
> My grandma, my great-grandmother, was born on the shores of the Lake,
> pre-contact ...
> She remembered what it was like to
> NOT live on a reservation.
> Remembered what it was like to ...
> go to the rice paddies,
> go to the deer camp,
> go to the sugar bush and travel around ...

She also knew
what it was like to be pushed onto the rez.
That was the only safe place for them to be.
She was difference,
'cause
she knew what tradition was.

In the following I-poem, Chukʋsh (Chunkash) identifies positive two-spirit role models in the community who honour themselves and their communities by fulfilling their ancestral roles as helpers. Being a two-spirit person does not in itself entitle a person to respect or accord special status; rather, it is how one conducts oneself, and how one's actions align with traditional values and knowledges (authenticity, generosity, humility, service) within the community that earns the respect of others and the right to esteemed roles.

I-Poem version (Chukʋsh)
One of the things I know that two-spirit people do . . . that I know
are getting wide respect . . .
It's a grace that people carry.
The honouring they give themselves,
their ability to stand tall and straight and be really open to people . . .
They have consistency that other people don't necessarily have.
They have honesty because they keep coming back and they keep saying . . .
'I'm here to help.
I'm here.
I want to be the community member that's available to you.'
They offer them some hope.
The two-spirit people I know are successful . . .
They have their faith.
They have their spiritualness.
They have a job.
They have some learnings they're willing to share with other people,
not hoard it and keep it to themselves.
Placing themselves in the midst of all those people . . .
you see people respond.
You see them start listening.

Chukʋsh's I-poem personifies relational generative practices that embody love and nurture belonging in one's family, including ancestors and future generations. For Chukʋsh, love and spirit were passed on to her through embodied teachings of generosity and kindness. Traditionally, teaching is done through observation and practice. The child is often asked to do a task that embodies the spirit of the lesson, and in this case Chukush prepares a cup of tea for her grandmother, which nurtures the spirit of giving and kindness and provides a sense of relational purpose. The emphasis remains on giving as opposed to receiving. Chukush's grandmother modelled the behaviour in her everyday living, helping to solidify the teaching for Chukush.

I-Poem (Chukush)
A lot of us have in our lives some grandparent, aunty, uncle, somebody who gave us their spirit too.
We have a spirit already.
When we walk into the world, someone keeps reminding you that you belong.
The thing that probably saved me is up until the time I was taken from my grandmother,
I was always . . . given a lot of love.
It wasn't all hugs and smooches.
One of the things my grandma always had me do was . . .
give her a cup of tea.
Now how loving is that? That you would ask this little child to do that . . .
it gave me a purpose,
it gave me a chance to take care of my grandma.
To be taught about giving.
I'd watch her give things to people,
give food to people walking by,
you never hoarded stuff that could be used by other people.

Chukush offers another I-poem, below, that identifies how the passage of Indigenous values, teachings and practices across generations can be drawn upon in times of distress. Chukush is able to invoke childhood memories of traditional practices (such as never raising one's voice, cleaning roots, beading bags) and the safety and comfort of those memories, as if they were a protective shield.

I-poem (Chukush)
Somewhere in there that value was instilled in me
came from this grandma
whose grandma instilled it in her, and . . .
whose grandma instilled in her, and . . .
in me.
I carry that today . . .
Whenever I get really frightened or scared, angry
I would just step back into looking at my grandma's house.

It always brought comfort.
I could always see her,
watch her as she is beading.
How strong her hands were,
how lovingly she put that beaded bag together,
how she would clean the roots . . .
Time . . .
when she was talking about what the world was about . . .
She never raised her voice at me.
Never.
At that little tiny age
I was given all those values and more that were engrained and instilled
in me
to carry me into adulthood.

Some of the two-spirit women shared stories of being disowned or kicked out of their family of origin's homes because they were two-spirit. While all described this experience as initially painful, nearly all identified a relative who stepped in to claim them, provide a safe space for them, and share with them traditional ways of being and loving in the world. In many cases, as Maiya's I-poem below reflects, the relatives shared traditional teachings through their actions (embracing them as two-spirit relatives) and lessons (such as beadwork and ceremony).

I-poem (Maiya)
I had an aunt- my mom's sister.
I've always called her 'Aunt Mom' because . . . when
I was disowned . . .
She called me within an hour and said:
'I will be your mother until your mother can be your mother again.'
'You're welcome to come to my house.'
'Welcome to be a part of my family . . .'
My aunt taught me everything she was taught.
She taught me how to dance.
How to make a shawl.
How to do beadwork and all of that stuff.
It was almost a second childhood
Becoming one of her family, one of her kids.

For two-spirit peoples, chronic stress combined with proximal and historical traumas has the potential to activate lifelong suffering, including depression, substance use, and death by suicide. In the HONOR Project, 39% of the two-spirit women had attempted suicide and 63% expressed risk of death by suicide (plan, thoughts, self-harm) (Walters, 2010). A number of the two-spirit women leaders talked about suicidality and identified key cultural and spiritual factors that had interrupted their attempts, such as an adult relative who stepped in and valued them, giving them a sense of cultural belonging and purpose, as well as divine interventions from the spirit world. In Ahnichi's I-poem, she identifies a moment in which she was about to take her life when her ancestors intervened. The critical factors that disrupted such despair and distress were feelings of being valued, having significance, having purpose, and a sense of belonging. As other women noted, one's ancestors are not only prominent figures in their teachings but in providing love as intervention.

I-poem (Ahnichi)
I was going to take my life.
I was getting ready to . . .
All of a sudden . . .
I heard this chanting and singing
Up over the hill came all these women
They were singing a song
They were chanting
They were circling around me
The sun came out so bright that it [vision] stopped.
That was such a profound experience.
I was ready to . . . and they stopped me.
The women told me . . .
That there was importance in my life
That I was significant
That I was valuable
There were many things in my life that
I needed to do
To get through the tough times
I think about that moment.

A common theme in the narratives involved transformative resistance actions, such as standing up for oneself, walking away from unhealthy relationships and community members, or refusing to accept anti-Native or anti-two-spirit attitudes from Native community members or the non-Native LGBTQI+ community. However, the women did not walk away into isolation, but instead turned towards love.

As Chukush's I-poem reflects, this also meant walking towards self-love and healing, as well as finding people who have healthful practices that support their well-being.

I-Poem (Chukʋsh)
Some of the Native community truly don't understand
about who people are who are gay.
That's okay.
I've found ways of just walking away from that.
Going to places where
I'm welcomed . . .
I'm always surrounded by the people who
I care about and who care about me.
There's a buffer of sorts . . .
my friends know who
I am . . .
I bring my partner, and my family is very receptive, very welcoming . . .
I'm not shunned.

Land-based healing

Indigenous research has shown that the land serves as 'a therapeutic site for healing through reconnecting people to both ancestral knowledges and stories of resilience, as well as viewing self as part of a larger collective and supporting transformation of trauma narratives' (Johnson-Jennings et al., 2020). Reconnecting to land, water and the elements fosters ancestral commitments to cultural continuity and healthful behaviours and practices – particularly when places in nature are approached relationally and/or in or with ceremony. Historically traumatic events or ongoing settler-colonial stress can be transformed in reconnecting to land and nature. Moreover, it can invoke or awaken ancestral memories and love that has been held for generations.

Nearly all of the women discussed the importance of connecting to the land, water, sky, and the elements for their healing, recentering and reconnecting to the ancestors. This I-poem from Kʋli describes how land-based healing and connecting has helped her mental health and well-being.

I-poem (Kʋli)
What they call the natural world . . .
We're a part of too.
Has always been, my solace.
My healing.
I trust the earth and the trees and the sky and the sea in a way
I can't trust people.
Those people – the earth is people to me.
Those people are my family,

my home.
I went to the forest . . .
It gave me this whole new feeling . . .
The water of the earth is in a continuous cycle . . .
It's always moving . . .
We're part of that too . . .
I'm getting real . . . that's how
I stay sane . . .
From that part of my life.

Narrative transformation

How we think and talk about our story matters. Through storytelling, we can acquire knowledge with respect, holism, and experience (Caxaj, 2015; Smith, 2019). Embedded in Indigenous stories are frameworks for well-being across generations (Johnson-Jennings, 2020; Jennings et al., 2021). Stories hold acts of transformative resistance as well as colonial trauma, and by sharing them, meanings and truths begin to emerge (Caxaj, 2015).

Settler colonialism has sought to disrupt our stories and how we think and talk with and about one another. This disruption frequently manifests as internalised colonisation or lateral violence. Embracing narrative transformation practices serves to decolonise internalised and embodied narratives of victimisation into indigenist narratives of resistance, persistence and thrivance: 'Indigenous re-storying can shift historical trauma narratives towards ancestral love, resilience, and sacrifices to improve individual health' (Johnson-Jennings & Walters, 2021). For centuries, tribal communities have utilised narrative transformation through art, song, dance, and ceremonies such as naming ceremonies. Storytelling is a major form of narrative transformation, as we see in creation/origin stories, ceremonial stories for sacred rites, humorous life-lesson stories, legends and poems. Nelson (2008, p. 5) notes that stories are 'possessed with such power that they have survived for generations despite attempts at repression and assimilation'. Today, we can find narrative transformative strategies in podcasts, blogs, digital stories, film, and other media (Jennings et al., 2018; Johnson-Jennings at al., 2019). These are also ways of transmitting Indigenous Knowledges, Original Instructions, and relational world views. As Johnson-Jennings and Walters (2021) found among Choctaw women, the stories we tell can transform trauma and grief into perseverance and resilience, and the need to continue to heal for future generations.

Many two-spirit communities are building creative, safe, healing spaces where they can narrate their whole being into the world, recommit and reconnect to tribal ways and knowledges, participate in ceremony without fear of harassment or shunning, and build a positive and vibrant community. Increasingly, stories, songs, dances, and other arts-based practices are finding their place in Indigenous health practices among two-spirits.

Many Indigenous nations and communities also value naming. Naming situates one in ways of kinship and relationality, and renaming serves to transform or heal among many communities (Compton, 2004). In particular, naming something makes a being or concept tangible and visible, and fights colonial erasure. Naming ceremonies, as a traditional practice, serve to identify the name's responsibility to the community, ancestors and spirit world (Exner, 2006). Naming reveals the role and gifts of the person in relation to the greater whole and allows for transformation to occur.

> **I-Poem (Ahnichi)**
> Part of my healing has been [being] able to name things.
> Define language for what has happened culturally.
> To me and a lot of people in my family . . .
> the biggest part of my healing has been [being] able to understand history,
> to have words to call it and help me to go through those experiences
> with language.
> I feel that's something that some of our people don't have
> the opportunity to do that, define language.
> To deal with the anger and the continuation of trauma,
> either in the urban or on the rez.
> Having language has been beneficial
> to be able to name things for what they are . . .

As can be seen in Ahnichi's poem, the power of naming and renaming in a contemporary context addresses colonial erasure and invisibility. Here, Ahnichi uses the 'we' voice in expressing transformative resistance, refusing to be made invisible. The use of 'we' suggests a connectedness across time and space to Indigenous histories, culture and spirituality, rejecting erasure.

One's story, one's truth, is another critical component of narrative transformation. Storying and re-storying provide an opportunity for transformative resistance – transforming internalised colonial attitudes as well as storying oneself to the outsider world to challenge colonial structures and attitudes (Johnson-Jennings & Walters, 2021). This storying is critical for healing.

> **I-Poem (Ahnichi)**
> For my personal experiences being out in the world as a two-spirit person.

As a person period.
As a Native woman.
Being out in the world in a sea of whiteness . . .
it's not about the label who I am . . .
it's about coming from my heart.
If I come from my heart and speak my truth,
talk my truth,
walk my truth,
honour my truth . . . that is what's going to keep me safe.
I can present that in a non-threatening way.
It gives me great freedom . . .
I need to choose my battles very carefully . . .
You have a choice – either stay in this flood and try to stop it
or step aside and let the flood go through and then step in
and pick up the pieces.
My choice has been . . .
I step aside
I have the choice – the decision of which pieces
I will pick up . . .

At times, narrative transformation involves taking a stand and enacting transformative resistance through action. In her I-Poem, Ahnichi recognises that if she is to do the community work and service she has committed to, she will need to take a stand and 'come out' as two-spirit. She did so in a communal setting to a Native audience and found her voice. She contextualises this action within a traditional values context, noting that she was able to stand in her identity in a way that is culturally resonant ('being calm about it') and from a spiritual place. It is about coming in and becoming out – in other words, becoming who she was meant to be and standing strong in her identity (Walters et al., 2008).

I-Poem (Ahnichi)
I said to myself,
if you're going to do this work,
you need to make a stand in your identity on some level.
You just cannot skirt around it anymore.
I remember standing in front
of the Native [health-related conference] group
they were talking . . . this homophobia was coming up . . . finally
I said, enough is enough.
I came out as a two-spirit person.
Everybody in the audience was like, mouths open, like, 'What?'
That was the greatest day,

because from that moment on
that's what carried me through . . .
I've always said
I was a two-spirit person.
I was able to do it in such a way that it wasn't like
HERE I AM . . .
I'm going to be in your face about it . . .
but with a mannerism of bringing it up and talking about it.
Being calm about it.
I've always felt very blessed that I was able to do that.
Present myself with
my identity.
To be strong in
my identity.

The participants discussed narrative transformation as transforming thoughts into prayerful action and strength. In her I-poem, Otapi actively takes her stress and pain and transforms those feelings into prayers.

I-Poem (Otapi)
I pray.
I do my ceremonies.
I do my beadwork and artwork . . .
Mostly pray . . . every morning and night . . .
In stressful times
I just try to think about living my day . . .
I could change now
I learned that through my mother
I don't think pain ever goes away but
you learn how to live with it
you learn how to change it for you
and
make it a strength.

Ceremony and spirituality

Many Indigenous cultures tie ceremony and spirituality to good health. Engaging in rituals of ceremony and spirituality has been found to support positive behavioural changes and mindfulness (Johnson-Jennings et al., 2018; Johnson-Jennings et al., 2020; Johnson-Jennings & Walters, 2021), and has been linked to lower disease risks and overall well-being (Garroutte et al., 2003; Dill et al., 2016).

The I-poem of Otapi, like other narratives from two-spirit women, reveals that a strong spiritual and ceremonial foundation provides a stronger sense of identity and well-being. The cultural lessons of caring for one another were transferred through ceremony and family time together. These teachings persist in two-spirit women's lives.

I-Poem (Otapi)
My most vivid memory
I have as a child . . .
we sweat daily . . . grandmother, my mom,
and aunts and all my little cousins
We'd go to the sweat lodge . . . the fire and the stones . . .
and pass them in . . .
We'd be in there talking and laughing and listening to the stories . . .
I could hear my relative breaking the ice in the creek.
You run out as little children into the creek and rinse off
and run into the house.
That spiritual time . . .
They'd talk about life.
Things we need to do to take care of each other as a family.
How we need to look at our little cousins and watch them
and take care of them.
We need to listen to older cousins because they had [more] time here . . .
It just was a spiritual kind of time.
At the time . . .
I didn't realise it was spiritual . . . just listening to the songs
and feeling all that presence that was there.

Two-spirit women did not passively enter into ceremony or spirituality. They discussed the need to 'meet the medicine halfway'. Though at times they were reluctant, desiring a quick fix, overwhelmingly the women reported the need to sacrifice and give to receive healing and clarity. As can be seen in Ahnichi's I-poem, at times this was directed by a loving relative.

I-poem (Ahnichi)
I remember
I was going through a tough time.
I went home.
I was just so disjointed, so angry . . .
My grandmother
she'd give me a big hug
she looked at me and said, 'Yup, [NAME], come home.'
I went to the cabin.

I said, 'Grandmother,
I really need your help.'
She says, 'Go fast.'[2]
I said . . .
'I don't want to go fast.
I don't want to do it.'
She said, 'You have to do it.'
I remember leaving the cabin,
I was really mad, going up trails, mumbling all the way down the trail.
That went on for a few days.
each time I went in the cabin,
she'd say, 'Go and fast.'
'I don't want to do it.'
Actually
I said, 'I don't want to hear what that fucking spirit has to say! [laughs]
I want to hear it from you.
I want human interaction, not spirit interaction!' [laughs]
I was mumbling, so angry,
I didn't want to do anything,
I didn't want to sit down to dinner,
I was so pissed.
On the fourth day
I got up and
something happened,
clicked into place before daylight.
I went in the cabin
She said, 'Come here, I'll mark a place for you.'[3]
So, she did.
I went out and that was a really tough time.
I was very fortunate.
I'm glad I did go out.
I did receive
what I needed to help me get through
it's really simple . . .
I say thanks for another day of life and breath –
it's the simple things
not the complicated things that gets me through the tough times . . .
family and friends and people who have like minds
who are clear can help you get through
the real tough times.

2   Carry out a ceremonial fast.
3   Ceremonial place outside for the fast.

In Indigenous communities, spirituality and ceremony often involve a community as opposed to an individual (Struthers et al., 2004). Two-spirit women indicated that a sense of collective spirituality within the community was beneficial for their health and well-being. They also indicated that ceremony can occur both informally and formally, as shared in Kʊli's and Aianli's I-poems.

I-Poem (Kʊli)
Two-spirit gatherings every year are really helpful to me.
It feels like that's the only time in the year
I get to be how whole self in one place.
Joking and laughing.
I wish we could have one that lasted a whole year.
We'd all be really different people when we came out of there . . .
that, to me, is really healing.
The ceremonies that happen within that context at least twice
have saved my life.
I was in really, really terrible shape.
Ceremonies there just changed everything . . .
I would say that ceremony is absolutely crucial to my survival.
I am really grateful whenever
I can be a part of ceremony.
It's so good.

I-poem (Aianli)
I pray often and without preaching.
I pray while I'm arguing.
I pray while I'm peeing.
I pray when I'm scratching.
I pray [laughs] all the time.
I talk
I talk to the Creator
like the Creator's sitting right next to me.
Well, the Creator is . . .
I mean, like,
I can see the Creator in front of me,
that literally keeps me afloat and has
all my life.
Yeah.

The powerful narratives of weaving thrivance led the authors to consider the transformative power of survivance, transformative resistance and persistence that swirl around Indigenous Knowledges and act as a war shield in battling settler colonialism and trauma (see Figure 2).

'Thrivance' is the outer weaving (fabric) or braid (sweetgrass). It surrounds and upholds indigenist and decolonising actions, enacted to grow Indigenous healing and health. Two-spirit women can be seen to engage in the weaving of thrivance to counter historical trauma and to create and regenerate love and knowledge. All the while, they centre their Indigenous Knowledges, which centres acts of thrivance.

At the centre of the shield, we see indigenist action and agency. These support health and well-being via relational restoration, the use of Original Instructions, narrative transformation, ceremony, traditional health practices and living our spiritual lives. Ancestral feathers on the war shield, with sub-themes identified, guide the women's shield of thrivance. Each feather has a corresponding act of thrivance. A common Original Instruction sub-theme entailed walking away from unhealthy interactions and towards love, whether ancestral, community, grandmother or aunty.

The women exercised narrative transformation while simultaneously re-storying, re-naming and claiming their identity as a manifestation of ancestral roles, which served to further disrupt settler-colonial narratives While they often discussed ceremony and spirituality, the women also reflected on collective healing and the importance of continuing their

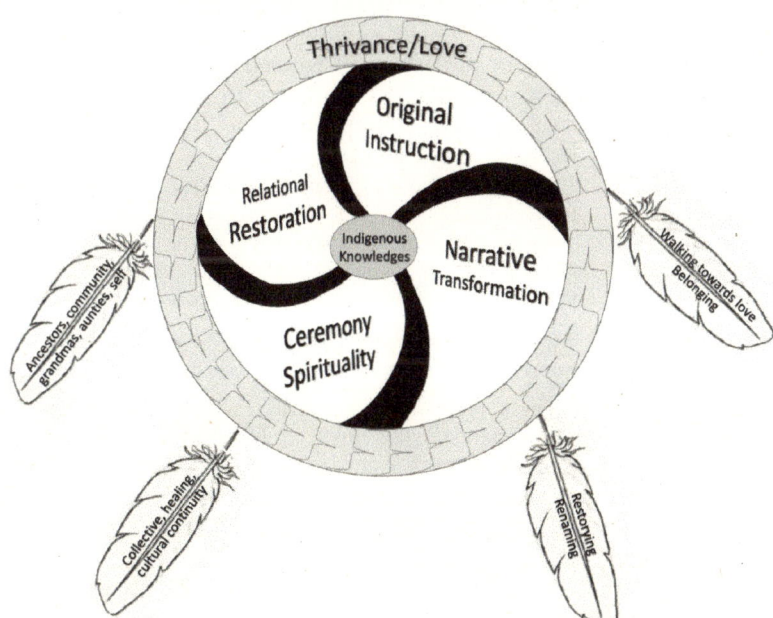

Figure 2: *The thrivance war shield is modelled on our ancient Southeastern Ceremonial Moundbuilder design, representing the wind and transformation.*

culture, as found among other Indigenous women in a previous study (Johnson-Jennings et al., 2021). Finally, relational restoration served as a protective factor in restoring connections to ancestors, community, grandmothers, aunties, and self.

In the centre of this shield is the sign for continuation in balance and transformation. This implies that Indigenous Knowledges as well as acts of transformative resistance, persistence and survivance create thrivance, but are not independent or stagnant. These four acts co-exist and mingle within the women's lives to form a balanced whole.

This shield wards off and disrupts settler-colonial trauma. It protects the women as they contribute meaningfully to their communities and ultimately, through such actions, uphold their health and well-being.

Conclusion

Overall, the two-spirit women in this study voiced their stories and acts of thrivance. By drawing from survivance and transformative resistance and being within Indigenous Knowledges, the women were able to engage in four overall acts: Original Instructions, narrative transformation, ceremony and spirituality, and relational restoration. In doing so, they created a shield of thrivance that guided their balance and health.

Though this study was limited by a smaller participant pool, this is one of the first studies to focus on two-spirit women's thrivance and healthy coping strategies. Like Apanukfila, the women in this study moved from a state of trauma to collective strength of helping self, others, and ancestors, both past and future.

References

Ballinger, F. (2000). Coyote, He/she was going there: Sex and gender in Native American trickster stories. *Studies in American Indian Literatures, 12*(4), 15–43.

Balsam, K. F., Huang, B., Fieland, K. C., Simoni, J. M., & Walters, K. L. (2004). Culture, trauma, and wellness: A comparison of heterosexual and lesbian, gay, bisexual, and two-spirit Native Americans. *Cultural Diversity and Ethnic Minority Psychology, 10*(3), 287–301. doi.org/10.1037/1099-9809.10.3.287

Bishop, R. (2005). Freeing ourselves from neocolonial domination in research: A Kaupapa Māori approach to creating knowledge. In N. K. Denzin & Y. S. Lincoln (Eds.), *The SAGE Handbook of Qualitative Research* (3) (pp. 109–138). Sage Publications.

Brayboy, B. M. J. (2005). Toward a tribal critical race theory in education. *The*

Urban Review, 37(5), 425–446. doi.org/10.1007/s11256-005-0018-y

Briggs-Cloud, M. (2010, December 26). Native languages, decolonization and social justice advocacy. *iNative*. inative.wordpress.com/author/fekecvte/

Cajete, G. (1999). Reflections on Indigenous ecology. *A people's ecology: Exploration in sustainable living*. Clear Light.

Cassels, S., Pearson, C. R., Walters, K. L., Simoni, J. M., & Morris, M. (2010). Sexual partner concurrency and sexual risk among gay, lesbian, bisexual, and transgender American Indian/Alaska Natives. *Sexually Transmitted Diseases, 37*(4), 272–278. doi.org/10.1097/OLQ.0b013e3181c37e3e

Chae, D., & Walters, K. L. (2009). Racial discrimination and racial identity attitudes in relation to self-rated health and physical pain and impairment among Two-Spirit American Indians/Alaska Natives. *American Journal of Public Health,* 99 (s1), s144–s151. doi.org/10.2105/AJPH.2007.126003

Compton, E. L. (2004). *An exploratory analysis of personal naming practices of Western North American Indians*. West Virginia University.

Dill, E. J., Manson, S. M., Jiang, L., Pratte, K. A., Gutilla, M. J., Knepper, S. L., Beals, J., Roubideaux, Y., & Special Diabetes Program for Indians Diabetes Prevention Demonstration Project. (2016). Psychosocial predictors of weight loss among American Indian and Alaska Native participants in a diabetes prevention translational project. *Journal of Diabetes Research,* 1546939. doi.org/10.1155/2016/1546939

Elm, J. H. L., Lewis, J. P., Walters, K. L., & Self, J. (2016). 'I'm in this world for a reason': Resilience and recovery among American Indian and Alaska Native two spirit women. *Journal of Lesbian Studies, 20*(3–4), 352–371. doi.org/1080/10894160.2016.1152813

Exner, F. K. (2006). *The impact of naming practices among North American Indians on name authority control* [Doctoral dissertation, University of Pretoria].

Evans-Campbell, T., Walters, K. L., Pearson, C. R., & Campbell, C. D. (2012). Indian boarding school experience, substance use, and mental health among urban two-spirit American Indian/Alaska Natives. *American Journal of Drug and Alcohol Abuse, 38*(5), 421–427. doi.org/10.3109/00952990.2012.701358.

Evans-Campbell, T., Fredriksen-Goldsen, K., Stately, A., & Walters, K. L. (2007). Caregiving experiences among American Indian Two-Spirit men and women: Contemporary and historical roles. *Journal of Gay and Lesbian Social Services, 18*(3–4), 75–92. doi.org/10.1300/J041v18n03_05

Fieland, K. C., Walters, K. L., & Simoni, J. M. (2007). Determinants of health among two-spirit American Indians and Alaska Natives. In I. H. Meyer and M. E. Northridge (Eds.), *The health of sexual minorities: Public health perspectives on lesbian, gay, bisexual, and transgender populations* (pp. 268–300). Springer / Kluwer Academic Publishers.

Garroutte, E. M., Goldberg, J., Beals, J., Herrell, R., Manson, S. M., & AI-SUPERPFP Team. (2003). Spirituality and attempted suicide among American Indians. *Social Science & Medicine, 56*(7), 1571–1579. doi.org/10.1016/s0277-9536(02)00157-0

Gilley, B. J. (2006). *Becoming two-spirit: Gay identity and social acceptance in Indian country*. University of Nebraska Press.

Gilligan, C., Spencer, R., Weinberg, M. K., & Bertsch, T. (2003). On the listening guide: A voice-centered relational method. In P. M. Camic, J. E. Rhodes, & L. Yardley (Eds.), *Qualitative research in psychology: Expanding perspectives in methodology and design* (pp. 157–172). American Psychological Association. doi.org/10.1037/10595-009

Hill, D. L. (2006). Sense of belonging as connectedness, American Indian worldview, and mental health. *Archives of Psychiatric Nursing, 20*(5), 210–216. doi.org/10.1016/j.apnu.2006.04.003

Huber, L.P. (2009). Disrupting apartheid of knowledge: Testimonio as methodology in Latina/o critical race research in education. *International Journal of Qualitative Studies in Education, 22*(6), 639–654. doi.org/10.1080/09518390903333863

Jennings, D., Little, M. M., & Johnson-Jennings, M. (2018). Developing a tribal health sovereignty model for obesity prevention. *Progress in Community Health Partnerships: Research, Education, and Action, 12*(3), 353–362. doi.org/10.1353/cpr.2018.0059

Jennings, D., Johnson-Jennings, M., Sanders, R., & Porter, L. (2021). (Under Review). Storytelling of Indigenous patient and family advocates engaged in a patient-oriented research initiative in the field of inflammatory bowel disease.

Johnson-Jennings, M., Belcourt, A., Town, M., Walls, M. L., & Walters, K. L. (2014). Racial discrimination's influence on smoking rates among American Indian Alaska Native two-spirit individuals: Does pain play a role? *Journal of Health Care for the Poor and Underserved, 25*(4), 1667–1678. doi.org/10.1353/hpu.2014.0193.

Johnson-Jennings, M., Billiot, S., Walters, K. L. (2020). Returning to our roots: Tribal health and wellness through land-based healing. *Geneaology, 4*(3), 91. doi.org/10.3390/genealogy4030091

Johnson-Jennings, M., Walters, K., & Little, M. (2018). And [they] even followed her into the hospital: Primary care providers' attitudes toward referral for traditional healing practices and integrating care for Indigenous patients. *Journal of Transcultural Nursing, 29*(4), 354–362. doi.org/10.1177/1043659617731817

Lang, S. (2016). Native American men-women, lesbians, two-spirits: Contemporary and historical perspectives. *Journal of Lesbian Studies, 20*(3–4), 299–323. doi.org/10.1080/10894160.2016.1148966.

Lehavot, K., Walters, K. L., & Simoni, J. M. (2009). Abuse, mastery, and health among lesbian, bisexual, and two-spirit American Indian and Alaska Native women. *Cultural Diversity and Ethnic Minority Psychology, 15*(3), 275–284. doi.org/10.1037/a0013458

McMahon, E. M., & Rogers, K. L. (2013). *Interactive oral history interviewing*. Routledge.

Nelson, K. M., Simoni, J. M., Pearson, C. R., & Walters, K. L. (2011). 'I've had unsafe sex so many times why bother being safe now?': The role of cognitions in sexual risk among American Indian/Alaska Native men who have sex with men. *Annals of Behavioral Medicine*, 42(3), 370–380. doi.org/10.1007/s12160-011-9302-0

Pantalone, D. W., Lehavot, K., Simoni, J. M., & Walters, K. L. (2011). I ain't never been a kid: Early violence exposure and other pathways to partner violence among sexual minority men with HIV. In J. L. Ristock (Ed.), *Intimate partner violence in LGBTQ lives* (pp. 182–206). Routledge.

Parker, M., Duran, B., & Walters, K. (2017). The relationship between bias-related victimization and general anxiety disorder among American Indian and Alaska Native lesbian, gay, bisexual, transgender, two-spirit community members. *International Journal of Indigenous Health*, 12(2), 64–83. doi.org/10.18357/ijih122201717785

Pearson, C. R., Walters, K. L., Simoni, J. M., Beltrán, R., & Nelson, K. M. (2013). A cautionary tale: Risk reduction strategies among urban American Indian/Alaska native men who have sex with men. *AIDS Education and Prevention*, 25(1), 25–37. doi.org/10.1521/aeap.2013.25.1.25

Petrovic, S., Lordly, D., Brigham, S., & Delaney, M. (2015). Learning to listen: An analysis of applying the Listening Guide to reflection papers. *International Journal of Qualitative Methods*, 14(5). doi.org/10.1177/1609406915621402

Roberts, R. L., Harper, R., Tuttle-Eagle Bull, D., & Heideman-Provost, L. (1998). The Native American medicine wheel and individual psychology: Common themes. *Journal of Individual Psychology*, 54(1), 135–45.

Roscoe, W. (1988). *Living the spirit: A gay American Indian anthology*. St. Martin's Press.

Simoni, J. M., Walters, K. L., Balsam, K. F., & Meyers, S. (2006). Victimization, substance use, and HIV risk behaviors among gay/bisexual/two-spirit vs. heterosexual American Indian men in New York City. *American Journal of Public Health*, 96(12), 2240–5. doi.org/10.2105/AJPH.2004.054056

Smith, L. T. (2005). On tricky ground: Researching the Native in the age of uncertainty. In N. K. Denzin & Y. S. Lincoln (Eds.), *The SAGE Handbook of Qualitative Research* (3) (pp. 85–107). Sage Publications.

Steinman, E. W. (2016). Decolonization not inclusion: Indigenous resistance to settler colonialism. *Indigenous Sociologies*, 2(2), 219–236. doi.org/10.1177/2332649215615889

Struthers, R., Eschiti, V. S., & Patchell, B. (2004). Traditional Indigenous healing: Part I. *Complementary therapies in Nursing and Midwifery*, 10(3), 141–149. doi.org/10.1016/j.ctnm.2004.05.001

Town, M. A., Walters, K. L., & Orellana, E. R. (2018). Discriminatory distress, HIV risk behavior, and community participation among American Indian/Alaska Native men who have sex with men. *Ethnicity and Health*, 26(5), 646–658. doi.org/10.1080/13557858.2018.1557115

Tuck, E., & Yang, K. W. (2012). Decolonization is not a metaphor. *Decolonization: Indigeneity, Education, and Society*, 1(1), 1–40.

Walters, K. (2010). *Critical issues and LGBT-two spirit populations: Highlights from the HONOR Project Study*. Indigenous Wellness Research Institute, University of Washington. qiclgbtq2s.org/critical-issues-and-lgbt-two-spirit-populations-highlights-from-the-honor-project-study/

Walters, K. L., Johnson-Jennings, M., Stroud, S. Rasmus, S., Charles, B., John, S., Allen, J., Koholokula, J. K., Look, M. A., de Silva, M., Lowe, J., Baldwin, J. A., Lawrence, G., Brooks, J., Noonan, C. W., Belcourt, A., Quintana, E., Semmens, E. O., Boulafentis, J. (2020). Growing from our roots: Strategies for developing culturally grounded health promotion interventions in American Indian, Alaska Native, and Native Hawaiian communities. *Prevention Science*, *21*(Suppl 1), 54–64.

Walters, K. L., Casey, C. M., Evans-Campbell, T., Valdez, R. B., & Zambrana, R. E. (2019). 'Before they kill my spirit entirely': Insights into the lived experiences of American Indian Alaska Native faculty at research universities, *Race Ethnicity and Education*, *22*(5), 610–633. doi.org/10.1080/13613324.2019.1579182

Walters, K. L., Mohammed, S. A., Evans-Campbell, T., Beltrán, R. E., Chae, D. H., & Duran, B. (2011). Bodies don't just tell stories, they tell histories: Embodiment of historical trauma among American Indians and Alaska Natives. *Dubois Review*, *8*(1): 179–189.

Walters, K. L, Beltrán, R., Huh, D., & Evans-Campbell, T. (2011). Dis-placement and dis-ease: Land, place, and health among American Indians and Alaska Natives. In L. M. Burton, S. P. Kemp, M. Leung, S. A. Matthews, & D. T. Takeuchi (Eds.), *Communities, neighborhoods, and health: Expanding the boundaries of place* (pp. 163–199). Springer. doi.org/10.1007/978-1-4419-7482-2_10

Walters, K. L., Chae, D. H., Perry, A. T., Stately, A., Old Person, R., & Simoni, J. M. (2008). 'My body and my spirit took care of me': Homelessness, violence, and resilience among American Indian two-spirit men. In S. Loue (Ed.), *Health issues confronting minority men who have sex with men* (pp. 125–156). Springer.

Walters, K. L., Evans-Campbell, T., Simoni, J. M., Ronquillo, T., & Bhuyan, R. (2006). 'My spirit in my heart': Identity experiences and challenges among two-spirit American Indian women. *Journal of Lesbian Studies*, *10*(1–2), 125–49.

Walters, K. L., Simoni, J. M., Evans-Campbell, T. A. (2002). Substance use among American Indians and Alaska Natives: Incorporating culture in an 'indigenist' stress-coping paradigm. *Public Health Reports*, *117*(Suppl. 1), S104–S117.

Walters, K. L., Simoni, J. M., & Horwath, P. F. (2001). Sexual orientation bias experiences and service needs of gay, lesbian, bisexual, transgender, and two-spirited American Indians. *Journal of Gay and Lesbian Social Services*, *13*, 133–149. doi.org/10.1300/J041v13n01_10

Wilson, A. (1996). How we find ourselves: Identity development and two-spirit people. *Harvard Educational Review*, 66(2), 303–318.

Yuan, N. P, Duran, B., Walters, K. L., Pearson, C., & Evans-Campbell, T. (2014). Alcohol misuse and associations with childhood maltreatment and out-of-home placement among urban Two-Spirit American Indian and Alaska Native People. *International Journal of Environmental Research and Public Health*, *11*(10), 10461–10479. doi.org/10.3390/ijerph11101046

13

Does Pain Play a Role?: The Influence of Racial Discrimination on Smoking Rates Two-Spirit Indigenous Persons

Michelle Johnson-Jennings, A. Belcourt, M. Town, Melissa Walls and Karina Walters

Introduction

In the United States, tobacco smoking remains 'the single most preventable cause of disease, disability, and death' (National Center for Chronic Disease Prevention and Health Promotion, 2010). Little research exists on smoking rates among American Indians/Alaska Natives (AIANs) despite AIANs having the highest rate of active smokers (31.5%) compared with all other US racial/ethnic groups (19.0%) (CDC, 2011). These rates are alarming, given that tobacco smoking was identified as a causal factor for 30% of all US cancer deaths and 80% of cardiovascular-related deaths during 2000–2004 (Adhikari et al., 2008). The fact that most AIAN deaths are attributable to cancer and cardiovascular diseases (National Center for Health Statistics, 2013) underscores the urgency of developing effective smoking prevention and intervention programmes. However, psychological factors such as chronic stress can be a barrier to the prevention and cessation of tobacco smoking (Slopen et al., 2012). When individuals from non-AIAN populations experience racial discrimination, psychological stress has been found to increase (Williams et al., 2008). Racial discrimination has been seen to increase smoking rates by nearly two-fold (Jamieson et al.,

2013; Purnell et al., 2012; Nakajima & al'Absi, 2011; Bennett et al., 2005). Given that racial discrimination is significantly higher for AIANs than for other US racial/ethnic groups (Les Whitbeck et al., 2004; Johansson et al., 2006), this may explain why their smoking rates are increasing rather than declining, as seen among other US racial/ethnic groups (Adhikari et al., 2008; King et al., 2011).

The discrimination that AIANs experience may vary inter-tribally based on sexual orientation and/or gender group status. Until colonisation, most if not all tribes valued and respected diverse AIAN sexual and gender expression (including lesbian, gay, bisexual, transgender/LGBTQI+ as well as heterosexual), with some tribes acknowledging three or more genders (Lang, 1998). However, after colonisation and within the US majority context, AIAN LGBTQI+ groups have faced ongoing violence, marginalisation and discrimination (King et al., 2011). Researchers, tribal community members and AIAN individuals commonly refer to AIAN LGBTQI+ persons as 'two-spirit', underlining the balance, or bridge, between male and female spirits and recognising the multiple sexual and gender roles that exist among tribes (Walters et al., 2006; Walters et al., 2008; Chae & Walters, 2009). Though not all AIAN LGBTQI+ individuals identify as two-spirit, this term will be used herein as a placeholder to reflect the Indigenous belief that AIAN cultural, sexual, and gender identity are inherently inseparable (Wilson, 1996; Gilley, 2006). Given this, two-spirit populations may have increased risks for non-ceremonial smoking that have not been previously explored among LGBTQI+ or aggregated AIAN populations (Walters et al., 2006).

Specific smoking risks among two-spirit people

Two-spirit individuals may encounter increased racial discrimination and smoking risks associated with their racial/ethnic and sexual orientation, as well as gender identity. Typically, researchers have targeted one sociodemographic variable at a time (such as those differing by gender, race, ethnicity, age) for smoking intervention, prevention, and cessation campaigns (Fu et al., 2008). While these campaigns may address racial discrimination stressors for AIANs or homophobia discrimination stressors for LGBTQI+ persons, these campaigns may fail to reach two-spirit populations, who experience racism in LGBTQI+ communities and increased homophobia in mainstream culture (Walters et al., 2008; Balsam et al., 2004; Walters, 1997). It has been argued that, for two-spirit people, the effects of racism and homophobia are inseparable (Walters et al., 2006; Chae & Walters, 2009). Hence, two-spirits' experience of racial discrimination and the resultant smoking risk may vary from other AIANs based on their tribal and sexual orientation and gender identities.

Firstly, as tribal members, two-spirit persons may experience disproportionate rates of smoking in relationship to their tribal community norms. For instance, some tribal communities endorse low-harm risk perceptions and lenient attitudes towards smoking, which may influence their increased smoking rates (Hodge & Struthers, 2006). Furthermore, two-spirits' tribal communities are more likely to be targeted by tobacco company advertisements. Tobacco companies have been seen to intentionally target AIAN cultural activities and provide monetary support of pow-wows and other tribal gatherings (Surgeon General, 1998), thereby potentially increasing tribal allegiance and subsequent individual use. Moreover, many tribal communities use tobacco for ceremonial and religious purposes. However, tribal communities often differentiate between everyday use and ceremonial use, and most communities discourage abuse (Struthers & Hodge, 2004; Nadeau et al., 2012). Therefore, this study's use of the term *smoking* will refer to non-ceremonial tobacco smoking and to a form of tobacco abuse. Depending on the tribal community and individual views, two-spirit individuals may or may not view smoking as abuse. Thus, complex AIAN group-related factors may influence two-spirits' use of tobacco and should be considered during research.

Secondly, two-spirit persons' sexual orientation/gender identity may contribute to an increased smoking risk. In the US, LGBTQI+ groups have higher smoking rates than non-LGBTQI+ groups (Case et al., 2004; Greenwood et al., 2005; Tang et al., 2004). A recent review found anywhere between 11% and 50% of LGBTQI+ adults smoke (Ryan et al., 2001). These high rates may be associated with tobacco industry advertisements that specifically target LGBTQI+ populations (Sell & Dunn, 2008), like their targeting of AIAN communities. In addition, the prevalence of smoking in LGBTQI+ groups may include health risks of marginalisation, fear of violence, reduced social support, internalised homophobia, and discrimination (Sell & Dunn, 2008). Furthermore, several demographic factors among LGBTQI+ groups have been associated with high smoking rates, such as one's HIV/AIDS status and education level. HIV/AIDS positive status, as opposed to a negative status, has been correlated with higher smoking risk (Rahmanian et al., 2011; Berg et al., 2014). Two-spirit populations have a much higher prevalence of HIV than non-Native populations, on par with rates found in sub-Saharan Africa; the percentage was highest for two-spirit men who had sex only with men (36%), followed by men who had sex with men and women (19%), two-spirit women who had sex with men (15%), and two-spirit women who had sex only with women (2%) (Cassels et al., 2010). Higher levels of education have also been seen to increase the risk of smoking among LGBTQI+ groups, contrary to non-LGBTQI+ groups (Ryan et al., 2001). Two-spirits may experience all of these LGBTQI+ related risk factors, as well as risks related to the effects of AIAN intergenerational trauma (Walters et al., 2008; Balsam et al., 2004; Walters et al., 2013). Through understanding the complex relationship between LGBTQI+ and AIAN smoking risk, effective smoking interventions may be developed for two-spirit populations.

Racial discrimination and pain

Two-spirit individuals who have experienced high rates of racial discrimination also reported increased physical pain and related impairment (Chae & Walters, 2009). One explanation may be that the stress from racial discrimination directly increases sensitivity to pain, as we have seen in other studies on stress and pain (Buchwald et al., 2005; Hassett & Clauw, 2011; Anderberg, 1999). Furthermore, pain has been associated with chronic smoking and smoking cessation relapse (Nakajima & al'Absi, 2011). Hence, two-spirit people who experience racial discrimination without pain may have lower smoking risks than those who experience racial discrimination with accompanying levels of pain. These cumulative risks highlight the need to investigate whether racial discrimination influences smoking rates within two-spirit populations.

This study sought to determine whether pain mediates the association between discrimination and current smoking status among two-spirit individuals. We selected self-reported pain, due to supporting evidence that racial discrimination is associated with high self-reported pain levels (Cassels et al., 2010). We further expanded the definition of 'pain' to include pain-related impairment, as a way to reduce self-report bias, modelling this on Chae & Walters (2009). This information may be applicable to other vulnerable populations who face high rates of racial discrimination and increased risk of smoking.

Methods

This study involved a secondary analysis of data from the HONOR Project (R01MH65871), a multi-site cross-sectional national survey of lesbian, gay, bisexual, transgender, trans* and two-spirit (LGBTQI+, T-S) American Indians/Native Americans (AIAN; as previously described by Chae and Walters (2009)). Local recruitment and interviewing were conducted at community-based cultural and social centres serving the AIAN communities.

Participants

From July 2005 to March 2007, we used a combination of targeted, partial networks and respondent-driven sampling techniques designed to maximise coverage of the heterogeneity of the population and to minimise selection bias. AIAN adults who identified as being enrolled in a tribe and as gay, lesbian, bisexual, transgender, trans* and/or two-spirit, or engaged in same-sex behaviour over the previous 12 months, were recruited from seven metropolitan areas across the US (Seattle-Tacoma, San Francisco-Oakland, Los Angeles, Denver, Tulsa – Oklahoma, Minneapolis-St.Paul, and New York City). The HONOR Project achieved a total response rate of 80.1% and there were no significant differences between respondent-driven sampling (seeds and nominees) and volunteer respondents by city or on key sociodemographic variables (i.e., gender, education, employment, income, or housing) that might reflect regional or sampling differences. Specifics regarding the recruitment and study procedures have been detailed elsewhere (Walters et al., 2006; Chae & Walters, 2009). A total of 447 AIAN participants completed a computer-assisted three- to four-hour interview and were compensated $65 for their time and effort.

Measures

Our dependent variable, smoking, was measured by participants' self-reported non-ceremonial use of tobacco. Those who indicated smoking at least daily during the previous 12 months = 1, and all others = 0. 'Pain' was measured as both 'subjective bodily pain' and 'pain-related impairment' via two items that asked for a) subjective ratings of bodily pain in the previous 4 weeks and b) the level of interference with work inside or outside of the home. Those who reported pain that interfered with work = 1, all others = 0. Self-reported stress due to experienced racial discrimination, including episodes of physical and verbal violence and harassment or mistreatment, was assessed as the mean of responses to 33 items from the Microaggressions Distress Scale developed by Walters (2002), whereby 0 indicates 'not at all' and 5 indicates 'extreme'.

Control variables

Sociodemographic variables and those that might influence smoking were controlled. These variables included: self-reported age and, as aforementioned due to the possible influence on smoking, HIV status (positive = 0, all else = 1). Health insurance status was controlled, as were sexual orientation (0 = gay/lesbian; 1 = bisexual; 2 = two-spirit; 3 = heterosexual, i.e., who self-identified as heterosexual but also may have same-sex sexual relationships; 4 = other), and gender.

Descriptive results

Participants within this sample identified as gay/lesbian (n = 202), bisexual (n = 129), two-spirit (n = 70), heterosexual (n = 29), and other (n = 15). Nearly half (45%) of the study sample reported smoking daily or more during the past 12 months, and 57% said they had experienced pain. The average age of participants was 39.8 years. The mean score for the racial discrimination measure was 1.5 (SD = 1.1). Table 1 displays bivariate associations among all study variables. Racial discrimination and pain were both positively and significantly associated with past year daily smoking. Sexual orientation and reports of pain were both positively associated with racial discrimination, while education and age were negatively associated with racial discrimination.

Mediation / regression analyses

We followed Baron and Kenny's suggested steps for testing mediation by running a series of multivariate regression models among a set of three variables: x, y, and m (see Baron & Kenny, 1986; Judd & Kenny, 1981; James & Brett, 1984), where x = racial discrimination (independent variable), y = smoking (outcome), and m = pain (the proposed mediator).

Firstly, we tested associations between x and y, net the control variables (Table 2, Step 1). We found that racial discrimination was significantly associated with smoking. Secondly, we ran a regression to determine whether x was associated with the mediator, m (Table 2, Step 2). Results revealed that discrimination was indeed significantly related to pain, even after accounting for several control variables. Finally, we investigated a model (Table 2, Step 3) in which both x and m are regressed on the outcome, y. After including pain in the model, the odds ratio for the relationship between discrimination and pain was reduced from 1.48 to 1.21 and dropped from statistical significance. Those reporting pain were

78% more likely to report smoking daily or more, even after accounting for all control variables and discrimination. Sobel test (1982) results (2.12, SE = .11; p < .05) indicated that this mediating effect was statistically significant.

Table 1: Descriptive statistics and bivariate associations for AIAN two-spirit population from the HONOR Project

	1	2	3	4	5	6	7	8
1. Daily smoking (past year)	1							
2. Racial discrimination	.10*	1						
3. Pain / impairment	.14**	.15**	1					
4. Insurance status	.06	-.04	-.07	1				
5. Education	-.17***	.17**	-.14**	-.24***	1			
6. Age	-.10*	-.03	.23***	-.16**	.14**	1		
7. HIV status (Positive = 1)	-.04	-.19**	.06	-.09	-.10*	.13**	1	
8. Sexual/gender orientation	.02	.15**	.16**	.11*	-.13**	.06	-.04	1
% / mean (s.e.)	45.2%	1.5 (1.1)	57%	2.5 (1.0)	2.5 (1.0)	39.8 (10.8)	21.5%	.93 (1.1)

* p< .05, ** p< .01, *** p < .001

Descriptive statistics

	N	Min	Max	Mean	Std. Deviation			
Smoke daily or more last year	424	0	1	.45	0.5			
Racial discrimination	444	0	4	1.5	1.1			
Pain and related impairment	447	0	1	0.6	0.5			
Education	447	1	4	2.5	1.0			
HIV positive, all else 0	446	0	1	0.2	0.4			
Age	443	18	67	39.79	10.76			
Sexual/gender orientation	445	0	4	.93	1.08			
Insurance	447	1	4	2.53	1.03			
Valid N (list wise)	416							
% / mean (s.e.)	45.2%	1.5(1.1)	57%	2.5(1.0)	2.5(1.0)	39.8 (10.8)	21.5%	.93 (1.1)

Table 2: Test of mediating effects of pain-related impairment on the association between discrimination and smoking for AIAN two-spirit population from the HONOR Project

	Model A (Step 1)		Model B (Step 2)		Model C (Step 3)	
	Smoking		Pain-related impairment		Smoking	
Outcome variable	b(SE)	exp(b)	b(SE)	exp(b)	b(SE)	exp(b)
Education	-.42(.11)	0.66***	-.47(.12)	0.63***	-.36(.11)	0.70**
HIV status (Positive = 1)	-.23(.26)	0.80	0.24(.26)	1.27	-.26(.26)	0.78
Age	-.01(.01)	0.99	0.05(.01)	1.05***	-.02(.01)	0.98
Sexual/gender orientation	-.07(.11)	0.93	0.27(.11)	1.31*	-.10(.11)	0.90
Insurance status	0.002(.10)	1.00	-.21(.11)	0.81*	-.03(.11)	1.03
Discrimination	0.24(.10)	1.27*	0.40(.11)	1.48***	.19(.10)	1.21
Pain and related impairment					.58(.22)	1.78**

* $p<0.05$, ** $p<0.01$, *** $p<0.001$

Table 3: Cross tabulation of self-reported sexual orientation by pain-related impairment for AIAN two-spirit individuals from the HONOR Project

	Orientation				
	Gay / Lesbian	Bisexual	Two-spirit	Heterosexual	Other
% Reporting Pain-Related Impairment	49%	59.7%	60%	82.8%	80%

$x2 = 16.994$, $df = 4$, $p = .002$

Discussion

Our study among urban two-spirit individuals illustrates the significant impact of racial discrimination on health behaviours, particularly health risk behaviours such as smoking, and mediating factors such as self-reported pain. From 2005 to 2007, we found that daily smoking rates for two-spirits (45.2%) were higher than US AIAN smoking rates (up to 36.4%). Furthermore, most of the two-spirit people sampled suffered from pain (57%). These findings are supported by a recent literature review indicating that AIAN consistently report higher pain levels than other racial/ethnic groups (Jimenez et al., 2011). As hypothesised, racial discrimination and smoking were correlated among two-spirit people. Specifically, two-spirit people who experienced racial discrimination appeared more likely to smoke. Our results further indicated that those individuals experiencing racial discrimination *and* pain were more likely to have increased smoking rates versus those who reported no pain. Overall, our findings indicate that racial discrimination, and resulting stress, likely increases the risk of pain and subsequently smoking.

An unexpected finding within the two-spirit sample was that pain varied significantly with sexual orientation and gender. While self-identifying gay and lesbian AIAN individuals had the lowest pain impairment rates, self-identified heterosexual (i.e., those in Table 3 who identified as heterosexual but also engaged in same gender sexual activity) and self-identified other AIAN groups had the highest pain impairment rates. Those self-identifying as either bisexual, two-spirit or transgender reported mid-level pain. Racial discrimination did not appear correlated with sexual orientation. One explanation may relate to significant experiential differences between these subgroups, where two-spirits who identify as heterosexual may experience greater levels of social or cultural distress, given the greater latitude between sexual identity and behavioural sexual expression (i.e., internalised heterosexism or lateral oppression from LGBTQI+ groups for heterosexual identity). Disaggregated two-spirit groups' experiences of marginalisation and coping may result in differences in stress, which may influence health behaviours for pain and smoking. Recent literature has also identified gender-specific risks for increased pain experiences and addiction; for instance, emotional distress and trauma for men was a higher risk than for women (Spertus et al., 1999). More research is needed in this area.

Several implications arose regarding smoking among two-spirit people. First given that racial discrimination has been found to increase pain among two-spirit people (Chae & Walters, 2009), smoking and stress have been associated with smoking cessation relapse and increased sensitivity to pain (Nakajima & al'Absi, 2011). Therefore, if pain increases smoking and smoking increases pain, this cyclical effect may result in higher smoking risks and lower likelihood of smoking cessation (Figure 1). Secondly, our findings indicate a need for tobacco cessation interventions to be culturally tailored and directed towards two-spirit populations. The promotion of effective tobacco cessation and interventions should consider this complexity, especially given the unique risk aetiology between racial discrimination and smoking, as mediated by pain. There is also a need to systematically examine the risk factors within frameworks that dually consider marginalisation status of two-spirit people and the biology of inequality. Consideration of the intersectionality of identities may assist in future research among two-spirit populations (Chae & Walters, 2009).

Finally, the Indigenist stress coping model (Hassett & Clauw, 2011) shifts the focus from individual risks to the influences of historical trauma (Walters et al., 2013; Brave Heart, 2003; Evans-Campbell et al., 2012) and ongoing oppression on a population. Our findings suggest that two-spirit populations have higher smoking risks within a context of historical trauma that cannot be ignored. Their self-reported pain could further be considered the embodiment of distress resulting from discrimination (Walters et al., 2013; Chae & Walters, 2009) and thus the potential mediator between racial discrimination and health-risk behaviours. Studying the embodiment of discrimination distress as manifested through self-reported pain will allow us to determine the driving forces for smoking behaviours and patterns among AIANs (Walters et al., 2013; Krieger, 1999). Such research may yield important directions for developing culturally relevant smoking policies and prevention practices to reduce AIAN smoking disparities and improve AIAN health.

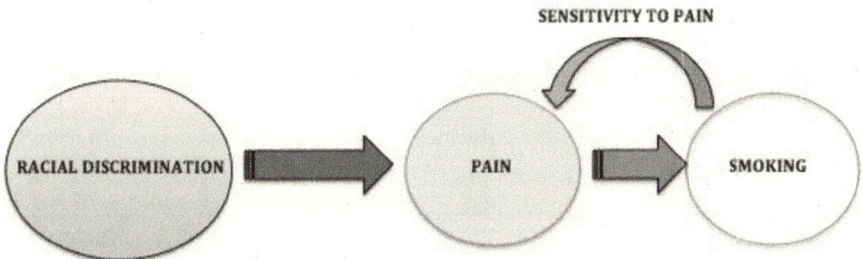

Figure 1: The complex relationship between racial discrimination and smoking as mediated by pain among an AIAN two-spirit group from the HONOR Project

There are several caveats to this study. First, only aggregated data for urban two-spirit people were analysed, which limits generalisation to rural and specific tribal groups that may differ by specific tribal affiliations. Furthermore, as noted by Chae and Walters (2009), we cannot infer causality from pain and smoking, as there may be unmeasured latent constructs at work (such as social support) that were beyond the scope of this paper. For instance, other studies have found that dynamic, culturally supportive behaviours are associated with lower substance use than those receiving less support among AIAN groups (Baldwin et al., 2011). Therefore, the influence of cultural affiliation and social support on two-spirits' smoking should be considered for future research. Nonetheless, this is the first known study to indicate that racial discrimination, as mediated by pain, increases the likelihood of non-ceremonial smoking for AIANs.

In conclusion, the Indigenist stress coping model and resulting approach outlined in this study allows for a rational way of merging social, cultural and biological experiences in order to understand how racial discrimination continues to be a determinant of health and health behaviours. The intersections of cultural, social and biological experiences form a complex arena for population patterns of health, disease and well-being among two-spirit populations. Pain continues to be a significant factor, and one that may embody the stress of discrimination, requiring culturally appropriate consideration in treatment and/or prevention planning. Interventions that are tailored for only race, sexual orientation or gender may not effectively reduce smoking among this population.

Acknowledgments

This project as supported by the National Institute of Health, National Institute of Mental Health, Indigenous HIV/AIDS Research Training (5R25MH084565-03) and the National Institute on Minority Health and Health Disparities (5P60MD006909). The data was provided from the HONOR Project Study as funded by the National Institute of Mental Health (R01MH65871).

This essay was originally published in 2014 as 'Racial discrimination's influence on smoking rates among American Indian Alaska Native two-spirit individuals: Does pain play a role?', *Journal of Health Care for the Poor and Underserved*, 25(4), 1667–78. doi.org/10.1353/hpu.2014.0193. Reproduced with kind permission.

References

Anderberg, U. M. (1999). Stress kan ge neuroendokrina störningar och smärttillstånd [Stress can induce neuroendocrine disorders and pain]. *Lakartidningen*, *96*(49), 5497–5499.

Baldwin, J. A., Brown, B. G., Wayment, H. A., Nez, R. A., & Brelsford, K. M. (2011). Culture and context: buffering the relationship between stressful life events and risky behaviors in American Indian youth. *Substance Use & Misuse*, *46*(11), 1380–1394. doi.org/10.3109/10826084.2011.592432

Balsam, K. F., Huang, B., Fieland, K. C., Simoni, J. M., & Walters, K. L. (2004). Culture, trauma, and wellness: a comparison of heterosexual and lesbian, gay, bisexual, and two-spirit native Americans. *Cultural Diversity & Ethnic Minority Psychology*, *10*(3), 287–301. doi.org/10.1037/1099-9809.10.3.287

Bennett, G. G., Wolin, K. Y., Robinson, E. L., Fowler, S., & Edwards, C. L. (2005). Perceived racial/ethnic harassment and tobacco use among African American young adults. *American Journal of Public Health*, *95*(2), 238–240. doi.org/10.2105/AJPH.2004.037812

Berg, C. J., Nehl, E. J., Wang, X., Ding, Y., He, N., Johnson, B. A., & Wong, F. Y. (2014). Healthcare provider intervention on smoking and quit attempts among HIV-positive versus HIV-negative MSM smokers in Chengdu, China. *AIDS Care*, *26*(9), 1201–1207. doi.org/10.1080/09540121.2014.892565

Brave Heart, M. Y. (2003). The historical trauma response among natives and its relationship with substance abuse: A Lakota illustration. *Journal of Psychoactive Drugs*, *35*(1), 7–13. doi.org/10.1080/02791072.2003.10399988

Buchwald, D., Goldberg, J., Noonan, C., Beals, J., Manson, S., & AI-SUPERPFP Team. (2005). Relationship between post-traumatic stress disorder and pain in two American Indian tribes. *Pain Medicine*, *6*(1), 72–79. doi.org/10.1111/j.1526-4637.2005.05005.x

Case, P., Austin, S. B., Hunter, D. J., Manson, J. E., Malspeis, S., Willett, W. C., & Spiegelman, D. (2004). Sexual orientation, health risk factors, and physical functioning in the Nurses' Health Study II. *Journal of Women's Health*, *13*(9), 1033–1047. doi.org/10.1089/jwh.2004.13.1033

Cassels, S., Pearson, C. R., Walters, K., Simoni, J. M., & Morris, M. (2010). Sexual partner concurrency and sexual risk among gay, lesbian, bisexual, and transgender American Indian/Alaska natives. *Sexually Transmitted Diseases*, *37*(4), 272–278. doi.org/10.1097/OLQ.0b013e3181c37e3e

Centers for Disease Control and Prevention (CDC). (2008). Smoking-attributable mortality. Years of potential life lost, and productivity losses – United States, 2000–2004. *Morbidity and Mortality Weekly Report*, *57*(45), 1226–1228. pubmed.ncbi.nlm.nih.gov/19008791/

Centers for Disease Control and Prevention (CDC). (2011). Current cigarette smoking among adults. *Morbidity and Mortality Weekly Report 2012*, *61*(44), 889–894. cdc.gov/mmwr/preview/mmwrhtml/mm6144a2.htm

Chae, D. H., & Walters, K. L. (2009). Racial discrimination and racial identity attitudes in relation to self-rated health and physical pain and impairment among two-spirit American Indians/Alaska Natives. *American Journal of Public Health, 99*, S144–S151. doi.org/10.2105/AJPH.2007.126003

Evans-Campbell, T., Walters, K. L., Pearson, C. R., & Campbell, C. D. (2012). Indian boarding school experience, substance use, and mental health among urban two-spirit American Indian/Alaska natives. *The American Journal of Drug and Alcohol Abuse, 38*(5), 421–427. doi.org/10.3109/00952990.2012.7 01358

Fu, S. S., Burgess, D. J., Hatsukami, D. K., Noorbaloochi, S., Clothier, B. A., Nugent, S., & van Ryn, M. (2008). Race and nicotine replacement treatment outcomes among low-income smokers. *American Journal of Preventive Medicine, 35*(6), S442–S448. doi.org/10.1016/j.amepre.2008.09.009

Gilley, B. J. (2006). *Becoming two-spirit: Gay identity and social acceptance in Indian country.* University of Nebraska Press.

Greenwood, G. L., Paul, J. P., Pollack, L. M., Binson, D., Catania, J. A., Chang, J., Humfleet, G., & Stall, R. (2005). Tobacco use and cessation among a household-based sample of US urban men who have sex with men. *American Journal of Public Health, 95*(1), 145–151. doi.org/10.2105/AJPH.2003.021451

Hassett, A. L., & Clauw, D. J. (2011). Does psychological stress cause chronic pain? *The Psychiatric Clinics of North America, 34*(3), 579–594. doi.org/10.1016/j.psc.2011.05.004

Hodge, F. S., & Struthers, R. (2006). Persistent smoking among Northern Plains Indians: Lenient attitudes, low harm value, and partiality toward cigarette smoking. *Journal of Cultural Diversity, 13*(4), 181–185.

Jamieson, J. P., Koslov, K., Nock, M. K., & Mendes, W. B. (2013). Experiencing discrimination increases risk taking. *Psychological Science, 24*(2), 131–139. doi.org/10.1177/0956797612448194

Jimenez, N., Garroutte, E., Kundu, A., Morales, L., & Buchwald, D. (2011). A review of the experience, epidemiology, and management of pain among American Indian, Alaska Native, and Aboriginal Canadian peoples. *The Journal of Pain, 12*(5), 511–522. doi.org/10.1016/j.jpain.2010.12.002

Johansson, P., Jacobsen, C., & Buchwald, D. (2006). Perceived discrimination in health care among American Indians/Alaska natives. *Ethnicity & Disease, 16*(4), 766–771.

Krieger, N. (1999). Embodying inequality: A review of concepts, measures, and methods for studying health consequences of discrimination. *International Journal of Health Services: Planning, Administration, Evaluation, 29*(2), 295–352. doi.org/10.2190/M11W-VWXE-KQM9-G97Q

Lang S. (1998). *Men as women, women as men: Changing gender in Native American cultures.* University of Texas Press.

Les Whitbeck, B., Chen, X., Hoyt, D. R., & Adams, G. W. (2004). Discrimination, historical loss and enculturation: Culturally specific risk and resiliency factors for alcohol abuse among American Indians. *Journal of Studies on Alcohol, 65*(4), 409–418. doi.org/10.15288/jsa.2004.65.409

Nadeau, M., Blake, N., Poupart, J., Rhodes, K., & Forster, J. L. (2012). Circles of tobacco wisdom: Learning about traditional and commercial tobacco with Native elders. *American Journal of Preventive Medicine, 43*(5 Suppl 3), S222–S228. doi.org/10.1016/j.amepre.2012.08.003

Nakajima, M., & al'Absi, M. (2011). Enhanced pain perception prior to smoking cessation is associated with early relapse. *Biological Psychology, 88*(1), 141–146. doi.org/10.1016/j.biopsycho.2011.07.006

National Center for Chronic Disease Prevention and Health Promotion. (2010). *Tobacco use, targeting the nation's leading killer.* stacks.cdc.gov/view/cdc/5527

National Center for Health Statistics. (2013). *Health, United States, 2012, with special feature on emergency care.* pubmed.ncbi.nlm.nih.gov/23885363/

Purnell, J. Q., Peppone, L. J., Alcaraz, K., McQueen, A., Guido, J. J., Carroll, J. K., Shacham, E., & Morrow, G. R. (2012). Perceived discrimination, psychological distress, and current smoking status: Results from the behavioral risk factor surveillance system reactions to race module, 2004–2008. *American Journal of Public Health, 102*(5), 844–851. doi.org/10.2105/AJPH.2012.300694

Rahmanian, S., Wewers, M. E., Koletar, S., Reynolds, N., Ferketich, A., & Diaz, P. (2011). Cigarette smoking in the HIV-infected population. *Proceedings of the American Thoracic Society, 8*(3), 313–319. doi.org/10.1513/pats.201009-058WR

Ryan, H., Wortley, P. M., Easton, A., Pederson, L., & Greenwood, G. (2001). Smoking among lesbians, gays, and bisexuals: A review of the literature. *American Journal of Preventive Medicine, 21*(2), 142–149. doi.org/10.1016/s0749-3797(01)00331-2

Sell, R. L., & Dunn, P. M. (2008). Inclusion of lesbian, gay, bisexual and transgender people in tobacco use-related surveillance and epidemiological research. *Journal of LGBT Health Research, 4*(1), 27–42. doi.org/10.1080/15574090802615703

Slopen, N., Dutra L. M., Williams, D. R., Mujahid, M. S., Lewis, T. T., Bennett, G. G., Ryff, C. D., & Albert, M. A. (2012). Psychological stressors and cigarette smoking among African American adults in midlife. *Nicotine & Tobacco Research, 14*(10), 1161–1169. doi.org/10.1093/ntr/nts011

Spertus, I. L., Burns, J., Glenn, B., Lofland, K., & McCracken, L. (1999). Gender differences in associations between trauma history and adjustment among chronic pain patients. *Pain, 82*(1), 97–102. doi.org/10.1016/S0304-3959(99)00040-8

Struthers, R., & Hodge, F. S. (2004). Sacred tobacco use in Ojibwe communities. *Journal of Holistic Nursing: Official Journal of the American Holistic Nurses' Association, 22*(3), 209–225. doi.org/10.1177/0898010104266735

Surgeon General. (1998). Tobacco use among U.S. racial/ethnic minority groups – African Americans, American Indians and Alaska Natives, Asian Americans and Pacific Islanders, Hispanics. A report of the Surgeon General. Executive summary. *MMWR. Recommendations and reports: Morbidity and mortality weekly report. Recommendations and reports, 47*(RR-18), v–16.

Tang, H., Greenwood, G. L., Cowling, D. W., Lloyd, J. C., Roeseler, A. G., & Bal, D. G. (2004). Cigarette smoking among lesbians, gays, and bisexuals:

How serious a problem? (United States). *Cancer Causes & Control: CCC*, *15*(8), 797–803. doi.org/10.1023/B:CACO.0000043430.32410.69

Walters, K. L. (1997). Urban lesbian and gay American Indian identity. *Journal of Gay & Lesbian Social Service*, *6*(2), 43–65. doi.org/10.1300/J041v06n02_05

Walters, K. L., Evans-Campbell, T., Simoni, J. M., Ronquillo, T., & Bhuyan, R. (2006). 'My spirit in my heart': Identity experiences and challenges among American Indian two-spirit women. *Journal of Lesbian Studies*, *10*(1–2), 125–149. doi.org/10.1300/J155v10n01_07

Walters, K. L., Horwath, P., & Simoni, J. (2008). Sexual orientation bias experiences and service needs of gay, lesbian, bisexual, transgendered, and two-spirited American Indians. *Journal of Gay and Lesbian Social Services*, *13*(1–2), 133–149. doi.org/10.1300/J041v13n01_10

Walters, K. L., Mohammed, S. A., Evans-Campbell, T., Beltrán, R. E., Chae, D. H., & Duran, B. (2011). BODIES DON'T JUST TELL STORIES, THEY TELL HISTORIES: Embodiment of historical trauma among American Indians and Alaska Natives. *Du Bois Review: Social Science Research on Race*, *8*(1), 179–189. doi.org/10.1017/S1742058X1100018X

Walters, K. L., Simoni, J. M., & Evans-Campbell, T. (2002). Substance use among American Indians and Alaska natives: Incorporating culture in an 'indigenist' stress-coping paradigm. *Public Health Reports*, *117 Suppl 1*, S104–S117.

Williams, D. R., Neighbors, H. W., & Jackson, J. S. (2003). Racial/ethnic discrimination and health: Findings from community studies. *American Journal of Public Health*, *93*(2), 200–208. doi.org/10.2105/ajph.93.2.200

Wilson, A. (1996). How we find ourselves: Identity development and two-spirit people. *Harvard Educational Review*, *66*(2), 303–317. doi.org/10.17763/haer.66.2.n551658577h927h4

14

Body Sovereignty: A Collaborative Reflection on Two-Spirit Methodologies

Sarah Hunt, Sandy Lambert and Alex Wilson

Introductions and intentions

We write this article on two-spirit research methodologies[1] as three two-spirit identified people from diverse Indigenous nations. Sarah Hunt is a Kwagu'ł scholar, community activist and writer who has developed Indigenous methodologies over the past 15+ years in her work on issues of violence, justice, self-determination, and land- and water-based praxis. Sandy Lambert is a member of the Tall Cree Nation, with more than 15 years' experience working in Indigenous HIV/AIDS education, advocacy, research and community-building. Sandy lives and works on Musqueam, Tsleil-Wa-Tuth and Squamish territories (Vancouver, BC) and Sarah lives and works on Lekwungen and W̱SÁNEĆ territories (Victoria, BC). Alex Wilson (Opaskwayak Cree Nation) is a full professor and the academic director of the Aboriginal Education Research Centre at the University of Saskatchewan. Her first academic article published on the topic of two-spirit identity in 1996 and subsequent scholarship has greatly contributed to building and sharing knowledge about two-spirit identity, history and teachings, Indigenous research methodologies, and the prevention of violence in the lives of Indigenous peoples.

---

1   This paper is based on a presentation by Sandy Lambert and Sarah Hunt at the National Canadian Aboriginal AIDS Network (CAAN) Conference, July 2015, in the territories of the Musqueam, Tsleil-wa-tuth and Squamish peoples (Vancouver, BC) with attendees from across Turtle Island.

We begin by locating ourselves in this way in order to recognise that all knowledge is situated in our own experience, personal and familial histories, and scholarly and community training. The diversity of our knowledge, as two-spirit scholar-activists and community members, strengthened the writing of this paper. Just as 'two-spirit' has diverse meanings, reflecting the vibrant cultural, linguistic, and historic diversity of Indigenous peoples across North America, we aim for this paper to reflect the diversity of approaches and situated knowledges inherent in developing two-spirit methodologies across institutional and community contexts, particularly those focused on issues of health. Our work together conceptualising two-spirit methodologies was first initiated for a joint presentation at an international conference on HIV/AIDS, hosted by the Canadian Aboriginal AIDS Network (CAAN). From our diverse community and research perspectives, we approach health within a holistic framework that situates two-spirit health within broader social determinants.

What we mean by methodology: Thinking, action and practices

We understand research methodology to mean the thinking, action and practices that are related to a particular set of knowledges – in this case, two-spirit knowledges. In this paper we seek to develop guiding principles that can be used to frame how we interact with the world as we engage in two-spirit research methodologies. Indigenous methodologies tend to approach cultural protocols, values and behaviours as integral to methodology (Smith, 1999). Here, we see relationality, accountability, body sovereignty and gender self-determination as the central protocols, values and behaviours which comprise two-spirit methodologies. Body sovereignty and gender self-determination have been threads throughout our collective work on diverse issues related to health, anti-violence work and the revitalisation of Indigenous law at an intimate level, with Alex's work in this area spanning over a decade (for example see Wilson, 2015a, 2015b, 2016c; Hunt, 2015, 2016b). While relationality and accountability are shared among many Indigenous knowledge systems, body sovereignty and gender self-determination arise from the specific lived realities and historic position of two-spirit people. Indigenous sovereignty is often imagined in relation to territories or nations, but, alongside other feminist and two-spirit artists, activists and scholars, we understand sovereignty as extending outward from the body. The body is the site through which Indigenous people assert sovereignty over all aspects of our lived experience, including our intimate relationships and our sexual health. Relatedly, gender self-determination is an affirmation of our ability to name, reclaim and express our gender roles and identities on our own terms. Taken together, two-spirit methodologies situate individual bodies, and the relationship between bodies, land, water and ancestors, at the centre of Indigenous systems of knowledge.

In the second half of this essay, we share specific methods – tools to gain information (Smith, 1999) or practical ways of creating or gathering knowledge – which we have found useful when working with two-spirit people in health research, services and education. Moreover, we have focused on methods rooted in the methodological approaches outlined above, aimed at fostering cultural safety and wellness for two-spirit people. We will first discuss the diverse meanings of 'two-spirit' and the impact of colonisation on two-spirit ways of knowing and being.

Two-spirit: Reclamation and emergence

The term 'two-spirit' has a specific history, and its meaning has changed over time.[2] Its popular use originates at the 1990 North American gathering of Aboriginal gay and lesbian people in Winnipeg, Manitoba, where it was embraced due to the meaning, origin and cultural significance of the term as explained by a traditional Indigenous teacher. (For more on this history, see McLeod, 2003.) Today, there is great diversity in two-spirit identity, across generations and across culturally specific teachings and geography (urban/rural). As an umbrella term, 'two-spirit' is meant to include diverse Indigenous LGBTQI+ (lesbian, gay, bisexual, trans* and queer) identities, and an array of culturally specific gender and sexual identities that don't fit heteronormative models. Many Indigenous people are looking to their own cultural teachings or languages to better name their identities within a decolonial framework and, increasingly, these Indigenous terms are being used instead of, or in addition to, the term 'two-spirit'. Therefore, 'two-spirit' is itself a contested term. Today we are reclaiming our history: who two-spirit people are and who we were prior to colonisation. We were the leaders in some Indigenous communities – healers, cultural practitioners, knowledge keepers – while in other communities we were just ordinary people. In many places, we are now being accepted and regenerated again, both in building community as two-spirit people and in taking up our specific cultural roles within our Indigenous nations. It is with this intention

2   For a complete discussion of the genesis of the term and the two-spirit movement, please see Wilson, 1996; Tafoya 1999; Driskill 2011; and McLeod, 2003.

of two-spirit reclamation, celebration and revitalisation that we engage in our work, including the collaborative writing of this essay.

Understanding the impact of colonisation on two-spirit people

Colonisation is understood as the key social determinant of Indigenous health (Greenwood et al,. 2015). It has shaped historic factors contributing to Indigenous well-being and continues to shape all other health determinants for Indigenous people and communities today. Colonisation has had specific impacts on the health of two-spirit people, particularly through the introduction and enforcement of Western models of gender and sexuality, which pathologised two-spirit bodies and relationships (McLeod, 2003; Wilson, 2015b). Colonisation has involved attempts at erasing Indigenous expressions of gender and sexual diversity rooted in cultural teachings and practices, replacing them with colonial gender and sexual norms. For example, with implementation of the Indian Act, residential schools imposed strict categories of heteropatriarchal gender, race and sexuality simultaneously. Leadership within the schools imposed rigid boundaries between men and women and what was considered acceptable expressions of sexuality, rooted in Christian beliefs about morality, while at the same time facilitating abuse. Residential schools caused the loss of Indigenous languages and, in turn, in some communities, the loss and marginalisation of the knowledge of two-spirit cultural roles. This further introduced notions of homophobia, which became internalised in Indigenous communities. Beyond residential schools, state-run child welfare regimes extended to the Sixties Scoop, during which thousands of Indigenous children were removed from their homes and communities and placed in largely white foster homes. Beginning in the 1960s, the Sixties Scoop is arguably echoed in today's discriminatory child welfare practices. Through these practices of raising children and youth without a sense of identity or community, generations of two-spirit people were taught that they did not fit in. These early experiences, combined with frequent abuse at the hands of the state, are related to the high incidence of mental illness among two-spirit people. Additionally, many people who were removed from their families during the Sixties Scoop figured out only later in life that they are two-spirit. These historical and ongoing colonial efforts to assimilate Indigenous people and to remove Indigenous children from their families and communities, paired with the lack of recognition of sexual and gender diversity (as seen in major gaps in data collection about LGBTQI+, trans* and two-spirit health), are related to the epidemic rates of HIV/AIDS among two-spirit people in Canada.

Indigenous people represent 3.8% of the population in Canada yet account for 8% of people living with HIV and 12.5% of all new HIV infections since 2008 (PHAC, 2010). In addition, HIV infection rates are 3.5 times higher for Indigenous people than non-Indigenous people (PHAC, 2011). While there is no available data on HIV/AIDS rates for two-spirit people, research and community initiatives identify HIV/AIDS as a key health concern (Bauer, Travers, Scanlon, & Coleman, 2012; Monette, et al. 2011; Taylor, 2009; Zoccole et al., 2005). Through their leadership and activism in the HIV/AIDS movement (Hunt, 2016a), it is evident that the two-spirit community has taken it upon themselves to address this health issue.

Rates of HIV/AIDS are fastest growing among Indigenous young people. Two-spirit youth are often framed solely by discourses of 'risk'. However, youth leaders increasingly emphasise that colonial attitudes, systems and relationships marginalise Indigenous youth, including two-spirit people, and that this colonialism is where risk is located, rather than within two-spirit people themselves (NIYCHA, 2017). Thus, we understand the leadership and vitality of two-spirit people within Indigenous sexual health, including HIV/AIDS movements historically and today, as a key site of two-spirit health, well-being and healing. Indeed, two-spirit people have resisted the stigma around their sexualities and gender identities, as well as around HIV/AIDS. They have asserted self-determination over their bodies, sexualities and relationships. Two-spirit people's increasing visibility is a sign of healing from historic and ongoing colonial abuses and attempted erasure.

Historic shifts in two-spirit community presence

Working together, we have identified recent shifts in the way two-spirit people are valued in diverse spaces focused on Indigenous health and well-being, including those focused on sexual health and HIV/AIDS. We have witnessed an increasing acceptance of two-spirit people in cultural spaces. This is significant, because colonisation has led to the imposition of taboos and shame around sexuality in cultural and ceremonial spaces, and undoing these harms involves dialogue and education in the valuation and acceptance of people of all genders and sexualities. Key to this shift is the importance of sharing culture with and among two-spirit people and other members of our communities. In some communities, elders are beginning to welcome two-spirit people as knowledge holders and as cultural practitioners once again. Acceptance and respect are growing in rural as well as urban areas, as noted by co-author Sandy Lambert, who was recently gifted an eagle feather with rainbow beading while speaking in a rural community.

Further, we have witnessed two-spirit people's leadership within Indigenous organisations, including as staff and on boards of directors. Rather than side-lining two-spirit people, some organisations are working to create culturally safe spaces in which their voices are valued. For example, in formal institutional spaces focused on Indigenous sexual health, we have witnessed meetings that are opened with a prayer and that use a circle model to set a tone of respect for all voices, rather than replicating top-down power dynamics.

These cultural and institutional shifts require cultural safety, training and education to break down heteropatriarchal[3] gender norms and the stigma around Indigenous sexuality. This does not mean simply 'including' or 'tolerating' two-spirit people but normalising the presence of people of diverse genders and sexualities. Everyday practices to foster this safe and inclusive space includes reflecting on gendered language, interrogating assumptions about sexual relationships and family make-up (de-normalising the heterosexual nuclear family) and considering the accessibility of gendered spaces such as washrooms, gender-specific housing or groups, and cultural and ceremonial spaces. Indigenous organisations need to develop competency in two-spirit issues and actively decolonise gender and sexuality within their programme models so to avoid erasing or further marginalising two-spirit community members.

Decolonising gender and sexuality also means considering the language we use, from everyday terms to the language of programmes, policies and research. The English language continues to limit the expression of culturally specific knowledge, but some two-spirit people are reclaiming words in their own languages to self-define their roles or identities. Like the term 'two-spirit' itself, new terms are being developed all the time; the

---

3 Heteropatriarchy is the combination of patriarchal and heteronormative belief systems, in which people are understood to fall into distinct and complementary genders (men and women) and heterosexuality is the norm. This belief system is culturally biased in favour of opposite-sex relationships and positions men and women in a hierarchy, with men occupying a dominant social position.

use of 'gender non-conforming'[4] is an example of this kind of innovation. We advocate practices which foster individual self-determination or self-identification, allowing people to decide what words to use to describe their identity today (Hunt, 2016a). For some people, especially youth, this may change if their gender identity changes, or as they decide to use different pronouns or come into a new understanding of their sexuality. Importantly, terminology is often context-specific, as someone might identify as two-spirit in one space, and at other times identify as gay. We follow the Native Youth Sexual Health Network (nativeyouthsexualhealth.com) in calling for adults to meet young people where they are, and reducing stigma around sexual health so to foster young people's self-determination in all areas.

Methods for working with two-spirit people and communities

Given the emergent and shifting nature of two-spirit leadership across diverse community contexts, there is an ever-growing set of ways of creating or gathering knowledge that are particularly relevant for two-spirit people or those working with two-spirit people. Here we share some of the methods that we see as important in the context of health research, services and education, while recognising that the application of these methods will vary greatly across geographies and cultural contexts. The methods we discuss here are 1) inviting self-identification, 2) fostering safe spaces, 3) de-linking ceremony and the gender binary, 4) applying a geographic lens, and 5) nothing about us without us.

Inviting self-identification

Nurturing gender self-identification and body sovereignty requires the creation of methods that avoid replicating colonial assumptions, rooted in heteropatriarchal models, about gender and sexuality. Foundational to these methods is not making assumptions about gender identity, pronouns, and gender expression, instead allowing people to name their own gender and sexuality, knowing that this might change over time. Organisations,

4   'Gender non-conforming' is a term used to describe or self-identify individuals who do not conform to expected gender norms within the binary gender model. Broadly speaking, it describes people who do not follow expected gender stereotypes about how 'men' and 'women' should act or what they should look like. Related terms include 'gender variant', 'gender diverse', and 'gender creative'.

communities and individuals will need to look at how the categories of male/female, man/woman, and assumptions of heterosexuality are embedded in their everyday language, policies and practices. For example, most forms of data gathering, like surveys or intake forms, limit the available categories. Allowing people to self-define rather than including only two gender options is one way to avoid this. Further, inviting everyone to name their preferred pronouns can help to destabilise assumptions without singling out people who may stereotypically appear to be two-spirit. Additionally, given that the English language has limited terms to describe gender and sexuality, and that due to colonisation gender diversity within many Indigenous languages have been lost, arts-based methods such as music, film, and photography can allow people to express the fullness of their identities (for examples, see Women's Earth Alliance and Native Youth Sexual Health Network, 2016).

Fostering safe spaces

Two-spirit people often belong to multiple communities, including Indigenous and queer or gay communities, and may feel stigmatised within the communities they are part of. For example, two-spirit people often face racism from the gay community as well as homophobia or transphobia from their Indigenous community (Wilson, 1996; 2009). Thus, two-spirit people may face lateral violence in both the Indigenous and non-Indigenous worlds they move between. With this in mind, there are methods that communities and organisations can use to ensure it is each person's own choice to 'out' themselves – and then only if, when and how they want to. Further, it should not be assumed that all Indigenous organisations are safe spaces for two-spirit people. While communities and organisations should take it upon themselves to meaningfully unpack and address racism, homophobia and transphobia, it must be recognised that undoing the harms of colonisation will take time. The significance of anonymity for two-spirit people across these diverse community spaces should be honoured, with individuals taking the lead on how much information to share about themselves. This is especially important when including two-spirit people who are HIV positive or have AIDS, given the potential harms of combined social stigma. Through these practices, self-determination can be fostered in the creation of safe spaces for two-spirit people.

De-linking ceremony and the gender binary

Ceremony and culture can be sites of empowerment, reclamation and healing, but for two-spirit people they can also be sites of oppression if they follow heteronormative[5] and cis-normative[6] models. The gender binary is often embedded in 'traditional' ceremonial practices, such as through strictly gendered rules about what to wear in ceremonial spaces (such as that all women must wear skirts – a practice known as 'skirt shaming' (Wilson, 2015c) – and that 'woman' equals 'female'). In de-linking ceremony and the gender binary, it is important to question how bodies are regulated through the imposition of binary gender norms. There is great variation in how two-spirit people are accepted, celebrated and invited into ceremonial spaces across cultural contests. In some communities, two-spirit people are seen as cultural leaders and work alongside elders in leading ceremonial practice, while in other contexts two-spirit people are shunned or are made to conform to binary gender practices in order to participate. In some communities, two-spirit people are working with elders to create their own ceremonial spaces so to reclaim spiritual wellness, with body sovereignty at the core of cultural revitalisation. Two-spirit methodologies foster the teaching that all bodies are sacred.

Applying a geographic lens

A geographic lens is key to understanding the specific needs and realities of two-spirit people across diverse sites. In rural areas, research or programming that focuses on two-spirit issues and perspectives can be challenging because of local internalised homophobia and transphobia. In small communities, two-spirit people don't necessarily have safe spaces in which to identify themselves, so methods must be developed in an inclusive

---

5   Heteronormativity is the belief that people fall into distinct and complementary genders (men and women) and that heterosexuality is the norm. This belief is embedded across social institutions, including in health policies and programs, such as in providing sexual health education that privileges heterosexual relationships or relationship counselling that assumes all clients are straight.
6   Cisnormativity is a term used to describe the ways in which institutional norms and social practices reproduce assumptions of a gender binary, along with assumed alignment of gender identity and physical sexes. Cisnormativity gives rise to the belief that gender non-conformity is not normal or is a 'problem'.

way to avoid perpetuating stigmatisation. In rural areas, we find it useful to develop and nurture local networks, and only advertise initiatives through word of mouth. If initiatives are advertised publicly, it is wise to keep the wording open or general so that people who participate aren't inadvertently outed without their consent. Further, we find it useful to learn about and then adopt the language that a specific community uses to talk about and name their gender and sexual identities, rather than to impose wording from afar. (For example, in some rural areas, the term 'two-spirit' is not used, in favour of local cultural terms, LGBTQI+, or simply not using names at all to talk about sexual practices). Meeting the local community where it's at is key.

Nothing about us without us

Two-spirit involvement in sexual health movements has taught us that you cannot do the work without us. In other words, rather than speaking about or for two-spirit people, we must be invited to speak for ourselves, taking up key leadership roles in any initiative or organisation concerned with two-spirit health. Further, you cannot take knowledge and then shelve it and run away; you must take a relational approach and ensure that all initiatives give back to the community. This is something we have seen slowly changing in the contexts in which we work, with researchers ensuring they avoid extractive approaches to two-spirit health. One example is co-author Sandy Lambert's work with The DUDES Club Society (dudesclub.ca), which now has 32 sites, primarily in British Columbia. Founded in 2010 in Vancouver's downtown east side, the DUDES Club fosters a peer-led space focused on the spiritual, physical, mental, emotional and social health of self-identified men, including two-spirit and trans* men. As part of the team, Sandy helps to connect men with local healthcare and other support services, instilling a sense of solidarity and pride within the community. The society has grown from four sites to 32 in the past few years through a 'train the trainer' model, which provides a knowledge bundle to facilitators and elders from the local community, who can then adapt the bundle to meet local needs. Growing in an organic way, this model has grown out of local desire to provide spaces for the well-being of Indigenous men, inclusive of two-spirit and trans people.

Research has also been a key part of the DUDES Club Society, with team members co-authoring papers and presenting at numerous health conferences (see for example Gross et al., 2016). The DUDES Club team continually brings knowledge back to the community in meaningful ways.

Sharing is key to Indigenous methodologies, and two-spirit men such as Sandy play a key role in all aspects of knowledge sharing. This upholds the belief that it is the responsibility of researchers and practitioners to maintain relationships beyond the end of a project, not simply cut off community relations when funding runs out or a project wraps up. Further, methods must be developed to involve two-spirit people in envisioning, carrying out and analysing research, not only in research on two-spirit issues but research on all Indigenous issues, to be more inclusive. It is of vital importance to have two-spirit people in leadership roles in organisations and individual projects to further the principles which are key to two-spirit methodologies.

Summary of methods for fostering two-spirit research methodologies

1. Inviting self-identification
- Avoid making assumptions based on appearances or perceived social norms.
- Allow people to name their own gender and sexuality, understanding that this might change over time.
- Avoid having only two gender options.
- Invite people to name their preferred pronouns.
- Use arts-based methods to allow greater self-expression.

2. Fostering safe spaces
- Recognise that two-spirit people face social stigma and discrimination.
- Ensure two-spirit people can choose when and if to 'out' themselves.
- Do not assume Indigenous organisations are safe spaces for two-spirit people.
- Identify trusted allies who can be called upon to provide support.
- Develop long- and short-term initiatives to address racism, homophobia and transphobia.
- Honour two-spirit people's anonymity across diverse community spaces.

3. De-linking ceremony and the gender binary
- Question how expected binary gender norms are perpetuated in concepts of 'tradition'.
- Recognise the diversity of roles that two-spirit people play in cultural spaces and in conducting ceremony.
- Foster the knowledge that all bodies are sacred.

4. Applying a geographic lens
- In rural and small communities, develop local networks through which to advertise to two-spirit people.
- In rural, remote and urban communities, build up local leadership in men's, queer and two-spirit wellness through providing training for local champions.
- Keep wording general on advertisements to avoid inadvertently outing participants without their consent.
- Adopt the local terminology and language to talk about gender and sexuality.

5. Nothing about us without us
- Rather than speaking for two-spirit people, invite us to speak for ourselves.
- Invite two-spirit people to take up key leadership roles in initiatives concerned with two-spirit health.
- Avoid extractive approaches to research by ensuring all initiatives give back in a meaningful way.
- Involve two-spirit people in envisioning, carrying out and analysing Indigenous research.

Moving forward

As two-spirit people walking side by side in this collaboration, we are excited about the changes unfolding in the revitalisation of two-spirit knowledge and leadership in our communities. However, ongoing marginalisation of two-spirit people – evident in a lack of statistics on two-spirit health, lack of consideration of two-spirit people in educational resources on Indigenous health, families and relationships, and the everyday treatment of two-spirit people as abnormal – serves as an imperative to foster decolonial methodologies that reflect the vibrancy, strengths and knowledge of all our two-spirit relations. We call on health organisations, researchers and practitioners to evaluate policies for their consideration of two-spirit lives and issues, and to develop appropriate models for implementation and accountability. Further, we encourage organisations to look internally at the way two-spirit people are supported in leadership positions. Are there two-spirit people on your board and in key staff positions? How are they supported in this work? What measures do you have in place to foster a respectful working environment and to consider two-spirit people as valued members of your team, not just as an 'at risk' group?

Funding

This research was funded by a grant from the Canadian Institute for Health Research (CIHR).

References

Driskill, Q. (2011). D4Y DβC (*Asegi Ayetl*): Cherokee two-spirit people reimagining nation. In Q.-L. Driskel, C. Finley, B. J. Gilley, & S. L. Morgensen (Eds.), *Queer Indigenous studies: Critical interventions in theory, politics, and literature* (pp. 97–112). University of Arizona Press.

Greenwood, M., de Leeuw, S., Lindsay, N. M., & Reading, C. (2015). *Determinants of Indigenous peoples' health in Canada: Beyond the social.* Canadian Scholars Press.

Gross, P. A., Efimoff, I., Patrick, L., Josewski, V., Hau, K., Lambert, S., & Smye, V. (2016). The DUDES Club: A brotherhood for men's health [Le *DUDES Club*]. *Canadian Family Physician, 62*(6), e311–e318.

Hunt, S. (2015). Embodying self-determination: Beyond the gender binary. In M. Greenwood, S. de Leeuw, N. M. Lindsay, & C. Reading (Eds.), *Determinants of Indigenous peoples' health in Canada: Beyond the social* (pp. 104–119). Canadian Scholars Press.

Hunt, S. (2016a). *An introduction to the health of Two-Spirit people: Historical, contemporary and emergent issues.* National Collaborating Centre for Aboriginal Health.

Hunt, S. (2016b). Decolonizing the roots of rape culture: Reflections on consent, sexual violence and university campuses. emmatalks.org/video/sarah-hunt/

McLeod, A. (2003). The experience of Aboriginal peoples. In B. Ryan (Ed.), *A new look at homophobia and heterosexism in Canada* (pp. 27–37). Canadian AIDS Society.

National Indigenous Youth Council on Sexual Health and HIV/AIDS. (2017). *Beyond 'at risk': Indigenous youth speak to service providers.* Information sheet. Canadian Aboriginal AIDS Network.

Smith, L. T. (1999). *Decolonizing methodologies: Research and Indigenous peoples.* Zed Books.

Tafoya, T. (1997). Native gay and lesbian issues: The two-spirited. In B. Green (Ed.), *Ethnic and cultural diversity among lesbians and gay men* (Vol. 3) (pp. 1–9). Sage Publications.

Wilson, A. (1996). How we find ourselves: Identity development and two-spirit people. *Harvard Educational Review, 66*(2), 303–317.

Wilson, A. (2009). Two-spirit identity: Active resistance to multiple oppressions. *Directions: Research and policy eliminating racism, 5*(1), 44–46.

Wilson, A. (2015a). Interview: Alex Wilson. *Journal of Global Indigeneity, 1*(1). ro.uow.edu.au/jgi/vol1/iss1/15

Wilson, A. (2015b). Our coming in stories: Cree identity, body sovereignty and gender self-determination. *Journal of Global Indigeneity, 1*(1). ro.uow.edu.au/jgi/vol1/iss1/4

Wilson, A. (2015c). Two-spirit people, body sovereignty and gender self determination. *Red Rising Magazine.* redrisingmagazine.ca/two-spirit-people-body-sovereignty-and-gender-self-determination/

Women's Earth Alliance and Native Youth Sexual Health Network. (2016). *Violence on the land, violence on our bodies: Building an Indigenous response to environmental violence.* landbodydefense.org

15

Gidoo-Imishinkoowenden ('You Have a Strong Mind'): Reflections on the 2-Spirit HIV/AIDS Wellness and Longevity Study (2SHAWLS)

Randy Jackson, Doris Peltier and David J. Brennan

We begin with excerpts from two different published stories. Written a few years before we wrote this chapter, the first story was the grounding inspiration for us to discuss *Amishakoowendamo'awag*[1] ('they have a strong mind'). This story was penned by a traditional two-spirit man named Manitou Waashask, who was living with HIV and who also worked in the Indigenous HIV movement in Canada. Manitou Waashask considered himself a warrior, as did his community. He was a leader, an advocate, and passionate about how culture might buffer negative experiences and heal our peoples. Highly respected in our two-spirit community in Canada, Manitou Waashask passed to the spirit world a few years after sharing the excerpt below.

> I've always [heard] people saying that being gay is a choice. I'm not sure if that statement is a result of homophobia or an unwillingness on their part

1   Several variations of *amishakoowendamo'awag* are used in this chapter, including *amishakoowendamowin* or 'strongmindedness' (the gift); *amishakoowendamo'awag* or 'they have a strong mind' (this addresses the collective), and *gidoo-imishinkoowenden* or 'you have a strong mind' (individual). It is important to note that these words have no gender, are used interchangeably, and reflect grammatical differences in the ways they are used in this paper.

to ask why someone would choose a life of ridicule, rejection, hatred, and violence [. . .] inflicted upon them. The choice, my friends, is not whether [. . .] to be gay. [It's about . . .] whether [. . . one is being] honest and therefore free.

How could someone working in HIV and AIDS prevention seroconvert? As careful as I was, the truth is, I'm [now HIV]-positive. After me and my old world died, I [. . .] continued this work with the same passion – just [now – I have] a new worldview. [I'm] still the strong, to-the-point, warrior I always was. Just now, [I'm] doing it with lived experience.

Regardless of where I go or what job I have, I am who I am and [I always] end up confronting homophobic remarks and actions, even from cultural experts, educating and advocating. This is my role in life. This is my passion. This is who I am. This is how I do it. My way of life is my job. Luckily, I just happen to get paid for it – Manitou Waashask (Ontario First Nations HIV/AIDS Education Circle, n.d.)

This second excerpt – from Thomas King's Massey Hall Lecture series, *The Truth about Stories: A Native Narrative* – propelled and inspired us to deeply reflect and critically think, not only about the first excerpt from the story shared above, but also about the kinds of stories that we, as Indigenous peoples living with HIV, share with HIV scholars. These research stories are then repackaged and told back to us in new and sometimes troubling ways.

I tell stories not to play on your sympathies but to suggest how stories can control our lives, for there is part of me that has never been able to move past these stories, a part of me that will be chained to these stories as long as I live. [. . .] Stories are wonderous things. And they are dangerous. [. . .] For once a story is told, it cannot be called back. Once told, it is loose in the world. So, you have to be careful with the stories you tell. And you have to watch out for the stories that you are told – Thomas King (2003, pp. 22–23).

It is from these two stories that we begin our journey, using an Indigenous lens, to think more critically about what is meant by resilience and the concept of *amishakoowendamo'awag* (they have a strong mind) or *gidoo-amishakoowendam* (you have a strong mind). By further examining some of our previous work together as people with a variety of identities and life experiences – Indigenous, settler, two-spirit, queer, non-queer, academic, community, and varying HIV statuses – we focus on the ways two-spirit people and those living with HIV provide leadership. Our goal is to bring these concepts to a new level of understanding and advance our thinking about the strengths, resources, and gifts Indigenous knowledges and communities bring to meaningfully lived cultural lives as Indigenous peoples.

Background

It is common in research reports – and we (Jackson and Peltier) consider these stories not from us, but about us, and as told to us by HIV scholars – to highlight Indigenous peoples as disproportionately impacted by HIV. In 2018, according to a recent Canadian HIV surveillance report, 'of [new HIV] cases with known race/ethnicity information [(N = 1196)], 19.3% were reported as Indigenous' (Haddad et al., 2019, p. 308), despite Indigenous peoples comprising only 4.9% of the Canadian population (Statistics Canada, 2017). Scholars often relate the over-representation of Indigenous peoples in HIV surveillance to the devastating experiences of colonisation and other Western-defined social determinants of health. Colonisation has been linked to an array of health and social disparities between Indigenous and non-Indigenous peoples (Gracey & King, 2009; King et al., 2009; Negin et al., 2015). Indigenous peoples are more likely to have a later HIV diagnosis (Stokes et al., 2006); slower uptake of anti-retroviral treatments (Wood et al., 2006); and less access to HIV-experienced physicians (Miller et al., 2006). Challenges related to care-seeking behaviour by HIV-positive Indigenous peoples have also been demonstrated to contribute to higher morbidity, shorter survival times, and a mortality rate three times higher than that of non-Indigenous people (Lima et al., 2006). Two-spirit men, who represent a majority of those living with AIDS and a sizeable proportion of new HIV infections, experience several unique factors (such as homophobia and gender-diverse or non-binary phobias and/or erasure) that also influence their health and well-being in negative ways.

Although such scholarly works provide much needed and valuable knowledge about how HIV is impacting Indigenous communities, and can inform the development of policy and programs, they are not the entire story. An exclusive focus on our pathologies as Indigenous peoples, stripped of any discussion surrounding structural barriers, potentially contributes to our oppression and creates an overall picture focused only on our perceived dysfunction and suffering. It is a picture that effectively shapes how Indigenous identity is socially constructed, and in turn, how policymakers and community agencies shape and provide health and social support services to Indigenous peoples (Bond, 2005; Lavallee & Poole,

2010; Peltier et al., 2011; Reading & Nowgesic, 2002). As such we have too few Indigenous community practice models that support Indigenous conceptional frameworks and allow us to talk about and live our lives in thriving health (Peltier et al., 2011; Richmond et al., 2007; Wilson & Young, 2008). These models and frameworks are especially lacking when considering how to support the wellness of two-spirit men living long-term with HIV. Such an observation is vitally important, for without it we fail to explore the ways in which Indigenous peoples continue to display remarkable resilience in the face of ongoing adversity (Stewart-Harawira, 2018). To be absolutely and unequivocally clear: when we voice stories focused on Indigenous and two-spirit cultural strength, we locate ourselves within them and we establish ourselves and our ecologies in ways that can't be severed by colonialism (McLeod, 2007).

Brennan and Jackson, along with two community organisations (2-spirit People of the First Nation and the Ontario Aboriginal HIV/AIDS Strategy), responded to the idea of sharing a more complete story. Together we designed a study to explore what makes it possible for two-spirit men to live successfully long-term with HIV. Aware that rates of HIV infection and poor quality of Western-defined care were central to, but only partially explained their disparities in health, we were also influenced by literature that described 'devaluation of culture' and 'lack of access to culturally appropriate health care and services' as contributing factors (PHAC, 2010, p. 33; see also Loppie, 2017). Following this critical evaluation of current knowledge, we decided to focus our research efforts on a range of unique and Indigenous determinants of health. We began this study fully understanding that Indigenous cultures can act as protective factors that promote resilient responses (Greenwood et al., 2018). Although our study was welcomed because it seemed to focus on the strengths of Indigenous people living in challenging circumstances, it also received critical community feedback. In the words of one community member, 'I never wanted to be resilient in the first place.' Although it was common for community members to agree with our findings, such support was often qualified with 'yes, but' statements, suggesting we did not go nearly as far as we could have with this line of inquiry to better understand how the notion of resilience itself has deeply colonising implications.

Inspired by the excerpt from the first story that opened this chapter, through conversation we (Brennan, Jackson and Peltier) explored the importance of *Anishinaabe-inendaamowin* (*Anishinaabe* worldview and understanding) of *amishakoowendamo'awag* (they have a strong mind) in reframing Western understanding of resilience. Our conversation contributes to critiques by Indigenous scholars of the way the West has conceptualised resilience as simply and only 'positive adaptation despite adversity' (Fleming & Ledogar, 2008, p. 8; Luthar, 2006). Grounded in Indigenous cultures, 'a strong mind' is something that is nurtured and supported in the relational context of Indigenous communities with a lived connection to the land. Indigenous languages not only shape how we think about the world – as with all cultures – but they also support our identities, contribute to our self-esteem, and (despite structural challenges we encounter) shape and sustain our cultures as strong and thriving Indigenous peoples (Marmion et al., 2014). Prior to exploring these ideas, we first review details from our earlier study, the *2-Spirit HIV/AIDS Wellness and Longevity Study* (see http://www.2shawls.com/; Brennan, Georgievski et al., 2021; Brennan, Jackson et al., 2021; Jackson et al., 2021). Finally, we situate our conversation within the literature by Indigenous scholars who critique the Western theory of resilience.

2-Spirit HIV/AIDS Wellness and Longevity Study (2SHAWLS)

Despite numerous obstacles, anecdotal evidence gathered by our community partners suggested that many two-spirit men living long-term with HIV and accessing services were doing well. Many two-spirit men accessing services were connected to their cultures and involved in their communities, and they generally accessed services only rarely, when periodically in crisis. Our community partners expressed the desire to push back against the published research that focused on Indigenous peoples' deficits, described above, as woefully inadequate and biased. They felt that negative descriptions of Indigenous health, although potentially useful in advocacy efforts, were only partial stories about the lives of Indigenous peoples. Research that focuses solely on challenges experienced by Indigenous peoples potentially constructs Indigenous identity and personhood only in terms of suffering and dysfunction (Bond, 2005; Lavallee & Clearsky, 2006; Reading & Nowgesic, 2002). The fear (often grounded in experience) was that such research findings could also then be used to justify continued paternalism (the idea that 'we're here to help') in ways that ignore principles of self-determination. Instead, building on earlier community work that resists racism, homophobia, colonisation, and gender violence against two-spirit men, our community partners asked us: 'How do we design services that support and encourage two-spirit men's health and resilience?' Rather than develop services based on pathology, they instead wanted information that they could mobilise to design support services grounded in the cultural strengths of two-spirit men. As Newhouse argued, 'Part of the healing journey is to begin to see ourselves differently, to move from seeing ourselves as wounded, to seeing ourselves as resilient' (Newhouse, 2006, p. 2).

In response, we (Brennan, Jackson, and community partners) designed a study that enabled us to better assess the factors, skills, resources, knowledges, and practices that contribute to the health and well-being of two-spirit men living long-term with HIV. Manitou Waashask, whose story is told in the first paragraphs of this chapter, was a two-spirit, long-term HIV-positive man who was an integral leader in Ontario for ensuring that services and programs for Indigenous people, including two-spirit people and those living with HIV, were providing care that was grounded in Indigenous knowledges and cultures. He was central to the development of the 2SHAWLS study. He often spoke of how we 'do not need another study to gather dust on a shelf', but one that would initiate change and overturn the impacts of colonisation upon Indigenous peoples. Manitou Waashask, who has since passed into the spirit world, lives on in the legacy of his work in this study. Drawing on principles of community-based research (Cochran et al., 2008), coupled with decolonising and Indigenous methodologies (Brant Castellano, 2000; Smith, 2014), with recruitment assistance provided by our community partners, we hosted three focus groups with 14 two-spirit male participants who indicated they had lived with HIV for at least 10 years. Re-envisioning our focus groups as traditional sharing circles (Baskin, 2005; Poff, 2006; Rothe et al., 2009), we asked one question: 'What is allowing you to live well long-term with HIV?' All sharing-group participants were offered an honorarium, sharing circles were audio-recorded, and full verbatim transcripts were produced. Symbol-based inquiry (e.g., a floor map of the medicine wheel) in data collection was used to elicit dialogue centred on strengths, assets and resilience (Graveline, 2010; Jackson et al., 2021). The medicine wheel provides many Indigenous people in Canada with a conceptual framework focused on 'spiritual, emotional and physical well-being [as enmeshed in the broader] political, social, and economic positioning of Indigenous peoples and communities' (Martin-Hill, 2009, p. 36). Ethical review was provided by the University of Toronto and McMaster University.

We used the medicine wheel again to guide participatory analysis, as a way of grounding our emerging understanding, because we wanted to derive understanding 'through the lens of those who originally experienced' the phenomena (Brant Castellano, 2000; McLeod, 2007, p. 17). As Graveline (2010) suggests, the medicine wheel in qualitative research works to transform Eurocentric consciousness by combining research processes with Indigenous teachings, worldview and values. We felt that this approach had value in research work with Indigenous communities because it 'incorporate[d] culturally appropriate protocols' (Lavallee & Poole, 2010, p. 276). Similarly, the medicine wheel also provided a potent visual reminder of the power of oral tradition that is grounded in different ways of knowing (Walker, 2001; Wenger-Nabigon, 2010) and potentially attended to meaning grounded in an 'inter-connected, inter-related holistic approach to addressing and analyzing social phenomena' (Martin Hill, 2009, p. 36).

Of the 14 participants, 12 indicated that they belonged to a First Nation group and 2 reported a Métis identity. The average age of the participants was 46 years (with an age range between 32 and 61 years). Our sample did not include any participant who self-identified as Inuit – the third main Indigenous group in Canada as defined by the Canadian Constitution. Through our participatory analysis, seven truths of resilience emerged in our findings: (1) Worldviews; (2) Finding One's Strength; (3) Walking towards Balance; (4) Recognising One's True Power; (5) *Mino-Bimaadiziwin* (Living the Way of the Good Life); (6) Self-Care; and (7) Living our Truth. Below we provide a summary of each of these themes.

1. Indigenous **worldviews** were considered fundamental to living well, and many participants provided sophisticated descriptions that recognised value in balancing the holistic aspects of self. It was a focus that supported participants to develop as mentally strong, emotionally present, physically healthy, and spiritually grounded persons. Here participants often referenced the cultural resources provided by their communities, such as connection with other two-spirit men, seeking guidance from elders, and making concerted efforts to connect with their spiritual worlds through ceremony. As one participant shared, 'I see it as the balance of those things.' The power of Indigenous worldviews guided participants to overcome challenges and to think about their wellness journeys as connected to community cultural strengths.

2. Connected to worldview, the theme of **finding one's strength** was centred on efforts participants made toward coming to terms (i.e., self-acceptance) with their identities and life circumstances (i.e., gay, gender diverse, Indigenous persons living with HIV).

They described that being honest with themselves, being vulnerable and open with significant others in their lives, and self-acceptance were necessary for living well. As one participant described, 'It's part of why I'm the unique individual I am [and] now [it's] probably my most cherished possession, [. . .] my unique sexuality.' Finding one's strength was described as being firmly connected in community relationships, and as a result, being able to navigate life challenges more efficiently and to grow as individuals.

3. Like the Indigenous teaching 'all my relations', participants described **walking towards balance** as expressing an active sense of individual agency, and it was considered integral to resilience. Here, social support was considered fundamental. Though the walk towards balance is an individual one, many participants described 'all my relations' as deep connections with friends, family, and community as equally important. As one participant shared, 'That's what I love about the HIV community – it's one big family. We have that one thing that connects us all – HIV.'

4. For many participants **recognising one's true power** hinged on being mentally, emotionally, and spiritually ready to hear the positive things about themselves as seen through the eyes of others. As one participant described, it's about learning to 'keep one's eyes open', becoming more honest, open, and vulnerable with others, and mobilising this new way of being to inspire self-acceptance. As another participant described, 'It's like my whole life [I] have been trying to learn how to love myself, and I'm there now.' Many participants recognised the power of connecting to the natural environment (i.e., the land) as 'the best therapy' that facilitated the translation of this experience to their friends, family, community, and nation.

5. The *Anishinaabe* word ***mino-bimaadiziwin*** (living the good life) described participants' journeys where they actively cultivated space in their lives for healing. Ultimately, *mino-bimaadiziwin* is a way of life, a sense of a commitment to well-being, and a spiritual way of knowing, being, and doing. Many participants talked about the importance of humans and laughter as effective coping mechanisms. Participants often described how they

became active and involved in the two-spirit health movement, or how they drew on the power of relationships with intimate others, friends, family and community as necessary for living the good life. As one participant shared, 'living [the] good life [lets me focus on] different ideas of what is success – different things work differently for different people – [and] success [for me] comes from working within that.'

6. For participants, **self-care** was broadly defined and extended beyond the individual to encompass family, community and nation. It is an orientation to life where participants described how their actions in the present, while drawing on traditional knowledge, could potentially benefit generations to come. It was expressed as an active sense of the profane – of acknowledging how one is ultimately connected, draws on, and supports all of creation – and how this supports the individual in return. Like 'recognising one's true power', as one participant shared about being out in nature, '[It helps] just to accept who we are and then move forward.'

7. For participants, being the person who the Creator meant you to be was described as **living our truths**. This theme was expressed by participants as a sense of coming 'full circle', embodying, and 'living comfortably' with their full selves, including their sexual and/or gender identity, HIV diagnosis, Indigeneity or HIV status. Ultimately living our truths drew on traditional teachings and was expressed as an imperative. It was through laughter and expressions of joy that were deployed by participants as a mechanism to connect their health to community. As one participant shared, 'I needed to learn to love myself, and I knew if I didn't learn how to love myself that my dislike of myself would kill me. I started to learn to how to love me . . . I love my two-spiritedness. I love my gayness.'

A conversation about Amishakoowendamo'awag

The decision to write a portion of this chapter as conversation was driven by our desire to impart the personal as a basis for truth from within *Anishinaabe* knowledge systems. We recognise ourselves as authors who actively contribute to pivoting the dialogue about resilience through an Indigenous lens by using a first-person narrative style (McGuire-Kishebakabaykwe, 2010). We also wanted to improve accessibility in our writing by largely avoiding Western scientific jargon and, as King (2003) did, 'to recreate an oral storytelling voice and craft [a] story [about resilience] in terms of a performance for a general audience' (p. 21). Our recorded and transcribed conversation centred on three themes: (1) How the West's definition of resilience is problematic in Indigenous contexts; (2) What we mean when we say *amishakoowendamo'awag*; and (3) Whether *amishakoowendamo'awag* shifts how we conceptualised Indigenous resilience in our earlier study, 2SHAWLS. Our exploration of these themes, introduced early in our conservation, led to a free-flowing and unstructured three-hour-long dialogue. As such, presented below is an edited version of this conversation that was also later organised around our three themes.

1. Challenges with resilience as conceptualised in 2SHAWLS

Peltier: Can I say something about my take on resilience? It's not a word that I really look at or even used [. . .]. It was through research where I started hearing the word. [. . . Researchers] would unpack and regurgitate our trauma as part of the [word and] it [is] very illness based. [. . . But] in the back of my mind, I'm [also] thinking we need to hear this stuff right now. We need to validate people's experiences in their journeys. [But] it just didn't sit comfortable with me. It – I was – it gave me some unease in my spirit and in my body. [. . . We] really [need] to push back against that a little bit, and maybe understand the real meaning of it, the true meaning, because I think it's overused, and [these academics] aren't there with us yet, quite often.

Jackson: I think for me, I first heard the word – [. . .] the critique of the word [. . .] – in [a journal] editorial that David Newhouse (2006) had written. [. . . In it] he critiqued the idea of resilience from an Indigenous lens [. . .] as placing the responsibility on the individual to respond. [. . . But] we never really unpacked that very well in the work we did [with 2SHAWLS]. I held my tongue [but I knew] we need to explore that. [At the time we did that study . . .] I thought it was more important [. . .] to have this conversation about [how . . .] Indigenous men who are living long term with HIV [. . . are] doing well, because [many of us] are, you know. [Our community partners on 2SHAWLS also . . .] wanted to push back against that [. . .] and I remember [them] telling us one day very early on, before we even got funding, that it was important to [. . .] understand how Indigenous people do well, so that they could design services that are grounded in strengths, as opposed to these other deficits that we hear about from Western research.

Brennan: What is interesting is that really, in truth, this entire project came about because [our community partners...] very directly said, '[we're] tired of researchers telling us how bad things are for us, when there are so many of us who are doing well.' [...] Not everybody [is doing well], and it's not perfect, but people are doing really well, and we don't have that story told yet. [At the time, resilience] was a bit of a buzz word. I remember thinking this is incredible, we need to do this for so many reasons, but to be able to do this, in particular, for two-spirit LGBTQ [...] We knew right away [...] as we were putting the grant together, we were talking about this as about people connecting to community. This is about people connecting to their culture and resources. And that's exactly what – of course – it's exactly what we found. [...] All along, I thought, oh, it's tremendous that we can spend time also critiquing these ideas and concepts, because just the structure of resilience, to me, as a Westerner or as a settler, really assumes that something has happened outside of you that has caused you pain and suffering, and you, as an individual, have figured out your internal resources to survive and/or thrive in that context. I knew right away that was going to be a problem because – at least my understanding and the way I think about Indigenous knowledge and Indigenous practice, if you will – I'm thinking research practice in a way, but even service delivery, is that it's not about an individual. It's never been about an individual. It's about a community. It's about a culture. It's bigger than an individual, which, of course, is exactly how we framed it, or tried to frame it.

2. What do we mean when we say 'Strong Mind' is Indigenous resilience?

Peltier: I really like [the excerpt from the first] story [we shared above at the beginning of this chapter]. I think there's – I see some of what we're talking about in that story.

Jackson: I had a conversation with Manitou Waashask and I asked for his perspective, 'what are the two-spirit teachings around this?' I remember him, very bluntly – [he] just told me straight out that there are no traditional teachings for two-spirit. It's about being [a] human being. It's about accepting who you are.

Peltier: [I have family who are two-spirit] living [. . .] in the community [. . .] and – they're accepted in that way. So, they're part of the spectrum. [. . .] I think in youth – youth are – what I'm seeing the last years as I come to know youth, [. . .] they'll stand up and say and identify with who they are. There's a strength in some of the youth.

Jackson: 'All my relations' continues to operate, even encouraged.

Peltier: Okay. [It's] just who a person was, and I loved that, because that spoke to me about kind of a – just sort of an acceptance, or maybe, [it's] in the 'all my relations' concept where it's just [. . .] – this is a person that's part of the family. This is a person that's part of the world, part of the community. I loved that little piece at the end of his story, because [. . . it speaks] to [an] Indigenous concept of accepting, and where this is part of, 'we're all connected'. This is where we are connected. I thought that was awesome.

Brennan: I think there's something to be learned from the idea that everyone has a place in the circle, everyone has a place. [I'm] trying to think about [. . .] resilience and [the] strong mind concept – [but it] came up a lot in the 2SHAWLS data, which was people figuring out ways to live in a certain context, to be true to who they were, be part of something, not to just be who I am for the sake of being me, but [to] be who I am as part of a larger context. [In 2SHAWLS,] we had our disagreements, and we had our fights, and some of it was about worldview, [. . . and our community partners would be,] 'No, this is how it has to be.' [It was a focus on resilience that was the] clear vision for [them]. Yeah, [so] that to me was an example of a strong mind.

Jackson: Another aspect of strong mind, I read it expressed by an activist [Alexander Leon] in the UK, when he posted on Twitter, and it went viral [. . .] What he wrote resonated: 'Queer people don't grow up as ourselves, we grow up playing a version of ourselves that sacrifices authenticity to minimise humiliation & prejudice. The massive task of our adult lives is to unpick which parts of ourselves are truly us & which parts we've created to protect us.'

Peltier: Wow, that's powerful.

Jackson: It's a powerful quote, but it still places the onus on the individual and ignores the social context that gave rise to this need in the first place. I [still] think it's a task that needs to happen. We still need to be authentically who we are, and forgive ourselves for protecting ourselves, and [allowing this to shape] the way we live – but that doesn't let social structures off the hook. It doesn't let social attitudes about two-spirit people off the hook. Those things also [still] need to shift too.

Peltier: [But, it's where] strongmindedness dwells [. . .] and when we come into this world, we carry that, we bring that with us. Through the course of living, and the journey that we experience, we begin to uncover that gift, and that's been one of [my] revelations. It is an individual work in a sense because what the individual needs to do, to find a way to tap into that or recognise that it's there, and begin to tap into that, and be more successful, because they're capable of tapping into what's under all those layers that the mask [we wear] has covered up.

Brennan: The way that quote reads is very much like [. . .] at least some of what I learned from 2SHAWLS and from my other work is how much that happens in response to others. It's not just that person trying to do that. Its [. . . people in our lives] trying to sort that out with you in this way. That's a 'demasking' there, a little bit of an attempt to do that, but not just in [your] own head, it's also in relationship to you [as someone in your life].

Jackson: I got sick once and went to an elder who took me into the sweat lodge. It was a powerful experience, and the elder gave me my spirit name in Cree and tells me, 'It's your life's work now to understand what that name means and how you live it.' He translated the word in English, but also tells me, 'You'll find that that translation will become inadequate' of what that name means, and how it connects to you as a person, and who are as a person, and what your gifts are.

Peltier: I go to [a traditional] fast, [something I started a year ago for a specific purpose]. [Our ceremonies] help us develop that good mind and that strong mind. [In taking part in ceremonies] you're honing – you're developing that good mind and that strong mind. That's what you're doing when you [join in ceremonies]. After that elder [from the fast] told me I had a strong mind, and when I translated it into my own language – *gidoo-amishakoowendam* – I realised that's what got me through most of my life, through everything bad that has happened to me.

Brennan: I think language is incapable of being precise, because almost all languages are. Because how do you – we try to use [language] to make things as precise as possible, but just the experience, or like you said, the context of any word could change what its meaning is in almost any language. What – I just wanted to get a sense about – because I have a feeling it's more than – [. . .] it's clearly deeper, and as you said, connected to other things such as the Creator or other context that make it very rich, and allows, I think, for – this is why it's kind of a really perfect concept to look at in relationship to this question of resilience because, again, there's – as you both have shared, there is a way in which this is occurring or that people are engaging with whatever they're engaging within their life, but again, they're not doing it alone. There is a piece that is about themselves, trying to make meaning of what's happening or draw upon whatever inner strength, but then also trying to do that in connection with other people.

3. Does 'Strong Mind' shift resilience as used in 2SHAWLS?

Brennan: How does this shift how we understand resilience? The 'demasking' – what we started talking about, all of that – I wonder if it's really about knowing who you are, but then having to hide it for all those reasons that we touched on, and coming to a place along your life journey and saying, 'Okay, I'm going to embrace who I am.'

Peltier: There's a humanity piece in there too. There's that bigger humanity part – heart [knowing] that comes with recognising you're part of the human family, [but] not everybody has that heart [they feel that they connect with to get to that meaning]. I was asking my sister the other day – because I do this quite often – I reflect on words, [. . .] in *Anishinaabemowin* (*Anishinaabe* language), what does *Anishinaabe* actually mean? If you break down the sounds, and if you break it down, and I thought it would be something very unique. I asked her about it, and what it actually means is a person that's Indigenous to the land that you're on. That's what it means.

Brennan: Can you say that again?

Peltier: A human being that's Indigenous to the land that they're on. It's everybody.

Brennan: Yeah, I'm just thinking about this, how we, how my understanding of resilience, and I think this is, we've articulated maybe this already is, yes, I go through these things, and then I become better somehow. Resilient, there's a judgement behind resilient and resilience. I hear less of a judgement about the way we're using the concept of having a 'strong mind'. Maybe I'm wrong, your words made me think about this. Do you hear a judgement behind that construct?

Peltier: No.

Brennan: Whereas 'resilient', I hear judgement that you're better. You're better off maybe for 'having experienced that and come through it' kind-of-thing, [it] goes right down to just how people use resilient or resilience, but I don't hear that in how you're talking about strong mind. I don't hear a judgement about you're better. . . I hear it's available to everyone, and it's not on – boom! – an experience or something. It's not based on you doing the right thing, at the right time, in the right place. It's deeper than that. Does that make sense? I don't know if what I said just now makes sense.

Jackson: I was just thinking about that report back, the community report back we did, and that guy standing up and saying, 'I never wanted to be resilient in the first place.' It was like, bam!

Brennan: A strong mind is many things. It's patience. It's that sense of connection to all things in creation. Those moments when they do come, and they do come, are such profound moments to live through. They're fleeting. They don't last very long. At least not for me they haven't, but I'm thankful that they do come. I just get this profound sense of connection to everything and everyone, and it's unshakable for the moment that I'm in it. I always take away the memory of that sense of connection. It helps me do the work that I do. It helps me think in a collective kind of way, I think.

Peltier: When we hear the words, 'all my relations', people are actually calling out to all of creation, acknowledging creation. When people say 'all my relations', sometimes people – I think people think it's just humans, but it's all of creation that you're actually acknowledging, and that's the word there, and I actually have that word broken down by sound, and that explains the meaning of that word, and – but it's really a call out, an acknowledgement of all creation, all life. When you reach that understanding, it's really profound, and I don't know if I'm reaching some of that understanding at my age now, but it still goes back to that 'all my relations', and it's connected to that as well, and that's a gift of creation.

Brennan: It really does shed our understanding of resilience. A strong mind is a gift from Creator. It's connected to everything and everyone in the broadest sense of the word. It isn't simply about an individual who is strong and able to cope with challenges. I think there's a lot that we talked about that shifts our understanding of resilience, and also adds, I think, to that emerging body of Indigenous scholarship, which is critiquing resilience, because the few articles I've read from Indigenous scholars, that first critique resilience, are talking more instead of that it's about connection. It's about connection to your community, to your elders. It's about participating in ceremony. It's about being able to speak your language, those kinds of things. I think of the story that we have shared today just starts to add – starts to nuance that discussion that other Indigenous scholars have paved for us to have this conversation, I think, in some ways.

Discussion

Our conversation focused on *amishakoowendamo'awag*, and below we situate our ideas about a strong mind in the context of earlier Indigenous scholars' critiques of resilience. In many ways, our chapter pushes back against a Western theory of resilience as 'positive adaptation' (Fleming & Ledogar, 2008), individual ability to 'absorb shocks and being able to bounce back' (Alexander, 2013), 'ability to rebound' from life's challenges (Weley-Esquimaux, 2009), or ability to 'recover and surmount' difficult conditions (McGuire-Kishebakabaykwe, 2010). In pushing back against these Western definitions of resilience, as do other Indigenous scholars, we underscore the need to conceptualise *amishakoowendamo'awag* and Indigenous resilience. This reframing, we believe, illuminates the 'strength and power of Indigenous collective and cultural knowledge' (Thomas et al., 2015, pp. 1–2). It is an idea that has already found broad and far-reaching support from other Indigenous resilience scholars. As Alexander (2013) writes, such a position opens the possibility that we might 'focus not on what [is] wrong with [Indigenous] people, but on their strengths' (p. 3).

As authors of this chapter, we were compelled to devote time, energy, and other resources to examine resilience through Indigenous knowledge systems. In this, we potentially identified and now better understand how aspects of the Indigenous cultural world protect our communities to situate their own gifts, gifts given by the Creator, and to mobilise these in difficult contexts (Lam et al., 2020; McGuire-Kishebakabaykwe, 2010). To be clear, while the word 'resilience' has been used to describe the ways in which Indigenous peoples respond to adversity, the lived meaning of this word is best grounded in Indigenous languages, such as *amishakoowendamo'awag* or *gidoo-amishakoowendam*. Using *Anishinaabe* words to talk about resilience refocuses our attention on the power of 'all my relations' and recognises that we 'are part of the circle'. To embody *amishakoowendamo'awag* is to be human, to live one's authentic self with a clear vision, and to unmask and untangle oneself through ceremony. Strand and Peacock (2003, p. 1) describe this protective factor as 'cultural resilience', which involves 'the use of traditional life-ways to overcome negative influences of oppression, abuse, poverty, violence, and discrimination.' Such culturally grounded frameworks also receive broad support in the literature (Duran & Duran, 1995; HeavyRunner, 2003). As highlighted in our conversation, *amishakoowendamowin* (strongmindedness) is a gift from the Creator, is something all humans are born with, and is activated and mobilised through ceremony. In other words, when we use enduring land-based cultural traditions and ceremonial practices (McGuire-Kishebakabaykwe, 2010), we ground our individual development to facilitate the embodiment of the notion *gidoo-amishakoowendam* (Burnette et al., 2018; Hamby et al., 2016; Wexler, 2013).

Conclusion

Our chapter highlights a need to shift our focus away from the perceived individual deficits so often attributed to Indigenous peoples, and even from the Western notion of resilience. Rather, we argue that Indigenous peoples possess formidable cultural strengths, and we can mobilise health services to turn their attention to 'unrecognised and neglected sources' of Indigenous well-being (Gone & Kirmayer, 2002). *Gidoo-amishakoowendam* is facilitated through a connection to land, ceremony, traditional medicines and spirituality. As McIvor and colleagues (2009) assert, when Indigenous peoples are offered community resources and are 'supported by elders and spiritual leaders', such offerings inspire a deeper connection to something they already possess, a gift from the Creator: *gidoo-amishakoowendam* you have a strong mind!

Dedication

We dedicate this paper to Tony Nobis – who is now on his spirit journey – this paper is for your wise, gentle and inspiring authority. Having had you in our lives has helped us shift in how we think about, witness and live Indigenous resilience. You have changed us for the better and for good.

References

Alexander, D. (2013). Resilience and disaster risk reduction: An etymological journey. *Natural Hazards and Earth System Science*, 2707–2716. doi.org/5194/nhess-13-2707-2013.

Baskin, C. (2005). Storytelling circles: Reflections of Aboriginal protocols in research. *Canadian Social Work Review*, 171–187.

Bond, C. (2005). A culture of ill health: Public health or Aboriginality? *Medical Journal of Australia, 183*(1), 39–41. doi.org/10.5694/j.1326-5377.2005.tb06891.x

Brant Castellano, M. (2000). Updating Aboriginal traditions of knowledge. In G. Sefa Dei, B. Hall, & D. Goldin Rosenburg (Eds.), *Indigenous knowledges in global contexts: Multiple readings of our world*, pp. 21–36. University of Toronto Press.

Brennan, D., Georgievski, G., Jackson, R., Horemans, C., Zocole, A., & Nobis, T. (2021). Resilience among two-spirit males who have been living with HIV long term: Findings from a scoping review. *Journal of Indigenous HIV Research, 12*, 5–28.

Brennan, D., Jackson, R., Georgievski, G., Zocole, A., & Nobis, T. (2021). Indigenizing scholarship to examine resilience among HIV-positive two-spirit men: Lessons learned from the 2-spirit HIV/AIDS wellness and longevity study (2SHAWLS). *Journal of Indigenous HIV Research, 12*, 29–45.

Burnette, C., Clark, C., & Rodning, C. (2018). 'Living off the land': How subsistence promotes well-being and resilience among Indigenous peoples of the southeastern United States. *Social Service Review, 92*(3), 369–400. doi.org/10.1086/699287

Cochran, P., Marshall, C., Garcia-Downing, C., Kendall, E., Cook, D., McCubbin, L., & Gover, R. (2008). Indigenous ways of knowing: Implications for participatory research and community. *American Journal of Public Health, 98*(1), 22–27. doi.org/2105/AJPH.2006.093641

Duran, E., & Duran, B. (1995). *Native American Postcolonial psychology.* State University of New York.

Fleming, J., & Ledogar, R. (2008). Resilience, an evolving concept: A review of literature relevant to Aboriginal research. *Pimatisiwin: A Journal of Aboriginal and Indigenous Community Health, 6*(2), 7–25.

Gone, J., & Kirmayer, L. (2002). Advancing Indigenous mental health research: Ethical, conceptual and methodological challenges. *Transcultural Psychiatry, 57*(5), 235–249. doi.org/10.1177/1363461520923151

Gracey, M., & King, M. (2009). Indigenous health part 1: Determinants and disease patterns. *The Lancet, 374*, 65–75. doi.org/10.1016/S0140-6736(09)60914-4

Graveline, F. (2010). Circle as methodology: Enacting an Aboriginal paradigm. *International Journal of Qualitative Studies in Education, 13*(4), 361–370. doi.org/10.1080/095183900413304

Greenwood, M., de Leeuw, S., & Lindsay, N. (2018). *Determinants of Indigenous peoples' health: Beyond the social.* CSP Books, Inc.

Haddad, N., Robert, A., Weeks, A., Popovic, N., Siu, W., & Archibald, C. (2019). HIV in Canada – Surveillance Report, 2018. *Canadian Communicable Disease Report, 45*(12), 304–312. doi.org/10.14745/ccdr.v45i12a01

Hamby, S., Banyard, V., & Grych, J. (2016). Strengths, narrative, and resilience: Restorying resilience research. *Psychology of Violence, 6*(1), 1–7. doi.org/10.1037/vio0000027

HeavyRunner, I. (2003). *Nurturing resilience in American Indian and Alaska Native children, youth, and communities.* CYC-Online, 1–3.

Jackson, R., Brennan, D., Georgievski, G., Zocole, A., & Nobis, T. (2021). 'Our gifts are the same': Resilient journeys of long-term HIV-positive two-spirit men in Ontario, Canada. *Journal of Indigenous HIV Research, 12,* 46–64.

King, M., Smith, A., & Gracey, M. (2009). Indigenous health part 2: The underlying causes of the health gap. *The Lancet,* 78–85. doi.org/10.1016/S0140-6736(09)60827-8

King, T. (2003). *The truth about stories: A Native narrative.* House of Anansi Press.

Lam, D., Hinz, E., Lang, D., Tengo, M., von Wehrden, H., & Martin-Lopez, B. (2020). Indigenous and local knowledge in sustainability transformations research: A literature review. *Ecology and Society, 25*(1), 3. doi.org/10.5751/ES-11305-250103

Lavallee, B., & Clearsky, L. (2006). From woundedness to resilience: A critical review from an Aboriginal perspective. *Journal of Aboriginal Health, 1*(4–5), 4–5.

Lavallee, L., & Poole, J. (2010). Beyond recovery: Colonization, health and healing for Indigenous peoples in Canada. *International Journal of Mental Health Addiction, 8,* 271–281. doi.org/10.1007/s11469-009-9239-8

Lima, V., Kretz, P., Palepu, A., Bonner, S., Kerr, T., Moore, D., Daniel, M., Montaner, J. S. G., & Hogg, R. (2006). Aboriginal status is a prognostic factor for mortality among antiretroviral naïve HIV-positive individuals first initiating HAART. *AIDS Research and Therapy, 3*(14), 1–9. doi.org/10.1186/1742-6405-3-14

Loppie, C. (2017). Promising practices in Indigenous community health promotion. In I. Rootman, A. Pederson, K. L. Frohlich, & S. Dupéré (Eds.), *Health promotion in Canada: New perspectives on theory, practice, policy, and research,* pp. 184–202. Canadian Scholars' Press.

Luthar, S. (2006). Resiliency in development: A synthesis of research across five decades. In D. Cicchetti & D. J. Cohen (Eds.), *Developmental psychopathology: Risk, disorder, and adaptation,* pp. 740–795. Wiley.

Marmion, D., Obata, K., & Troy, J. (2014). *Community, identity, wellbeing: The report of the second National Indigenous Languages Survey.* Australian Institute of Aboriginal and Torres Strait Islander Studies.

Martin-Hill, D. (2009). Traditional medicine and restoration of wellness strategies. *International Journal of Indigenous Health, 5*(1), 26–42.

McGuire-Kishebakabaykwe, P. (2010). Exploring resilience and Indigenous ways of knowing. *Pimatisiwin: A Journal of Aboriginal and Indigenous Community health, 8*(2), 117–131.

McIvor, O., Napoleon, A., & Dickie, K. (2009). Language and culture as protective factors for at-risk communities. *Journal of Aboriginal Health, 5*(1), 6–25.

McLeod, N. (2007). *Cree narrative memory: From treaties to contemporary times.* Purich Publishing Ltd.

Miller, C., Spitall, P., Wood, E., Chan, K., & Schechter, M. (2006). Inadequacies in antiretroviral therapy use among Aboriginal and other Canadian populations. *AIDS Care, 18*(8), 968–976.doi.org/10.1080/09540120500481480

Negin, J., Aspin, C., Gadsden, T., & Reading, C. (2015). HIV among Indigenous peoples: A review of the literature on HIV-related behaviour since the beginning of the epidemic. *AIDS and Behavior, 19*, 1720–1734. doi./org.10.1007/s10461-015-1023-0

Newhouse, D. (2006). Editorial: From woundedness to resilience. *Journal of Aboriginal Health, 3*, 2–3.

Ontario First Nations HIV/AIDS Education Circle. (n.d.). *My heart and spirit have come home: In our own words* (Vol. 2). Anishinabek Nation: Union of Ontario Indians.

Peltier, D., Jackson, R., Prentice, T., Masching, R., Monette, L., Fong, M., & Shore, K. (2011). When women pick up their bundles: HIV prevention and related service needs of Aboriginal women in Canada. In J. Gaghagan (Ed.), *Women and HIV in Canada: Implications for research, policy and practice*, pp. 85–104. Canadian Scholars' Press.

PHAC. (2010). *Population-specific HIV/AIDS status report: Aboriginal peoples.* Public Health Agency of Canada (PHAC).

Poff, D. (2006). The importance of story-telling: Research protocols in Aboriginal communities. *Journal of Empirical Research on Human Research Ethics, 1*(3), 27–28. doi.org/10.1525/jer.2006.1.3.27

Reading, J., & Nowgesic, E. (2002). Improving the health of future generations: The Canadian Institutes of Health Research, Institute of Aboriginal Peoples' Health. *American Journal of Public Health, 92*(9), 1396–1400.

Richmond, C., Ross, N., & Egeland, G. (2007). Social support and thriving health: A new approach to understanding the health of Indigenous Canadians. *Amercian Journal of Public Health, 97*(9), 1827–1833. doi.org/10.2105/AJPH.2006.096917

Rothe, J., Ozegovic, D., & Carroll, L. (2009). Innovation in qualitative interviews: 'Sharing circles' in a First Nation community. *Injury Prevention, 15*, 334–340. doi.org/10.1136/ip.2008.021261

Smith, L. T. (2014). *Decolonizing methodologies: Research and Indigenous peoples* (2nd ed.). Zed Books.

Statistics Canada. (2017). *Aboriginal peoples in Canada: Key results from the 2016 Census.* Statistics Canada.

Stewart-Harawira, M. (2018). Indigenous resilience and pedagogies of resistance: Responding to the crisis of our age. In J. Kinder & M. Stewart-Harawira (Eds.), *Resilient systems/resilient communities: Intersections of sustainability*, pp. 158–179. Kule Institute for Advanced Study, University of Alberta.

Stokes, J., Pennock, J., & Archibald, C. (2006). *Factors associated with late HIV diagnosis in Canada*. International AIDS Society.

Strand, J., & Peacock, R. (2003). Resource guide: Cultural resilience. *Tribal College Journal, 14*(4), 28–31.

Thomas, D., Mitchell, T., & Arseneau, C. (2015). Re-evaluating resilience: From individual vulnerabilities to the strength of cultures and collectivities among Indigenous communities. *Resilience: International Policies, Practices and Discourses, 4*(2), 116–129. doi.org/10.1080/21693293.2015.1094174

Walker, P. (2001). Journeys around the medicine wheel: A story of Indigenous research in a Western university. *Australian Journal of Indigenous Education, 29*(2), 18–21.

Weley-Esquimaux, C. (2009). Trauma and resilience: Notes on decolonization. In G.G. Valaskakis, E. Guimond, & M. Dion Stout (Eds.) *Restoring balance: First Nations women, community, and culture*, pp. 13–34. University of Manitoba Press.

Wenger-Nabigon, A. (2010). The Cree Medicine Wheel as an organizing paradigm of theories of human development. *Native Social Work Journal, 7,* 139–161.

Wexler, L. (2013). Looking across three generation of Alaska Natives to explore how culture fosters Indigenous resilience. *Transcultural Psychiatry, 51*(1), 73–92. doi.org/10.1177/1363461513497417

Wilson, K., & Young, K. (2008). An overview of Aboriginal health research in the social sciences: Current trends and future directions. *International Journal of Circumpolar Health, 67*(2/3), 179–189. doi.org/10.3402/ijch.v67i2-3.18260

Wood, E., Kerr, T., Palepu, A., Zhang, R., & Strathee, S. (2006). Slower uptake of HIV antiretroviral therapy among Aboriginal injection drug users. *Journal of Infection, 52*(4), 233–236. doi.org/10.1016/j.jinf.2005.07.008

16

Two-Spirit Return: Intergenerational Healing and Cultural Leadership among Mixed-Race American Indians

Andrew Jolivétte

> I mostly turn to my friends, um . . . I do a couple different things though, every year. I go to Oklahoma, go to ceremonies. I'm very involved with like the local Cherokee community. I've been like asked [by the] Cherokee nation to do community organising for San Francisco and the Bay Area. So I've recently went through like a leadership training. I got sent back to Oklahoma to um . . . to um to do leadership training. [*Indian Blood* respondent, 2012]

Indigenous cultural mentoring networks

Indigenous cultural mentoring networks (ICMNs) offer a counter-hegemonic model for stress-coping and high-risk behaviour among mixed-race, lesbian, gay, bisexual, transgender, queer, and/or two-spirit (MLGBTQ2s) populations in the San Francisco Bay Area that can reduce rates of HIV infection among this population. ICMNs can also serve as a mechanism to achieve decolonisation and a two-spirit return. Striving for two-spirit return, however, entails an acceptance of the regionally specific context of the term 'two-spirit' as created, maintained and practiced with the Traditional Urban Indian Cultural Knowledge Systems (TUICKS) within the San Francisco area. The term two-spirit as discussed throughout this book is not a fixed, universal category that can be applied to all American

Indian tribes and nations. However, within TUICKS, two-spirit return can and should include a process for self-determination and self-definition articulated by MLGBTQ2s people who, together with other Indigenous people, engage in urban Indian kinship networks.

Many of the *Indian Blood*[1] respondents speak to the need for stronger kinship networks that include local Native friends with shared identities, as well as a balance between these networks in urban areas and ceremony within their respective nations. The quotation that opens this chapter raises important and fundamental questions about leadership, ceremony, and reciprocity as healing. While there are very few studies that assess the efficacy of peer-mentoring programmes as a measure to reduce high-risk sexual behaviour, those studies have demonstrated that peer mentoring interventions (PMIs) can mitigate injection drug use and other high-risk behaviours associated with HIV seroconversion (Purcell et al., 2007). Social learning, along with ICMNs, is effective in both disease management and prevention among marginalised groups, according to Purcell et al. (2007):

> The peer mentoring intervention [PMI, the intervention condition] was developed based on a combination of theories and concepts, including empowerment (Zimmerman, 1995; Hays et al., 2003); peer leadership or advocacy (Kelly et al., 1997); Social Learning Theory (SLT, Bandura, 1986); Social Identity Theory (Latkin et al., 2003); and the Information, Motivation, and Behavioral Skills (IMB) Model (Fisher & Fisher, 1992). Participants were told during the first session that we wanted to help them try out a new social role as informal peer mentors and that learning this role would help them to protect themselves and their communities (using the slogan 'power to protect').

The PMI they developed for injection drug users provides some insight into the possible ways to organise PMIs for MLGBTQ2s populations to reduce the transmission of HIV. Modifications to this model should consider MLGBTQ2s priority concerns and cultural knowledge, and include a scale to measure and address historical and intergenerational trauma, as well as stress-coping mechanisms. The Purcell model relies quite heavily on traditional Western approaches to mentoring and prosocial behaviour, and does not necessarily consider the ramifications of psycho-social traumas on populations that experience Post-Traumatic Invasion Syndrome (PTIS). PTIS is the result of two-spirit dissolution after European invasion in the Americas, a process that began in American

---

[1] Andrew Jolivétte, *Indian Blood: HIV and colonial trauma in San Francisco's two-spirit community* (University of Washington Press, 2016).

Indian societies that continues to produce painful memories of a history and on-going condition that is seldom discussed, but is very evident when we look at American Indian health and pathways to healing. PTIS is the negative colonial affect that European invasion in the United States has cause since this first contact into the contemporary period. An effective and responsible approach to PMIs among Indigenous peoples must centre cultural knowledge, harm reduction and community leadership through social and political participation. Many MLGBTQ2s respondents speak of their experiences with revictimisation and weak health and wellness networks. The fear of revictimisation, coupled with a fragile health support network, gives many vulnerable populations pause when deciding whether to participate in new studies, including interventions. Consider the following statements made by *Indian Blood* participants:

> I couldn't tell you, besides my brother . . . I couldn't tell you any of my brothers' and sisters' birthdays. I don't know them. I don't keep those kinds of things in my brain. But um . . . yeah it's as if we're going to doctors and stuff regularly . . . It's only until recently that I've actually needed to go to the doctor, and it's like, I didn't know where to go. I don't have the money. I don't have insurance. So I was like, where am I gonna go? But I'm not enrolled, so I was like, can I go to the Indian health centre? Will they take me? Or Valley Medical, where they'll just charge you later . . . Lots and lots of money! But it was like, hmmm, no I've always just muddled through like my boss says about me, 'I don't know how you always do it, you just keep marching on!' It's like, well there's not too many other choices. You either just lay down and die or keep going. And I keep going, usually with a smile on my face. [*Indian Blood* respondent, 2012]

> Uh . . . I don't know . . . I actually . . . the last time I saw a doctor it was re-traumatizing, it was at the health centre. He wanted to do a genital examination, and I said I have a history of sexual abuse. Absolutely not! When I'm down on the table, he does what he wants to do. And when I brought it up with the health centre, then it's . . . victimise, or re-victimise, or . . . blame the victim type, type of thing. After that point it's just, ya know what, it is . . . No matter where you go, it's Western medicine. Um . . . It's a long history of abuse, um, and until it really approaches a position of holistic care, then I might consider it. But I deal with that a lot and um I just keep going. So and I do get a lot of lectures, but ironically a lot of women understand why I refuse services. Cause I'm not . . . ya know I did the adult thing, I did the 'right' thing and yet even though I went and done what was supposed to be the 'right' thing it like um . . . Don't disempower me! Cause that could be deadly at some point, more so for the other side. [*Indian Blood* respondent, 2012]

These responses not only convey the ongoing challenges of policing Indian identity for those who are mixed-blood and/or unenrolled, they also demonstrate that many people in the Native community of the San Francisco Bay Area are struggling to just 'keep going on' with few healthcare options. The participants' quotes also condemn the fact that even within some Native-specific organisations there may be doctors and non-Native staff who treat patients with the same kind of care that they might receive from non-ethnic-specific hospitals. As one man points out, he doesn't want to feel disempowered or revictimised as a survivor of sexual violence.

So how do we balance the needs of MLGBTQ2s populations within the context of ongoing colonial medical practices? There are at least two essential steps that must be taken when we consider the potential benefits of developing a PMI model, or any intervention, for MLGBTQ2s-identified Natives. First, it is important to structure interventions that consider ethnic, tribal and cultural affinity. While many of the factors associated with the IBPN (Indian Blood Psychosocial Nexus of Risk) model (a model that identifies six interrelated factors in contributing to HIV/AIDS disparities among American Indians. These six factors include: two-spirit cultural dissolution, historical and intergenerational trauma, gender and racial discrimination, mixed-race cognitive dissonance, sexual violence, and impaired stress coping in urban settings) can be traced back to tribal communities of origin, or within families, causing distrust among younger and elder generations or between those who share particular ethnic, gender, or sexual orientation affinities, it is still more significant that PMIs pair MLGBTQ2s individuals with mentors who have a similar background and experience if we are to expect intervention participants to feel safe sharing their stories and experiences. Second, HIV support groups or prevention models within mainstream hospitals do not meet the cultural competence needs of many MLGBTQ2s people, nor do these facilities consider the impact of white racism within queer communities as potentially destructive to peer mentoring that is inter-racial. In other words, mainstream and ethnic-specific health organisations that house support groups must consider how they lack the infrastructure to support ethnic, gender and culturally specific peer mentoring groups. One participant spoke about his experience with Kaiser Hospital's HIV support group and how whiteness and the fear of white sexual predatory behaviour impacts his choices in selecting a peer support group in the San Francisco Bay Area:

> Kaiser has like two HIV support groups, and it had like a gay men's group and like a mixed group of people. And I decided, after I heard things about both groups, that I really didn't want to go to the gay one because I felt

> that it was mostly an older, long-term survivor sort of group; of mostly gay white men. And I just felt I didn't, I wasn't going to relate to them. And at that point I was really so vulnerable, being recently like seroconverted, that like I didn't want to deal with white dudes . . . Basically . . . and white dudes hitting on me, ya know, in this moment of like . . . where I felt like vulnerable sexually or whatever. I'd rather deal with the straight dude at the HIV positive group, ya know who was like ya know whatever. So I went to like the straight support group. Which actually turned out to be more people of colour, and a little younger set; and a quarter of them were gay anyway. [*Indian Blood* respondent, 2012]

This statement suggests that the importance of Indigenous mentoring networks should be central to any HIV intervention model for MLGBTQ2s populations. This individual, rather than choosing a group of other gay men, chose a heterosexual group because of the stigmas associated with white colonialism, sexual abuse and objectification. While there are many concerns and potential problems with non-ethnic-specific peer mentoring models, I do not want to understate the complexities also associated with the development of an Indigenous cultural mentoring network. Some participants raise significant concerns about the ongoing stereotypes and pan-Indian reductionist approaches of urban Indian organisations that lack tribal specificity.

> How can it be better? I come in and everyone is all friendly and stuff, but sometimes they . . . I wish there was more money for staff and there was no restrictions on blood quantum, or are you enrolled? Or this or that. It's like, just if you need help, we are here to help you. That would be lovely. Like okay, that's the restrictions I'm talking about, it's like if you need . . . 'Cause that's what I would do, if you need help, let me help you. 'Cause there was a lady crying the train station today, just this old woman sitting in the corner crying on the ground. And I went and talked to her and I offered to buy her some cold medicine or whatever she needed. And she was doing alright and says, 'Will you just talk to me?' So I sat for 15 minutes and talked to her. She said thank you! And I shook her hand and I said, 'I hope you feel better.' But she goes, 'That helped.' Even that little tiny bit, even though I didn't do anything, I just talked to her. But to offer no restrictions, you don't have to give me any money, whatever you need please let me help you. That would be nice . . . In a perfect world. [*Indian Blood* respondent, 2012]

Internalising the ideologies of colonising nations continues to deeply impact the delivery of health care services in Indigenous communities, as the previous quote demonstrates. If Native-specific organisations are to effectively reduce HIV/AIDS risk, there has to be a shift from colonial policies and practices, which focus more on blood quantum and enrolment restrictions, to a shared sense of community-based urban cultural affinities, participation and high quality services. Cultural competence as discussed thus far is a primary and foundational component of building an urban American Indian kinship network of support, but without a high degree of service delivery, cultural competence may not be enough to prevent MLGBTQ2s people from choosing non-ethnic-specific efficiency over ethnic-specific cultural competence:

> I think, like some basic competence would help, first of all. Sometimes I go into a clinic or something, and there might be staff, they might be ethnically, culturally competent. But when you wanna get something done, they have no clue of how to treat people. Like, ya know it takes them forever to do something for you that should, that they should just know how to do what needs to be done. So like there's this baseline of confidence, ya know, that should exist. Um . . . and they should be efficient. That's why I'd rather go to somebody who is not culturally competent who is gonna be efficient with my care. Then on top of that, it's icing on the cake if like they have some competence . . . Ya know 'cause I go to Kaiser and my physician is really competent. My nurse calls back when I call her, she picks up the phone, she answers me. She tries to do the best that she can, and I feel that. And that's what gives me confidence, ya know, in the services. Yeah. And then like, secondly, it's like um . . . yeah it would be nice to like have ya know folks who were like gay in the end. At all levels of the staff, not just the frontline staff. Cause often you go to like a Native organisation and the frontline staff is like maybe, Indian, and the middle management are like White or Asian, and then the very top are like ya know these Indian moguls. Who like lorded over everybody else and used the middle management to like control everybody else. I think that's actually the case here in San Francisco at the health centre, and stuff like that. And I think that's a problem. Um . . . I think you need to have like Indian people in every single area of the organisation. [*Indian Blood* respondent, 2012]

While this participant raises important points about the significance of having culturally competent and efficient services that include gay and Native staff at all levels of Native organisations, there is a possible lack of awareness about the ability of American Indian organisations and health agencies to hire all-Native staff, due to the overall size of the population and a shortage of Native Americans in the field of HIV/AIDS and medicine in general. This is not to suggest that Native organisations should not re-assess the institutional culture and structure of their facilities, but it is equally important to point out that many of the ethnic-specific organisations lack the external funding to build stronger capacity or must compete with other organisations for grants to produce more efficient programmes that include more Native and MLGBTQ2s staff.

Constructing tribally specific ICMNs remains difficult in urban American Indian communities because there is often a shortage of potential mentors from the same tribes as those who would need mentoring. One possible solution to this dilemma is the co-construction and co-development of a shared definition of Traditional Urban Indian Cultural Knowledge Systems among MLGBTQ2s mentors and mentees. Sharing the responsibility for co-creating TUICKS in the San Francisco Bay Area would address at least two of the major concerns of MLGBTQ2s. First, the conflation of Indian/Pan-Indian with tribally specific nations can finally be taken off the table as a concern if we make space for at least two forms of regional/culturally specific traditional knowledge: urban and tribal nation. Second, a co-creation process of TUICKS can provide the space to deconstruct tribal-specific hegemony in the construction of Pan-Indian narratives of 'authenticity'. In other words, certain tribes such as the Lakota and Cherokee are often cited by other Natives in the Bay Area as being dominant in the construction of Native cultural practices and representations visible to non-Natives as well as other Indigenous people. An exchange between two focus group participants highlights these tensions as a call for new narratives and organisational/community-based approaches to defining urban Indian identity:

> Um . . . No, I think it's good to have a mix of people. But when I go back to Oklahoma and to Cherokee Services . . . Our Nation is different from other Indian Nations, so you can't lump all American Indians in the same group. People in Oklahoma who have a longer history of assimilation and contact with whites are more assimilated to white culture, even blood quantum-wise. My tribe is, there are very few full-bloods left. And most everybody is mixed race, that's just the way it is. Whereas if you go to like Navajo land, there's tons of full-bloods. So, to try to just lump, like, Navajos and Cherokees just because we are both Native American Indians, it's like, you're gonna be looking for different things. The Navajos are gonna expect different things than the Cherokee. Um . . . So . . . I don't know how to solve that. Yeah, I think that would be a conundrum. [*Indian Blood* respondent, 2012]

> And actually you bring up an excellent point, it's kind of ethnic domination ya know . . . I think I said honouring and respecting, and if I didn't one of the things I meant is honouring and respecting. And it's the assumptions that you're Dine or Lakota, and these are the ways and . . . That's part of the urban dynamic, especially within San Francisco and . . . Red Power, Pan-Indianism, and those other ism-schisms . . . I if on one hand, as a community,

um ... sometimes we forget to honor and embrace our differences. We'd much rather focus in on, um ... what our ethereal commonalities are, and it's actually that re-practising of racism. And just this blank stereotype of what it is, and rather than dealing with the human being. 'Cause that's what it's really about, is embracing the human being. And if there are those commonalities of, our cultural commonalities, then, ya know, great! That's all the gravy, but human services ... Two key words. [*Indian Blood* respondent, 2012]

These respondents criticise the over-homogenisation of Indigenous peoples and tribal nations into one generic 'Indian' category while missing their unique histories and experiences with colonialism and whiteness. They also indict the ways that singular nation hegemony takes form in urban Indian environments, where the influence, cultural practices and histories of larger tribes such as the Lakota, Cherokee and Dine can sometimes overshadow other Native groups, especially those who are Native to a particular urban area; in this case, California Indians are often overshadowed by nations from other regions of the country. These monolithic representations of 'the Native' as always Lakota or Cherokee, for example, can also lead to cultural appropriation of Lakota and Cherokee language and traditions by urban Indians who lack a tribally specific connection to their own Nations. Therefore, it is urgent that as we discuss and trace a dual- or multi-national tradition among urban Indians, we accept their ability to be culturally fluent in respect to their own tribes and in regards to their own traditional urban Indian communities, where they, their parents and grandparents may have grown up and participated in the development of TUICKS.

In this way, MLGBTQ2s can continue to demonstrate a deep commitment to the decolonisation of gender, sexuality and mixed-race identity as a necessary process for reducing HIV risk and building intergenerational networks of support, peer mentoring and cultural leadership that will strengthen the urban Indian community in the San Francisco Bay Area.

Intergenerational healing and cultural leadership: An intervention model – toward urban two-spirit return

Well, when I first came out here [San Francisco] there were so many different Indian people from so many different tribes, you know. And we were just so young and wide-eyed ... Many of us had been through boarding schools and then relocation. And so, um, many of us, you know, we had strong ties to our tribes and our traditions and we brought that traditional knowledge with us to the Bay Area. There were gay American Indians at Alcatraz and many of us joined in the Red Power Movement to make our voices and stories more, like, visible, you know. We had a strategy to go to the media to be sure people saw us, ya know, at, like, Pride Parades and Powwows and what not, and today a lot of that generation that started groups like Gay American Indians, we're getting older and dying off and there is like a gap or disconnect sometimes that I worry about in terms of that leadership and tight community that I felt we had. But I also see some hope, you know, with these young people in BAAITS [Bay Area American Indian Two Spirits] and others that organise the two-spirit powwows and other Wellness types of things. We need to, well, I would like to . . . Um, before it's too late, see more intergenerational spaces to ensure that gay Indians and lesbians, and two-spirits, don't stop the momentum that we built up over so many years. It's like, I worry sometimes, and I feel blessed that I learned all those ceremonies and ways of my tribe, and at the same time when I came here we made these new traditions. We struggled a lot and with the AIDS epidemic, I saw a lot of those young Indian activists die before their time and I wish they could see how things have . . . how things are kinda changing, but I know we have to get together, more the elders and [the] new generation, and get past any drama created by non-Indians and sometimes, to be honest, that we create ourselves, so we can live with more dignity and more honour, ya know what I mean? We need to have leaders so we don't lose everything we've gained through the years. I try to do my part, and I'll talk to any young person interested in this Indian community, and if I can help them learn about their own tribe I've done that too. [*Indian Blood* respondent, 2012]

MLGBTQ2s elders are a difficult population to define and identify – not everyone is simply an elder because they reach a certain age. In the context of the San Francisco Bay Area urban Indian community, I define an elder as someone who has been identified by the community as an elder as a result of their participation, leadership and cultural knowledge of Native history in the region over an extended period of time from the 1970s onward. The quote above reflects a sentiment I often hear within the two-spirit and LGBTQI+ American Indian community in the Bay Area. I've been told by elders, young people, educators and activists that intergenerational trauma can be healed if the community can deal with divisions and internal struggles that exist as a result of adopting non-Native ideologies of tradition, race, gender and sexuality. As this elder Native man expresses his concern about the future leadership of the community and protecting some of the important strides that have been made by previous and contemporary ethnic- and LGBTQI+-specific organisations, he also implicitly suggests that mentoring and preserving urban traditions alongside tribally specific traditions is possible if there is a space for this type of dialogue. I want to suggest as I conclude that questions of authenticity around what constitutes tradition create deeply embedded resentments and hostilities in some urban Indian communities (Fixico, 2000). When we attempt to understand MLGBTQ2s populations we can see why the term 'two-spirit' gives some Natives pause, as it is often oversimplified, generalised or otherwise used by outsiders in inappropriate ways. It is here that I want to open up a dialogue among scholars, activists and community members about the regionally specific meanings of the term, and how different communities come to understand and identify with the concept and practice based on how and where they were raised.

'Two-spirit' is a contested term that is not used here to represent all tribes or urban Indian communities. Urban Two-Spirit Return, in the context of this work, asserts that two-spirit identities and communities are always constructed within the genealogies of history, place and culture. I argue that two-spirit sensibilities, while diverse, do share common narratives that attempt to move away from Western colonial constructions of gender and sexuality as always fixed or binary. In the San Francisco Bay Area there is a two-spirit community, within which there are two-spirit organisations that create their own unique and specific traditional practices, in a return to non-colonial, Indigenous worldviews. There are many different tribal nations represented in this Indigenous region of the country, and this heterogeneity is becoming a central aspect of tradition for the generations of Native peoples who have relocated to the Bay Area over the past six decades, as well as those California Natives whose ancestors have lived here for centuries. In order to return to a decolonial practice of gender, sexual and ethnic diversity, urban MLGBTQ2s populations must enter into critical dialogues with one another about the ongoing impacts of intergenerational trauma.

These intergenerational dialogues, when centred on healing, can open up the conditions and possibilities for decolonisation through active and critical engagement of kinship networks working to restore the mistrust, pain and trauma associated with two-spirit dissolution and Post-Traumatic Invasion Syndrome. If MLGBTQ2s people are to reduce their risk for HIV infection, they must have a cultural structure in place to buffer the ongoing impacts of the IBPN risk factors. Based upon participant and community discussions during the course of my research collaboration with the Native American AIDS Project, at least one tangible intervention model rose to the surface as a possible stress-coping mechanism that would not only reduce HIV risk, but also strengthen community cohesion and self-determination among MLGBTQ2s American Indians in the San Francisco Bay Area.

The Intergenerational Healing and Cultural Leadership (IHCL) intervention model in the original proposal argued for a two-year, multi-site intervention, to provide empirical data to assess MLGBTQ2s service needs by implementing the model to address gaps in ethnic-specific, community-based networks of support. The modified research intervention design seeks to restore and increase the cultural networks of support that two-spirit people provide within American Indian communities. As the research has unfolded it has become clear that the intervention should begin as a one-site intervention in the San Francisco Bay Area, in order to understand the regionally specific context of two-spirit practices without assuming a priori knowledge of the other originally proposed sites in Los Angeles and Seattle. I propose a one-site intervention in partnership with the Native American Health Centers of San Francisco and Oakland. The goal of the intervention is to produce effective urban Indian kinship networks of support and healing between different generations of mixed-blood American Indians. If successful, this model will provide the community with another method to combat intergenerational trauma and two-spirit cultural dissolution while simultaneously reducing HIV risk among MLGBTQ2s people.

The IHCL Intervention Model will be proposed to the Native American Health Centers' (NAHC's) 2-Spirit Advisory Board, where I currently serve as a member, in 2014. Based on the findings of this book, I will collaborate with the NAHC to assess the feasibility of implementing the model by the end of 2014. The first year of the two-year intervention involves the recruitment of 25 elders (ideally elders will be 45 years of age and older, but the final definition of an elder will be determined by members of the advisory board, which includes community members, academics, and medical professionals), who will partner with 25 young people. Once the elders are recruited, phase two includes a focus group session and training co-designed by elder participants and NAHC staff to discuss and identify key themes and needs related to cultural retention, MLGBTQ2s leadership cultivation, and intergenerational trauma reduction. One of the anticipated challenges with this recommended intervention is identifying and recruiting the participants. In conversations with local tribal leaders, the desire for mentors has come up on numerous occasions: while there is a strong desire for peer and intergenerational mentoring programmes, there is often a lack of mentors available. To address this potential recruitment challenge I anticipate working with former members of Gay American Indians, Native American AIDS Project and BAAITS to ensure we cast a wide net to recruit participants. It will also be important to extend our recruitment efforts to local California tribal communities, reservations and rancherías that are often ignored due to distance and insufficient relationship development. Many of these members, while firmly rooted in their own specific tribal traditions, also actively participate in the cultivation and development of TUICKS and would therefore make for appropriate mentors/mentees.

The third and fourth phases of year one include the recruitment of 25 Native youth mentees (ideally under the age of 45, but the final definition of Native youth is to be determined by the 2-Spirit Advisory Board) followed by a focus group session and training co-designed by youth participants and NAHC staff to discuss key themes and needs related to cultural retention, MLGBTQ2s leadership cultivation and intergenerational trauma reduction. The second year of the IHCL Intervention Model will begin with a MLGBTQ2s cultural summit and ceremony of return and reconciliation. The ceremony will be co-created by participants, 2-Spirit Advisory Board members and NAHC staff to incorporate TUICKS and practices that are unique to the San Francisco Bay Area Indian community. During this phase, youth and elders will meet for one-on-one sessions to co-create a Native community mentors (NCMs) programme. The primary mode of interaction during meetings between mentors and mentees will be through talking circles and one-on-one sessions with elders, who will serve as NCMs. I anticipate that, as with all mentoring programmes, there will be bi-directional mentoring, and many of the youth participants will also provide important knowledge to their mentors. The most important aspect of this model, however, is that it is co-developed by MLGBTQ2s Natives and reflects their perspectives and experiences. As noted by many Indigenous scholars, we must place Indigenous knowledge creation, education and self-determination in research in the hands of the community members most directly impacted by colonisation (Smith, 1999; Mihesuah and Cavendar-Wilson, 2004; Wilson & Yellow Bird, 2005; Abu-Saad & Champagne; 2006; Wilson, 2009).

I envision the ceremony as a moment to recentre Indigenous epistemologies from both urban and tribal frameworks of cultural knowledge and community participation. Ideally the ceremony will offer an opportunity for MLGBTQ2s people to reconcile the antagonistic experiences of internal and external rejection in the face of colonial haunting; microaggressions based on race, gender and sexuality; as well as the unfinished influences of settler colonialism on Indigenous-determined group membership criteria. As elder and youth participants begin the mentoring process, they will be asked to create and complete risk-behaviour and stress-coping rubrics to measure the ways they currently deal with high-risk sexual and social behaviour as well as stress. They will be asked to identify potential goals for reducing stress and mitigating high-risk behaviour in the context of collective and communal healing, as opposed to individual therapies and intervention approaches. To this end, they will collectively establish community participation action plans (CPAPs) at the beginning of the programme for assessment at the end of the first six months of the mentoring programme. After 12 months of participation in the IHCL intervention model, all participants will report on the status of their CPAPs during a summit meeting. Youth mentees will report on their progress on taking up cultural leadership positions within the community and elders will discuss their efforts in supporting mentees with CPAPs. Each youth and elder will present an impact statement about the experience, in terms of behaviour, stress and wellness. A stress and wellness rubric will be developed to measure differences from the beginning of the intervention to the end of the first year and to assess the effectiveness of the IHCL model for the wellness of participants. The IHCL intervention seeks to create a model for American Indian healing among MLGBTQ2s individuals who are currently at risk for HIV/AIDS. If successful, this model can be used to bring new knowledge and practices to the fields of queer studies, public health and Native American studies. As a co-created, co-owned model, the approach in and of itself addresses many challenges identified throughout this book for MLGBTQ2s people. Decolonisation is ultimately a question of obtaining and sharing the power to define our experience, history and identity with other members of our community without Western, colonial influence. In co-creating this intervention, MLGBTQ2s will obtain and share the power to name their own experiences – an important first step in healing from and ending colonial haunting.

The IHCL intervention model seeks to queer public health discourse by offering new ethnic-specific and culturally competent approaches to HIV/AIDS prevention from an inter/trans-disciplinary perspective. As MLGBTQ2s people move from the most marginalised spaces in communities of Indigenous people and people of colour, to the centre of studies dealing with HIV/AIDS, there will be an emergence of more nuanced and pragmatic critical interrogations of anti-Indianism and public health disparities. The IHCL model is but one recommended step in a long process toward decolonisation and cultural healing. Every step towards wellness, inclusivity and holistic health interventions in the face of colonial haunting and HIV brings us closer to the day when gender, sexuality and mixed-race identities will not only lead to decolonisation, but toward an actualisation of a truly sovereign, self-determined American Indian community.

References

Abu-Saad, I., & Champagne, D. (2006). *Indigenous education and empowerment: International perspectives*. AltaMira Press.

Bandura A. (1986). *Social foundations of thought and action*. Prentice-Hall.

Fisher, J. D., & Fisher, W. (1992). Changing AIDS-risk behavior. *Psychology Bulletin, 111*, 455–474.

Fixico, D. (2000). *The urban Indian experience in America*. University of New Mexico Press.

Hays, R. B., Rebchook G. M., & Kegeles S. M. (2003). The empowerment project: Community-building with young gay and bisexual men to prevent HIV1. *American Journal of Community Psychology, 31*, 301–312.

Jolivétte, Andrew. (2016). *Indian Blood: HIV and colonial trauma in San Francisco's two-spirit community*. University of Washington Press.

Kelly, J. A., Murphy, D. A., Sikkema, K. J., et al. (1997). Randomised, controlled, community-level HIV-prevention intervention for sexual-risk behaviour among homosexual men in US cities. *Lancet, 350*, 1500–1505.

Latkin C. A., Sherman S. & Knowlton A. (2003). HIV prevention among drug users: Outcome of a network-oriented peer outreach intervention. *Health Psychology, 22*, 332–339.

Mihesuah, D., & Cavendar-Wilson, A. (2004). *Indigenizing the academy: Transforming scholarship and empowering communities*. University of Nebraska Press.

Purcell, D., Metsch, L., Latka, M., et al. (2004). Behavioral prevention trial with HIV-Seropositive injection drug users: Rationale and methods of the INSPIRE study. *Journal of Acquired Immune Deficiency Syndrome, 37*(2), S110–S118.

Purcell, D. W., Latka, M. H., Metsch, L. R., Latkin, C. A., Gómez, C. A., Mizuno, Y., Arnsten, J. H., Wilkinson, J. D., Knight, K. R., Knowlton, A. R., Santibanez, S., Tobin, K. E., Rose, C. D., Valverde, E. E., Gourevitch, M. N., Eldred, L., Borkowf, C. B., & INSPIRE Study Team (2007). Results from a randomized controlled trial of a peer-mentoring intervention to reduce HIV transmission and increase access to care and adherence to HIV medications among HIV-seropositive injection drug users. *Journal of Acquired Immune Deficiency Syndromes (1999), 46*, S35–S47. doi.org/10.1097/QAI.0b013e31815767c4

Smith, L. T. (1999). *Decolonizing methodologies: Research and Indigenous peoples*. Zed Books.

Wilson, W. A. & Yellow Bird, M. (2005). *For Indigenous eyes only: A decolonization handbook*. School of American Research Press.

Wilson, S. (2009). *Research is ceremony: Indigenous research methods*. Fernwood Publishing.

Zimmerman, M. A. (1995). Psychological empowerment: Issues and illustrations. *American Journal of Community Psychology, 23*, 581–599.

17

Honouring Our Ancestors: Two-Spirit Resurgence in the 21st Century

Albert McLeod

Born and raised in the colony

On 28 November 2017, the prime minister of Canada, Justin Trudeau, apologised to LGBTQ2 Canadians for the homophobia and transphobia perpetrated by the state since the early days of colonisation and the formation of Canada as a nation (Trudeau, 2017). Leading up to the apology, Canada added the numeral 2 to the end of the internationally recognised LGBTQ initialism, thus acknowledging the existence of Indigenous LGBTQ (two-spirit) people as part of the nation's history and contemporary civil society. 'Two-spirit' is an umbrella term used in North America to describe Indigenous people who may identify as LGBTQ. This chapter describes the 40-year path that two-spirit people took to be included in Canada's apology and be recognised as unique allies in the broader LGBTQ community. The narrative centres on my personal journey and experiences as an Indigenous gay man living and working in western Canada.

I was born in 1955 and raised in the small Métis village of Cormorant in northern Manitoba. My parents were of Métis ancestry; my father was a McLeod who originated from Norway House and my mother was a McIvor, originating from Cross Lake.[1] The McLeod and McIvor Half Breed clans had worked in the Hudson's Bay Company (HBC) fur trade for generations and the women of these families were primarily First Nation and Métis.

1 Norway House and Cross Lake were early Hudson's Bay Company fur trading posts.

As a cis-male child, I was attracted to feminine things like dolls, make-up and high heels at an early age. My father, Bill, was a Provincial Game Officer and I lived with my parents and five siblings on Cormorant Lake on a plot of government land. Within this family dynamic, my feminine expression was not seen as deviant or odd even though my father followed the Anglican faith and my mother was a Roman Catholic. There was little pressure for me to conform to that era's ideals of masculinity considering my family descended from generations of hunters, trappers and HBC factors.[2] A reason for this acceptance is the Indigenous philosophy referenced by Ojibwe language specialist Roger Roulette in the short film *Deb-we-win Ge-ken-am-aan, Our Place in the Circle* (National Film Board of Canada, 2008) by two-spirit film maker Lorne Olson: 'In traditional Aboriginal communities, regarding gay people, the whole notion was to value the person. Because, in their philosophy; everybody's got a purpose, everybody's got a destiny, and everybody's got a role in this world.'

My parents, aunts and uncles, and grandparents were raised within a predominantly Cree culture and were fluent speakers. This was a period of intense pressure for the northern Cree people to conform to Euro-Christian values and beliefs and Western ways of living, in order to be assimilated into Canadian society. Despite this, the worldview of my parents and immediate extended family was still imbued with the pre-contact ethic of non-interference. Brant (1990) identifies the importance of this approach: 'The ethic of non-interference is a behavioural norm of North American Native tribes that promotes positive, interpersonal relations by discouraging coercion of any kind . . . A high degree of respect for every human being's independence leads the Native to view instructing, coercing or attempting to persuade another person as undesirable behavior' (p. 535).

From the earliest days of my childhood, my grandmother, Mary Madeline McIvor (née Moose), greatly influenced my identity and sense of purpose. She was born in 1897, at the Nelson House HBC Post, into a large Cree family who were closely allied with the fur trade. In 1937, Madeline married my grandfather, Albert Bethune McIvor, after she had been recruited to help him raise his three children after his wife Alice (Madeline's younger sister) had died. My grandmother was part of a generation that transitioned from a pre-contact belief system to a Euro-Christian one by converting to Catholicism. However, she had maintained her language and the traditional sewing and food preparation skills passed on to her by her mother and grandmothers. Despite being the wife of an HBC factor, she never spoke English, perhaps because throughout her

---

2   'Factor' is a term used to describe a man in charge of an HBC trading post.

life she had been surrounded by people who were fluently Cree. Madeline was renowned for her skill in making brain-tanned hides, and sewing and decorating moccasins and jackets with her beadwork. In her smokehouse, she smoked fish and dried moose meat for making pemmican, a food staple in the fur trade. In many ways, my grandmother was a mentor to me; she heightened my interest in artistic expression and appreciation of Cree design and showed me the value of hard work. In the Ojibwe world, each person is understood to possess a divine gift (Roger Roulette, in National Film Board of Canada, 2008). In my case, the gift was my artistic abilities that mirrored those of my grandmother and her generation.

As Western assimilation continued into the 1960s and 70s, my grandmother and I soon became relics of a bygone era and we were both ostracised. With modernisation that brought electricity, airplanes and other technologies, her knowledge and skills were no longer needed or valued. For me, the traditional acceptance of gender and sexual diversity inherent in the Cree culture had dissipated and I was soon to experience the homophobia that underpinned colonisation in my community. It was in high school in the nearby town of The Pas, where we had relocated in 1963, that I first experienced the intersection of race, homophobia and classism. The pressure to affirm our heterosexuality among my male peers was intense, to the extent that other students who were gay or bisexual were forced to take on a heterosexual identity just to be physically safe and to belong.

Unwilling and unable to conform to these social ideals, I quit high school at 16 and began to experiment with alcohol and drugs. At the time, my family was in no condition to provide any mental or emotional support to a young person coming out as gay. They were stuck between two identities and two worlds, and children were considered liabilities. Living in a rural town, away from the extended McLeod and McIvor clans in the traditional territory, my family did not have access to family elders and historians, and we were treated as outsiders. Because our ancestral grandmothers had lost their Indian status when they married white men, my immediate family, for the most part, didn't talk about the past or identify any of the stresses and schisms that may have occurred then.

Although the previous generations were fluent in the Cree language, in the 1950s and 60s some families chose, consciously or unconsciously, not to pass the language to my generation. Assimilating from a Half Breed culture to that of the mainstream culture required staying under the radar, not making waves, and passing as white or assimilated. By then, the northern clan families had converted to Christianity as the church and state collaborated to settle western Canada. As such, my family had been indoctrinated to follow homophobic Christian beliefs and attitudes, as well as those introduced by the HBC. Homosexual stigma, fear and alienation permeated Canadian society. The word 'bugger' was commonly used in northern communities to express annoyance or anger toward another person. Its historic link to the term 'buggery', which describes a male engaging in anal sex with another male, had been lost by the 1950s, to the point that it had become a benign, teasing comment. But homosexual acts were still illegal in Canada, and there was no recourse for my family to deal with my situation because we were surrounded by social ostracism, racism, poverty, addictions and historic trauma.

During the early colonial period, Canada empowered various church groups (Anglican, Baptist, Mennonite Pioneer Mission, Methodist, Presbyterian, Roman Catholic, United Church) to instil homophobic and transphobic attitudes among Indigenous nations. The churches were also allowed to promote patriarchy, consequently lowering the status of Indigenous women and promoting misogynistic beliefs among the young men. This aversion to the 'power of the feminine' was then directed toward gay men and transgender women through ridicule, bullying, incest, sexual exploitation and violence. The historical record about Indigenous lesbian women, bisexual people and transgender males and females in this region is non-existent, due to intentional erasure and the criminalising and pathologising of their identities and roles.

However, one account from 1801 by Alexander Henry informs us about an Ojibwe person, Yellow Head (also known as Berdash) who would today be considered a transgender female: 'This person is a curious compound between a man and a woman. He is a man both as to members and courage, but pretends to be womanish, and dresses as such. His walk and mode of sitting, his manners, occupations, and language are those of a woman' (Henry & Thompson, 1897, p. 347). According to Roulette, 'berdash' or 'berdache' (the translation for Henry's reference to the Ojibwe term *agookwe*) means 'a hidden woman'. Henry goes on to describe the sexual mores of the Cheyenne and the sexual activity between heterosexual men and transgender women. There are no historic descriptions or identifiers of Indigenous males who would fit into the modern definition of homosexual or gay, although some of the so-called 'berdashes' in Henry's journals could have been in this category. These rare accounts describe acts of oral and anal sex, which were considered deviant by the settlers and prohibited by the various churches who ruled over Indigenous communities and the fur trade:

> Upon the whole they ['Schians' – Henry's spelling of 'Cheyenne'] appeared to me to be a fierce and savage set of scoundrels, still more loose and

licentious than the Mandanes [Mandan]; the men appeared to take pride in displaying their nudities. I am also informed that they are much given to unnatural lusts and often prefer a young man to a woman. They have many berdashes amongst them, who make it their business to satisfy such beastly passions. (Henry & Thompson, 1897, pp. 347–8)

Laws created by Canada's colonial government, such as the Indian Act (1867) and various other policies, introduced a binary gender system that held no space for two-spirit people. The censuses that included Indian reserves established the concept of a male 'head of household', thus framing extended Indigenous families within a patriarchal, nuclear-family construct to mirror that of the state (see Census of Canada, 1911). Church-sanctioned marriages, and conversion rituals like baptisms and confirmations, made it impossible for any gender and sexual diversity to openly exist. As colonisation progressed, traditional Indigenous names were soon replaced in the censuses by colonial ones, many chosen from the Bible. After the signing of treaties in Western Canada, treaty annuity paylists initially recorded traditional, non-gender-specific personal names like Kahkahpeeweenin, meaning 'Come and Eat' (Indian Affairs Canada, 1876), until enumerators and churches ultimately changed the names to European gender-specific ones. Public discourse in local newspapers was mainly about Western settlements, farming and the growth of commerce and industry. It was primarily controlled by regional politicians, federal agencies and churches, who provided a narrow, patriarchal view of society.

While new institutions like commerce, law and education began to influence the morals and values of small colonial enclaves such as the Red River Settlement in southern Manitoba, there were still remnants of an earlier colonial consciousness that was not as puritanical or censored. Toronto poet Charles Mair references a berdache identity in his 1888 poem, 'The Last Bison'. Albert Braz's review of Mair's writing establishes that the Métis, and likely the settler community, were well aware of Indigenous constructions of multiple genders: one of Mair's notes about 'The Last Bison' explains that 'A huge animal called by the half-breed plain hunters the burdash (the hermaphrodite) was occasionally found in a large bison herd. It was called by the Indians ayaquauy [*ayahkwêw*], namely of either sex.' Braz explains further: 'Unlike other androgynous bison, the burdash that appears to Mair's poet possesses not merely exceptional beauty and colossal strength but also a "voice", a voice with which he is able to produce its bygone kin's song' (Braz, 2001, p. 1). Mair's mention of the berdache in his lament about the intentional extermination of the bison from the prairies is perhaps a metaphor for the erasure of the Cree *ayahkwêw* (transgender female) identity (Vowel, 2012) and the increasing intolerance of same sex people of that era.

As European colonisers moved into Indigenous territories around the world, anthropologists and other academics shone light on the diversity they found in these ancient cultures; for example, Matilda Coxe Stevenson (1849–1915) was an American ethnologist from this era who profiled the life of We'wha, a Zuni *lhamana* (two-spirit person) and notable fibre artist, weaver and potter. Later, anthropologists like Sabine Lang and writers like Will Roscoe researched and documented the history and lives of two-spirit/ Indigenous LGBTQ people in the pre- and post-contact eras.

LGBTQ researcher Rictor Norton reveals that in the late 17th century the rise of militarisation, social policing and surveillance in European society began to reveal the extent of gender and sexual diversity there:

> The widespread appearance of queer subcultures across Europe around the year 1700 is almost certainly linked not to the rise of capitalism but to the rise of surveillance. Efficiently organized 'police forces' hardly existed before then. The subculture was uncovered as a result of new social regulations rather than created by some tenuous link with economic structures or changing gender conceptions. (Norton, 2013, p. 1)

The same policing and surveillance was embedded in the colonisation process and imported to North American colonies. Since 1841 the Canadian Criminal Code had imposed the death penalty for all persons engaging in same-sex sexual relationships (Canadian Centre for Gender and Sexual Diversity, 2018, p. 1). As the Canadian government instituted Indian Residential Schools and sent the North-West Mounted Police to combat American whiskey traders in the west, any representation outside of heteronormativity and binary gender categories was suppressed. Later, Canada sent its militia to quell the Northwest Rebellion in Saskatchewan in 1885, further suppressing Indigenous sovereignty through violence and intimidation.

Canada and its churches implemented gender segregation in their Indian Residential Schools that functioned from 1880 to 1996. In the words of the Truth and Reconciliation Commission of Canada (2015):

> These residential schools were created for the purpose of separating Aboriginal children from their families, in order to minimize and weaken family ties and cultural linkages, and to indoctrinate children into a new culture – the culture of the legally dominant Euro-Christian Canadian society, led by Canada's first prime minister, Sir John A. Macdonald. The schools were in existence for well over 100 years, and many successive

generations of children from the same communities and families endured the experience of them. That experience was hidden for most of Canada's history, until Survivors of the system were finally able to find the strength, courage, and support to bring their experiences to light in several thousand class-action lawsuit in Canada's history. (p. v)

According to Roulette, some pre-contact words are known to be archaic (i.e. no longer used), and in the case of words that would describe sexual or gender diversity, it is likely they became so during the Indian Residential School era. An intersecting policy, embedded in these institutions and that within the policing of fur traders and the military, was the focus on enforcing celibacy through social control. Certainly, any same-sex behaviour or intimacy among the many men living together in isolation on the prairies and in the north would be condemned outright and Indigenous sexual practices and mores were deemed uncivilised. It can be assumed that, in arranged and polygynous marriages among the Cree, that *ayahkwêws*[3] would have been married to heterosexual men.

Pre-contact storytelling provides a lens into Indigenous concepts that scandalised settler societies who sought to erase them entirely. Puritanical settlers were vehemently opposed to nudity, eroticism and so-called promiscuity. In the mid-1970s, with the assistance of my aunt Helene, who translated, I had the opportunity to interview my grandmother about her early life, however she was not able tell me about the Weesageechak[4] stories she was familiar with. As a Catholic, she considered them too explicit to pass on to my generation. The stories were humorous parables that informed children about their bodies, sexuality and procreation, and social codes of conduct. The modern versions of these stories are heavily censored, and in many instances, they do not make much sense due to the absence of context and a moral lesson. For the Cree, these stories were pragmatic ways of transmitting to the next generation cultural knowledge about the fertility of nature and the process of cyclical procreation.

Invocations and petitions to the spirit world were delivered through ritualised fertility ceremonies, offerings and dances. Despite the laws that prohibited them, the northern Cree continued to practice their rituals in

---

3 *Ayahkwêw*: A balanced being / a reprimanding being; a being who corrects breaches of laws (Leigh Thomas, personal communication, 19 April 2020).
4 'The Trickster goes by many names and has many forms. In Cree, the Trickster is called "Weesageechak". This figure can choose any form and disguise that it wishes. This is primarily a clownish figure whose role is to teach the people about the nature and the meaning of existence on the planet' (Indigenous Peoples Literature, 2022).

secret, far from the eyes of the colonists and informants. Certainly, early colonists in northern Manitoba were afraid of the immensity of the boreal forest they sought to subdue, but they didn't fully understand the Cree, Dene and Inuit rituals and ceremonies that bound them to the seasonal cycles and renewals that came with each summer and winter. The annual procreation of plants, animals and humans was centred on fertility and sexuality. This uncensored, explicit view of nature created tension with colonists who positioned themselves near Cree settlements to facilitate conversion to Christianity and assimilation to the colonial culture. A review of the surviving diary of Reverend Henry Budd, the first Indigenous Anglican priest in Manitoba, gives insight into this mindset:

> Although James Mackay believed that many of the traditional beliefs had been undermined, he doubted their complete elimination . . . Since conversion to Christianity not only involved the worship of a new god, but also a commitment to a new system of ethics, the strategy employed by Budd and other missionaries was the abrogation of the traditional belief system. (Pettipas, 1974, p. xxi)

At the town of The Pas, where Budd established an Anglican mission, he describes the extent of northern Cree spiritual belief and practices in the mid-1880s. At the time, the Ojibwe Midewiwin culture from the south would have arrived in this area through the fur trade routes. It is only now that these ceremonies are returning to the north.

> To the southeast in the proximity of Muddy Lake there was an island in the Saskatchewan River which grew poplar and contained the only substantial stand of wood for miles. Here the Swampy Cree were reputed to have held their councils, dog feasts, and Medicine ceremonies. Its name in Swampy Cree was Kash-Ke-Bu-Jes-Pu-Qua-Ne-Shing, translated by Hind as 'Trying [sic] the mouth of a drum.' (Pettipas, 1974, p. xxxv)

The puritanical attitude toward sex and sexuality espoused by Christian missionaries and colonists confused and frustrated Indigenous people. Elder Willie Ermine, from the First Nations University of Canada, talks with Roulette about how Indigenous culture evolved over 20,000 years in North America and the human condition had been figured out. The idea of moralising about sexuality and the need for taboos is something that settler society still struggles with. 'Although Aboriginal people valued many of the goods they received through trade with Europeans, they did not see Europeans as possessing a superior civilization, and were often appalled by such aspects of missionary life as celibacy' (Truth and

Reconciliation Commission of Canada, 2015, p. 42).

Patricia Ningewance and her mother, Christine, provide insight into the Ojibwe philosophy toward sharing cultural norms and morals through storytelling. In her recent book, *Gii-Nitaa-Aadisooke: Ojibwe Legends from Lac Seul* (2018), Patricia shares 19 legends she heard from her mother as a child in northern Ontario. Pat does not apologise for how explicit these stories are, because they were crafted to instruct young minds about the community's values and morals. However, we can see below how Western society continues to judge, edit and censor Indigenous practice and knowledge.

> Note that since many children use this site, we have tried to avoid linking to any Native American legends or stories which deal explicitly with sex or contain bad language, including slur words for Native Americans. However, like the folklore of any culture – including European fairy tales – there is often violence and bad behavior in American Indian folklore, so please use discretion about sharing them with younger children. (Native Languages of the Americas, n.d.)

As I increasingly came to accept my homosexuality, I sought out gay references on television, magazines and in the movies. The portrayal of gay lives in popular media at the time was focused on victimhood and tragedy, and usually ended in the death of the principal character. As a youth, I was unaware of changes occurring in the larger political arena, such as Prime Minister Pierre Trudeau's amendments to the Criminal Code, decriminalising homosexuality in Canada, which passed into law in 1969. The first time I saw a positive portrayal of a two-spirit person was in the 1970 Hollywood film *Little Big Man*. The character Little Horse, played by Robert Little Star, is a Lakota *winkte* (transgender female) who wishes to marry the lead character Jack Crabb, played by Dustin Hoffman. I believe this scenario is drawn from a historical account described in the 1830 publication, *A Narrative of the Captivity and Adventures of John Tanner*, where Tanner recounts a meeting with Yellow Head, who is described above. At the age of 16, I was elated to finally find validation of my identity. My only gay cultural references were through television, where the flamboyant entertainer Liberace and the former US soldier and transsexual Christina Jorgenson were popular personas. I remember distinctly in 1973, while watching the 45th Academy Awards on black-and-white television, I was fascinated to see Sacheen Littlefeather walk across the stage in full traditional women's regalia to relay a message from Marlon Brando, who had just won the Best Actor Award for *The Godfather*. She stated that he would not accept the award because of the industry's stereotypical portrayal of American Indians and incidents at Wounded Knee. I was struck by the fact that an Indigenous woman was standing up to the Hollywood elites to bust their make-believe world and their myths about American history. I remember the following year that two men were married in Winnipeg: Chris Vogel and Rick North, gay rights activists, who married in the Unitarian Church.

Depressed and desperate to escape from my life of isolation in the north, I signed up for a commercial art course in the southern city of Brandon, and left home at the age of 19. In 1976, after completing the course, I moved to Winnipeg, the capital of Manitoba, where I soon met other two-spirit men through the bar scene at places like the St Regis Hotel, Giovanni's Room, Happenings, the Detour and the Silver Slipper Lounge. Men sought out casual sex and male hustlers at the Hill, and at bathhouses like the Office Sauna Bath and Obee's. Gay people in Winnipeg were very closeted, and queer Indigenous folk were segregated and tolerated at the fringes of cliques. Further, young gay men who had migrated from nearby reserves were vulnerable to sexual exploitation by older white males (known as chicken hawks), and were soon discarded in favour of new recruits. Because my earlier socialisation in the north was heteronormative, I hung out primarily with straight friends and eventually met two-spirit people, who I became fascinated with because of their humour and self-confidence.

The course of my life changed in 1977, when I saw the Canadian film *Outrageous!* starring Craig Russell as a Toronto drag queen who finds fame and fortune in the New York gay scene. The film sparked my desire to explore my feminine identity; however, drag and cross-dressing were risky and rare occurrences in Winnipeg, and the transgender identity had not yet been introduced. Facing a future of low-paying jobs, drinking parties and living a closeted life, I decided to move west to Vancouver.

> The failure of an adequate gay scene to develop in Winnipeg has severely limited the development of a gay identity and a sense of community. What happens is this. After people have come out in this city and have developed a sense of their identity as gay people, they want to live gay lives. They quickly realize that Winnipeg has very little to offer the gay person who is Out and About. Consequently, they leave Winnipeg for Toronto, Vancouver, Montreal, or even Saskatoon – places where a more developed gay scene exists. (Korinek, 2018, p. 152)

Escaping to the Hollywood of Canada

In the spring of 1979, after a two-day train ride, I arrived in Vancouver with two travelling buddies and $40 in my pocket. We soon found a social community in bars like the Castle Pub and Ambassador Hotel and gay bars like the Shaggy Horse, Faces, Luv-A-Fair Cabaret, Gandydancer, Numbers Nightclub, the Central and BJ's Club. I began to meet other two-spirit men who had similar stories to mine. They had come to Vancouver from small rural towns, Métis communities and Cree, Dene, Mohawk, Micmac and Ojibwe reserves in Canada. Many also belonged to the West Coast First Nations such as the Musqueam, Squamish, Tsleil-Waututh, Kwakiutl, Coast Salish, Tsimshian, Kaska and Chilcotin. Eventually, I was introduced to a local two-spirit group called the Greater Vancouver Native Cultural Society (GVNCS), of which many of my new friends were members. The GVNCS was founded in 1977 as a response to a First Nation candidate being denied the title of Empress of Vancouver because of racism (Dowson Buffalo, 2005). Laurie McDonald, from Alberta, created the society, which elected a Princess and Chief figurehead each year at an annual ball called the Legacy.

> Involvement in the GVNCS allows the individual to be part of a strong organization that often becomes a 'surrogate family'. This helps to create a strong identity, which is maintained through social activities, including the altruistic behaviour of fundraising for various charities. This contribution not only breaks down societal barriers, but also builds bridges between the larger society and the gay community, and from within the gay community, between First Nations and non-First Nations peoples. (Dowson Buffalo, 2005, p. 8)

I met two people who were from my home province and we became quick friends: Harvey McGillivary, who was born on the Opaskwayak Cree Nation, across the river from the town of the Pas where I was raised, and Richard Dennahardt, from a community near Brandon. In 1981, Harvey became a candidate for the GVNCS Princess title and established a family clan called the White Owl. Harvey's drag name was HaZzZel de Pontiac and she adopted me into her White Owl Clan as her surrogate daughter.[5] I took the name Annie as I established a female persona in the

---

5   A common practice among some circles of cisgender gay men was to use female pronouns to refer to one another. It was a term of acknowledgement of the person's feminine side and was not seen as a slight or judgement. I believe verbal gendering practices like this pre-date European colonisation, and it was likely something that existed in ancient cultures. It can be understood as an alignment of a person's feminine power/identity with the lineage of their female

GVNCS. I chose this name when I left Manitoba because Annie was my grandmother Madeline's aunt. At the time, I felt it was important to call on a spirit guide to protect me on my journey west, and her story resonated with me. There were other members of the GVNCS who lived primarily as cis males but also developed a female persona as part of the GVNCS community collective. Some gay cis-male members didn't follow this path; other members identified and lived solely as transgender females. Within the safety of the GVNCS gay sub-culture, it was possible for me to fulfil a gender identity that I inherently possessed but was not otherwise able to express. It was a continuation of a trajectory influenced by my knowledge of Yellow Head, Sacheen Littlefeather's resistance, and Robin Turner's performance in *Outrageous!* It is hard to know how different our lives would have been if we were raised in Indigenous communities that had not been influenced by colonisation. As I have both Cree and Scottish ancestry, could there be similar gender identity options in both ancient cultures?

The GVNCS royalty (Chiefs and Princesses) and their clan members were involved in many drag shows and socials throughout the year. Their female drag was a combination of glamorous make-up and dresses complemented at times with traditional female dress that included moccasins and other adornments. The cis-male entertainers also performed in both mainstream and traditional male regalia. However, in formal GVNCS occasions, traditional regalia was worn to represent the various nations they belonged to. The Chief and Princess wore faux eagle feather headdresses along with West Coast button blankets to recognise the traditional territory they were in. In 1982, I became the fifth GVNCS Princess with the title of Princess V, White Owl II. By then I too had a surrogate drag daughter, known as Sarah Blanket, who would become Princess VI the following year. Those of us who were new to the fast-paced life of Vancouver were vulnerable to addiction and exploitation, but with the interventions of Harvey and her husband John, many of us survived. GVNCS's Tsimshian Princess I (1978–79), White Feather Georgina Ross, was another two-spirit elder who demonstrated her culture, in that she too was wise enough to adopt me and two other Prairie people into her life and home. Establishing chosen or surrogate families and clans for social orphans is a tradition and a way to honour our ancestors' teachings. As a Cree person living in southern Manitoba in a prominently Ojibwe

> ancestors: mothers, grandmothers and great-grandmothers. Heterosexual cis-male siblings would align with the masculine attitudes and attributes of their ancestral grandfathers and great-grandfathers.

community and culture, I too have been adopted by them in my homeland.

Unbeknownst to us, the global HIV pandemic had reached Vancouver in the late 1970s and many of our friends and colleagues would soon become infected. I remember seeing an article about GRID (Gay-related Immune Deficiency) in *Time* magazine but didn't take much notice of it. GRID was later called AIDS, and as the cases steadily grew, scientists theorised about what caused the disease. Some attributed it to using poppers (amyl nitrate) or having too much sex. It wasn't until 1983 that doctors reported AIDS was caused by a retrovirus (HIV) that could be sexually transmitted. By then I was deep into the party scene and had quit my job to complete my reign as Princess. Unemployed, burnt out and afraid of contracting the virus, I decided to return to Manitoba that summer.

Return to Winnipeg (the Murky Water)[6]

In Winnipeg, I returned to living a quieter life and connecting with friends in the local gay scene. While the reality of HIV and AIDS was unfolding in gay centres in North America, it seemed far away from the small prairie city. My drinking finally caught up with me in the spring of 1986 when I joined the gay Alcoholics Anonymous group, New Freedom, and became sober. The group was composed of gay men and lesbian women, and some were Indigenous like me. It was a good group and I thrived mentally and socially within this circle of like-minded people.

That year a group of two-spirit friends and I established the Nichiwakan Native Gay Society to support Indigenous youth living in the city. Two 17-year-olds in our circle had committed suicide within months of each other, shocking us and galvanising us into doing something to support other youth. We negotiated the use of a local gay cabaret, Giovanni's Room (Gio's), to host weekend 'Tea and Bannock' socials each month. The socials were alcohol and drug free and included a drag show and a meal. Slowly we began to learn more about each other and identify the things that our community needed and was interested in. We were a mix of Cree, Ojibwe and Ojibwe Cree gay men, lesbians, and transgender men and women.

Members of the Nichiwakan Native Gay Society were interested in learning about traditional Indigenous culture and ceremonies because they had no knowledge or experience with them. One of our members, Vernon Paul, invited a knowledge keeper named Barbara Daniels to teach us. She was surprised to learn we were all gay, however because her spiritual

---

6   In the Ojibwe language, 'Winnipeg' means 'murky water'.

role was to teach the culture, she agreed to help us. Barbara taught about sharing circles, smudge ceremonies and sweat lodge songs. Myra Laramee, who had taught many two-spirit youth at Argyle Alternative High School, joined our group and we began to host sharing circles in our community.

Then one day my friend Paul Packo called me from the local hospital. He had recently returned to Manitoba from Vancouver and was working in a northern camp. Jokingly, I asked if he had AIDS and he said he did. This moment began my journey with HIV/AIDS which has lasted to this day. Paul died nine months later at the age of 28, with only his mother at his side. He was the first Indigenous person to be diagnosed with AIDS in Manitoba. Paul's death heralded an approaching decade of similar deaths of two-spirit friends and acquaintances, many of whom never made it home. The fear, shame and stigma associated with HIV/AIDS was intense in mainstream society and even more so in Indigenous communities. Because AIDS cases among Indigenous people were prominent in two-spirit men, myths persisted that it was a gay disease or that people caught it because they lived a gay lifestyle.

While there was a degree of acceptance and tolerance in the broader Winnipeg LGBTQ community, First Nations leaders were not as progressive. In 1987, Manitoba's New Democratic Party (NDP) introduced legislation that prohibited discrimination based on sexual orientation. Opposition came from the Christian-right faction as well as from some First Nation Chiefs who were vehemently opposed to linking homosexuality with an Indigenous identity. At the time, Indigenous LGBTQ people were not only dealing with racism and exclusion, they were also dealing with homophobic attitudes expressed by their own people.

In 1990, federal and provincial expropriation of traditional lands for the purposes of resource extraction, and attempts to diminish First Nations sovereignty, were met by resistance. That summer brought the Oka Crisis in Quebec and the quashing of the Meech Lake Accord by Manitoba MLA (Member of the Legislative Assembly) Elijah Harper. The Nichiwakan Native Gay Society was also active, organising the Third Annual Gathering of Native American Gays and Lesbians in Beausejour, Manitoba. It was at this time that member Myra Laramee received the vision of the name 'two-spirits', which would be introduced later at the gathering. This spiritual name resonated so well with the participants, it was quickly adopted by many of the Indigenous LGBTQ groups in Canada and the United States.

Leaders in the AIDS movement

Canada's federal programme for First Nations and Inuit health, Medical Services Branch (MSB), prioritised education and prevention to address the growing HIV epidemic in Canada. Dr Jay Wortman, a Métis physician from Alberta, was recruited to lead the response. At the local level in Winnipeg, the Nichiwakan Native Gay Society was involved in the development of the Village Clinic, a specialist HIV/AIDS clinic. (The original name proposed for the clinic was the Winnipeg Gay Men's Health Centre, modelled on the one in New York, but due to the homophobic nature of the provincial government at the time, that name was rejected.) This alliance opened the door to the further development of the two-spirit community. Myra Laramee and I were members on the first provincial AIDS advisory committee.

Glen Murray, an educator from the Village Clinic, recruited Myra, Dorland McKay and me to provide HIV/AIDS 101 education to First Nation communities throughout Manitoba. Glen and Myra also supported a group of Indigenous two-spirit youth. In 1991, a group of two-spirit volunteers established the Manitoba Aboriginal AIDS Task Force (MAATF) non-profit organisation, which functioned until 2001, when it was amalgamated into the Nine Circles Community Health Centre. The relationship with governmental programmes and community organisations increased the profile of two-spirit people and created many opportunities for engagement and support. Connie Merasty from Opaskwayak Cree Nation was featured in the 1993 National Film Board of Canada documentary, *Out: Stories of Lesbian and Gay Youth in Canada*. Billy Merasty, originally from Brochet, Manitoba, played a two-spirit character called Nathan in the TV series *Liberty Street*.

The intersection of the two-spirit movement and the response to HIV/AIDS established a strong foundation that introduced the two-spirit identity back into the First Nations and Métis cultures. With the support of Health Canada, two-spirit men and women like Kecia Larkin led the Indigenous response to HIV/AIDS. Their work culminated in the creation of the Canadian Aboriginal AIDS Network (CAAN) in 1997. CAAN further enhanced the ability of two-spirit people to participate in research and advisory committees, and to connect with other two-spirit people in other parts of Canada.

HIV/AIDS education provided a rare opportunity for LGBTQ sexual health information and safer sex practices to be delivered in First Nations communities. As many of the speakers were two-spirit men who have sex with men (MSM), the sharing of their lived experience and living with HIV/

AIDS dispelled stereotypes and myths about the pandemic. The MAATF also had the support of elders and knowledge keepers like Velma Orvis, Leslie Spillett, Barbara Daniels, Beverly Littlethunder, Linda McEvoy and May Louise Campbell, who were gay-positive and not intimidated by the stigma of HIV/AIDS.

The two-spirit movement intersected with the Indigenous women's movement because of the similar impacts of patriarchal oppression on both groups. In many cases, women's gatherings provided safe spaces for two-spirit and transgender people to gather, and Indigenous women began to advocate on behalf of their two-spirit children. One of those safe spaces was Ms Purdy's Women's Club, a lesbian bar in Winnipeg where two-spirit women connected and strengthened their involvement and voices.

While a transgender identity existed in pre-contact Indigenous cultures, it was only in the 1990s that it became recognised within the broader gay community. The initialism expanded to 'LGBTQ', which inclusively represented lesbian, gay, bisexual and transgender people. The presence of transgender men and women was rare in Manitoba history and society and even more rare in First Nation and Métis communities. The role and purpose of transgender people had been erased to the point that it became dangerous to be out as transgender. For many transgender youth, their journey began in Winnipeg's gay bars like Giovanni's Room, Happenings and The Detour, where many identified as gay and lesbian and later transitioned to be either transgender male or female. Gender fluidity was common in the gay sub-culture, where drag kings and queens rubbed shoulders with cross-dressers and transgender people.

The two-spirit population was often sexually exploited because of their vulnerability and lack of employment and stable housing. Many of the two-spirit youth who came to the city from the north, excited to be able to openly express themselves, soon became caught up in a cycle of alcohol and drug use and prostitution. They had been bullied out of school and, with no education or work experience, they rarely experienced the independence that comes with being employed. Some, overwhelmed with culture shock, regret and frustration, moved even farther away, overdosed or committed suicide. Their story is portrayed in the play *Hectic*, written by current and former sex workers from Winnipeg, in which three of the characters describe the journey of two-spirit people in the sex trade.

Despite the challenges, the Annual International Two-Spirit Gathering provided a thread of continuity and support for two-spirit people in Canada and the US. The gathering has been held in 1990, 1998, 2010 and 2018 at the Sandy-Saulteaux Spiritual Centre in Beausejour, Manitoba. Two-spirit people from Manitoba have also travelled across North America to attend the various gatherings held over the years.

Two-spirit activism

The 2-Spirited People of Manitoba (2SPM) group became a registered non-profit society in March 2006. Their organisational structure provided a mechanism for communication, outreach and advocacy. While there was some level of knowledge about two-spirit people as members of First Nations and Métis communities, political and service organisations resisted any acknowledgement, support or inclusion due to entrenched homophobia and transphobia at all levels. In 2005, the National Aboriginal Health Organization's First Nations Health Centre published a First Nations suicide prevention toolkit without including two-spirit people as a priority population. The 2SPM wrote a letter to the First Nations Health Centre identifying this exclusion and the centre responded by publishing the supplemental manual *Suicide Prevention and Two-Spirited People* in 2012.

The above scenario describes how Indigenous pedagogy, history, life philosophy and languages had been co-opted by academia, governmental research funding systems and Indigenous political organisations to hold up a colonial binary gender structure first imposed through the Indian Act and Indian Residential Schools. The personal and collective biases of high-level professionals and leaders effectively diminished and erased the two-spirit experience. They sought to promote an idealised Indigenous gender identity and sexual orientation that valued heterosexuality and binary genders, and wrap them in a culturally specific framework.

Two-spirit people began their own truth and reconciliation process back in 1988 with the launch of the Annual International Two-Spirit Gathering. Leaders like Barbara Bruce, Peetanacoot Nenakawekapo, Beverly Littlethunder, Raven Heavy Runner, Jamie Goulet, Connie Merasty, Dr Alex Wilson, Art Zoccole, Dr Myra Laramee and Sharon Day continued to educate and advocate on behalf of two-spirit development. Over 32 years, the gathering has been held in 11 states in the US and 7 provinces in Canada. Learning about traditional teachings, plant medicines and ceremonies was vital to the healing and strengthening of two-spirit people who had experienced a common traumatic history. The sweat lodge ceremony, powwow, sharing circles and pipe ceremonies became key components of the gathering. For many two-spirit people it was their first time learning about their traditional cultures, because they felt intimidated or excluded from them in their own territories. Also, the promotion of idealised binary gender roles in ceremonies made it difficult for two-spirit people who are transgender, lesbian or non-binary to wear the traditional long skirt to participate. Some elders and knowledge keepers do not believe in gender diversity and prohibit some two-spirit people from participating in various rituals and ceremonies. Because Indigenous governmental organisations like First Nations Band Councils and community programme services must comply with the Canadian Human Rights Act (2011), these incidents of discrimination are illegal and must be prevented and reconciled.

Over the past decade the 2SPM has had to advocate for fair representation and inclusion of two-spirit people in local and national events where two-spirit people have already been identified as a priority population. In 2015, Connie Merasty and I met with Perry Bellegarde, National Chief of the Assembly of First Nations (AFN) and presented him with three recommendations to support the inclusion of two-spirit First Nations people. A principal recommendation was that the AFN establish a Two-Spirit Council at the national level. The AFN amended its Charter in December 2021 to create a Two-Spirit Council.

Two-spirit elders Peetanacoot Nenakawekapo and Gayle Pruden have been leaders in reclaiming traditional two-spirit roles and opening doors in the broader Indigenous community. Peetanacoot, a long-term survivor with HIV, worked at Nine Circles Community Health Centre for 12 years and later at the Aboriginal Health and Wellness Centre for two years. Gayle, a transgender woman activist, joined the pow wow circle in 2009 as a jingle dress dancer. They exemplify the return of the Ojibwe *agookwe* identity and role. They have both travelled extensively in North America, teaching community elders, organisational staff and LGBTQ allies about the contributions and gifts of two-spirit people and how to make spaces safer and more respectful. They have also been instrumental in creating space at Sundance ceremonies in Manitoba. In 2015, the Blacksmith Family Sundance formally welcomed two-spirit people to participate in their Sundance without any gender restrictions.

The internet has brought more opportunities for two-spirit people to keep connected and reach people in rural, on-reserve, northern and remote communities. Today, there are 17 two-spirit groups in the US and Canada, and the 2SPM manages a website and Facebook group with over 1600 members. Over the past 30 years, a new generation of two-spirit people, or people who identify as Indigequeer or Indigenous LGBTQ, have risen and become leaders, activists and artists. The cathartic work of writers like Beth Brant, Chrystos and Tomson Highway is now merged with that of writers like Joshua Whitehead and Waawaate Fobister. Two-spirit youth today are more likely to finish high school, obtain a university degree and establish themselves in a career. They can also marry and have a family, with their rights recognised and protected by the state. Two-spirit youth of this generation do not have to hide their identities and can feel more confident in coming out as two-spirit at a younger age. Certainly, it is a freer time, in which two-spirit people can contribute to the wellness and growth of their communities.

Two-spirit resurgence

Over the years, the two-spirit activism that began in Manitoba influenced aspects of the Indigenous and non-Indigenous LGBTQ community beyond its borders. After 20 years, the two-spirit term slowly began to be integrated into the mission statements of mainstream LGBTQ centres in Canada. Eventually 'TS' or '2S' was attached to the end of the LGBTQ initialism. Canada eventually moved the '2S' to the front of the initialism (now including I+) in the launch of the 2SLGBTQI+ Action Plan. For the most part, the broader LGBTQ community was confused and frustrated with the term, and they didn't see why Indigenous people or Queer People of Colour (QPOC) should seek special status in the community. Conversations about Indigenous sexuality and the practice of spirituality was generally understated, and the concept of two spirits defining Indigenous LGBTQ people was challenging for many. However, the source of the name aligns with the Indigenous belief system that acknowledges the spiritual power of dimensions beyond that of human experience and perception. The churches invested in assimilating Indigenous people pathologised these beliefs and branded the unconverted as primitive devil worshippers. In Canada's history, Indigenous and non-Indigenous LGBTQ people were also branded as spiritually corrupt, deviant and unworthy of respect. It is ironic that over a century later, the two-spirit name not only affirms the spiritual aspect of LGBTQ lives, but also introduces spiritual connections to the natural world back into Canadian consciousness.

Moreover, education and research institutions, community service organisations and the federal, provincial and territorial governments have also adopted the term and initialism in their communications and programmes. The phenomenon of spirit-naming and the term 'two-spirit' were affirmed by the Canadian government in November 2017, with the prime minister's formal apology to two-spirit people and the formation of the LGBTQ2 Secretariat.

Canada's Truth and Reconciliation Commission (TRC) and the recent National Inquiry into Murdered and Missing Indigenous Women and Girls (NIMMIWG) addressed two-spirit issues to varying degrees. The TRC's 94 'Calls to Action' do not specifically provide solutions that address the binary gender construction imposed on First Nations people by the Indian Residential School System. However, after an unpromising start, the NIMMIWG broadened its mission to include two-spirit, lesbian, gay, bisexual, transgender, queer, questioning, intersex and asexual (2SLGBTQQIA) people in the consultations and in its 231 'Calls for Justice', an action that is reflective of decolonisation and reconciliation. The inquiry's final report identifies 32 calls in a section titled '2SLGBTQQIA-Specific Calls for Justice'.[7] In June 2018, as an expert witness on behalf of the 2SPM, I gave testimony to the inquiry about the history and experience of two-spirit people.

Historically, the two-spirit liberation movement began in the 1960s, when First Nations people in the US and Canada were relocated to large urban centres. In 1975, Randy Burns (Northern Paiute) and Barbara Cameron (Lakota) created the Gay American Indians group in San Francisco. Since then there have been various attempts to establish two-spirit organisations that provide support programmes. To date, the 2-Spirited People of the 1st Nations in Toronto has been the only group to achieve this status. In 2003, the Aboriginal Two-Spirit Working Group (Edmonton) and the Nechi Institute co-hosted 'Two Spirits in Motion: The First Canadian Forum on Two Spirit Peoples, HIV/AIDS and Health' in Edmonton. Two significant recommendations of the forum were to create a national two-spirit organisation and to continue hosting national forums on two-spirit people (Aboriginal Two-Spirit Working Group (Edmonton) & Nechi Institute, 2003). Initially, the 2-Spirited People of the 1st Nations agreed to amend their incorporation status to become the national organisation; however, interest lapsed and there was no further planning until 2018, when the Two Spirit Circle of Edmonton Society met at the 31st Annual International Two-Spirit Gathering in Manitoba to elect a board of directors for the national non-profit 2Spirits in Motion Society (2SiMS).[8]

After 30 years of lobbying First Nations leaders for support, two-spirit

---

7   In 2022, Canada moved '2S' to the front of the LGBTQI+ initialism: women-gender-equality.canada.ca/en/free-to-be-me/federal-2slgbtqi-plus-action-plan.html

8   The incorporated name was originally the 2Spirits in Motion Foundation, but was changed to the 2Spirits in Motion Society in January 2020.

First Nations people were finally able to receive the support they needed. At the Assembly of First Nations (AFN) General Assembly held in Vancouver in July 2018, delegate Chief Alan Polchies Jr, of St Mary's First Nation, and elder Ed Lavallee made a resolution for the AFN to support the development and subsequent funding of the 2SiMS to establish a national voice and presence for two-spirit peoples throughout Canada. The resolution passed unanimously.

Métis two-spirit people have also made progress in finding support from an Indigenous political base. In August 2019, the Manitoba Métis Federation (MMF) announced the 2Spirit Michif Local, the first organisation of its kind that represents two-spirit people. Institutions like universities have also been responsive by including two-spirit people in Indigenous history and working to make their institutions culturally safer. The University of Winnipeg Archives maintain a two-spirit collection and the university supported a forum, 'C2C: Two Spirit & Queer People of Colour Call to Conversation with LGBT & Allies', in October 2017. Many Inuit do not identify with the two-spirit term, and there is little information about LGBTQ activism among LGBTQ Inuit people.

In 1955, when I was born, my grandmother Madeline was already 58 years old. She lived to be 93, dying in 1990. I live in the 21st century, establishing the trajectory and narrative of my life and hers over three centuries. As a grandmother she intuitively gave me unconditional love and the nurturance of spirit that helped me survive colonial racism and homophobia. Today, I have my own surrogate extended family of two-spirit daughters who are in their thirties and forties and also have a 22-year-old godson and two adopted granddaughters aged 11 and 13. As we move forward together, we honour and claim the knowledge of our ancestors and the sacred ways we were forced to discard along our journey.

References

Aboriginal Two-Spirit Working Group (Edmonton) and the Nechi Institute. (2003). *Two Spirits in motion: 1st Canadian forum on two spirit peoples, HIV/AIDS and health* [Video]. YouTube. youtube.com/watch?v=7S5FwvcLf2Y

Brant C. (1990). Native ethics and rules of behaviour. *Canadian Journal of Psychiatry, 35*(6), 534–539. doi.org/10.1177/070674379003500612

Braz, A. (2001). Wither the white man: Charles Mair's 'Lament for the bison'. *Canadian Poetry, 49*, 40–55.

Canadian Centre for Gender and Sexual Diversity (2018). *Queer Canadian history timeline – Pre-colonization to present.* ccgsd-ccdgs.org/wp-content/uploads/2020/09/Canadian-History-Timeline.pdf

Countries and their Cultures. (2020). *North America, Cree/Western Woods.* everyculture.com/North-America/Cree-Western-Woods-Marriage-and-Family.html

Census of Canada. (1911). Northwest Territories, Nelson House, Manitoba, p. 17. automatedgenealogy.com/census11/SplitView.jsp?id=27355

Dowson Buffalo, D. (2005). *Decolonizing homosexuality: A history of the Greater Vancouver Native Cultural Society.* [Unpublished essay, First Nations Studies 490]. Vancouver Island University.

Henry, A., & Thompson, D. (1897). *New light on the early history of the greater Northwest: The manuscript journals of Alexander Henry, fur trader of the Northwest Company, and of David Thompson, official geographer and explorer of the same company. 1799–1814. Exploration and adventure among the Indians on the Red, Saskatchewan, Missouri, and Columbia Rivers.* Francis P. Harper.

Indian Affairs Canada. (1876). Treaty Annuity Paylists 1871–1876, Treaties 1, 2, 3 and 5. (Microfilm R.G. 10, Vol. 9351). St. Peters Band, Reel C-7315, p. 18, Manitoba, Library and Archives Canada. heritage.canadiana.ca/view/oocihm.lac_reel_c7135/18?r=0&s=4

Indigenous People's Literature. (2022). Weesageechak. In *Mythologies of the Cree. Indigenous people's Literature,* indigenouspeoplenet.wordpress.com

Korinek, V. (2018). *Prairie fairies: A history of queer communities and people in Western Canada, 1930–1985.* University of Toronto Press.

Medicine, B. (2002). Directions in gender research in American Indian societies: Two spirits and other categories. *Online Readings in Psychology and Culture, 3*(1). doi.org/10.9707/2307-0919.1024

National Aboriginal Health Organization. (2005). *Assessment and planning tool kit for suicide prevention in First Nations communities.* First Nations Health Centre. npaihb.org/images/epicenter_docs/suicide_prevention/2008/First%20Nation%20ToolKit%20for%20SuicidePrev.pdf

National Aboriginal Health Organization. (2012). *Suicide prevention and two-spirited people.* First Nations Health Centre. ruor.uottawa.ca/bitstream/10393/30544/1/Suicide_Prevention_2Spirited_People_Guide_2012.pdf

National Film Board of Canada. (2008). *Second stories – Deb-we-win Ge-ken-am-aan, our place in the circle.* Written and directed by Lorne Olson. nfb.ca/film/second_stories_-our_place_in_the_circle/

Native Languages of the Americas. (n.d.). *Native American Indian legends and folklore.* native-languages.org/legends.htm

Ningewance, C., & Ningewance, P. (2018). *Gii-Nitaa-Aadisooke: Ojibwe legends from Lac Seul.* Mazinaate.

Norton, R. (2013, July 12). The gay subculture in early eighteenth-century London. *The gay subculture in Georgian England.* rictornorton.co.uk/eighteen/molly2.htm

Pettipas, K. (1974). *The diary of the Reverend Henry Budd, 1870–1875.* Manitoba Record Society Publications.

Tanner, J. (1830). *A narrative of the captivity and adventures of John Tanner (U.S. interpreter at the Saut de Ste. Marie) during thirty years residence among the Indians in the interior of North America.* G. & C. & H. Carvill.

Trudeau, J. (2017). Remarks by Prime Minister Justin Trudeau to apologize to LGBTQ2 Canadians. Ottawa, Ontario, 26 November. pm.gc.ca/en/news/speeches/2017/11/28/remarks-prime-minister-justin-trudeau-apologize-lgbtq2-canadians

Truth and Reconciliation Commission of Canada. (2015). *Canada's residential schools: The history, part 1, origins to 1939.* McGill-Queen's University Press.

Vowel, C. (2012, March 29). Language, culture, and two-spirit identity. *âpihtawikosisân.* apihtawikosisan.com/2012/03/language-culture-and-two-spirit-identity/

18

Unknown Devotions: Trans* and Indigena Freedom Dance

Rafael/a Luna-Pizano

Axcan, c_nc_ nimitz, mo_____en Tlahuitzlampa xan_que. Tzotzonalli ce! Axcan, cenca n_____, _____lia en Cihuatlampa _aneq_e. ____tzonalli ome! Tlazocamati_____. ____cama___ Tonanzin. Tlazocam_ti Ton_tiuh, Coy_xuahqui. Tlazo_____Eh_katl. _____Chalch_huitlique. Ometeotl!

Ko Cebu te moana.
Ko Tongva ngā pae maunga nāna ahau i whakaruruhau.
I tipu ake ahau ki ngā tahataha o dxʷdəwʔabš.
Ko Ilocano, ko MeXicano, ko Chiricahua Apache, ko Visaya ōku iwi.
Ko Salvacion Barruga Luna rāua ko Stella Rojas Pizano ōku kuia.
Ko Vivian Luna rāua ko Caesar Pizano ōku mātua.
Nō reira ko Bakla ahau. Soy Indigena, soy dos espiritu.
Ko Rafael/a Lucia Luna-Pizano tōku ingoa.

> The holes mark a beginning. An invitation to taste the gap. An affirmation of unknowing – a link between their memory and ours.

In an aging tradition of bridging loss, I offer a dance: an exercise in surrender to the power of the unknown. As a creative practitioner, bodyworker and listener, I have been collecting my reflections of body sovereignty from a trans* and Indigena perspective. Below, you will find a collection of spaces-between that ask Indigenous communities to consider an ever-evolving decolonial project (Smith, 2012) of embodiment. Whose experiences of body-spirit can tell us of freedom? How do we prepare ourselves to listen (Q'um Q'um Xiiem, 2020)?

> *trans freedom is the commitment to staying alive and in our bodies as trans people. trans freedom is the survival of our knowledge, our creativity and our dreams as trans people. trans freedom is 'thrivance' (Walters et al., 2010); the ability to imagine a future, the ability to connect with our relations across time and space. trans freedom is the power to say no and to say yes, the surrender to rest, locating the unknown in the known.*

Perilous knowledge, the kind that sifts your fingers with its weight, spreads your hair with its electricity, makes you look over your shoulder after you lock the door.

> Thus, Trans* Body Freedom is moving between spaces and states of being with an understanding of ancestral (more-than-human) relationship and embodiment. This understanding guides our ability to navigate and create within spaces like Vā, or the 'realm of potential being and ultimate reality' (Joseph, 2020).

The shifting and traversing that is foundational to trans freedom begs the question: What is trans experience, beyond an identity? Beyond a Western concept that still responds to a binary that is to be crossed, blended, or altogether resisted? Are there 'trans practices' of living, survival, relationality and resistance? I am answered by Latinx trans and queer scholars from Turtle Island (an Indigenous name for North America) who offer *transmovimientos* as 'embodied movements across time, space, and memory . . . inspired by social movement activism and by the multiple daily physical and ephemeral crossings of queer and trans bodies' (Hernandez, 2021, p. xvii).

Transmovimientos are about critical creativity that bear new frameworks to bridge generational gaps where queer, trans and gender-diverse lives are centered, creating a future (meaning inter-generational growth and exchange of trans peoples' knowledge) where intersections for tangible change and intervention exist (Hernandez, 2021, p. xvii). Black trans and feminist scholars in Turtle Island, Kai Green and Treva Ellison, offer another trans practice or movement: *tranifesting*, or 'transformative manifesting', which 'calls attention to epistemologies, sites of struggle, rituals, and modes of consciousness, representation, and embodiment that summon into being flexible collectivities' (Green & Ellison, 2014, p. 222).

They describe 'flexible collectivities' as those capable of surviving and mobilising across 'normative and violative configurations' of colonial categories such as race, gender and class (Green & Ellison, 2014, p. 222).

Such collectivities are people that exist at the intersection of Indigenous, Black and trans experience; collectivities who enact a resistance that is birthed at the intersection of 'trauma, injury, and the potential for material transformation and healing' (Green & Ellison, 2014, p. 222). The keyword here is 'material' with reference to transformation and healing, highlighting the importance of tangible shift, which is not as vulnerable to institutional commodification as theoretical shift. Ultimately, transmovimientos and tranifesting are just a few ways to begin to articulate the 'grace and grit' (personal correspondence, Acca Warren, creat@r, 2020) necessary to navigate the swells of being in diaspora (from land or body) as Indigenous trans* peoples.

I am interested in the practice of trans existence as an evolving tradition, just as ancient as birth (we rebirth ourselves all the time), a practice based in a place that is far from static. Drawing from the same puna that gives us transmovimiento, this 'place' from which trans practice emerges is the intersection of disparate energies or elements – such as water, fire and wind – that unite to destroy and recreate balance. A sense of 'place' is something that many displaced Indigenous people have lost during our generations of forced removal and assimilation. As Walters and her colleagues note, 'place and land are directly tied to indigenous identity and health – it is the site where dynamic interactions occur among humans and all of creation' (Wildcat, 2001, cited in Walters et al., 2010, p. 173). Being removed from our lands is to be removed from our bodies, but trans people have a specific task to reconnect or stay connected with our bodies if we are to stay alive. Thus, Indigenous trans* people contain information and practices that are essential to the return of Indigenous communities to our bodies/lands. As a landless Native, my trans resistance has brought me to a sense of place that I did not think possible, ultimately keeping me alive long enough to realise that my first teachers and guardians are water and land. The loop between trans embodiment and elemental movement is clear and unending.

I have my body, my last piece of land and one of the burial sites of my ancestors' bones.
Their bones have become mine,
holding me up, resonating like a dowsing rod
the correct path or direction at each step.
Because I am a trans person surviving in a transphobic world,
I have had to practice this art of (re)connection with my body
as a site of ancestral teaching and strategy. My body is the place
to which I return when I want to visit my ancestors' lands and waters,
yet this return is not without difficulty or sacrifice.

What is your devotion that grants you access to return home?
What makes you believe that you ever left?

Indigenous people continue to fight for the protection of our lands and connection to land-based traditions. 'Ko au te whenua, ko te whenua ko au'. This whakataukī echoes an understanding that is central to Indigenous body autonomy – 'I am the land, the land is me'. As we protect the land and waters, we protect our bodies, which come from and depend upon these lands and waters. To protect our bodies by meeting the needs of our body-spirits as Indigenous trans people – whether it is relearning our languages or transforming our bodies – allows us to remain alive and connected so that we may understand why and how to protect our lands and waters. Indigenous trans bodies house specific relationships, responsibilities and roles that are also place-based (Simpson, 2017, p. 127). Engaging the practices necessary to survive in our bodies as Indigenous trans people is an act of freedom and self-determination that directly affects the continuation of Indigenous technologies and knowledge. The forced removal and disconnection of Indigenous trans people from our lands, our families (via assimilation), and our bodies (via transphobia, homophobia, transmisogyny) has resulted in a large disturbance to the Indigenous collective capacity to uproot and resist deeply embedded colonial practices. As Indigenous scholars have observed of two-spirit people's historical trauma in the HONOR Project study,

'Place-associated role loss potentially affects all Native community members, particularly those [often two-spirit people] who hold roles associated with specific place-based responsibilities such as agricultural development, working with and taking care of plant medicines, and funerary responsibilities' (Walters et al., 2010, p. 191).

Indigenous trans* people, who may also be two-spirit, continue to find ourselves drawn to practical roles that sustain community health and transitions (i.e. rites of passage), but often struggle to find the mentorship necessary to fulfill our traditional roles as ceremonial leaders, healing practitioners or guardians. Therefore, the displacement of trans people from Indigenous lands and cultural practices is detrimental to community health on many levels. It is up to our global Indigenous community to better understand and value the roles of trans and gender-diverse people within our communities if we are going to restore power and freedom to our land-bodies.

Although some Indigenous trans* people may have the good fortune to be mentored by other Native elders who are not threatened by our resistance to colonial gender, many of us never find community support or are often ejected from Native spaces when transphobia finally surfaces. I have experienced all of these possibilities and have witnessed other Indigenous transfolks endure the same cycle of reunion, disillusionment, harm and eventually, exile. These experiences have been with non-trans and trans leaders of ceremonial spaces, alike. None of us, as Indigenous peoples, are free from transphobia if we have been raised in a settler-colonial society that is predicated upon transphobic belief systems transplanted to our homelands. Transplanted to our bodies. Despite the social and spiritual barriers that Indigenous trans* people face on our journey towards reclaiming ancestral knowledge, we continue to unearth our traditional practices by connecting to our last pieces of ancestral lands: our bodies. The privilege of being trans is the deep and ongoing relationship we must establish with our bodies, which house ancestors, in order to stay alive. Because we must do so much work to stay alive and in our bodies (a daily resistance to assimilation), we have the honour of knowing our lands and therefore our ancestral practice in a way that many non-trans people may never experience. Despite and perhaps even because of the body and 'gender dysphoria' we may experience (an indicator of the harm of colonial gender systems), Indigenous trans* people have had to connect deeply to embodied practices of home. There is a particular knowing and skill that comes from such practice, trans practice, and we have a responsibility to share these teachings with our elders, our young people and each other. The responsibility to share or teach incites a contract with those who are willing to learn or listen. Who among us is ready to listen, to trust and to transform with the leadership of Indigenous trans* freedom seekers?

The steps that I and so many of my trans and Native relations have taken to reclaim power with our body-lands are as diverse as our ancestors. Our physical sacrifices, sometimes associated with gender-affirming surgeries or hormone replacement therapies, are often the focus of non-trans perspectives on trans experiences. These offerings of flesh and blood in exchange for (re) connection with our body-lands are just one layer in unfolding an ancestral practice that even many trans people may not ever fully understand. From my trans* Indigena perspective, our journey to become our full, trans selves, is a form of (re)birth or passage necessary to retrieve knowledge that is important for the collective as well as the individual. Gender-affirming and trans* rites of passage include many forms of shift, from choosing our names in our native tongues to allowing our bodies to take shape. We see these journeys repeat throughout pūrākau and other creation stories enacted by our elemental ancestors, whether they are shapeshifting to gain eternal life for humanity, or shedding an entire name, role, and body in order to fulfill their destiny (Yates-Smith, 1998; Murphy, 2013). All the forms of (re)claiming our body-lands are in alignment with the body sovereignty that our elemental ancestors enacted and our human ancestors fought to protect. Even if our forms of body reclamation do not make sense to our non-trans relatives, or seem to uphold colonial expressions of gender (binary presentations that allow us to 'pass' as a certain colonised gender), our decisions must be respected with the belief that we are doing exactly what we need to survive and carry on our ancestors' ways. Tiwala sa mga Bakla. Tiakina ngā tāngata Irawhiti. Trust and believe trans people. Although our relationships and responsibilities cannot always be understood by non-trans people (and sometimes not by other trans relatives), we cannot uncover this knowledge alone. Indigenous cosmologies remind us that we do not exist in isolation, even if many Indigenous trans* people may feel isolated in an acute way. If we are to locate the meaning of our experiences, we must look to the web of relationships in which we are held.

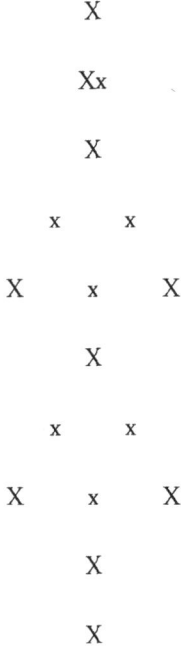

When I am asked to speak about my top-surgery experience or anything related
to gender transition, I always return to spirit, a wairua –
the two waters that reunited to create me and ground me into the land.
Since the first time I was born, I only felt half-here.

I always wanted to return 'home', or what I figured was the life I had just come from, the after-life or between-life.
I found that I could not return unless I killed myself, so I was always flirting with that passageway through my teenage years and into my early twenties.
I started to see another path home when I began to understand that my feelings of disconnection could be due to hosting white forms of gender in my body (among other forms of colonisation). I did not find much resonance in white transgender narratives, but through my own instincts I began to find readings and artworks that whispered of more ancient lineages of fluidity.
These resources told me of Two-Spirit and later of Whakatama, Bakla, and I would cherish these glimpses like my own blood, no matter what their origin. I saw pieces of myself in these articulations of gender, fluidity and liminal power. I would continue to follow these traces until I could create the dance that would lead me home. It was not just a path that emerged, but a dance, a way of being and practice of life.
As my auntie reminds me, ". . . the practice is not for later, it is now. This is the practice of living" (personal correspondence, Shar Palacio, attorney and Judo practitioner 2021).
For me, to be trans is not a static identity or even state of being, it is a way of being, an art,
a practice of life that some people develop in order to stay alive, in order to be happy, in order to breathe, in order to be an ancestor.
Ultimately, to be trans is to be free. To be trans is to be sovereign.
To be trans is a movement, a dance, an energetic, an expression of wairua, mauri, mana, puna waihanga
that is both beautiful and rare to behold.
For those of us that have the privilege to manifest these expressions, we must take the utmost care to love ourselves through it, for it is not an easy practice, although powerful, necessary.
For those of us who are lucky enough to witness our relations express trans power and embodiment, we must also do all that we can to nurture, protect and believe in the power of our *own liminality*. Mana Irawhiti. Mana Ira Tāngata.

=

=

=

By understanding the cosmic relationships that have been observed by our ancestors, Indigenous trans* people can begin to see our trans practices as part of a larger legacy of Indigenous technology and resistance. The experiences and wisdom gathered by Indigenous trans* rites of passage are imperative to the continued recovery of Indigenous knowledge, but these pieces of the 'eggshell' (Smith, 2020) are being ignored or even rejected because many Indigenous communities are not yet free from transphobia or homophobia. Indigenous trans* people not only have the task of recovering the ancestral practices in our body-lands, we must also convince our communities that our practices are 'traditional' and maintain the essence of our original instructions. Indigenous trans* practice descends from an elemental lineage that was preserved by the ceremonies and rituals of our ancestors, therefore our practices are preserved in land and water epistemologies (body-based, somatic learning). The more we can understand trans embodiment as a form of Indigenous epistemology, the more we can trust the practices that arise from our experiences as recovered ancestral knowledge. We still need the wisdom of elders and young ones to decipher what knowledge and practices truly serve the well-being of our peoples, but our communities need to dissolve internalised transphobia in order to continue these processes of recovering cultural sovereignty. It is not enough to 'accept' trans and gender-diverse people in our communities. How do we embrace gender diversity (decolonial forms of embodiment) within each of us, regardless of perceived identity? Until each of us begins to listen to the power of fluidity within ourselves and support the evolution of decolonial genders in new generations, all the subtleties (and not-so-subtleties) of transphobia will continue a colonial agenda of separation and subjugation within our communities. The individual and collective trauma of being shut out from ancestral inheritance and practice is a continuing legacy that has resulted in spiritual and physical deaths throughout trans community. Out of death, we continue to birth – to create forms of rituals and resistance too liminal to be found ...

{{ }}

We hovered in that echo of light that you can't always distinguish from streetlamps or the last ramblings of sun. I picked the simplest piece of writing in my notebook – more of a message that I was still deciphering on a half-torn sheet. I asked the pod to listen to all the sounds travelling through and around us, the back-up choir for our poetry that night. I began to walk around the perimeter of the circle, testing my footing while balancing a flame in one hand and my notebook in the other. Footsteps in the grass preceded my first spoken whenu, or strand. I picked up the first line and like a stutter dance of two steps forward, one step back, I was Huitzilopoxtli in motion. Looping back through the half strands, caring for this small flame, seeing the ground with my feet, I began to circle in the opposite direction as the second half of the message worked its way out of me. I was no more powerful than the witnesses, despite seeming to be in control of the reading or the 'performance'. I was just as vulnerable as they were, just as uncertain and curious. My role was to keep going until the spell was complete, until the message had reached its natural exit into the sea of memory. I had never read this channelled, scrap message aloud before, and although I thought I knew what it was about, it was not until I began reading it in the round, circling and uncircling this pod of human energy, this portal, that I began to understand this message with my entire being. After we decided that we had finished our duty of welcoming te pō, we gathered our blankets, empty glasses and tiny flames. Like ants feeling our way home, we filed back into the tiny whare to turn up some te reo jams, eat leftovers and write on the walls again.

{{ }}

Is this tranifesting? 'The ceremony that must be found' or the 're-writing of knowledge such that it is "availing to the needs of mankind"' (Wynter, 1984, p. 21, as quoted by Green & Ellison, 2014, p. 223). The ceremony that tears down, clears the ground and reframes the portal for a future of transmovimiento, of Irawhiti, of Bakla, of Black, Brown, Indigena Trans Power. Why be afraid of our future anymore? Instead of resigning ourselves to our martyrdom, what if we stopped dying before we were ever reborn? What are the ceremonies that only trans people can do? The rituals that come from our possession of memories, memories that cis bodies (assimilated bodies) deny or suppress. These rituals give us access to unknown doors that cannot be co-opted or replicated by settler-colonial thieves. Our rituals are keys, maps and instructions; training grounds, oracles and tools (for planting or defending). Our rituals are beautiful, terrifying and binding. For 'We hate them too / We hate everyone who hates you. We are possessed by a ma'i aitu. We are possessed by a ma'i maliu. We can fall. We can die any time' (Avia, 2020, p. 62). We can and do channel . . . for all of our missing and murdered children. Indigenous trans* people fight through our untouchable bodies, whether too profane or too sacred, we are the body between death and life. Look to us for the ritual to reframe, watch the borders from which we make clay and fashion new bodies, untraceable and in(di)visible. We are made of wind and water, ash and bone, mascara and dawn, precariously positioned and ready to live, do not let us fall in vain. To protect land, to defend our bodies, Indigenous communities must continue to grow gender-diverse and gender-sacred people.

'ko hine-tii-tama koe
ko hine-rau-angiangi koe
ko hine-nui-te-pō koe
mana ▓▓▓, *mana ira tangata e!'*
(personal correspondence, Alé Jensen-Whakataka, kaimanioro, 2021)

Kuputaka and glossary: Interpretations and inspirations

bakla: queer, trans (feminine), used as an umbrella for all queer and trans-ish expression from what I have left of Ilocano, Cebuano culture. From *babae* (Filipino 'woman') + *lalaki* (Filipino 'man').

gender-diverse: embodying a lived resistance to colonial genders.

Huitzilopoxtli: a Mexican deity associated with warriors and the sun, often depicted as a hummingbird. The danza (Azteca) associated with Huitzilopoxtli follows the movements of a hummingbird – flying forward and then stopping mid-air to suddenly fly in reverse.

irawhiti: (n) transgender [person]. From *ira* ('life principle, gene') + *whiti* ('to change, turn, transfer, transpose, swap, exchange; to cross over; to reach the opposite side; cross piece'). *Whiti* can also mean 'to shine (of sun)'.

mana: (n) prestige, authority, control, power, influence, status, spiritual power, charisma – a supernatural force in a person, place or object. There are many types of mana (i.e. mana whenua, mana atua, mana takatāpui).

mauri: (n) life principle, life force, vital essence, special nature, a material symbol of a life principle, source of emotions – the essential quality and vitality of a being or entity. Also used for a physical object, individual, ecosystem or social group in which this essence is located.

puna: (v) to well up flow; (n) spring (of water), well, pool.

pūrākau: 'Pūrākau, a traditional form of Māori narrative, contains philosophical thought, epistemological constructs, cultural codes, and worldviews that are fundamental to our identity as Māori. Pūrākau are a collection of traditional oral narratives that should not only be protected, but also understood as a pedagogical-based anthology of literature that are still relevant today' (Lee, 2009, p. 1).

trans(*): 'It is important to make this distinction between trans-gender and trans because many transgender people do not identify as transgender, but rather identify as man or woman, not asking to remake or add a new gender category, but rather fit into one that already exists. In this case, I would not say that transgender people are actually undoing the categories that produce the boundaries of a gender binary, though changing one's location on the binary does challenge the notion that gender is fixed, because some people are able to change genders. I think what might be more useful in this conversation is to think about gender non-conforming bodies, bodies that do not fit and actively refute a binary legibility. Not because these people are necessarily more radical, but their existence often poses a critique to the gender-binaried-order of the land' (Green & Bey, 2017, p. 444).

waihanga: (v) create, to make, build, develop, generate, erect, construct.

wairua: (n) spirit, soul – spirit of a person which exists beyond death. It is the non-physical spirit, distinct from the body and the *mauri*.

whakataukī: (n) proverb, significant saying, formulaic saying, cryptic saying, aphorism.

All kupu Māori interpretations (with the exception of pūrākau) have been sourced from *Te Aka Māori Dictionary*: maoridictionary.co.nz, October 2021.

Note

The opening lines of this chapter are parts of an invocation (Nahuatl) used to open danza Azteca ceremonies, calling in the energies of the seven directions. I chanted these words as the sahumadora, or fire-keeper, during many danza Azteca ceremonies. Because I have found it difficult to return to most danza spaces that still struggle with transphobia, I am no longer speaking these words regularly. Thus, there are pieces missing because I cannot always remember each word as it fades in and out with lack of practice.

The second opening is my current pepeha, or formal way in introducing myself in Māori spaces. I have had to learn how to provide this oral evidence of my origins after living in Aotearoa–New Zealand and building relationships with tangata whenua. It has been a challenging and vulnerable process to create a pepeha as an Indigenous person in diaspora. I do not know my ancestral mountains or bodies of water, but it is healing to locate which elements have raised me, nonetheless.

References

Argüello, T. M., & Walters, K. (2018). They tell us 'we don't belong in the world and we shouldn't take up a place': HIV discourse within two-spirit communities. *Journal of Ethnic & Cultural Diversity in Social Work, 27*(2), 107–123. doi.org/10.1080/15313204.2017.1362616

Avia, T. (2020). *The savage coloniser book*. Victoria University Press.

Cajete, G. (2000). *Native science: Natural laws of interdependence*. Clear Light Publishers.

Fernandez, A. R., Evans-Campbell, T., Johnson-Jennings, M., Beltran, R. E., Schultz, K., Stroud, S., & Walters, K. L. (2020). 'Being on the walk put it somewhere in my body': The meaning of place in health for Indigenous women. *Journal of Ethnic & Cultural Diversity in Social Work, 30*(1–2), 122–137. doi.org/10.1080/15313204.2020.1770652

Green, K. M., & Bey, M. (2017). Where black feminist thought and trans* feminism meet: A conversation. *Souls (Boulder, Colo.), 19*(4), 438–454. doi.org/10.1080/10999949.2018.1434365

Green, K. M., & Ellison, T. (2014). Tranifest. *Transgender Studies Quarterly, 1*(1-2), 222–225. doi.org/10.1215/23289252-2400082

Johnson-Jennings, M., Billiot, S., & Walters, K. (2020). Returning to our roots: Tribal health and wellness through land-based healing. *Genealogy (Basel), 4*(3), 91. doi.org/10.3390/genealogy4030091

Joseph, K. (2020). Review of *Diagrammatic*, an installation of artworks by Leafa Wilson, 2018–2020. Gallagher Academy of Performing Arts Gallery, Nov 2020–Feb 2021.

Krieger, N. (2005). Embodiment: A conceptual glossary for epidemiology. *Journal of Epidemiology and Community Health, 59*(5), 350–355. doi.org/10.1136/jech.2004.024562

Lee, J. (2009). Decolonising Māori narratives: pūrākau as a method. *MAI Review, 2*.

Murphy, N. (2013). *Te awa atua: Menstruation in the pre-colonial Māori world*. He Puna Manawa Ltd.

Parker, M., Duran, B., & Walters, K. (2017). The relationship between bias-related victimization and generalized anxiety disorder among American Indian and Alaska Native lesbian, gay, bisexual, transgender, two-spirit community members. *International Journal of Indigenous Health, 12*(2), 64–83. doi.org/10.18357/ijih122201717785

Q'um Q'um Xiiem, J. (2020). *Indigenous storywork for performance, practice and pedagogy*. International Indigenous Research Conference, 18 November 2020, University of Auckland.

Simpson, L. B. (2017). *As we have always done: Indigenous freedom through radical resistance*. University of Minnesota Press.

Smith, L. T. (2012). *Decolonizing methodologies: research and indigenous peoples* (2nd ed.). Zed Books.

Walters, K. L., Beltran, R., Huh, D., & Evans-Campbell, T. (2010). Displacement and dis-ease: Land, place, and health among American Indians and

Alaska Natives. In L. M. Burton, S. P. Kemp, M. Leung, S. A. Matthews, & D. T. Takeuchi (Eds.), *Communities, neighborhoods, and health; Expanding the boundaries of place*, 163–199. Springer New York. doi.org/10.1007/978-1-4419-7482-2_10

Walters, K. L., Mohammed, S. A., Evans-Campbell, T., Beltrán, R. E., Chae, D. H., & Duran, B. (2011). Bodies don't just tell stories, they tell histories: Embodiment of historical trauma among American Indians and Alaska natives. *Du Bois Review, 8*(1), 179–189. doi.org/10.1017/S1742058X1100018X

Yates-Smith, G. R. A. (1998). *Hine! e Hine!: Rediscovering the feminine in Maori spirituality*. [Doctoral thesis (Maori), University of Waikato].

Contributing Authors

Clive Aspin (Ngāti Maru, Ngāti Whanaunga, Ngāti Tamaterā) is the inaugural associate dean, Māori, in the Faculty of Health at Te Herenga Waka—Victoria University of Wellington, where he is also a senior lecturer in Health and postgraduate studies director. He was born in Waiuku and grew up on his ancestral land of Hauraki. Clive is a Māori public health researcher whose work focuses on Māori and Indigenous health, HIV, sexuality, and suicide prevention. He was the executive research officer at Ngā Pae o te Maramatanga, New Zealand's centre of Māori research excellence. He served as a ministerial appointment to the Board of the Health Research Council and as chair of the Māori Research Committee and is a founding member of the International Indigenous Working Group on HIV and AIDS.

Annie Belcourt, PhD (Aminiisiaki/Mdeboge/Otterwoman) is an American Indian clinical psychologist and professor at the University of Montana's College of Health. She holds a joint appointment in the departments of Pharmacy Practice and Community/Public Health, serves as a faculty senator and is a senior fellow in the JPB TH Chan Harvard School of Public Health's Environmental Health programme. Her research emphasises the intersection of health disparity and equity within indigenous communities. She is a member of the Blackfeet Nation Institutional Review Board and an enrolled tribal member of the Three Affiliated Tribes (Blackfeet, Chippewa, Mandan, and Hidatsa).

David J. Brennan is a settler on Turtle Island and originally from the traditional land of many Indigenous peoples and languages, including Mohegan, Mashantucket Pequot, Eastern Pequot, Schaghticoke, Golden Hill Paugussett, Niantic, and the Quinnipiac, as well as other Algonquian-speaking peoples, what is now known as the state of Connecticut. He lives on the traditional land of the Huron-Wendat, the Seneca, and the Mississaugas of the Credit, also known today as Toronto, Canada. His family comes from Germany, Ireland and England. David is a social worker with 40+ years of experience working in the HIV field as an advocate, case manager, clinical services director, hospice social worker, bereavement coordinator, and researcher. He is currently a professor at the Factor-Inwentash Faculty of Social Work at the University of Toronto. He also serves as the associate dean, Research, and the director of the CRUISElab, an interdisciplinary social work research lab focused on the health and wellness of gay, bi, queer, two-spirit, cis, trans guys and non-binary people. He holds an OHTN Endgame Leadership Chair in Gay and Bisexual Men's Health in Social Work. He is actively seeking ways to address the issues of truth and reconciliation between Indigenous and settler peoples. He is honoured to be part of the book and to work with his colleagues on this chapter.

Nicholas (Nick) Kenneth Gerald Garrett (Ngāti Maniapoto) is an applied biostatistician with over 27 years of experience in health research (nine years senior biostatistician at ESR, 17 years at AUT as senior research fellow, now associate professor). He collaborates on many health and environmental research projects, mainly as lead biostatistician. Most of the research that he has been involved with has been based on the general population or examining impacts on minority populations. He is actively engaged in Māori health research and supporting Māori researchers. Some of his current research projects include development of a Māori specific screening tool for dementia, investigating the impact of hearing status on educational outcomes for Pacific youth, and an audit of district health boards for family violence screening processes.

Alison Green (Ngāti Pūkeko, Ngāti Awa, and Ngāi Tamarawaho, Ngāti Ranginui) is a professor at the School of Indigenous Graduate Studies, Te Whare Wānanga o Awanuiārangi. She holds a PhD in Māori and Pacific Development (2018) and a Master of Māori and Pacific Development (First Class Honours) from the University of Waikato. In 2019, Alison was awarded the inaugural Misiweskamik Indigenous Post-Doctoral Fellowship to the University of Saskatchewan, Canada, where she taught at the Department of Indigenous Studies, University of Saskatchewan. She is also the chief executive of a Kaupapa Māori organisation that delivers sexual and reproductive health promotion, policy and advisory services, and research. Alison lives with her partner and whānau on a dusty backroad on the west coast of Te Ika a Māui (North Island). She is proud of her three children, their children, and the legacies left by her tipuna (ancestors).

Tłaliłila'ogwa / Sarah Hunt is a Kwakwa̱ka̱'wakw (Kwagu'ł) 2SQ activist scholar who is passionate about creating alternatives to violent state systems through nurturing community networks with shared orientations toward decolonisation, self-determination and solidarity. She is a Canada research chair in Indigenous Political Ecology and assistant professor in the School of Environmental Studies at the University of Victoria, located on the unceded lands of the Lekwungen & W̱SÁNEĆ peoples. Tłaliłila'ogwa's current research focuses on fostering justice across the nested scales of lands/waters, homes and bodies via engagement of coastal peoples' embodied knowledge and land-based cultural practice. As a grassroots organiser and a scholar, she has collaborated with two-spirit, queer and non-binary youth and communities on projects that seek to redefine well-being, safety and healing via decolonising approaches. Her writing has been published in the anthologies *Keetsahnak: Our Missing and Murdered Indigenous Sisters* and *Indigenous Research: Theories, Practices and Relationships*, the journals *Atlantis*, *The Journal of Lesbian Studies* and *Cultural Geographies*, and numerous research reports, podcasts and other media. Most days you can find Tłaliłila'ogwa at the shoreline talking to the whales.

Randy Jackson is an assistant professor in the School of Social Work at McMaster University with a joint appointment in the Department of Health, Aging and Society. Originally from Kettle and Stony Point First Nation (Anishinaabe), Jackson explores lived experience among Indigenous peoples living with HIV and AIDS (IPHAs) using Indigenous knowledge, perspectives, and values. Jackson is the Nominated Principal Investigator of the Feast Centre for Indigenous STBBI Research, which he co-leads with Renée Masching. Jackson's programme of research explores the use of Indigenous knowledge across diverse topics, including experiences of depression, Indigenous masculinity, Indigenous trans health, two-spirit resilience, and Indigenous peoples living with HIV. Randy is the recipient of a Queen Elizabeth II Diamond Jubilee Medal (2012) and a CANFAR/CAHR award (2020) for excellence in his community-based research work in HIV with Indigenous peoples.

Michelle Aihina Ikhinsh Holhpokunna Johnson-Jennings, EdM, PhD, is an enrolled citizen of the Choctaw Nation of Oklahoma. Michelle is a clinical health psychologist and is a professor of social work and public health, and director of the land-based healing division at the Indigenous Wellness Research Institute at the University of Washington. She holds joint/affiliate appointments at the University of Colorado's School of Public Health, the University of Saskatchewan, and the University of Waikato. As a clinical health psychologist, her therapeutic expertise lies in working with Indigenous communities and decolonising healing approaches. She recently served as the Canada Research Chair for Indigenous Community Engaged Research at the University of Saskatchewan, founded and directed the Research for Indigenous Community Health Center at the University of Minnesota, and was awarded a US Fulbright Scholarship to conduct research in Aotearoa.

Andrew Jolivétte (Louisiana Creole, Atakapa-Ishak Nation of Louisiana [Tsikip/Opelousa/Heron Clan], of Ishak, African, French, Spanish, Italian and Irish descent) is professor and chair of the Ethnic Studies Department at the University of California, San Diego, where he is also the founding director of the Native American and Indigenous Studies Program. Dr Jolivétte is the series editor of *Black Indigenous Futures and Speculations* at Routledge, the co-chair of the UC Ethnic Studies Council, the board president of the San Francisco American Indian Cultural Center and the author or editor of nine books, including *Indian Blood: HIV and Colonial Trauma in San Francisco's Two-Spirit Community* and *Louisiana Creoles: Cultural Recovery and Mixed-Race Native American Identity.* He is a former professor and department chair of American Indian Studies at San Francisco State University and was the 2020–21 MultiRacial Network Scholar in Residence for the American College Personnel Association. Professor Jolivétte accepted a new position at the University of California, San Diego in 2019 and is currently serving as Department Chair of Ethnic Studies and as Founding Director of Native American and Indigenous Studies at UC San Diego.

Elizabeth Kerekere MP was born in Gisborne, where she lives with her wife, Alofa Aiono, and their furry babies. On her father's side, she is Whānau a Kai, Ngāti Oneone, Te Aitanga a Māhaki, Rongowhakaata and Ngāi Tāmanuhiri. On her mother's side, Elizabeth hails from Clare and Tipperary in Ireland. Elizabeth is a lifelong grassroots activist, focused on kaupapa Māori and Te Tiriti issues relating to health, mental health, suicide and violence prevention and youth development for over 40 years. Elizabeth has represented Rainbow and Indigenous human rights issues, including at the United Nations in Geneva. She is a fierce voice for takatāpui and young people, and founded Tīwhanawhana Trust in 2001 to advocate for takatāpui to 'tell our stories, build our communities and leave a legacy'. As a leader within Rainbow and youth development sectors for over 30 years, Elizabeth has mentored more than 50 young people. Her PhD on takatāpui identity and well-being is required reading in universities across Australia,

America and Europe, and her takatāpui suicide prevention resources are used in health and school settings across the country. Her research projects include assisted reproductive health and family formation; LGBTQI+ youth health and well-being; trans and non-binary health and well-being; and gender inclusive perinatal care. In February 2021, she launched a record-breaking petition to ban conversion therapy; the law passed a year later. Trans, intersex and non-binary people can now easily self-identify their gender on the birth certificate. Elizabeth is determined to amend the Human Rights Act and criminalise gender normalising surgery on intersex infants.

Sandy Lambert is from Cree and Dene ancestry with membership to TALLCREE First Nation. Sandy was raised off reserve and now resides in Vancouver, BC. He has spent many years of volunteering with non-profit, non-government organisations, attending HIV/AIDS conferences, and planning and organising participation on research committees and projects provincially and nationally. In 2013 he received a Lifetime Achievement award from the Canadian Aboriginal AIDS Network (CAAN) for his advocacy work for people living with HIV/AIDS. His latest project has been working as the External Liaison and Elder for DUDES Club, a model for Indigenous men's wellness promotion that builds solidarity and brotherhood, enabling men to regain a sense of pride and purpose in their life. It began as an initiative to promote health awareness among men of the Vancouver's Downtown East side and has since established branches across British Columbia.

Rebekah Laurence descends from Ngāti Unu hapū and Ngāti Maniapoto iwi in the King Country of Aotearoa. She is an emerging researcher in the field of takatāpui and Māori LGBTQI+ well-being, with an interest in supporting their sexual and reproductive health. Rebekah works as the knowledge dissemination lead for Te Whāriki Takapou, a Māori organisation which provides Māori sexual and reproductive health promotion, research, and policy and advisory services. She holds an MSc in psychology; her thesis explored Māori LGBTQI+ youth gender and sexual identities. She has contributed to recent literature on takatāpui and Māori LGBTQI+ identity and well-being, and has been involved in several research projects regarding Māori sexual and reproductive health, including research on HIV and long-acting reversible contraception. In 2022 Rebekah returned to university to complete training as a community psychologist. She lives with her fiancé and their cat Bella in Hamilton, Aotearoa.

Rafael/a Luna-Pizano grew up along the coasts of Te Moana-nui-a-Kiwa, in the shelter of Tongva, Chumash and Coast Salish lands. Rafael/a is a bakla, two-spirit/ed descendant of Ilocano, Visayan, Xicano and Chiricahua Apache peoples. He is a lover, reluctant healer, and future nanay. Through a playful practice that draws on all aspects of ritual, Rafael/a offers creative methodologies to decompose academic barriers to trans* and Indigenous scholarship. He is currently in love with the vibrations of taonga pūoro and is working towards an underwater sound residency that brings him closer to the musical practices of his islands and deserts.

Kim McBreen (Waitaha, Kāti Māmoe, Ngāi Tahu, Pākehā) is a kaimahi at Te Wānanga o Raukawa. She lives in a small coastal town with her partner and two children and dreams of community. Kim's essay explores her resistance to the term 'takatāpui' and to building takatāpui community as a long-term strategy for decolonisation. She argues that whatever else we do, we must confront and dismantle heteropatriarchy if we want a better world for ourselves and future generations. She imagines a future that returns to a tikanga of whakapapa and whānau where we are not judged by gender or sexuality. Where there is again no need for takatāpui identity. Kim is picking at heteropatriarchy in several projects. She contributes to Te Wānanga o Raukawa's *Whāngai and the Adoption of Māori* and *He Ara Mataora* projects, and teaches in the Ahunga Tikanga programme.

Albert McLeod is a Status Indian member of the Nisichawayasihk Cree Nation in northern Canada and has ancestral connections to the Métis communities of Norway House and Cross Lake in the province of Manitoba. He has lived in Winnipeg for over 40 years and is the president of the 2-Spirited People of Manitoba and one of the founders of the Canadian Aboriginal AIDS Network. As a gay youth growing up at a time of intense western assimilation of Indigenous peoples and the erasure of Indigenous languages, spirituality and philosophies, he was guided by the resilience of his grandmother, who was born in 1897: Madeline McIvor (née Moose) was a gifted traditional artist who practised her skills until she died at 93. His inherent and inalienable rights as a 2Spirit person were instilled in him by the natural world and ecosystems in which he was raised. Coming out of a hostile patriarchal hunter society that disdained LGBTQ+ people, he established safer spaces for 2Spirit peoples at the highest levels of Canada's colonial structure and Indigenous governance. Albert was in Vancouver when transmission of HIV was spreading in gay populations across the Western world. Indigenous gay men were the first wave impacted, and one response in 1988 was the founding of the Annual International Two-Spirit Gathering. Held in Canada and the US for the past 34 years, this gathering is a place where 2Spirit people can connect to the land, their elders, ceremonies, and their spirituality. In 2018, Albert received an Honorary Doctorate of Laws from the University of Winnipeg. He continues to provide advice and direction on HIV/AIDS, 2Spirit leadership, and decolonisation and reconciliation as an Indigenous cultural consultant. (albertmcleod.com)

Carl Mika is Māori from Tuhourangi, and is professor in Aotahi Māori and Indigenous Studies, University of Canterbury, Aotearoa. A former lawyer specialising in criminal and Treaty of Waitangi law, he now works almost entirely in the area of Māori thought/philosophy, with a particular focus on its revitalisation within a colonised reality. Committed to investigating Indigenous notions of holism, Carl is currently working on the Māori concepts of nothingness and darkness in response to an Enlightenment focus on clarity, and is speculating on how they can form the backdrop of academic expression. He also writes and presents on western Continental philosophies.

Tawhanga Nopera's iwi affiliations are Ngāti Whakaue, Ngāti Wahiao, Tuhourangi, Ngāti Tuwharetoa, Ngāti Tarawhai, Ngāti Whaoa, Ngāti Aamaru and Ngāi Tawake. Tawhanga was the first student to graduate with a PhD with creative practices from the University of Waikato. Today, he is a research fellow on the WERO: Working to End Racial Discrimination Project at Te Ngira: Institute for Population Research, University of Waikato, where he is also the health promotions coordinator at Student Health Services. As an artist and academic, Tawhanga intends for his research to support wellness pathways through Kaupapa Māori knowledge and practices. His research and art investigates marginality and is grounded by te pā harakeke, through raranga – a creative Māori approach toward socially accountable communities. Tawhanga has a particular interest in ways that individuals are impacted by notions of power, and seeks out transformative pathways from traumatic experiences.

Doris Peltier is Anishinaabe from Wikwemikoong, a First Nations community located on the Odawa, Ojibway and Pottawatami peoples' territory on Manitoulin Island in Ontario. In adulthood, Doris honed her storytelling skills as one of Canada's pre-eminent Indigenous performing artists, and was instrumental in amplifying the importance of Indigenous people telling their own stories. She recognises that storytelling is an Indigenous knowledge tool that has always been utilised to transmit knowledge, and that story is a transferable skill that brought her into Indigenous health research. She believes research is also about storytelling. Doris is the community engagement coordinator with the Feast Centre for Indigenous STBBI Research, a partnership between McMaster University and Communities, Alliances and Networks. She is co-creator of Visioning Health I & II, a research project by and for HIV-positive Indigenous women, focused on strengths-based stories of her peers. Doris is also a Community Advisory Council member with the Waakebiness-Bryce Institute for Indigenous Health at the Dalla Lana School of Public Health (University of Toronto), and a member of the Women Living with HIV Advisory Group with World Health Organization. Doris has worked for almost two decades within the Indigenous HIV movement in Canada, including many years in Indigenous community-based health research. Doris was recently awarded an honorary doctorate from the University of Ottawa's Faculty of Social Sciences for her contributions to Indigenous health and wellness in Canada. She is a mother, grandmother, and great-grandmother, and has grandchildren who identify as two-spirited or transgendered, for whom she helps ensure strong familial supports. She is fluent in Anishinaabemowin, framing her worldview in Indigenous health research. Doris advocates for researchers to further explore Indigenous languages, to find strengths and gifts that Creator gives each of us.

Mera Penehira is Ngāti Raukawa ki Ōtaki and Rangitāne. Mera is a professor and the head of school of Indigenous Graduate Studies at Te Whare Wānanga o Awanuiārangi. In 2010 she was awarded the Health Research Council's Hohua Tutengaehe Research Fellowship in Māori health, which she is undertaking in the Te Kotahi Research Institute at the University of Waikato. Mera has a background in Māori and special education, and has been researching in Māori health for six years. Her doctoral thesis centred on traditional knowledge and healing practices, studying Māori women with hepatitis C. In particular the research examined the process of moko (traditional Māori skin carving) and notions of mouri as legitimate components of Māori well-being. In her postdoctoral research Mera will explore Māori views on sexual and reproductive health, developing a Kaupapa Māori model of resistance and well-being in this context. Mera is also involved in Kura Kaupapa Māori and has a daughter attending Te Kura Kaupapa o Hoani Waititi Marae in Auckland.

Leonie Pihama (Te Ātiawa, Ngā Māhanga a Tairi, Waikato) is a mother of six and grandmother of six mokopuna. She is a professor of Māori and Indigenous research, director of research at Tū Tama Wahine o Taranaki, and director of Māori and Indigenous analysis. She has held roles as professor of Māori research at Ngā Wai a Te Tūī Research Institute, and director at Te Kotahi Research Institute (Waikato) and the Indigenous Research Institute for Māori and Indigenous Education (University of Auckland). She was a recipient of the Hohua Tūtengaehe Post-Doctoral Research Fellowship and the inaugural Ngā Pae o te Māramatanga Senior Māori Fulbright Scholarship at the University of Washington. In 2015, Leonie was awarded the Te Tohu Pae Tāwhiti Award and the Te Tohu Rapuora Award. She has served on the boards of the Māori Health Committee for the Health Research Council, Māori Television, Te Māngai Pāho and Ngā Pae o te Māramatanga.

Matt Roskruge (Te Ātiawa and Ngāti Tama) is an associate professor with the School of Economics and Finance and co-Director of Te Au Rangahau at Massey University. He currently holds a Rutherford Discovery Fellowship to explore social capital in Aotearoa, with a particular focus on the relevance for Māori. Dr Roskruge has broad research interests across the applied quantitative social sciences with a focus on the Māori economy and economic issues, particularly those related to health and social wellbeing. He contributed to the quantitative design and analysis of the Honour Project Aotearoa, and learned a lot on Kaupapa Māori research design, becoming a much better researcher through involvement in the project. Matt has two wonderful young boys and a large garden to keep him occupied, and still enjoys playing an occasional video game in the evening.

Shirley Simmonds is a descendant of the Raukawa, Ngāpuhi and Ngāti Tūwharetoa nations in Aotearoa. She is the mother of two young boys, and a self-employed Kaupapa Māori researcher. Shirley led the chapter on Kaupapa Māori survey design in this publication, alongside the research team, and had a key role in the quantitative research aspect of the Honour Project Aotearoa. Shirley is a keen gardener and is dedicated to raising her boys in their native language and living the values of our ancestors in everyday activities.

Herearoha Skipper (Ngāti Hako, Ngāti Tamaterā, Ngāti Pāoa, Ngāti Tara Tokanui Tawhaki, Ngāti Whanaunga, Ngāpuhi). Herearoha has held senior leadership roles at the University of Waikato for over 20 years, is the director of Te Ara Tupu, serves as a trustee for Ngāti Tamaterā Treaty Settlement Trust (PSGE), Ngāti Pāoa Iwi Trust (PSGE) and Te Whāriki Manawāhine o Hauraki, and sits on several governance boards representing iwi as a Treaty partner. She has extensive networks with community organisations, the business sector, and government agencies throughout Aotearoa, and Indigenous communities internationally. She specialises in strategy, business development, leadership transformation, governance, finance, transformative praxis, policy, and te reo Māori revitalisation. Herearoha manages major research projects in environment, health, whānau well-being, education and te reo Māori, including the Honour Project Aotearoa, with the aim of improving life experiences of takatāpui. She provides leadership in Kaupapa Māori research that promotes the vision, values, and aspirations of whānau, hapū and iwi.

Matthew Town, PhD, MPH, is a citizen of the Choctaw Nation of Oklahoma. He is an assistant professor at the School of Social Work at Portland State University. Dr Town is a behavioural health scientist whose research focuses on the impacts of psychosocial and cultural factors on health behaviours of American Indian and Alaska Natives (AIAN), sexual minorities, and AIAN sexual minorities. His research interests include HIV prevention, treatment, and care; substance use prevention; health disparities; American Indian and Alaska Native health; LGBTQI+ health; intervention development and evaluation; and community-based participatory research.

Melissa Walls, PhD (Bois Forte and Couchiching First Nation Anishinaabe) is the director of the Great Lakes Hub for the Johns Hopkins Center for American Indian Health, and associate professor of International Health at the Johns Hopkins Bloomberg School of Public Health. She is a social scientist committed to collaborative research and has over a decade of experience working with tribal communities in the United States and Canada. Her involvement in community-based participatory research (CBPR) projects to date includes mental health epidemiology; culturally relevant, family-based, substance-use prevention and mental health promotion programming and evaluation; and examining the impact of stress and mental health on diabetes. Dr Walls' collaborative work has received funding from the National Institutes of Health and the Public Health Agency of Canada.

Alex Wilson, EdD (Neyonawak Inniniwak from the Opaskwayak Cree Nation) is professor and academic director at the Aboriginal Education Research Centre, University of Saskatchewan. She completed her BA (Psychology) at California State University, Sacramento, in 1994; her EdM (Human Development and Psychology: Psycho-social and Cultural Development) from Harvard University in 1995; and an EdD (Human Development and Psychology) from Harvard University in 2007. Dr Wilson's scholarship has greatly contributed to building and sharing knowledge about two-spirit identity, history and teachings, Indigenous research methodologies, and the prevention of violence in the lives of Indigenous peoples. She is one of many organisers with the Idle No More movement, integrating radical education movement work with grassroots interventions that prevent the destruction of land and water. Dr Wilson is a recipient of the University of Saskatchewan Provost's Award in Aboriginal Education for connecting research to pedagogy and practice, the Avenue Community Centre for Gender & Sexual Diversity's 2014 Affinity community service award, the 2015 Provost's Award for Community Outreach and Engagement, the 2016 Nellie Award, and the 2016 Peter Corren Award. She was recently recognised by the Legislature of Manitoba for her extensive ongoing work with Indigenous communities revitalising Cree culture through land-based education.

Glossary

Page numbers in **bold** indicate photographs; *italics* a graph or table; 'n' indicates a footnote.

A Narrative of the Captivity and Adventures of John Tanner, 312
Aboriginal Education Research Centre, 255
Aboriginal Health and Wellness Centre, 321
Aboriginal Two-Spirit Working Group (Edmonton), 323
abortion, 89
absence, 55–57
abuse, 157, 206, 258–259, 292–294
academia, orthodox, 43
Academy Awards, 312–313
acceptance, 38–40, 70, 136, 147, 217–218, 259–261, 280, 306, 317
accessibility, 260, 278
accountability
    research, 23, 105, 256
    settler, 212
activism, 153–155, 157–158, 160, 173, 207, 255–256, 259, 280, 298, 313, 320–324
addictions, 136, 138, 207, 307, 315
Adelaide, 196–197
adoption, 62–63, 66, 199, 314–316
advisory group, 100, 105, 107
advocacy, 182–183, 200, 273, 291, 320–321
affirmation, 38
Africa, 157, 243
agookwe, 307, 321
agricultural development, 330
Ahakoa Te Aha, 19

Ahnichi, 213–214, 216–218, 224, 227–229, 231–232
Aianli, 233
AIDS. *see* HIV/AIDS
AIDS Epidemiology Group, 156
AIDS Foundation, 143
AIDS Network, 36, 137, 143
Alberta, 314
Alcatraz, 298
alcohol, 116, 133, 136, 213, 306, 316, 319
Alcoholics Anonymous, 316
'all my relations,' 276, 280, 283, 285
American Indians
    mixed race, 24, 290–291, 293–294, 296–297
    over-homogenisation of, 297
    tribal differences, 296–297
    urban, 291, 293–296, 299
amishakoowendamo'awag, 269–270, 269n1, 272, 277–285
ancestors, elemental, 331–332
ancestral entities, 45
ancestral generations, 12, 205, 207, 211, 214–215, 219, 222–223, 225–227, 234, 257. *see also* whakapapa
ancestral marae, 78, 122–123, *123*, 130
ancestral practice, 331–332
ancestral predestiny, 218
ancestral relationship, 328–329, 333–334
anger, 139

Anishinaabe-inendaamowin, 23, 272, 282, 285
Annual International Two-Spirit Gathering, 317, 319–320, 323
anonymity, significance of, 262, 265
anthropologists, 309
anti-trans campaigners, 85n15
anxiety, 133, 206–207
Aotearoa New Zealand Sex Workers Collective, 19
Apalachi ('giving help'), 204
Apanukfila ('Whirlwind'), 204–206, 215, 234–235
Apela ('helper'), 204
Apeli ('act of storming'), 204
Argyle Alternative High School, 317
aroha, 191
artefact label, 168
arts-based practices, 215, 227, 262, 265, 306, 327, 334–335
Asia, 85, 157
aspirational well-being. *see* pae ora
Assembly of First Nations (AFN), 321, 323–324
assigned at birth, sex, 78n9, 80, 85
assimilation, 24–25, 258, 296, 305–307, 311, 329–331
assumptions, 33, 43
Auckland, 118, 143, 155
Auckland Pride Festival, 39, 124
Australia, 154, 157, 160, 196
authenticity, 280–281, 285, 296, 299
ayahkwêw, 308–309, 310, 310n3

balance, 18, 275–276, 329
Bangkok, 76
baptisms, 308
bar scene, 313–314
bathhouses, 313
Bay Area American Indian Two Spirits, 298, 301
Bay of Plenty, 182
beadwork, 223–224, 229, 306
Beausejour, 317, 319

becoming, 54n7
behavioural health, 206–207, 230. *see also* health risk behaviours
being, Māori metaphysics perspective, 51, 55–56
belief systems, 184, 260n3, 305, 307, 311, 322, 331
Bellegarde, Perry, 321
belonging, 12, 30, 62–64, 133, 216–219, 222, 224–225, 306, 314
berdache, 307–308
binary constraints, 184–185, 188–189, 191–192
binary gender norms, 263, 265, 308, 309, 320–321, 323, 328, 330
biphobia, 18, 73–74
birth certificate, changing, 76
Blacksmith Family Sundance, 321
blood quantum, 294–296
boarding schools, 206–207, 212–213, 258, 298, 309–310, 320, 323
body sovereignty, 23, 256–257, 261, 263, 327, 332–333
body-lands, 331–332
body-spirit, 327, 330
Brando, Marlon, 312–313
Brandon, 313, 314
Brant, Beth, 321
Brochet, 318
Bruce, Barbara, 320
Budd, Reverend Henry, 311
bullying, 61, 71, 83, 116–117, *116*, 126, 138, 307, 319
bunker community, 64–65, 71
Burnett Clinic, 143
Burns, Randy, 323
business management, 196

calendar cycles, 215
Calls for Justice, 323
Cameron, Barbara, 323
Campbell, May Louise, 319
Canada, 24, 154, 157, 304
Canadian Aboriginal AIDS Network

(CAAN), 318
Canadian Criminal Code, 309
Canadian Human Rights Act (2011), 321
cancer deaths, 240
Cape Town, 76
capitalism, 64, 70
cardiovascullar-related deaths, 240
caretaker role, 216–218
Caribbean Women and Sexual Diversity Conference, 76
Carmen, 196
carvings, 87
casual sex, 313
Catholicism, 305, 310
celebration, two-spirit, 258
celibacy, 310–311
censorship, 312
Census, 83
ceremonies
    fertility, 310–311
    importance of, 22, 160, 211–212, 225, 227, 334–336
    leadership role in, 25, 215–216, 330–331
    learning about, 316–317, 320–321
    rite of passage, 219
    and well-being, 230–234, 275, 281, 284–285, 290–291, 298, 301
ceremony, delinking, 261, 263, 265
Chaney, Ange, 75
Cherokee nation, 290, 296–297
Cherokee services, 296
Cheyenne, 307–308
Chicago, 76
chicken hawks, 313
Chilcotin, 314
child welfare regimes, 258
children, 61, 64, 71, 185, 217, 219, 222–224, 230, 305–306. *see also* boarding schools
    and discrimination, 135, 194, 199
    pre-colonisation, 62, 310
    removal of, 258, 309–310
Chile, 160
Choctaw, 211, 227
Choctaw Okla Hannali, 204
Christchurch, 76, 118
Christianity, 37–38, 64–65, 192, 207, 213, 221, 258, 305–307, 311
Christian-right factions, 317
Chrystos, 321
Chukush, 213–214, 221–223, 225
churches. *see* religious institutions
circle, part of, 280, 285
cisgender men, 88
cisnormativity, 263, 263n6
classism, 306
Coast Salish, 314
Coates, Natalie, 191–192, 200–201
Code of Health. *see* New Zealand Code of Health and Disability Services Consumers' Rights
codes of conduct, 310
cognitive dissonance, mixed-race, 293
colonial ideology, internalising of, 294–295
colonial medical practices, 292–293
colonialism, settler
    categorisation by, 328
    embedded practices, 330
    erasure, 22, 205, 207
    historic trauma, 211–216, 220–221, 225–226, 233–234, 291–292
    and HIV/AIDS, 259, 272
    influences of, 301
    moral attitudes, 15–16, 294, 307, 310–311, 324, 331
colonial-washing, 30–31
colonisation
    apology, 304
    and belonging, 63–66
    dismantling, 71, 274
    and female traditions, 85, 170
    and gender understanding, 14–15, 21, 23, 60–61, 68, 138, 148, 181, 183–186, 200, 241, 258–259, 262
    and identity construction, 133, 257

impacts of, 73, 77, 81, 140, 160, 271, 301, 315
Indigenous names, 308
iwi development, 168–169
new illnesses, 154
philosophies, 45, 49, 52
policing and surveillance, 309
and resilience, 157
resisting, 273
and statistics, 97–99, 158–159
and tā moko, 163, 171–172
and tikanga, 90, 181, 184, 186, 190
and traditional healing practices, 165
coming out, 37–38, 41, 81, 138, 148, 196, 207, 228–229, 262, 264–266, 306, 313, 322
commerce, 308
common law, Aotearoa, 21, 181–182, 189–192
community
  acceptance in, 259–261, 276, 279, 284
  building of, 24, 60–61, 70–71, 181, 313–314, 318
  collective spirituality of, 232
  contemporary roles in, 124, 130, 218–219, 228–229
  exclusion, 13, 15, 159, 263, 306–307, 320–321, 330–331
  lack of, 63–64
  nature of, 64–65
  of origin, 293
  traditional roles in, 182, 216–219, 221–222, 227, 234, 241, 257–258, 260, 263, 305–306, 317, 321, 330
community focus, HIV response, 160
community participation action plans (CPAPs), 302
community practice models, 272
conceptional frameworks, 272
confidentiality, 105
confirmations, 308
confrontation, 70–71

connectedness, 14, 30, 34–35, 102, 113, 120, 129–130, 175–177, 213, 215, 220, 228, 234, 276, 279–280, 282, 284, 321, 328–330. *see also* whanaungatanga
contrapuntal voices, 211
conversion practices, banning, 76
conversion rituals, 308
Cormorant Lake, 304–305
Counting Ourselves study, 120–121
courts. *see* criminal justice system
COVID-19, 63–64, 76, 158–159, 161
Crabb, Jack, 312
creation, gift of, 283
creativity, 327–328
Creator, 220, 233, 277, 282, 284–285
Cree, 305–306, 308–311, 314–316
Cree spirit name, 281
criminal justice system, 128–129, 191
critical discourse analysis, 44, 44n2
Cross Lake, 304, 304n1
cross-sectional surveys, 98–99, 105
Crown, 70, 184, 186, 192–193
cultural acceptance shift, 259–261
cultural dissolution, 291, 293, 299–300
cultural distress, 248
cultural values, 74–75, 78–79, 88, 212, 228, 258, 274–275, 312
culture
  affinity, 293
  appropriation of, 297
  competency, 89, 140, 293, 295, 302
  connections, 121–124, 130, 273, 276, 279, 309
  devaluation, 272
  evolution of, 311
  safety, 201, 257, 260
  shock, 319

dance, 25, 321, 327, 333, 334–335
Daniels, Barbara, 316–317, 319
danza Azteca ceremonies, 337
data sovereignty, 105–106

Index 357

data underreporting, 156
Day, Sharon, 320
death penalty, 309
decolonial project, 327
decolonisation
    'Calls for Justice, 323
    data sovereignty, 105
    gender and sexuality, 260
    health-based processes, 168, 208, 266
    methodologies, 274
    and self-reflection, 90
    and takatāpui wellbeing, 16, 61
    thrivance narratives, 226, 233
    and tikanga Māori, 88–189, 191–193, 201
    two-spirit return, 290–291, 297, 299, 302–303
Deer Woman, 215
deficit-based research, 154, 157, 207, 273, 278
demasking, 281–282, 285
Dene, 311, 314
Dennahardt, Richard, 314
Denver, 209, 244
DePaul University, 76
depression, 83–84, 133, 136–138, 143, 207, 224, 313
designated at birth, sex, 78n9, 80, 85
destiny, 305
detachment, 46
diabetes, 171–172
difference, celebration of, 165
Dine, 297
disabilities, Rainbow people with, 83–84
Disability Resource Centre, 145
disconnection, 333
discrimination. *see also* racism
    American Indian and Alaskan Native experiences, 12, 206, 241–242, 301, 306–307, 317, 321
    disability-related, *127*, 128
    fear of, 89, 115–121

    forms of, 81
    gender identity, 127–128, 181–183, 194–196, 200–201, 293
    health services, 12, 126–128, 130–131, 140–142
    HIV/AIDS, 153, 160
    impacts of, 22, 126–130, 134, 193, 242
    and iwi participation, 123–124
    by Māori, 13, 190–192
    and mental health, 126
    overcoming, 74, 85–86, 126
    and parenthood, 121
    sexual identity, 127–128
disease management and prevention, 291
disenfranchisement, 15, 128
dishonour, 213
District Health Boards, 2, 124–125
Doctrine of Discovery, 212
drag and cross-dressing, 313–315
drug use, 116, 136, 153, 156, 196, 291, 306, 316, 319
DUDES Club Society, 264–265
dysfunction, perceived, 271, 273

earth-mother, 69
ecocide, 212
eco-social chronic stressors, 207
Edmonton, 323
education
    decolonisation of, 193, 301
    discrimination in, 88, 126–129, 131, 135, 200, 306, 319
    moral influence of, 308
    need for, 12, 259–261
    and racism, 245
    and smoking risk, 242–243
    survey, 106
    te reo Māori, 122
    tuakana/teina role, 101
    and two-spirit name, 322
educators, 298
Egypt, 196

elders. *see also* kaumātua
    access to, 275, 281, 284, 306
    AIDS work by, 319
    gender diversity views of, 216, 260, 263–264, 321, 330
    and Indigenous knowledge, 169–170, 311, 316–317, 334
    and tikanga Māori, 181–183, 189–190
    two-spirit, 315, 320–321, 331
    urban, 298, 300–302
electric shock treatment, 38, 136
electricity, access to, 206
Ellison, Treva, 328
embodiment, 25, 327–329, 334
emigration, 136
emotional health, 248, 264, 274–276
emotional support, 104
employment, 14, 118, 126–128, 131, 193, 195–196, 200, 319, 322
empowerment, 263, 291
Empress of Vancouver, 314
environmental hazard exposure, 206
epistemicide, 212
epistemology, Indigenous, 334
erasure, 22, 24, 207, 212–213, 215–216, 227–228, 258–260, 271, 307–310, 319–320
Ermine, Willie, 311
eroticism, 310
Erskine Fellowship, 76
essence, 52–54, 52n5
ethics, 45–46, 89, 305, 311
ethnic affinity, 293
ethnic domination, 296–297
ethnocide, 212
etymology, 48–49, 55
European society, 17th century, 309
exclamatory knowledge, 17, 51–52

fa'afafine, 31, 39
fakaleitī, 31, 39
families. *see also* whānau
    acceptance in, 305
    distrust within, 293
    extended, 305–306, 324
    nuclear, 308
    separation from, 309–310, 330
    and support, 306
    surrogate, 314–315, 324
Families Commission, 112
family harm, 157
female personas, 314–315
female traditions, 170
feminism, 86
fertility rituals, 310–311
fertility services, 14, 120, 135
films, influence of, 312–313
First Nations Band Councils, 321
First Nations Health Centre, 320
First Nations leaders, 317, 323–324
First Nations people, 154, 160, 171–172, 275, 304, 318–320
First Nations University of Canada, 311
flexible collectivities, 328–329
Fobister, Waawaate, 322
food preparation, traditional, 305–306
foods, healthy, 171–172, 206
forgiveness, 281
foster homes, 258
'Four Hs,' 153, 159
fragmentation, Western, 45–46, 51, 56
freedom, 25, 327–328, 330–331, 333
funding, ethnic specific organisations, 296
fundraising, 314
funerary rites, 217–219, 330
fur trade, 304–307, 310–311
future generations, 12, 133, 205, 207, 215, 219, 222, 227, 277

Gay American Indians, 298, 300, 323
gay culture, 312–313
gender
    and absence, 53–55
    binary, embedding of, 263
    categorisation of, 54, 56

confines of, 71
decolonisation, 16
equality, 86
and language, 56n10, 62
and Māori worldedness, 51–53, 60–61
non-binary, 16, 33, 85, 86n18, 205n1
roles, 184–187, 189–193, 198–201, 213, 241
segregation, 309
self-determination, 23, 256–257
Western understandings of, 65–67, 187, 258, 299, 333
gender diversity, 258–259, 262, 306, 308–310, 321, 334–335
gender expression, 184–187, 189–193, 198–201, 212, 215, 241, 261, 315, 332
gender fluidity, 13, 33, 73, 83, 85–86, 90, 185, 188, 319, 333
gender identity
  colonial gender structure, 320
  culturally specific, 257
  decolonisation, 303
  discrimination, 115–119, 126–127, 200–201, 242
  and health services, 126–127, 129, 142, 147–148
  importance of, 12–-13
  and Native Americans, 11
  role models, 138
  self-harm and suicide, 130, 134
  self-identification, 261, 314–315
  and smoking risk, 242
  and te reo Māori, 189
  and tikanga Māori, 181–185, 189–193
  and 'two-spirit' term, 205n1
Gender Minorities Aotearoa, 19
gender non-conforming, definition, 261n4
gender-affirming healthcare, 89, 331–332
gender-critical feminists, 85n15

gendered spaces, accessibility of, 260
gene, 52, 52n5, 54
general practitioners (GPs), 115, 119, 124–126, 129, 131, 146
General Social Survey, 119
Geneva, 76
genitalia, 65, 89, 184–185
genocide, 15, 186, 212
geographic lens, 261, 263–264, 266
geographical bias, 105
gidoo-imishinkoowenden, 23–24, 269n1, 270, 281, 285
Gii-Nitaa-Aadisooke: Ojibwe Legends from Lac Suel, 312
Gisborne, 80
Global Feminist LBQ Women*'s Conference, 76
Goulet, Jamie, 320
governance, Indigenous, 24, 105–106, 215
government, 128–129, 131, 184, 322
Greater Vancouver Native Cultural Society (GVNCS), 314–315
Greece, ancient, 65
Green, Kai, 328
Green Party, 76, 89n19
greetings, importance of, 147
grief, 35–36
ground
  divisible, 48–50
  Māori realities of, 46–53

Hamilton, Tom, 75
harm reduction, 292
Harper, Elijah, 317
Hastings, 40
hate crimes and speech, 135
Hati, Chanel, 80n12
Haunui, Kevin, 75, 86n18
hauora Māori, 30, 100–101, 106. *see also* well-being
He Korowai Oranga: Māori Health Strategy, 101, 106, 112
healing, 24, 206, 213–215, 220, 225–

226, 233–234, 259, 263, 276–277, 290–292, 297, 299–300, 302, 320, 329–330, 338
health, self-perception of, 114
health and well-being. *see* well-being
Health Canada, 318
health data autonomy, 19, 97–98
health determinants, Indigenous, 272
health disparities, 271–272
health interventions, Western, 167
health practices, traditional, 126, 165–168, 217–219, 227–228, 231–234, 330
health professionals, 19, 157
    takatāpui, 145–146, 148
health reforms, 76
health risk behaviours, 248, 250, 290–291, 302. *see also* behavioural health
health services
    access, 15, 19–20, 88–89, 101–102, 134–135, 138, 140–147, 155, 160, 206, 271, 292
    communication issues, 143–144
    culturally appropriate, 101–102, 272, 285, 293–295
    decolonisation of, 193
    discrimination, 126–131, 200
    education and training needs, 12, 15, 144–145, 148
    Indigenous, 271–272
    inequities, 12
    Māori, 141–142
    and parenthood, 121
    positive connections with, 146–147, 261, 264
    usage, 124, *125*
health services experiences (survey), 106
health support roles, two-spirit people, 218–219
health workforce (survey), 106
healthful living, 22, 166, 206–207, 209, 225, 276–277
Heavy Runner, Raven, 320

Hectic, 319
Henry, Alexander, 307
heritage, 170–171
Hero, 70
heteronormativity, 13, 66, 73, 86, 123, 135, 184–185, 189, 191–192, 213, 257, 263, 263n5, 309, 313
heteropatriarchy, 17–18, 60–62, 64–70, 85, 258, 260–261
    definition, 260n3
heterosexism, 14, 85, 207–208, 306, 320
Hidatsa miati (male in a woman's role), 207
Highway, Tomson, 321
Hine Te Ariki, 80–81
Hineahuone, 47
Hinemoa, 30
Hine-nui-te-pō, 55, 57
Hinetītama, 47, 55, 57
history, framing of, 79, 212
history, two-spirit, 216
HIV/AIDS
    Aotearoa experience, 20, 134, 155–156
    awareness, 155
    care and support, 115, 155–156, 218–219, 273
    conferences, 155, 157–158, 160, 183
    data issues, 156–159
    disparities, 154–155, 157, 160, 271, 293, 302
    early days of, 20, 153–154, 196–197, 298, 316–317
    education, 155, 318–319
    international Indigenous response, 20, 155, 157
    leadership, 318–319
    living with HIV, 23, 272–278, 321
    and Māori, 154–160
    morbidity and mortality rates, 271
    policy and programs, 271, 274, 290–291, 293–295, 297, 299–300
    prevention strategies, 154–155, 158,

160–161, 300–303, 318–319
and smoking risk, 242, 245
stigma and discrimination, 13–14, 20, 117–118, 143, 153, 183, 197, 317
'Two Spirits in Motion' forum, 323
two-spirit populations, 23, 242–243, 259, 262, 269–272, 290–291, 293–295, 297, 299–300, 302
Village Clinic, 318
Ho, Wai, 75
Hoffman, Dustin, 312
home, sense of, 63
homelessness, 114, 120, 131
homonormativity, 207–208
homophobia
   experiences of, 14, 196, 269–271, 306–307
   First Nations Chiefs, 317
   and health services, 115, 140, 143
   internalised, 16, 242, 258, 263
   and iwi participation, 123
   overcoming, 18–19, 36, 126, 183, 191, 193, 229, 262, 324, 334
   and parenthood, 121
   political and service organisations, 320
   and racism, 135–137
   state perpetration, 304
   and well-being, 41, 73–74, 117–119, 130–131, 134, 137–139, 148, 241–242, 273, 330
homosexual law reform, 70, 312
HONOR Project, 11–12, 21–22, 98, 100, 103, 115–116, 119, 124, 126, 129, 210, 224, 243–250, 330
HONOR Project Two-Spirit Health Study, 22, 209–212
Honour Project Aotearoa, 11–12, 16–17
   demographics, 112
   design, 97–107
   discrimination impacts, 126–129, 192–194, 201

healthy future requirements, 112–113
mauri ora, 112–119
mode, 103
ngā hononga, 121–124
objectives, 101–102, 133
questions, 103–104
sexual and gender identities, 111–112, 182–183, 188
summary, 129–131
wai ora, 124–126
whānau ora, 119–121
hormone treatment, 196, 331
Household Economic Survey, 83
housing inequities, 206, 319
Hudson's Bay Company (HBC), 304–305, 307
Huitzilopoxtli, 335
human behaviours, challenges of, 153
Human Rights Act, 193, 200–201
Human Rights Commission, 12
human rights issues, 14, 21, 89, 118, 134, 182
hustlers, male, 313

I poems, 210–211, 213, 216–233
ia, 54
ideas, conception of, 44–45
identity. *see also* gender identity; sexual identity
   collective, 14, 215
   construction, 133
   criminalising of, 307
   cultural and spiritual, 187, 205n1, 229–230, 234, 241, 258, 329
   erasure of, 212–213
   family influence on, 305–306
   impact of perceived dysfunction, 271
   importance of, 113, 131, 139
   and Indigenous languages, 273
   inseparable nature of, 241
   Māori, 64, 103, 113–115, 117, 121, 130, 139, 148

mixed race, 303
and rangatiratanga, 103, 107
reclamation of, 29–34, 40, 60–61, 147, 257–258
self-determination, 85, 103, 112, 188–189, 198, 259–261, 265, 291
social construction, 271
survey results, 111–112
and tā moko, 163–165, 171, 174–179
takatāpui, 65, 68, 71, 78–81, 187
and tikanga Māori, 189–192, 200
transgender, 313, 319
urban, 291, 293–297
Western understandings of, 187, 258
immigration, 129
immunity, 154
inclusion, 38, 136, 187
income, insufficient, 114, 120, 131, 155
independence, belief in, 305
Indian Act (1867), 258, 308, 320
Indian agents, 207
Indian Blood: HIV and Colonial Trauma in San Francisco's Two-Spirit Community, 24, 290–294
Indian Blood Psychosocial Nexus of Risk (IBPN) model, 293
Indian identity, policing of, 293–295
Indian status, 306
Indigenous cultural mentoring networks (ICMNs), 24, 290–291, 294, 296–297
Indigenous HIV conference, 155
Indigenous knowledges and practices, 211, 274, 279, 284, 334
Indigenous law, 256
Indigenous philosophy, 305
Indigenous Wellness Research Institute, 11, 21, 98
Indigenous women's movement, 319
inequities, 12, 15, 115, 131, 134, 182–183, 206–207
infant sleep patterns (survey), 106

Information, Motivation and Behavioral Skills (IMB) Model, 291
institutional commodification, 329
institutional shifts, 259–261, 322, 324
interconnectedness
of all things, 17, 44, 80, 282
and identity, 31, 76
intergenerational growth, 328
Intergenerational Healing and Cultural Leadership (IHCL) intervention model, 300–302
intergenerational needs, 297–299
intermarriage, 306
internalisation, colonial values, 138, 186, 208, 226, 228
international Indigenous networks, 157–158, 160–161
International Indigenous Pre-Conference on HIV/AIDS, 157, 183
International Indigenous Working Group on HIV and AIDS (IIWGHA), 157–158, 160
internet, 321
interphobia, 73–74, 86, 89
intersectional feminist analysis, 85, 88
Intersex Aotearoa, 76
Intersex community, 81
intersex infants and children, 89
Inuit, 154, 160, 275, 311, 324
invisibility, 12, 15, 228
ira, 51–55
isolation, 35–36, 69, 136, 138, 148, 313, 330–332
iwi, 35, 39, 70, 122–123, 130–131, 133

Jackson, Moana, 60
Jamaica, 76
Jehovah's Witnesses, 37
Johnson-Jennings, Dr, 204
Jorgenson, Christina, 312
judgement, 282

Kwagu'ł, 255
Kahukiwa, Robyn, 87

Kaiser Hospital, 293–295
kaitiakitanga, 82, 102, 113
kanohi kitea approach, 105
karakia, 126, 129
Kaska, 314
kaumātua, 21, 181–183, 191, 193–194, 198. *see also* elders
kaupapa Māori, 11, 17–19, 97–107
kaupapa whānau, 113, 119, 124, 130
Kerekere, Dr Elizabeth, 11
Kereopa, Hohepa, 166
King, Thomas, 270
Kingston, 76
kinship, 206, 215
kinship networks, Indian urban, 24, 291, 295, 297, 299–301
Kvli, 226, 232
knowledge, Indigenous. *see also* mātauranga
  censorship of, 312
  definition, 168–169
  and identity, 15, 257
  Original Instructions, 215–221
  reclaiming, 172, 208–209, 225, 227, 301, 320, 324, 331, 334
  storytelling, 310
  and thrivance, 22, 233–234
  in urban settings, 296, 298, 316–317
  and well-being, 271, 274, 277, 284, 292
knowledge keepers. *see* elders, 23
kōhanga reo, 61, 122
kura Kaupapa Māori, 61, 64, 69, 122
Kwakiutl, 314

Lakota, 296–297, 312, 323
land
  desecration, 206
  dispossession, 15, 25, 212, 317
  ownership, 186
  relationship with, 25, 215, 257, 273, 276, 282, 285, 329–330
land-based healing, 225–226

land-based traumatic events, 206
Lang, Sabine, 309
language. *see also* te reo Māori
  absence of, 62, 310
  confrontation with metaphysics, 52n5
  connection to, 284–285
  contributions of, 273
  Cree, 305–306, 308, 310n4, 311
  difficulty with, 281–282
  and diversity, 78–79, 83–84, 187–189, 216–217, 257, 264, 266, 307, 312
  eradication of, 24, 212, 258
  and gender, 56n10, 62, 183, 260, 262
  and healing, 227–228, 330
  innovation in, 260–261
  Māori worlded, 43–46
  Ojibwe, 305, 307, 316n6, 321
  retention of, 305–306
  separation from its objects, 52
  and silence, 45
  Western view of, 45
Laramee, Dr Myra, 317–318, 320
Larkin, Kecia, 318
laughter, 276–277
Lavallee, Ed, 324
lawyers, Māori, 181
leadership, 24, 85, 91, 185–186, 209–210, 259–261, 263–266, 270–271, 274, 290–292, 297–298, 300–302, 321–322
leadership pathway, 70
legal rights, 117
legal system, *117*, 184, 307–309
legends, 30–31, 312
legislation, 317, 321
  failures in, 21, 118, 121, 129, 131, 139, 147, 187, 191, 193, 200
Lekwungen territory, 255
LGBTQ2 Secretariat, 322
Liberace, 312
liberation, 69–71

Liberty Street, 318
life essence. *see* mouri
Lifeline, 136–137
Listening Guide method, 210–211
Little Big Man, 312
Little Horse, 312
Little Star, Robert, 312
Littlefeather, Sacheen, 312–313, 315
Littlethunder, Beverly, 319–320
Logie, Jan, 89n19
Los Angeles, 209, 244, 300
love, 206, 222, 224–226, 234
Love Life Fono, 39

Maaka, Dr Golan, 167
Macdonald, Sir John A., 309
Mackay, James, 311
māhū, 31
Mair, Charles, 308
Maiya, 218–219, 221, 223–224
mana, 62, 73, 78, 84–87, 101, 103–104, 185–187, 190–191, 333
mana kaitiakitanga, 165–166
mana motuhake, 102, 189
Mana Taiohi, 76
mana tipua, 73, 86, 91
mana wāhine, 18, 69, 73, 86, 91, 186
Mana Wāhine Kaupapa Inquiry, 86n17
manaakitanga, 71, 191
manaia, 87
Mandan, 308
Mangakāhia, Meri Te Tai, 186
Manifest Destiny, 212
manifestation of the remnant, 218
Manitoba, 257, 304, 308, 311, 313, 315–319, 321–323
Manitoba Aboriginal AIDS Task Force (MAATF), 318–319
Manitoba Métis Federation (MMF), 324
Manitoba MLA, 317
Māori analysis, 17, 43
Māori Data Sovereignty Network, 105

Māori dictionary, 77n8
Māori feminism, 86
Māori Language Commission. *see* Te Taura Whiri i Te Reo Māori
Māori language survey, 106
Māori men, changing attitudes of, 186, 190
Māori Parliament. *see* Te Kotahitanga
Māori population
 decline, 154
 youthfulness, 156
Māori Select Committee, 200
Māori society
 contemporary, 189–191, 193
 gender balance in, 86, 183–186, 189–191
 traditional, 31, 77, 85–86, 90, 138, 148, 181, 183–186, 198, 200
marae protocols, 90
marakihau, 80
marginalisation
 and disability, 83
 and HIV/AIDS, 160
 Indigenous youth, 259
 takatāpui, 13–14, 64, 138, 148, 187, 190–192, 201
 two-spirit people, 241–242, 248, 258, 260, 266, 302
marriages, 308, 310, 313
masculinity, 66, 68–69, 305
massacres, 206
Mataatua, 185
Matariki, 63
mātauranga, 76, 100, 102, 112–113, 118, 170, 184, 191–192. *see also* knowledge, Indigenous
Mate Arai Kore, Mate Ketoketo, 155
matter, unseen, 46
mauri, 73, 82–84, 85, 101, 112, 164, 333
mauri ora, 101–102, 106, 112–119. *see also* well-being
McDonald, Laurie, 314
McEvoy, Linda, 319

McGarvey, Te Aoterangi, 155
McGillivary, Harvey, 314–315
McIvor, Albert Bethune, 305
McIvor, Mary Madeline (née Moose), 24, 305, 324
McKay, Dorland, 318
McLeod, 304
McMaster University, 274
Mead, Sir Hirini Moko, 189–190
media, 76, 128–129, 312
mediation/regression analyses, 245–246
mediator role, 216–218
medical profession, 81, 184–185, 195–196
Medical Services Branch, 318
medicine wheel, 274–275
medicines, plant, 320, 330
Meech Lake Accord, 317
Mehlhopt, Soul, 86n18
memory, 170–171
mental health
    Rainbow people, 88
    self-harm and suicide, 118–119
    self-perception of, 114
    services, 124–126, *125*
    takatāpui, 74, 131, 133, 138
    treatment, 136
    two spirit people, 206, 258, 264, 316
    youth, 83–84, 219
Mental Health Foundation, 75
mental illness classification, 38
mentorship, 24, 101, 291–294, 296–297, 299–302, 306, 330
Merasty, Bill, 318
Merasty, Connie, 318, 320–321
metaphysical relationships, 43–45, 52, 55, 165, 167–168
Métis, 154, 160, 275, 304, 308, 314, 318–320, 324
Micmac, 314
micro-aggression distress, 22, 206–207, 244, 301

mihimihi, 147
military, 310
military combat exposure, 206
Ministry of Health, 124–125
Minneapolis-St. Paul, 209, 244
mino-bimaadiziwin, 276–277
mirimiri, 126
misogyny
    childhood experiences, 135
    escaping, 63, 196
    and iwi participation, 123
    overcoming, 148, 183, 191, 193
    and parenthood, 121
    self-harm and suicide, 118–119, 138
    and trauma, 85, 115–116, 307, 330
    and well-being, 19, 41, 131
missing and murdered Indigenous women, 206, 323
missionaries, 77, 85, 184–185, 207, 212–213, 311
Mitchell, Mani Bruce, 76
mixed race cognitive dissonance, 293
Mohawk, 314
morality, 15, 258, 310–311
morbidity and mortality rates, 206, 271
mouri, 163–165
movies, influence of, 312–313
MPs, Rainbow, 76
Murray, Glen, 318
Musqueam, 255, 255n1, 314
Mvskoke language, 216–217
My tapu head (1990), 87
mystification, 169–170

name-calling, 195
names, personal, 308
naming ceremonies, 227–228, 234, 331
narrative transformation, 22, 211, 226–229, 234
National Aboriginal Health Organization, 320
National Canadian Aboriginal AIDS

Network (CAAN) conference, 255n1, 256
National Collective of Independent Women's Refuges (NCIWR), 75
National Council on AIDS, 155–156
National Inquiry into Murdered and Missing Indigenous Women and Girls, 323
National Rainbow Strategy, 76
Native American AIDS Project, 24, 299–301
Native American Health Centers, 300–301
Native American/First Nations Gay and Lesbian conference, 205n1
Native Community Mentors (NCM) Program, 301
Native Youth Sexual Health Network, 261
natural world, 24, 215, 220, 226, 276–277, 311, 322, 330
Navajo, 296
Nechi Institute, 323
Neho, Manu, 20, 163, 172–179
Nelson, 76
Nelson House HBC Post, 305
Nenakawekapo, Peetanacoot, 320–321
neonatal intensive care, 14, 135
New Democratic Party, Manitoba, 317
New Freedom, 316
New York, 153, 209, 244, 313
New Zealand Code of Health and Disability Services Consumers' Rights, 121, 129, 147, 193, 200–201
New Zealand Health Survey (2017), 114
ngā hononga, 121–124
Ngā Uri o Uenuku Hui, 76
Ngāpuhi, 173
Ngāti Awa, 189, 191
Ngati Tuwharetoa, 31

Nichiwakan Native Gay Society, 316–318
Nignewance, Christine, 312
Nine Circles Community Health Centre, 318, 321
Ningewance, Patricia, 312
noa, 87
non-interference, ethics of, 305
normalisation, 38–39, 260, 328
North, Rick, 313
Northern Algonquin, 11
Northern Paiute, 323
North-West Mounted Police, 309
Northwest Rebellion, 309
Norton, Rictor, 309
Norway, 160
Norway House, 304, 304n1
nuclear families, 14, 63–64, 66, 85, 260, 308
nudity, 310

Oakley, 136
objectification, 293–294
Oceania, 157
Ojibwe Midewiwin culture, 311
Ojibwe people, 307, 312, 314, 316, 321
Oka Crisis, 317
Oklahoma, 290, 296
Oklahoma City-Tulsa, 209
Olson, Lorne, 305
Ontario, 274
Ontario Aboriginal HIV/AIDS strategy, 272
Opaskwayak Cree Nation, 255, 314, 318
openness, 117
ora, 101
oral history, 171
oral tradition, 275
orientation/whaka, 48–49
Original Instructions, 22, 211, 215–220, 227, 234, 334
orphans, social, 315

Orvis, Velma, 319
ostracism, 135, 306–307
Otapi, 229–230, 230
Ottawa, 160
Out: Stories of Lesbian and Gay Youth in Canada, 318
Outrageous! 313, 315

Pacific, 85
Packo, Paul, 317
pae ora, 101–102, 106
Pae Ora (Healthy Futures) Bill, 200
pain, 22–23, 243–246, 248–250, *249*
Pan-Indianism, 294, 296–297
Papatūānuku, 47, 50, 77, 84–85
paradoxes, 50
parenthood, 120–121, 130–131, 199–200
Parliament, 76
participants, research, 103–105, 182, 210, 244, 290–294, 300–301, 318
partnerships, 70
Pasifika, 83–84
paternalism, 273
patriarchy, 24, 66, 184–185, 192, 213, 307, 308, 319
Paul, Vernon, 316
peer mentoring interventions (PMIs), 291–293
pepeha, 338
perceptions, 44–45
persistence, 22, 208, 211, 213, 226–227, 233–234
Peru, 160
pharmacists, 124
phenomenology, Māori, 50
philosophies, 43, 52
    Māori, 49–51, 49n3, 54–56, 54n7
    Western, 44–48, 51, 54–56
physical being, 74
physical health, 264, 274–275
physical realm, 73, 86
pipe ceremonies, 320

place, sense of, 12–13, 329–330
Pʋlali, 219
Platonic Form, 48
Polchies, Chief Alan Jr, 324
police, 70, 128–129, 195–196
policing, social, 309
political participation, 292
pollutants and toxins, 206, 212
Post-Traumatic Invasion Syndrome (PTIS), 291–292, 299
potential, 54n7
pou (posts), 86–87, 86n18
poverty, 307
'power of the feminine,' aversion to, 307
Pow wows, 298, 320–321
practices, traditional, 223
prayer, 229–230, 233, 260
pre-colonisation, 31, 41, 62, 305, 319
predatory behaviour, 293–294
pregnancies, unwanted, 136, 138
prejudice, 13, 153, 216, 280
presence, 46, 55
pre-testing, 104
Pride Parades, 298
primary care services, 19, 115
Primary Health Strategy, 126
Primary Healthcare Organisation (PHO), 125
primordial ground, 17
procreation, 310–311
promiscuity, 310
pronouns, 55, 84, 210, 261–262, 265, 314n5
prosperity, 170–171
prostitution, 319
Pruden, Gayle, 321
psychology, 74, 240–241
puberty, 81
Public Health Commission, 155–156
public health services, 22, 114–115
public institutions, trust in, 128–129
puna waihanga, 333
punishment, 212–213

pūrākau, 17, 21, 181–183, 188, 193–201, 331
puritanical attitudes, 310–311
puritans, 77
purpose, sense of, 222–225, 305

qualitative methods, 22, 98, 209–211, 274–275
Qualtrics, 104
quantitative methods, 18–19, 97–99, 106–107, 156
Quebec, 317
Queen Victoria, 186
queer subculture, 17th century, 309
quilts, 36, 137

racism
  escaping, 63, 196
  experiences of, 306–307, 314, 317
  and health risk behaviours, 22, 248
  and health services, 126–127, 140–141, 160
  and HIV/AIDS disparities, 293
  overcoming, 86, 126, 183, 193, 262
  and pain, 243–245, *249*, 250
  and parenthood, 121
  re-practicing, 297
  resisting, 273
  and smoking, 245, *249*, 250
  and stress, 240–241
  and takatāpui, 13
  US ethnic groups, 241–242
  and well-being, 19, 115–116, 130–131, 134–137
Rainbow Policy, Green Party, 76
Rainbow representation, 76
rangatiratanga. *see also* sovereignty
  and HIV/AIDS, 161
  Honour Project Aotearoa, 99, 102–104, 107, 133
  and identity, 29–30, 61, 188–189
  and moko kauwae, 176–178
  pathways, 19
  and well-being, 113, 117, 130, 157
Ranginui, 55, 85
rank, 185
rationalism, 43, 46, 48–49, 50, 53–54
reciprocity, 291
reconciliation, 323
recovery, 207–208
recruitment, study participants, 103–105, 107, 244, 274, 300–301
Red Power Movement, 297–298
Red River Settlement, 308
regalia, 315
rejection, 62–64, 83, 117, 121, 136, 138, 223–224, 301, 306
relational restoration, 22, 211, 220, 234
relationality, 23, 220, 256, 264–266
relationships, 76–77, 305, 332
religious institutions, 129, 138, 142, 184, 307–308, 322
relocation, forced, 206, 329–330
re-Māorification, 61
reproductive justice, 89
research methodologies, 18–19, 22–23, 97–98, 158–159, 255–257, 261–266, 274–275
reservations, 221, 313–314
residential schools. *see* boarding schools
resilience, 23–24, 157, 160–161, 165, 207, 220, 225, 227, 270, 272–280, 282–285
resistance, 225–226, 317, 328–330, 334
resources, 69
respect, earning, 221–222
responsibilities, intergenerational, 215
re-storying, Indigenous, 226–228, 234
revictimisation, 292–293
revitalisation, two-spirit, 258, 266

rites of passage, 219, 330–331, 334
rituals, 25, 334–336
River Mist Maiden. *see* Hine Te Ariki
role models, 113, 116–117, *116*, 126, 130, 134, 138, 140, 148, 221–222, 312–313
Romans, 65
rongoā Māori, 126, 129, 166–168
Roscoe, Will, 309
Ross, White Feather Georgina, 315
Roulette, Roger, 305, 309, 311
rural areas, challenges in, 263–264, 266
Russell, Craig, 313

sacred-feminine, 69
safe spaces, 23, 24, 260–263, 265, 319, 321, 324
safety, 126, 195–196, 200, 293, 306
sample size, 103
San Francisco, 323
San Francisco Bay area, 24, 290–291, 293, 296–301
San Francisco-Oakland, 209, 244
Saskatchewan, 154, 309
Saskatoon, 313
schools, mainstream, 64
science-sex, 49–51
Scottish ancestry, 315
Seattle, 300
Seattle-Tacoma, 209, 244
security, 105
segregation, 61, 313
self, understandings of, 51, 55–56
self-acceptance, 275–276, 279
self-care, 143, 277
self-determination, 70, 86, 99, 114, 130, 168, 171, 273, 291, 300–301, 303, 330. *see also* rangatiratanga
self-esteem, 12, 273
self-harm, 20, 83–84, 118–119, 130, 134, 136–140, 148
self-hatred, 138–139

self-love, 225, 333
self-reliance, 143
service, role of, 216–219, 221–222, 235
service delivery issues, 295
settlers, 77, 184, 310–311
sex, etymology of, 49
sex work, 196–197
'sex-based rights,' 85n15
sexual attention, unwanted, 138, 307
sexual behaviours, 153, 156, 302
sexual diversity, 258–259, 306, 308–310
sexual exploitation, 313, 315, 319
sexual expression, 15, 212, 215, 241
sexual fluidity, 73, 85–86, 90
sexual health, 43–44, 47, 52, 114, 124, 138, 143, 256, 259–260, 264, 318
sexual health inequities, 115
sexual identity
  culturally specific, 257
  decolonisation, 16, 303
  and discrimination, 182
  and health services, 114–119, 126–127, 129, 142, 147–148
  importance of, 12–13
  and Native Americans, 11
  role models, 138
  self-harm and suicide, 130, 134
  and 'two-spirit' term, 205n1
sexual orientation, 115, 134, 218, 242, 245, 248, 320
sexual roles, 213, 241
sexuality
  and censorship, 310–311
  colonisation impacts, 60–61
  decolonisation, 16, 303
  and 'ground,' 47
  Indigenous, 15, 68, 259
  and language, 62
  Western understandings of, 12, 66–67, 258, 299
shame, 213

sharing circles, 260, 274, 301, 317, 320–321
Sixties Scoop, 258
skills, traditional, 305–306
skin carving. *see* tā moko
Smith, Lee, 77n8, 187
smoking, 240–250
   ceremonial and religious, 242
   cessation relapse, 248–249
   and gender identity, 242
   HONOR Project secondary study, 22, 243–250
   and pain, 243, 245–246, 248–250, *249*
   prevention and intervention programmes, 23, 240–241, 243, 249
   and racism, 240–242, 245, 248
   tobacco abuse, 242
   tobacco company targeting, 242
   tribal attitudes, 242
   two-spirit populations, 241–243
smudge ceremonies, 317
social attitudes, 280–281
social barriers, 314, 331
social behaviour, 302
social control, 310
social disadvantage, 157
social distress, 248
Social Identity Theory, 291
Social Learning Theory, 291
social media, 321
social participation, 292
social services, 12, 124, 129–130, 193, 271
social support, 124, 242, 250, 264, 276, 315
socio-economic barriers, 123–124
songs, traditional, 215, 227, 231, 317. *see also* waiata
South Africa, 160
South America, 157
South Canterbury, 36, 137
sovereignty, 25, 309, 317, 334. *see also* rangatiratanga
'Sowing Seeds' research, 158–159
Spillett, Leslie, 319
spiritual barriers, 331
spiritual health, 119, 264, 274–276
spiritual world, 73, 86, 215, 220, 224–225, 227, 275, 310, 322, 333
spirituality. *see also* wairuatanga
   body-spirit, 327–329
   and connectedness, 228
   Māori, 73–75, 78, 88, 164–165, 187
   and moko kauwae, 172–173, 175–178
   Northern Cree, 311
   Spirit Guides, 315
   two-spirit people, 22, 213
   and well-being, 211, 220, 230–234, 263
Squamish, 255, 255n1, 314
St Mary's First Nation, 324
staff, Native organisations, 295–296
statistics
   HIV/AIDS, 242–243, 259, 271
   Honour Project Aotearoa, 18–19, 97–107
   non-heterosexual Māori, 138
   and Rainbow people, 82–84
   smoking, 240–242, 245, *246–247*
Statistics Act 1975, 105
Statistics New Zealand, 83
Stevenson, Matilda Coxe, 309
stigma
   HIV/AIDS, 13–14, 20, 117–118, 134, 153, 160, 259, 294, 317
   homosexual, 307
   overcoming, 191, 259–262
   and sexual health inequities, 115
   transgender, 181–183, 193
Stonewall, 70
storytelling
   Choctaw, 204–206
   creation stories, 331–332
   as 'data,' 211
   erasure of, 213, 310

and moko, 164
Ojibwe, 312
Original Instructions, 215
power of, 269–270
and resilience, 278–279
and thrivance, 208–209, 234
well-being framework, 226–228
strategies, 61, 68–70, 208, 211, 234, 298
stress
  coping mechanisms, 22, 116–117, 290, 293, 300, 302
  'minority,' 135
  overcoming, 126, 226, 229–230
  racism and pain, 22, 243–244, 248
  self-harm and suicide, 130, 224
  and smoking, 240–241, 248–249
  and well-being, 12
'strong mind,' 23–24, 273, 279–284, 282
students, Polytech, 36, 137
substance use, 133, 157, 206–207, 224
suffrage, 186
suicide, 20, 75, 83–84, 118–119, 130, 134, 136–140, 146, 148, 224–225, 316, 319–320, 333–334
Suicide Prevention and Two-Spirited People, 320
Sundance ceremonies, 321
support services, 118–119, 126, 264, 273–274, 292, 294, 323. *see also* kinship networks, Indian urban
surgery, gender reassignment, 196
surveillance, 309
survey, quantitative, 31
surveys, Māori population, 106–107
survival strategies, 25, 63
survivance, 22, 207–208, 211, 233–234, 328–330
sweat lodges, 230, 281, 317, 320
Sydney, 183, 196
symbol-based enquiry, 274

tā moko

facial, 164, 168
and identity, 171, 174–179
meaning, 164–165
moko kauwae, 163, 163n1, 173–178
mouri moko, 163–164
safe landscape for, 172
and traditional healing practices, 165–168
and well-being, 20–21, 170–171
taboos, 311
taha hinengaro, 74
taha tinana, 74
taha wairua, 74
taha whānau, 15, 74
tāhuhu, 86–87
takatāpui, heteropatriachy entrenchment issue, 64–65, 67–71
takatāpui, term origins, 17, 29–32, 60–61, 67, 77–78, 77n8, 187–189
takatāpui rights, 192–193
Takipū Marae, 80
talking circles. *see* sharing circles
Tall Cree Nation, 255
Tamati, Te Whatinga, 198–199
tangata ira tāne, 77–78, 80, 88
tapu, 73, 87–90, 142, 167
Taranaki, 167
Taranaki Base Hospital, 154
target population, 102–103
Te Ao Māori, 100, 133
Te Arawa, 31
Te Awekotuku, Ngahuia, 77n8, 169–170, 187
Te Karaka, 80
Te Kotahitanga, 186
Te Kupenga national survey, 106, 113, 120–122, 124, 128–130
Te Mana Raraunga, 105
Te Pō, 55, 57
Te Puni Kokiri, 155
Te Rangikaheke, 31, 77, 187
Te Rau Hinengaro: New Zealand Mental Health Survey, 118, 137
te reo Māori, 106, 113, 121–122, *122,*

124, 129, 145, 178, 183, 187–189, 192
Te Rōpū Tautoko Trust, 155–156
Te Taura Whiri i Te Reo Māori, 189
Te Tiriti o Waitangi, 21, 79, 79n10, 86n17, 147, 184, 186–187, 189, 192–193, 201
Te Wānanga o Raukawa, 60
Te Wao, Manawaroa, 21, 181–183, 188, 193–200, **195, 197, 199**
Te Wao, Peri, 80n12
Te Whare Rokiroki Māori Women's Refuge, 75
Te Whare Takatāpui framework, 73–77, 86–87, 90, 91
Te Whare Tapa Whā health model, 73–74
teachers, 207
teaching, traditional processes, 218, 222–224
teachings, Indigenous, 211, 215, 222–224, 230, 255, 257–258, 275, 277, 279, 331
television, 312
'testimonios,' 209
The Godfather, 312
'The Last Bison,' 308
The Legacy Ball, 314
The Office Sauna Bath, 313
The Pas, 306, 311, 314
The Truth about Stories: A Native Narrative, 270
themes, narrative, 211
thing, as verb, 50
third/fourth genders, 213, 215, 241
thrivance, 22, 208–211, 226, 233–234, *234*, 328
tikanga Māori
  1950s life, 194
  colonisation impacts, 89–91
  and common law, 21
  Crown responsibilities, 192–193
  decolonisation of, 191–192
  definition, 189–190

Honour Project Aotearoa, 112–113, 129
and legal system, 191–192
subjugation of, 186, 190, 192–193
and Te Whatinga Tamati, 198–199
and well-being, 15–16, 73, 106, 181–184, 200–201
Tiki, 30–31
time, linear, 54n7
tipua, 80–82
tīpuna, 77, 80, 82
Tīwhanawhana Trust, 18, 19, 73, 75, 86n18, 90–91
tohunga, 87, 166–167, 173–174
Tokanui, 136
Tombi, 220
Toronto, 313, 323
Toronto Charter, 158
traders, 184, 311
trading posts, 304–305, 304n1
traditional knowledge. *see* knowledge, Indigenous
traditional medicines and ceremonies, 126, 129, 160, 285. *see also* medicines, plant; rongoā
Traditional Urban Indian Cultural Knowledge Systems (TUICKS), 290–291, 296–297, 301
tranifesting, 328–329, 335
trans existence, evolving tradition of, 329
trans practice, 331
trans-exclusionary radical feminists (TERFs), 85n15
transformative resistance, 22, 208–209, 211, 225–226, 228–229, 233–234, 329
transgender, categorisation of, 56
transition journeys, 80n12
transmovimientos, 328–329, 335
transphobia
  childhood experiences, 135
  colonisation impacts, 307, 330–331
  escaping, 196

internalised, 16, 263, 334
and iwi participation, 123
overcoming, 18–19, 73–74, 85–86, 126, 183, 191–193, 262, 329, 334
and parenthood, 121
political and service organisations, 320
self-harm and suicide, 118–119, 138
state perpetration, 304
and well-being, 41, 89, 115–116, 130–131, 148
trauma, contemporary oppression, 206–207, 224, 249
trauma, historical and intergenerational
and healthcare access, 15
impact on self-harm and suicide, 224
and Māori, 18, 73, 85, 178
and Native Americans, 12, 24, 293
overcoming, 233–234, 320, 334
and research protocols, 159–160
and smoking risk, 243
and two-spirit people, 22, 206–207, 209, 211–216, 220, 225–227, 249, 259, 291–292, 298–302, 307, 320
and well-being, 116, 171
treaties, 308
Treaty of Waitangi. *see* Te Tiriti o Waitangi
tribal affinity, 293, 298
tribal names, two-spirit people, 216–217
Trolove, Jack, 75
Trudeau, Justin, 304, 322
Trudeau, Pierre, 312
trust, patterns of, 128–129, 131
Truth and Reconciliation Commission of Canada, 309–310, 323
truths, living, 277
Tsimshian, 314
Tsleil-Waututh, 255, 255n1, 314
tuakana/teina role, 101
tuakiri, 113–115, 117, 130. *see also* identity
Tulsa-Oklahoma City, 209, 244
tūpuna, 18, 138, 164
tūrangawaewae, 74, 87
Turner, Robin, 315
Turtle Island (North America), 255n1, 328
Tūtānekai, 30–31
Twitter, 280
'Two Spirits in Motion' forum, 323
two-spirit, meanings of, 11, 205n1, 241, 256–257, 290–291, 299, 304
Two-Spirit Circle of Edmonton Society, 323
two-spirit name vision, 317
two-spirit resurgence, Canada, 24, 304, 322–324
two-spirit return, US, 24, 290–291, 299

Uganda, 160
unconditional love, 34
Underworld, 57
Unitarian Church, 313
United Nations
Convention on the Rights of the Child, 89
Declaration on the Rights of Indigenous People, 118, 192, 201
Freedom of Religion and Belief Conference, 76
Human Rights Council, 76
and IIWGHA, 157–158
Independent Expert on protection against violence and discrimination based on sexual orientation and gender identity, 82
United States, 154, 157, 212, 240, 244
University of Canterbury, 76
University of Otago, 156
University of Saskatchewan, 255
University of Toronto, 274
University of Washington, 11, 98
University of Winnipeg, 324

urban traditions, 299
urbanisation, 12, 24, 186, 291, 293–296, 323

Vā, 328
validation, 312
values
   European, 186, 191, 305, 307
   Indigenous, 216–218, 220, 223, 229
   influences on, 308
   Māori, 18, 30, 75, 134, 191, 198
Vancouver, 313–314, 316–317, 323
victimisation, 135, 208, 226
Village Clinic, 318
violence
   and colonisation, 90, 183, 213, 226, 241, 307, 309
   combating, 256
   experiences of, 14, 22, 116–117, 135, 206–207, 244
   fear of, 242
   gendered, 73, 83, 89, 215, 273
   physical, 206–207, 213
   sexual, 206–207, 293
   systemic, 88–89
visibility, 38–41, 134, 138, 148, 208, 215–216, 259, 298
visual art, Māori, 164
Vogel, Chris, 313
vulnerability factors, HIV, 156–157

Waashask, Manitou, 269–270, 274, 279
wai, 126
waiata, 31, 171. *see also* songs, traditional
Waikato, 182
Waikohu, 80
waiora, 80, 101–102, 106, 124–126. *see also* well-being
Wairaka, 185
wairua, 15, 73, 80–82, 85, 90, 112, 138, 176–178, 333
wairuatanga, 106, 113

Waitangi Tribunal, 192–193
Waituhi, 80
Walters, Karina, 11, 98, 101
wānanga, 100, 106–107
war shield heuristic, 211, 233–234, *234*
warfare, 185
water, 206, 212, 257
weaving analogy, 208–209, 233–234
Weesageechak stories, 310, 310n4
well-being. *see also* waiora
   access to health services, 15, 19, 133–148, 206, 271, 292–294
   ceremonies and spirituality, 230–234, 298
   coming out, 81
   Crown responsibilities, 193
   DUDES Club Society, 264–265
   health and social services, 12, 124–126
   health barriers, 82, 88–89, 102, 125–128
   health data autonomy, 97–98
   health risk behaviours, 248, 250, 290–291, 302
   healthful practices, 225, 276–277
   Honour Project Aotearoa, 97–107, 111–131
   and Indigenous knowledge, 215, 220
   Indigenous sources of, 230–234, 285, 329
   and intangible relationships, 112–113
   and mana, 85
   mental health, 74, 83–84, 114
   physical health, 114
   public places, 126–128, 131
   research protocols, 159, 256–257
   safety, 41, 63–65, 67, 71, 81, 88, 104, 107, 116–117, 126–128, 131
   self-care, 143, 277
   sexual health, 114, 259–260
   social determinants, 258, 271

spiritual, 263
strengths-based understandings of, 11
and tā moko, 163, 170–171, 176–177
takatāpui, 60–61, 63–65, 67–69, 73–74, 200–201
and tapu breach, 88
and tikanga, 181–182, 200–201
Toronto Charter, 158
traditional healing practices, 126, 165–168
trust in institutions, 128–129, 131
two-spirit men, 273–278
two-spirit women, 22, 211–212, 220
two-spirit youth, 290–291
Western framework, 12–13
and whānau, 29, 34–38, 176–177
youth, 322
Wellington, 40, 76, 118
West Coast First Nations, 314
Western assumptions, 17, 43, 46–47, 51
Western biomedical models, 16, 89
Western feminism, 86
We'wha, 309
Whaingaroa, 182
whaka (prefix), 48
whakaaro, 45, 53
whakanoa, 87
whakapapa. *see also* ancestral generations
  as defining factor, 103
  and HIV/AIDS, 155
  importance of, 121, 174–175, 198
  and mana, 84–85
  and Māori worldedness, 53, 54n8
  and moko kauwae, 163n1
  need for, 64, 67, 89, 113–114
  pre-colonisation, 62, 185
  responsibilities of, 41, 62, 71, 194
  and rongoā, 167
  and tā moko, 164
  and takatāpui identity, 187–188, 193
  understanding of, 60–61, 71, 77–79
  and Western metaphysics, 50n4
Whakatane, 143

whakataukī, 171, 330
Whakaue, 30
whakawāhine, 77, 80, 88
whānau. *see also* families
  attacks on, 14, 66
  composition of, 119–120, 194
  connection to, 120, 130, 148, 191, 215, 222
  healthy future requirements, 113
  and identity, 32–34, 40, 116–117, 139
  nuclear families, 63–64, 66, 260
  other takatāpui in, 35–37, 39–40, 197, 280
  rejection by, 14, 62–64, 83, 121, 136, 191, 223–224
  roles in, 219
  support from, 118–119, 136, 194, 199–200, 223–225, 230–232, 234
  and well-being, 14, 29–30, 34–38, 41, 113–114, 116–117, 120, 130, 133–134
whānau ora, 101–102, 106
Whanāu Rangatiratanga Measurement Framework, 112
whanaungatanga, 76, 105–107, 113–114, 129, 147
Whangarei, 64
Whare Takatāpui, 18, 77, 79, 82, 84
Whatawhata, 182, 194, 197
whiskey traders, 309
White Owl family clan, 314–315
Whitehead, Joshua, 322
Wilson, Dr Alex, 320
winkte, 312
Winnipeg, 257, 313, 316, 318–319, 319
Women's Refuge, 32, 75–76
workers, community, 156
workforce development, 101
workplaces, 184, 186
world record, 76
world view
  Indigenous, 23, 44, 49n3, 207–208, 212, 215–217, 220, 227, 272–273,

275–276, 280, 299, 305
  Māori, 43, 55, 106, 165–166, 168
  Ojibwe, 306
worlded analysis, 45
worldedness, 17, 44–45, 49n3, 51, 53–55
worthiness, 164, 170
Wortman, Dr Jay, 318
Wounded Knee, 312
W̱SÁNEĆ, 255

Yellow Head, 307, 312, 315
youth
  coming out, 83–84
  development, 76, 334
  HIV/AIDS, 156, 259
  language and identity, 261
  Māori, 18, 182
  mental health, 88, 139–140, 146, 219, 258
  mentorship, 301–302
  rites of passage, 219
  role models, 312–313, 331
  strength of, 280, 298, 322
  struggles, 319
  support for, 316–318

Zoccole, Art, 320
Zuni people, 309